International Action Research

This volume was written to celebrate practitioners around the world who dedicate their lives and their work for the education of themselves and others.

International Action Research:
A Casebook for Educational Reform

Edited by

Sandra Hollingsworth

 The Falmer Press

(A member of the Taylor & Francis Group)
London • Washington, D.C.

UK   Falmer Press, 1 Gunpowder Square, London, EC4A 3DE
USA   Falmer Press, Taylor & Francis Inc., 1900 Frost Road, Suite 101,
        Bristol, PA 19007

First published in 1997

**A catalogue record for this book is available from the British
Library**

ISBN 0 7507 0604 X cased
ISBN 0 7507 0605 8 paper

**Library of Congress Cataloging-in-Publication Data are
available on request**

Jacket design by Caroline Archer

Typeset in 10/12pt Times by
Graphicraft Typesetters Ltd., Hong Kong.

*Printed in Great Britain by Biddles Ltd., Guildford and King's Lynn on
paper which has a specified pH value on final paper manufacture of not
less than 7.5 and is therefore 'acid free'.*

Contents

Contents

Acknowledgments

We are deeply indebted to many who helped to make this volume become a reality. We'd like to recognize their contributions by naming them here:

Anna Clarkson, Falmer Press
Malcolm Clarkson, Falmer Press
Christina Le, Student Assistant, San Jose State University
Linda Leeper, San Jose State University
Robyn S. Lock, San Francisco State University

Foreword

Judyth Sachs and Susan Groundwater Smith (Australia)

This book is a collection of papers from some of the most respected practitioners and advocates of action research from around the world. It makes a significant contribution to our understanding of the scope of action research as a research methodology but also gives readers a strong appreciation of the political work of action research, namely its place in socially transforming organizations of all types. On the basis of the diverse range of examples presented in this book it is clear that there is no one form of action research, as Janet Miller writes to Marion Dadds and Sandra Hollingsworth 'action research does not conform to any predictable pattern' (p. 55). The great strength of this book is that it provides compelling examples of how action research has been applied in various settings ranging from the United States, the United Kingdom, South Africa, Malaysia, Australia, Canada, Mexico, Austria, Italy and Israel. Furthermore, it clearly indicates how action research has been used in a variety of professional contexts.

The volume demonstrates the power of action research as a research tool that has as much use in educational settings as in other organizations. It also provides examples of the structural, individual and personal dimensions of the action research project. It is clear that the intent of action research is political, both at the institutional and individual level.

All the contributors write with passion and commitment of their work in action research projects. The examples of what is possible using an action oriented approach is one of the singular strengths of this book. The experiences and successes of all the practitioners of action research are written clearly and accessibly. To this end the book is a valuable resource for people in a variety of contexts where action research is an appropriate methodology for improvement, whether this be at a micro, meso or macro level of organizations. It is a particularly useful resource for people in educational settings and those whose jobs have an educative dimension. However, this is not a 'how-to manual', there are enough of those around already. Rather it addresses theoretical and practical dimensions of action research.

The examples of action research practice as presented in the book speak of the courage, vision and passion of people working in a variety of settings and contexts. Some of the examples presented are deeply moving, while others are inspirational. It is clear from reading the examples presented in this book that action research is not for the faint hearted. It is for those who strive to improve their practice and that of others. More importantly however, the book makes clear the personal and professional rewards gained by those using action research for improvement purposes. We strongly commend this book to you.

Section I

Multiple Perspectives and Discourses on Action Research

Section Editor: Sandra Hollingsworth

Section I stands as an overview of different cultural/geographical and philosophical/ epistemological perspectives on educational reform issues addressed through action research. Authors briefly review the history/idea of action research as it evolved in different contexts, the theories of educational and societal change/reform which accompany varying perspectives, and the practical implications which accompany each view.

The chapters represent questions posed from different discourses/perspectives: Susan E. Noffke queries the origins of new methodological paradigms for practical/ political uses in the United States. John Elliott's chapter asks how effective different action research paradigms have been on educational change in the United Kingdom. Herbert Altrichter inquires into the importation of action research from England to German-speaking countries employing social science theories. The chapter by Stephen Kemmis and Shirley Grundy also refers to the different manifestations of action research around the world, then questions the relationship of action research to social and professional imperatives in Australia. Finally, Sandra Hollingsworth, Marion Dadds and Janet Miller explore the critical issues of personal transformational in action research across cultures.

1 Themes and Tensions in US Action Research: Towards Historical Analysis

Susan E. Noffke (United States)

Definitions of action research vary greatly. The term in its broadest sense refers to research conducted in a field setting with those actually involved in that field, often alongside an 'outsider', into the study of questions influenced by practitioners rather than solely by 'experts'. The burgeoning of interest in action research internationally over the past twenty years seems both to hold great promise and also to provide an occasion to consider why such a change in educational research is occurring and what it might involve.

The primary focus of the chapter is on the development of action research in the middle part of the twentieth century in the United States. Through analysis of some of the assumptions, intentions, and practices of educational action research as they emerged in this era, themes and contradictions in the development of action research are revealed. In its exploration of the antecedents of this research form, the chapter complements other writings on the history of action research (Adelman, 1993; Altrichter and Gstettner, 1993; Foshay, 1994; Kemmis, 1982; King and Lonnquist, 1992; McKernan, 1988; McTaggart, 1991; Noffke, 1994 and 1997; Peters and Robinson, 1984; Schubert and Lopez-Schubert, 1984; Wallace, 1987). In this chapter, however, central tendencies in action research emerge, not as a neat succession of intellectual traditions situated in an era of great social change, but as a complex web with contradictory themes.

It is important to emphasize that the 'telling' of this particular history of action research is only one of many other possible stories. As I have argued elsewhere (Noffke, 1997), action research can be seen as part of a long tradition among African-American, feminist, and other scholar- and grassroots activists to seek a strong and mutually constitutive relationship between research and social change. In addition, a look at action research traditions outside academically or US-based efforts (see Altrichter and Gstettner, 1993; Fals-Borda and Rahman, 1991; Gunz, 1996; Park, *et al.*, 1993) reveals very different forms of action research from those highlighted here. Yet, as will be apparent in the final section, an analysis of themes and tensions in this particular era and context, may provide a useful frame for many contemporary action research efforts. In that sense, this chapter is acknowledged as merely one story, a step towards further historical analyses.

In the various outlines of the history of action research noted earlier, there are several commonly cited antecedents for the ideas embodied in the practices of educational action research. Each of these will, in turn be examined in this chapter. One comes from the use of applied anthropology in the government services, especially the work of John Collier. A second is the work of Kurt Lewin and his followers in the field of social psychology. The third area is within education, particularly curriculum studies. All three of these have influenced the various forms of action research today, to varying degrees. The differing contributions of these three branches of the action research family, as well as their similarities deserve clarification.

Action research efforts in this era form a middle and a transition point for education and educational research in this century. Looking at them allows us an opportunity to look backward and forward into the history of educational efforts from a time when context is a clear factor in educational change. The context is one of international events — two world wars and the Great Depression, potentially influential in the development of education and educational research in many countries. Yet these larger events are only a part of the context. Education, its institutions and its participants have histories which, though influenced by great events, develop, too, as a result of other factors.

Of 'Democracy', 'Social Engineering', and Social Change Born

The work of John Collier, Commissioner of Indian Affairs from 1933–1945, seems at first to be vastly separated from the work of 'educationists' of the time, yet there were important connections. Early in his career, Collier was very active in education. With his wife, he started The Home School, which combined work, play, and study. He also worked with the People's Institute and other organizations in New York on community projects, often to benefit children. These projects involved field research and teaching, and focused on the development of methods which would 'insure a maximum degree of local democracy'. John Dewey was on the advisory board of Collier's New York Training School for Community Workers, and William Heard Kilpatrick met frequently with its students (Collier, 1963, pp. 84–7).

'Community' was important in Collier's plans for implementing the Indian Reorganization Act, part of the 'Indian New Deal', and was also salient in educational work in general during this era (Stephon, 1983, 1984; Everett, 1938). Collier's work in the movement to relocate Native American education from boarding schools into communities on the reservations was closely connected with W. Carson Ryan, Jr. and Willard Beatty, who were the first two Directors of Indian Education for the US Indian Service in the early 1930s and also served terms as president of the Progressive Education Association. The educational platform for the community schools focused on 'local culture and resource-centered education, flexibility of program, bilingual teaching, native language literacy, and the goal of native self-sufficiency' (Iverson, 1978, p. 235; Beatty, 1940) rather than 'mastery of the material culture of the dominant race' (Beatty, cited in Iverson, p. 236).

Collier's work is part of a general trend during the early part of the century towards documenting everyday lives and practices, often those of poor or minority peoples, and towards the development of 'applied' branches of research. It is important both in the sense that it responded to a need to facilitate social improvement rather than only to accumulate experimental data and theories, and in the sense that it opened up a whole new branch of opportunities for a generation of social scientists.

Collier described a form of 'action research, research-action' done in small Native American communities in the area of soil conservation. The chief characteristics of the work were the emphases on the need for the community to benefit concretely from the research and on the importance of a non-directive role for the consulting 'experts' (Collier, 1945, p. 294). Although not specific as to the research process, it was to 'be evoked by needs of action, should be integrative of many disciplines, should involve both administrator and the layman, and should feed itself into action' (p. 300). The problems of 'ethnic relations' were, to Collier, the major issues of the post-world war II era, and could be resolved only by recognizing and revitalizing the ethnic society and lands, and recapturing a sense of 'community'. This was to be accomplished through 'the experience of responsible democracy': 'the most therapeutic, the most disciplinary, the most dynamogenic, and the most productive of efficiency'. Democracy was 'the way of order' (1945, p. 275).

Collier was aware of the potential of research efforts to be used for social control, for example to provide bilingual education so that information would be more accessible, thus making outside-developed policies easier to implement. This contradiction between the potential of 'democratic means' being used both for 'engineered change' and for self-determination was particularly salient in the work of social scientists in the state service, both in Indian Affairs and later in the Japanese 'relocation' centers during the war (see James, 1986). The desire both for democratic means and for social improvement guided by principles determined outside the field setting, was to remain a central tension in later developments in action research. Collier referred to action research as being on the verge of 'social planning', which he saw as being in the beginning stages of development (Collier, 1945, p. 297). Aspects of a more fully developed form of social engineering (Graebner, 1987), can be found in the work of Kurt Lewin, whom Collier considered a close friend. It is Lewin who is the second and, at least from an international perspective, a most significant figure in early action research.

Research for Re-education

Lewin shared major interests with Collier: a faith in democratic forms and a concern for understanding the 'dynamics' of the group in order to resolve social problems. A Jewish refugee from Nazi Germany, Lewin was also keenly aware of the importance of what Collier had called 'ethnic relations'. He and his colleagues at the Iowa Child Welfare Station worked on topics which reflected not only the strong interest he had in democracy, but which were easily seen as having direct application to schools (Marrow, 1969). He wrote about his and others' work on autocratic, democratic, and *laissez-faire* atmospheres in children's groups in several progressive journals of the time (Lewin, 1938; Lewin and Lewin, 1942).

Lewin's concept of democracy, like Collier's, emphasized its efficiency, but without Collier's aversion to 'management'. Some of this connection may have been a response to criticisms of democratic means as inefficient (Lewin, 1944). Considering Lewin's life experiences, it would not be surprising if the lessons of the Weimar Republic may have led to a concern that democracy be efficient in addressing pressing problems and to an understanding that 'populist' programs do not always lead to democracy. Another factor may have been his connection to research in industry, which tied increased participation in decision-making by workers to greater productivity (Marrow, 1969; Adelman, 1993; Cunningham, 1993).

In many ways, this raises a contradiction between the uses of democratic methods for 'worthwhile democratic ends', what Collier considered the undemocratic specter of social engineering. Lewin, however, saw democracy and planning as interdependent:

> The survival and development of democracy depends not so much on the development of democratic ideals which are wide-spread and so strong. Today, more than ever before, democracy depends upon the development of efficient forms of democratic social management and upon the spreading of the skill in such management to the common man. (Lewin, 1947, p. 153)

Lewin's formulation of action research had a clear focus on instituting changes — taking actions, carefully collecting information on their effects, and then evaluating them, rather than formulating hypotheses to be tested, although the eventual development of theories was important (Lewin, 1946). This represents not only a clear distinction from the dominant research forms of the time, but also emphasizes Lewin's concern with resolving issues, not merely collecting information and writing about them. Yet the theory developed as a result of the research was theory about *change*, not solely about the problem or topic itself. The overriding theme of Lewin's post-war work was that of prejudice. Concerned with changing attitudes toward minorities, a process of 're-education', Lewin and his colleagues worked on projects related to problems of assimilation versus pluralism, of segregation versus integration, of discrimination, as well as of class stratification (Lewin and Grabbe, 1945; Lippitt and Radke, 1946).

Lewin envisioned a version of social science that would integrate social theory and social action. He saw good social theory as inevitably practical, and stressed the important function that he believed action research would play in its development:

> The research needed for social practice can best be characterized as research for social management or social engineering. It is a type of action research, a comparative research on the conditions and effects of various forms of social action, and research leading to social action. Research that produces nothing but books will not suffice. (Lewin, 1947, p. 150)

Social action and social theory were, to Lewin, an integrated whole whose goals were determined by notions of democracy and social justice. The methods of social science could be equally as rigorous as those of the natural sciences, and therefore equally as legitimate.

The Depression, the work with oppressed minorities, and the urgency of the wartime efforts may have contributed to the research form that both Lewin and Collier advocated. Such issues emphasized the need for social science to develop efficient means to gather information relevant to immediate social needs. In both Lewin's and Collier's work, such needs resulted in an emphasis on several themes, one of which is the necessity for research to be in the field, in all of its complexity. A concern with social justice is evident in both, as is a tension between 'democratic' ends and 'social engineering' means. All of these were also present in the later developments of action research in education.

Curriculum Studies and the Science of Education

Lewin shared with some progressive educators an interest in group processes and 'learning by doing'. Both supported efforts at setting up student self-government, learning by group work, and the development of democratic leadership. A melding of progressive education with emerging methods in the social sciences could provide one explanation for the emergence of action research in education. Yet, the education field itself, had, of course, been working out its own definitions of legitimate research. Although the dominant form of educational research in the early twentieth century could be typified by the testing and measurement movement, by 'activity analysis', and by the fact-finding of the US Office of Education, there was also a trend toward 'field study research'.

The trend toward field studies is an important link in the action research family. By the late 1930s and early 1940s, there were two important alternatives to laboratory experiments. One was typified by the Eight Year Study, an attempt on the part of the Progressive Education Association to analyze the impact of changes which loosened the control exerted by college entrance requirements over the high school curriculum (Aiken, 1942). A key aspect of that project relevant to the later development of action research, was that the changes, seen as experiments, were made at the school level, by the teachers and administrators, with the assistance of consultants (Schubert and Lopez-Schubert, 1984). Such school-based curriculum studies were part of '. . . the increasingly popular notion that curriculum revision should be undertaken by the participants who would be called upon to implement the innovations' (Kliebard, 1995, p. 223).

Second, the work of John Dewey has particular relevance as a conceptual basis for action research (Watson, 1949). Dewey held a vision of educational research method that contrasted starkly with the natural science-inspired experiments. Dewey asserted: 'Educational science cannot be constructed simply by borrowing the technique of experiment and measurement found in physical science' (Dewey, 1929/1984, p. 13). He sought, rather, 'methods which enable us to make an analysis of what the gifted teacher does intuitively, so that something accruing from his work can be communicated to others' (p. 5).

Dewey addressed the issue of the sources of an educational science and concluded:

> (1) that educational practices provide the data, the subject matter, which form the problems of inquiry. They are the sole source of the ultimate problems to be investigated. These educational practices are also (2) the final test of value of the conclusions of all researches . . . Actual activities in educating test the worth of scientific results. (1929/1984, pp. 16–17)

Dewey's emphasis on the defining of an educational problem and the inclusion of a hypothesis contrasted with Lewin's model, which seemed to focus more attention on the action step. It was Dewey's version of the process, combined with Lewin's understanding of 'group dynamics' in a democracy, that would gradually emerge in the post-war years.

Growing up in Educational Practice

Dewey also emphasized a role for teachers in educational research. Aware of the split between educational researchers and practitioners he concluded: '. . . it is impossible to see how there can be an adequate flow of subject-matter to set and control the problems investigators deal with, unless there is active participation on the part of those directly engaged in teaching' (1929/1984, p. 24). Involvement of teachers was to grow during the war-time and post-war era, building on the tradition of school-based curriculum development begun in the earlier decades. Why this occurred and what form it took is as yet unclear; but research during that time seems to have made a partial and temporary move from the universities towards schools and school districts.

One example of that move can be seen in the Horace Mann-Lincoln Institute for School Experimentation at Teachers College. Begun in the fall of 1943, the Institute established 'two basic study committees for the in-service education of teachers in local situations', focusing on two broad topics: understanding the social bases of the curriculum and the implications of child development for the curriculum (Horace Mann-Lincoln Staff, 1945, pp. 274–76). Plans were made to 'initiate a plan of cooperative experimentation with a group of associated schools' (Teachers College, 1946, pp. 521–23). Gordon Mackenzie, who, along with Stephen Corey, became a special consultant to the Institute in 1944, attributed this change from experimental schools to affiliations with school districts to three trends: growth in schools' use of 'experimentation as a means of curriculum improvement', the 'marked trend toward community-oriented schools which use and serve their community, as well as work directly for improved community living', and 'the phenomenal growth of enrollment in public schools, and the accompanying increase in the variability of pupils' (Mackenzie, 1946, p. 438).

The work of the Horace Mann-Lincoln Institute was part of a much larger family of projects that were underway during this time; of concern in many of these projects, was the wide gap between knowledge and practice. Yet there was another factor which influenced the course of educational research during this time. The curricular basis of the Horace Mann-Lincoln Institute was a critique of the 'conventional school subjects' approach to curriculum design. Rather than 'strictly logical and factual mentality' producing 'a mechanical and emotionally cold process', the staff sought to include more of the 'education of the emotions for moral and [a]esthetic living', previously the domain of 'the home and other influences', into the school curriculum (Goodson, 1946, p. 35). Besides an emphasis on 'active learning' and the 'whole child', democratic processes and individual differences were salient features. This description represents a major shift from the dominant form of curriculum and pedagogy actually practiced at the time and echoes the beliefs of Collier and Lewin.

While the school-based curriculum development projects shared a rejection of the traditional course of study, they, like the progressive education movement in general, were based on differing assumptions, what Kliebard (1995) refers to as developmentalist, social efficiency, and social meliorist approaches. Understanding the diversity in the progressive movement is crucial to understanding how conflicting forms of action research emerged in the later years. The curriculum vision behind action research, though loosely progressive, actually embodied a number of views. Some of the Horace Mann-Lincoln Institute staff clearly aligned themselves with efforts to produce 'a curriculum organized around the persistent life situations which learners encounter' (Horace Mann-Lincoln Staff, 1948). Although this action research work would later become a part of the efforts to create a 'life adjustment' curriculum (Kliebard, 1995), the early work shows influences of a cultural critique, including areas of economics as well as 'intergroup tensions' (Goodson, 1946), aimed at social reconstruction rather than adjustment.

Two other points lead to an understanding of how the social vision of the Horace Mann-Lincoln Institute included both a radical, democratic vision, particularly in the area of economics, and a social engineering aspect. In discussing the need for economic stability, the assumption was that such an economy depended on 'the equitable distribution of goods and services' to reduce the conflict-producing 'uneven distribution of economic opportunity and power'. In order to accomplish this, however, research into a kind of 'democratic social engineering' was seen as a necessity:

> Experimentation is needed to discover the ways in which the school can influence people to assure the development of a discipline, both intellectual and emotional in scope and influence, that meets the present urgency of public problems. (Goodson, 1946, pp. 37–8)

The overall goal was 'educating for a personality type' — a person who is socially sensitive, cooperative, thinking (i.e., can define problems, formulate plans, check plans against facts and values, and act upon tentative conclusions), creative and self-directing — the 'democratic person' (pp. 41–2).

In addition to working with the school districts, the staff and their graduate students were to conduct research which we would recognize today as 'action research on action research'. Their major areas of concern in this undertaking were group dynamics, the 'investigation of the barriers to curriculum change' and 'the means and methods by which change can be hastened' (Mackenzie, 1946, p. 445). In many ways, the work of the Horace Mann-Lincoln Institute represents a beginning point not only for action research in education, but also for later studies on the process of change. These studies were beginning to yield information about the function of the group in changing individual attitudes and behavior. Action research became both a way to better facilitate curriculum change (Horace Mann-Lincoln Institute Staff, 1948; Horace Mann-Lincoln Study Group, 1948; Benne, 1948), and also a way to change teachers' attitudes toward the use of more traditional research.

The earlier themes of community, of progressive education, of school-based curriculum development, of the need for a closer knowledge-practice connection, of the benefits of field research, as well as the continuing tension between democracy and social engineering, were all evident in the early work of the Horace Mann-Lincoln Institute. The theme of ethnic relations and the related focus on demographic changes in the school population were continuing aspects of action research, but for now, the concern was to be with the acceptance of this type of activity as a legitimate form of educational research.

The Method of Science: Depoliticizing Action Research

Stephen Corey, who from his post at the University of Chicago, had worked with the Horace Mann-Lincoln Institute and later moved to Teachers College, is probably the most well-known figure in the early action research work. Although seemingly very committed to the concept, he, like many others of the time, seemed to be ambivalent to the term itself: 'I hold no especial brief for the name, but it has some currency and is sufficiently descriptive' (Corey, 1953, p. viii). In contrast to the works of Collier and Lewin, the theme of democracy was not assumed by Corey to be an integral element of research: '. . . the use of the method of science in the solution of practical educational problems can be adequately defended for its own sake' (p. 17). The acceptance of action research as a legitimate research form seemed quite important to Corey. He argued that there was only a relative difference between research and everyday problem solving. He also felt that the quality of the research by teachers that he advocated, would gradually improve as they gained experience. Validity, to Corey, was to be judged 'by its effects on human welfare' (Corey, 1953, p. 17).

In the research Corey described, 'experts' might be called in to consult, but the major responsibility for the research lay on the cooperative group. Doing research in groups was, to Corey, the preferred method. His language in describing the advantages of group action research echoes the 'group dynamics' work of Lewin and his followers: 1) an increased commitment to change, 2) an increased probability that the actions proposed would be possible, 3) a greater range and variety of talent,

4) a reduction of individual risk, and 5) the prevention of feelings of manipulation (pp. 137–39).

That the potential in action research for social engineering also played a role in Corey's thinking is evident in the last point. For writers on action research at the time, the process of curriculum change through action research could be viewed as an engineering issue: 'The change of a curriculum reflects changes in attitudes, concept structure, skills and needs in the teachers' (Thelen, 1948, pp. 577–78). When viewed in this way, the knowledge produced through action research becomes not educational knowledge, but knowledge about the group process. The educational theory involved then becomes not a problematic to be explored through action research, but more of a body of knowledge to be adjusted to context.

Corey's emphasis on hypothesis testing and data gathering by the teachers themselves shows a view of action research as producing educational knowledge, not theory only about how to facilitate change. Corey's expectations for the outcomes of action research were clearly focused on educational improvement. To him, it was a vehicle to increase the possibility that teachers and administrators would change, and thereby improve their educational practices. Its purpose, however, seems primarily instrumental. The principled commitment to democracy that had accompanied earlier forms of action research, was missing, at least in Corey's writing. While some of the classroom projects reflect a desire to establish democratic processes either in the classroom or in the staff-administration relationship, Corey's commitment seemed to be the development of a body of knowledge and skills that would assist practitioners in adjusting to cultural change, rather than participating in it.

One can speculate a bit about the effect of the context. Corey, in his discussion of the democracy question in action research refers to Whittaker Chambers, a prominent figure in the McCarthy era, who equated the scientific method with communism (1953, p. 24). The years since the initiation of the Horace Mann-Lincoln Institute had brought a great deal of changes in the problems of schooling. They had also brought the Berlin Airlift and the beginnings of the 'Cold War', and were, at the time of Corey's writing, on the edge of the Korean War and McCarthyism. While this point is not clearly evidenced, there is a noticeable change of emphasis in the issues of educational journals of the time from the discussion of 'democracy' and 'one-world ideals' to the focus on the gap between theory and practice and the need for the 'reeducation' of teachers.

Into Inservice and Personal Development

Corey's work was only a part of a larger attempt to effect curriculum change during the post-war era and into the 1950s. The groups doing action research were complemented by others who also advocated the participation of teachers in curriculum planning and improvement (Miel, 1946; Passow, *et al.*, 1955; Sharp, 1951). Both at Teachers College and elsewhere, many people advocated the use of action research. Best known of these are Hilda Taba, at San Francisco State College, and Abraham

Shumsky, a student at Teachers' College and later on the faculty at Brooklyn College. With both, the efforts to establish action research as a distinct research form seem to have faded. Rather, perhaps as a result of the increasing teacher shortage in the 1950s, the emphasis was on the opportunities in action research for inservice education and personal development of teachers. In Taba's work, the legacy of the school based curriculum movement is evident, but there is more of a focus on classroom practices, especially issues of curriculum adjustment and classroom control (Taba and Noel, 1957).

Taba's writings show an explicit response to the changing composition of the school, at least on the issue of class. Race, though surely an issue nationally at the time, is not mentioned. Unlike Corey, she felt that action research 'should seek especially to enhance the democratic quality in teaching and in supervisory leadership' (Taba and Noel, 1957, p. 6). Shumsky saw action research as a way to restore a sense of community (McTaggart, 1991), he seems focused primarily on individual self-development, on research as having 'personal significance' (Shumsky, 1958).

For Taba, one of the purposes of action research was 'to change those who are making the changes, that is, to enhance the insights of the teachers, to alter their attitudes . . .' (Taba, 1957, p. 43). Shumsky's interests in action research were consciously not intended to be the manipulation of a social engineer. In discussing the formation of a teacher's action ideology through the process of action research, he asserted:

> The meaningfulness of this ideology to the investigator is determined by the extent to which it is derived under conditions of freedom, and the extent to which it is a product of a re-examination of the relationship between the teachers' system of values and his field problems. (1958, p. 122)

The 'conditions of freedom' in the 1950s may well have included a need for a more individualistic form of action research.

With Shumsky's work, what has been called the 'first generation' (McTaggart and Singh, 1988) of action research came to a close. Begun in an era emphasizing local curriculum development, especially that of a 'progressive' or 'life adjustment' type, its presence in the educational literature faded into the background of the new, nationally funded, 'expert'-designed curriculum, centered around the 'structure of the disciplines' (Kliebard, 1995).

Persistent Themes in Action Research

This chapter has focused on themes emergent in the development of action research through the 1950s. Field research, community, school-based curriculum development, progressive education, teacher-as-researcher, demographic changes, a knowledge-practice gap, and ethnic/human relations have been a part of the various forms of action research, and are a part of a tension between democracy and social engineering. These themes have great bearing on understanding the recent resurgence of interest in action research, particularly the dimensions along which current forms of action research vary. The themes that emerged continue to be part of current work, as does the tension between democracy and social engineering.

Action research seemed to decline in prominence in the late 1950s, although it is as yet unclear exactly how prevalent the practice was even in its heyday. It is, however, important to realize that action research did not die, it remained consistent and fairly common throughout the 1960s and 1970s in several areas. Significant to the recent increase in interest in action research in the UK, for example, is the continuance of community service research throughout the 1960s and 1970s, often addressing problems of working-class pupils in the new comprehensive schools. Although not considered by some to be successful (Whyte, 1986), such projects maintained the tradition of action research partly through the efforts of the Tavistock Institute, an organization with close connections to Lewin and his successors.

The field studies approach, illuminative evaluation, and the development of alternative, qualitative methodologies have carried further the theme from the 1930s of looking closely at everyday events. Many, but not all, action research projects carried out today employ an qualitative approach to data collection and analysis. Broadly defined to include questions of gender, race, and class, the theme of ethnic, or human relations, is present in the work of Stenhouse and in such projects as the 'Girls and Occupational Choice' and the 'Girls into Science and Technology' projects in the UK, and it has played a role in the work at Deakin University in Australia (Chisholm and Holland, 1986; McTaggart, 1991; Stenhouse, 1980; 1983). As in the earlier era, some of the interest can be attributed to the demographic changes in school populations experienced in some countries as a result of expanding the availability of secondary school education.

The strongest theme, not surprisingly, since many of the current definitions of action research require it, is the idea of the teacher as researcher. Perhaps the most influential of the recent writers on this topic has been Lawrence Stenhouse, but most action research today maintains the tradition. An often forgotten aspect, at least in the US, to Stenhouse's work was the thorough rejection of the dominant objectives based model for curriculum design, in favor of a more process-based approach (Stenhouse, 1975). Just as in the earlier era, much of action research today, but not all, is done within a framework that rejects the dominant mode of curriculum development in favor of a school-based, alternative model (See Carr and Kemmis, 1988; Elliott, 1991; Elliott and Adelman, 1973; Grundy and Kemmis, 1988). In the US, too, the 'process' approach to the teaching of writing has provided the core of many recent projects (Cochran-Smith and Lytle, 1993; Goswami and Stillman, 1987).

The knowledge-practice gap theme, too, is particularly salient in some US projects (Tikunoff and Ward, 1983). As in the earlier era, action research is seen as a way to bridge the gap between theory and practice. Yet even in action research forms which embody a different, often reflexive or dialectical, theory-practice relationship, the theme emerges as part of an explanation for the growth of action research. The inability of traditional research forms to adequately respond to the needs of expanded and changing schools is seen as part of a 'legitimation crisis', in which alternative forms of research compete (Schneider, 1980; Elliott, 1984).

Through these themes, the tension between democracy and social engineering continues to be worked out. From a concern that research topics emanate from teachers, through those involving equalizing relationships in classrooms, to an explicit emancipatory project, a democratic impulse in action research is evident. Yet within these projects, the social engineering element is also present. It can take the form of changing teachers' attitudes towards research, developing hypotheses about the ways teachers develop, or facilitating the research process. All of these, carried out 'above' the teachers' own action research, carry with them the potential for 'engineered' change. In action research, whether seeming to be guided by a technical logic, a moral position, or an emancipatory intent, the central contradiction remains. This contradiction must be addressed by all proponents of action research.

References

ADELMAN, C. (1993) 'Kurt Lewin and the origins of action research', *Educational Action Research*, **1**, 1, pp. 7–24.

AIKEN, W.M. (1942) *The Story of the Eight-year Study*, New York, Harper and Brothers.

ALTRICHTER, H. and GSTETTNER, P. (1993) 'Action research: A closed chapter in the history of German social science?' *Educational Action Research*, **1**, 3, pp. 329–60.

BEATTY, W. (1940, Nov.) 'Uncle Sam develops a new kind of rural school', *Elementary School Journal*, **41**, 3, pp. 185–93.

BENNE, K.D. (1948, April) 'An approach to issues underlying curriculum development', *Journal of Educational Research*, **41**, 7, pp. 561–76.

CARR, W. and KEMMIS, S. (1988) *Becoming Critical: Education, Knowledge and Action Research*, London, Falmer Press.

CHISHOLM, L. and HOLLAND, J. (1986) 'Girls and occupational choice: Anti-sexism in action in a curriculum development project', *British Journal of Sociology of Education*, **7**, 4, pp. 353–65.

COCHRAN-SMITH, M. and LYTLE, S.L. (1993) *Inside/outside: Teacher Research and Knowledge*, New York, Teachers College Press.

COLLIER, J. (1945) 'United States Indian administration as a laboratory of ethnic relations', *Social Research*, 12, pp. 265–303.

COLLIER, J. (1963) *From Every Zenith*, Denver, Sage Books.

COREY, S.M. (1953) *Action Research to Improve School Practices*, New York, Teachers College.

CUNNINGHAM, J.B. (1993) *Action Research and Organizational Development*, Westport, CT, Praeger.

DEWEY, J. (1929/1984) 'The sources of a science of education', in BOYDSTON, J.A. (Ed.), *The Later Works: Vol. 5, 1929–1930* (pp. 3–40), Carbondale, Southern Illinois University Press.

ELLIOTT, J. (1984) *Legitimation Crisis and the Growth of Educational Action Research*, Cambridge, Cambridge Institute of Education.

ELLIOTT, J. (1991) *Action Research for Educational Change*, Philadelphia, Open University Press/Milton Keynes.

ELLIOTT, J. and ADELMAN, C. (1973) 'Reflecting where the action is: The design of the Ford Teaching Project', *Education for Teaching*, 92, pp. 8–20.

EVERETT, S. (1938) *The Community School*, New York, D. Appleton-Century.

FALS-BORDA, O. and RAHMAN, M.A. (Eds) (1991) *Action and Knowledge: Breaking the Monopoly with Participatory Action Research*, New York, Apex Press.

FOSHAY, A.W. (1994, Summer) 'Action research: An early history in the United States', *Journal of Curriculum & Supervision*, **9**, 4, pp. 317–25.

GOODSON, M.R. (1946, Oct.) 'Charting a course for educational progres', *Teachers College Record*, **48**, 1, pp. 35–60.

GOSWAMI, D. and STILLMAN, P.R. (Eds) (1987) *Reclaiming the Classroom: Teacher Research as an Agency for Change*, Portsmouth, NH, Boynton/Cook-Heinemann.

GRAEBNER, W. (1987) *The Engineering of Consent: Democracy and Authority in Twentieth-century America*, Madison, University of Wisconsin Press.

GRUNDY, S. and KEMMIS, S. (1981/1988) 'Educational action research in Australia: The state of the art (An overview)', in KEMMIS, S. and McTAGGART, R. (Eds), *The Action Research Reader*, (3rd Ed.), (pp. 321–35), Geelong, Deakin University Press.

GUNZ, J. (1996) 'Jacob L. Moreno and the origins of action research', *Educational Action Research*, **4**, 1, pp. 145–48.

HORACE MANN-LINCOLN INSTITUTE OF SCHOOL EXPERIMENTATION STAFF (1945, Jan.) 'Departmental notes', *Teachers College Record*, **46**, 4, pp. 275–76.

HORACE MANN-LINCOLN INSTITUTE OF SCHOOL EXPERIMENTATION STAFF (1948, Feb.) 'A progress report', *Teachers College Record*, **49**, 5, pp. 305–62.

HORACE MANN-LINCOLN STUDY GROUP (1948, Nov.) 'Recommended: Group research for teachers', *Teachers College Record*, **50**, 2, pp. 108–113.

IVERSON, K. (1978) 'Progressive education for Native American: Washington Ideology and Navajo reservation implementation', *Review Journal of Philosophy and Social Science*, **3**, 2, pp. 231–55.

JAMES, T. (1986, April) *The Social Scientist and Minority Groups in Crisis*, History Department Faculty Seminar, Wesleyan University.

KEMMIS, S. (1982) 'Action research in retrospect and prospect', in S. KEMMIS, *et al.* (Eds), *The Action Research Reader* (2nd Ed.), pp. 11–31, Geelong: Deakin University Press.

KING, J.A. and LONNQUIST, M.P. (1992) *A Review of Writing on Action Research*, Minneapolis, Center for Applied Research and Educational Improvement, University of Minnesota.

KLIEBARD, H.M. (1995) *The Struggle for the American Curriculum*, 1893–1958 (2nd Ed.), Boston, Routledge.

LEWIN, G. and LEWIN, K. (1942, Oct.) 'Democracy and the school', *Understanding the Child*, **10**, 1, pp. 7–11.

LEWIN, K. (1938, July) 'Experiments on autocratic and democratic principles', *The Social Frontier*, **4**, 37, pp. 316–19.

LEWIN, K. (1944, Jan.) 'The dynamics of group action', *Educational Leadership*, 1, pp. 195–200.

LEWIN, K. (1946) 'Action research and minority problems', *Journal of Social Issues*, **2**, 4, pp. 34–46.

LEWIN, K. (1947) 'Frontiers in group dynamics: II. Channels of group life; Social planning and action research', *Human Relations*, 1, pp. 143–53.

LEWIN, K. and GRABBE, P. (1945) 'Conduct, knowledge, and acceptance of new values', *Journal of Social Issues*, **1**, 3, pp. 53–64.

LIPPITT, R. and RADKE, M. (1946, March) 'New trends in the investigation of prejudice. In Controlling group prejudice', *The Annals of the American Academy of Political and Social Science*, 244, pp. 167–76.

MACKENZIE, G.N. (1946, April) 'The Horace Mann-Lincoln Institute of School Experimentation', *Teachers College Record*, **47**, 7, pp. 438–45.

McKernan, J. (1988) 'The countenance of curriculum action research: Traditional, collaborative, and emancipatory-critical conceptions', *Journal of Curriculum and Supervision*, **3**, 3, pp. 173–200.

McTaggart, R. (1991) *Action research: A short modern history*, Geelong, Deakin University Press.

McTaggart, R. and Singh, M. (1988) 'A fourth generation of action research: Notes on the Deakin Seminar', in Kemmis, S. and McTaggart, R. (Eds), *The Action Research Reader*, 3rd Ed. (pp. 409–28). Geelong, Victoria, Deakin University Press.

Marrow, A.J. (1969) *The Practical Theorist: The Life and Work of Kurt Lewin*, NY, Basic Books.

Miel, A. (1946) *Changing the curriculum: A social process*, New York, Appleton-Century Co.

Noffke, S.E. (1994) 'Action research: Towards the next generation', *Educational Action Research*, **2**, 1, pp. 9–21.

Noffke, S.E. (1997) 'Professional, personal, and political dimensions of action research', in Apple, M.W. (Ed.), *Review of Research in Education*, **22**, pp. 299–337.

Park, P., Brydon-Miller, M., Hall, B. and Jackson, T. (Eds) (1993) *Voices of Change: Participatory Research in the United States and Canada*, Westport, Bergin & Garvey.

Passow, A.H., Miles, M.B. and Corey, S. (1955) *Training Curriculum Leaders for Cooperative Research*, New York, Teachers College, Columbia University.

Peters, M. and Robinson, V. (1984) 'The origins and status of action research', *Journal of Applied Behavioral Science*, **20**, 2, pp. 113–24.

Schneider, U. (1980) *Sozialwissenschaftliche Methodenkrise und Handlungsforschung*, Frankfurt, Campus Verlag.

Schubert, W. and Lopez-Schubert, A. (1984, April) 'Sources of a theory of action research in Progressive Education', paper presented at the Annual Meeting of the American Educational Research Association, New Orleans.

Sharp, G. (1951) *Curriculum Development as Re-education of the Teacher*, New York, Teachers College.

Shumsky, A. (1958) *The Action Research Way of Learning: An Approach to In-service Education*, NY, Teachers College.

Stefon, F.J. (1983, Fall; 1984, Winter) 'The Indians' Zarathustra: An investigation into the philosophical roots of John Collier's Indian New Deal educational and administrative policies', *Journal of Ethnic Studies*, **11**, 3 and 4, pp. 1–28, 29–45.

Stenhouse, L. (1975) *An Introduction to Curriculum Research and Development*, London, Heinemann Educational Books.

Stenouse, L. (Ed.) (1980) *Curriculum Development in Action*, London, Heinemann Educational Books.

Stenhouse, L. (1983) *Authority, Education and Emancipation*, London, Heinemann Educational Books.

Taba, H. (1957) 'Problem identification', in *Research for Curriculum Improvement* (pp. 42–71). Washington, DC, Association for Supervision and Curriculum Development.

Taba, H. and Noel, E. (1957) *Action Research: A Case Study*, Washington, DC, Association for Curriculum & Supervision.

Teachers College (1946, May) 'Teachers College proposes a new plan of school experimentation', *Teachers College Record*, **47**, 8, pp. 521–23.

Thelen, H.A. (1948, April) 'Engineering research in curriculum building', *Journal of Educational Research*, **41**, 7, pp. 577–96.

Tikunoff, W.J. and Ward, B.A. (1983, May) 'Collaborative research on teaching', *Elementary School Journal*, **83**, 4, pp. 453–68.

WALLACE, M. (1987) 'A Historical review of action research: Some implications for the education of teachers in their managerial role', *Journal of Education for Teaching*, **13**, 2, pp. 97–115.

WATSON, G. (1949, May) 'What are the effects of a democratic atmosphere on children?' *Progressive Education*, **17**, 5, pp. 336–42.

WHYTE, J. (1986) *Girls into Science and Technology*, London, Routledge & Kegan Paul.

2 School-based Curriculum Development and Action Research in the United Kingdom

John Elliott (United Kingdom)

Introduction

The idea of action research in the field of education emerged in the United Kingdom (UK) in the context of school-based curriculum development during the 1960s. At the time, curriculum development was perceived to be a solution to a widespread problem in basic education; namely, the alienation of large numbers of students in secondary schools from a form of schooling which emphasized the systematic transmission of bodies of knowledge organized around the 'subjects' taught in the universities. Following the 1944 Education Act, secondary modern schools were created for the 'non-academic' student, judged to be of only average or below average academic ability, on the basis of their failure to pass the 11+ IQ tests for entrance into the secondary grammar schools. Students in these schools followed a watered down curriculum modelled on the academic subjects taught in the grammar schools, with the addition of highly gendered practical craft subjects, e.g., metal and woodwork for boys and home economics (cookery and needlework) for girls. Those who passed the 11+ were prepared in the grammar schools for academic examinations at 16 years, and those with the best passes proceeded to specialize in a narrower range of academic subjects for further examinations at 18 years. The latter provided a passport into university.

It was a system designed for a society conceived as a meritocracy in which social goods — wealth, status, and privileges — were distributed on the basis of merit, measured in terms of standards for the acquisition of cultural capital set by the universities. Educational excellence consisted in the mastery of the knowledge produced in the universities. The system of tests and examinations were intended to ensure equality of opportunity but not equality of success. While fostering upward mobility within the class structure, the structure remained in place, for the function of schooling was primarily that of allocating students, albeit 'justly', to their future roles and positions within the social hierarchy.

Egalitarian equality, equality of success, implies an equal distribution of cultural capital. The post-war secondary school curriculum in the UK, based on academically defined educational standards, provided a basis for rationalizing the unequal distribution of cultural capital. Its major side effect was the disaffection of large numbers of pupils attending the secondary modern schools, particularly in relation to the humanities, conceived in terms of subjects like history, geography, and religion. Teachers in these schools were faced with two alternatives: develop them as systems of containment and control; or restructure the curriculum and thereby reduce its major side-effect on students. Those who moved to change the curriculum adopted either a reformist or an innovatory stance to the problem. The reformist stance resulted in attempts to make the curriculum less knowledge-based and concentrated on practical skills, e.g., through courses on motor vehicle maintenance, home decoration and child care. The innovatory stance instigated attempts to change the conditions under which students gained access to knowledge. Whereas reformist attempts accepted a dual conception of the basic education curriculum, an academic one for the most able and a practical one for the less able, innovatory schools and teachers tried to fundamentally reconceptualize the curriculum. In the 60s, as much curriculum theorizing took place in the schools as in the academy.

It was from attempts to restructure and reconceptualize the humanities curriculum in the innovatory secondary modern schools of the 60s within the UK, that action research emerged. These schools attempted to change the curriculum to make it more relevant to the experience of everyday living in contemporary society. Such attempts involved:

- restructuring the content of the curriculum around life themes rather than subjects;
- representing content as resources for thinking about the problems and issues of everyday living rather than simply information to be learned;
- transforming the teaching-learning process from the systematic transmission of information to a discussion-based inquiry;
- teachers monitoring the ways they select and represent content in classrooms by eliciting student feedback; and
- collaboration between teachers across subject specialisms.

The concern for relevance implied a form of curriculum change which we might describe as pedagogically driven, in contrast to currently fashionable standards-driven approaches. Such an approach problematized the prevailing interpretation of educational standards as sets of objective meanings enshrined in school subjects, and reconceptualized the relationship between knowledge, the teacher and the learner as a more interactional and dynamic process, in which the teacher continually tests, under certain pedagogical conditions, the educational value for students of the content she/he introduces. This imposed an obligation on teachers to reflexively transform their practice in order to establish the appropriate pedagogical conditions for conducting such curriculum experiments. Curriculum development implied pedagogical development, e.g., establishing conditions which fostered learning through discussion. It involved a form of action research performed by teachers in their classrooms and schools. In this context, action research took the form of a self-reflexive experimental process in which the teacher monitored his or her interactions with students in determining what constituted educationally worthwhile curriculum experiences. In the absence of such self-monitoring, teachers might erroneously conclude that the content they had selected was innapropriate as a learning resource, when the problem lay in the way they handled it pedagogically.

The kinds of innovative experiments described, increasingly took on an inter-disciplinary form. Teachers within different subject areas became aware that they were focusing on similar life themes, and that the students' learning experiences would be considerably enriched if they pooled their expertise and adopted an inter-disciplinary approach to the teaching of the humanities. In order to facilitate this, new patterns of curriculum organization emerged. The humanities subjects began to share blocks of time with whole year groups of students and this enabled teachers to experiment with different patterns of social organization for teachers and students. It enabled team teaching and peer observation to occur. For example, different sub-ject specialists could come together, with a large number of students within the same time slot, to present information which each considered to be relevant to any informed judgments about the theme or issue under discussion. In this situation they were able to observe each other's presentational methods and hold debates about the relevance and significance of their subject matter. Within the same time block students could be organized into discussion groups to examine the informa-tion presented, and its significance for their understanding of a particular theme or issue. Some blocks of time were organized to enable students to gather their own information through interdisciplinary research in their local communities and feed it back into their discussions.

In addition to their role as subject specialists, teachers took on new roles, and developed new skills connected with the collaborative planning of 'integrated' cur-ricula, team teaching, chairing discussions, and facilitating students' inter-disciplinary research and inquiry in the wider community. They found they could no longer depend on the routine skills they had acquired as transmitters of tightly bounded subject-matter. All involved experienced a measure of de-skilling and this moti-vated them to abandon the individualism that characterized subject teaching and to collaborate with each other in developing new professional knowledge, through sharing experiences and ideas. Innovative curriculum experimentation in the field of the humanities became more collaborative as it became less subject-based. As a form of action research it not only involved individual teachers in eliciting student perceptions of their performance, in addition to their own, but also in eliciting the perceptions of their peers. This is why the triangulation of data — understanding a situation from different points of view — emerged as a central element of the methodology of educational action research in the UK.

The kind of innovative curriculum experiments in the humanities subjects that I have described, which emerged in the UK as a response to widespread student disaffection in the secondary modern schools of the 60s, can appropriately be called a form of action research, rather than simply reflective practice, because the teachers who participated in these experiments wished to produce accounts of their actions. These teachers had an expectant audience in their peers, headteachers, local and national government officials, and school inspectors: all in search of solutions to the problem of educating the 'non-academic' student. They presented their work at conferences, wrote articles for professional journals, and appeared on radio and television. Their reputations as innovators advanced rather than impeded their careers, and publication was a means of establishing them.

The National Curriculum Project, Curriculum Theory and the Dissemination of Action Research

In the mid-1960s, the Schools Council for Curriculum Reform was established as an educational partnership between teachers (represented by their unions), local education authorities (the teachers' employers) and central government. Its object was to provide teachers and schools with support for curriculum development. This included developing the system of public examinations in ways which were consistent with the new curricula. Respect for the professional autonomy of teachers on questions of what and how to teach was a central principle governing the Council's work. It initiated a range of curriculum projects led by subject experts from academia but staffed by innovatory teachers on 'temporary release' from their schools. The project teams devised and piloted new content and materials in collaboration with volunteer schools and then tried to disseminate their curriculum packages more widely to potential users in the educational system.

This model of support for curriculum development failed, on the whole, to secure widespread adoption in schools. It rested on the assumption that curriculum innovations were transferable commodities, hence, the first task of dissemination was to 'sell' the package as a general solution to a curriculum problem. All teachers then had to do, to make the innovation work in their classrooms, was to follow the instructions for use which accompanied the package. However, according to those who constructed such packages, many teachers failed to read the instructions properly and assimilated the innovation to the norms governing their existing practices.

One project adopted a different approach to the problem of disseminating curriculum innovation in schools. This was the Humanities Project (1967–72), directed by Lawrence Stenhouse (see Stenhouse, 1968). The project was established by the Schools Council towards the end of an inquiry into young school leavers (those who left school at the minimum age of 15 without taking public examinations). The inquiry (1968), revealed that one of the major factors which switched many young adolescents off schooling was the perceived irrelevance of the curriculum, particularly in the area of the humanities, to their immediate vocational and practical concerns. Such concerns focused on the need to get a job, but this was not unrelated to the need to acquire adult status, a status students felt to be incommensurate with remaining in school. Entry into the world of work was perceived as synonymous with entry into the world of the adult.

Stenhouse, formerly a university and college lecturer, reconceptualized the humanities subjects as resources for adolescents to reflect about their experience of becoming adults in society, rather than bodies of abstract knowledge to be acquired through a continuing dependency relation with teachers. In doing so he hoped to dispel the students' perception that remaining at school impeded rather than supported their entrance into the world of the adult, and that the study of the humanities was an irrelevance.

Stenhouse recognized that such a reconceptualization had profound implications for teaching and learning. The subject matter of the humanities was not to be regarded as a source of objective knowledge accessed by learners on the basis of an authority relation with experts through a process of instruction. Regarding it as a resource for reflecting about their experience entitled learners to question the subject matter in the light of experience rather than be questioned about it, and to have opportunities for free and open discussion about the issues they raise. Such a learning process implied giving learners space in which to express the individuality and creativity of their thinking (Stenhouse, 1967) and become active constructors of their own understandings and insights through a process of enquiry and discussion. It implied that teachers protect students against the use of their traditional authority position to impose their prejudices, and that they protect divergence in discussion. Stenhouse and his team spelt all these implications out in the form of a set of pedagogical aims and principles which specified a role for the teacher as the manager of an educational process rather than an authoritative source of knowledge, as one in authority in relation to the handling of subject matter in classrooms, but not an authority.

Stenhouse vigororously and articulately denounced teaching by 'knowledge objectives' on the grounds that it was inconsistent with treating the humanities subjects as resources for individuals to use in making sense of their everyday experience (See Stenhouse; 1970). Although it protected students from the prejudices of their teachers and unwarranted interference in their personal lives, it did so at the cost of disconnecting knowledge from the knower's subjective experience of living. Stenhouse argued that rather than structuring curriculum materials in the humanities around pre-specified knowledge outcomes and thereby reinforce the traditional pedagogy in schools, they should be structured to support the innovatory pedagogy specified in the aims and principles of Humanities Curriculum Project (HCP).

The Humanities Project was therefore conceived as a form of pedagogically-driven, as opposed to objectives- or standards-driven curriculum change, and was therefore highly congruent with the logic that underpinned many of the more localized school-based curriculum initiatives which preceded it. The difference was the Stenhouse and his team articulated and made that logic publicly explicit, and thereby enabled HCP as an innovation to become the focus of significant debates within the teaching profession, amongst educationalists in the academy, and more widely through the media. The difference might be explained by the fact that, like other Schools Council projects, HCP was housed in a higher education institution and led by an academic. Such projects were therefore more inclined to methodological theorizing about their practice than teacher-led innovations in schools. However, it should also be noted that the project teams also consisted of teachers on release from their schools, and therefore provided a context in which methodology could be grounded in practical experience. This certainly appears to have been the case with HCP, for its explicit curriculum theory in many respects articulated a cluster of ideas, cited earlier above, that had been to varying degrees implicit in teacher-initiated innovations within the humanities curriculum (Elliott, 1991, Ch 1). It was to Stenhouse's credit that the theoretical rationale of HCP was grounded in the study of a certain kind of innovatory practice in schools.

The requirement by the Schools Council for the national dissemination of its projects, supplied the motivation for the emergence of curriculum theory. Innovations had to be conceptualized and justified as a basis for communication with potential users. I would contend that theoretical discourse in the curriculum field, in the UK at least, emerged in the context of national projects like HCP which operated at the boundaries between academia and the school system, and were required to disseminate innovations throughout that system.

One problem which confronted HCP's pedagogically driven model of curriculum change was that it appeared to prescribe a teaching and learning process, and this was seen by many teachers and their representatives on the Council to infringe the professional autonomy of teachers. Standards-driven models did not appear initially to constitute such an infringement. Their advocates argued that while learning outcomes were prescribed, teachers were free to select the methods for bringing them about. Few teachers at the time recognized that the options were restricted to instructional methods, since within the established professional culture teaching was equated with instruction.

Stenhouse and his team were able to resolve the dissemination dilemma of HCP by drawing on another idea implicit in school-initiated innovations in the humanities; namely, that they constituted innovative curriculum experiments. HCP was disseminated as such. The project team appealed not so much to the innovation enthusiast — change for change's sake — but to teachers with sceptical and critical minds. They were asked to suspend judgment for a period and generate and test strategies for realizing the pedagogical aims and principles of the project on the basis of evidence they gathered about the effects of their teaching on students. It was in this dissemination context that the ideas of teachers as researchers and action research were originally explicated, clarified, and elaborated as part of the nation-wide theoretical curriculum discourse which HCP stimulated. The idea of action research was an integral element of the curriculum change theory generated by HCP.

The Marginalization of the Academic Change Agent and the Merchandising of Action Research

From the UK Curriculum Reform movement in the UK during the 1960s and 70s a new field of educational enquiry and scholarship emerged in the universities and colleges and was called Curriculum Studies. It was founded on the discourses about curriculum change which were developed in the context of the Schools Council's projects and involved academics, teachers, and the local government advisory personnel responsible for disseminating projects to schools and supporting teachers trying to implement them. Many of the teachers and advisers involved, discovered new opportunities for career development as curriculum specialists in higher education institutions. The emergence of Curriculum Studies as an academic specialism posed a threat to the foundation disciplines of education — psychology, sociology, philosophy and history — as the basis for organizing research and scholarship in the field of education, and to the rationalist assumptions about the theory-practice relationship which underpinned this way of organizing the production and dissemination of educational knowledge. This was particularly evident in two major strands of the new specialism which arose out of the involvement of academics in the project-based curriculum reforms. The first was that of a new paradigm of curriculum evaluation, and the second a new paradigm of education research called action research.

The 'new evaluation' rejected what became known as the 'agricultural botany' paradigm, (Parlett and Hamilton, 1981) in which the gross yields of a programme were determined by comparing measurements of students' performance before and after the implementation of the curriculum. The latter assumed that a curriculum innovation operated in the same way regardless of the context of its implementation, and therefore that aggregated scores measured the effectiveness of the programme generally. The 'new evaluators' on the other hand observed that innovations shaped up differently in practice, and that their effects varied according to context. Hence, evaluators needed to study cases in order to understand the complex transactions which constituted the innovation in process.

The evaluation enterprise lost its foundations in a positivist and behaviourist science of psychology and developed as a form of naturalistic inquiry (Simons, 1987), using qualitative methods — such as unstructured interviews, participant observation, and triangulation — derived from social anthropology and naturalistic sociology, to provide a multifaceted portrayal of the change process in particular settings. Curriculum Evaluation was transformed into the study of change processes. The evaluators did not see it as their responsibility to judge the merits of an innovation but to portray it in a form which enabled a variety of 'stakeholders' to judge it for themselves in the light of their interests and evaluative standards. MacDonald (1976) conceptualized three different kinds of evaluation in terms of the kinds of audiences they sought to inform; namely, autocratic, bureaucratic, and democratic. He argued that the questions addressed in an evaluation should neither be determined by the evaluators themselves or bureaucrats. Rather, in a pluralistic democracy, they should stem from a variety of groups with a legitimate interest in the innovation. Democratic Evaluation with its idea of democracy as a stakeholder society (House, 1986) in which power is widely dispersed provided an alternative vision of quality assurance and educational accountability to the one embedded in the centralizing tendencies of the bureacratic state.

The second new paradigm of educational enquiry which academic institutions in the UK inherited from the curriculum reform movement was that of action research. It provided an alternative vision of quality development to the standards-driven reforms of the state, sometimes articulated as a bottom-up, as opposed to a top-down, change strategy. Educational enquiry within this paradigm was pedagogically-driven, inasmuch as it aimed to change the pedagogical conditions under which students gained access to knowledge and culture. This involved teachers gathering, sharing, and discussing evidence about problematic aspects of their practices in classrooms and schools with a view to changing these practices to effect a better match with their pedagogical aims.

Unlike the 'new evaluation', action research constituted an 'insider' rather than 'outsider' form of enquiry, not because it excluded outsiders from participating in the research process but because it adopted the action perspective of the educational practitioner. Researchers in higher education institutions were able to collaborate with teachers in the gathering and analysis of evidence when they shared a common vision of educational change. Such visions are articulated as pedagogical aims. For example, at the Centre for Applied Research in Education in the University of East Anglia and the Cambridge Institute of Education, collaborative action research projects have, over the past twenty years, focused on such topics as 'Inquiry/ Discovery Teaching', Mixed-Ability Teaching', 'Teaching for Understanding', 'Using Micro-computers to foster Autonomous Learning', 'Developing Environmental Awareness through Action-Learning in the Community'. Each of these topics represents a pedagogical aim embodying an idea of educational change that the researchers shared with many teachers inside the schools. The collaboration of researchers in academic institutions with teachers in schools on such action research projects was grounded in a view of the professional culture of teachers as dynamic rather than static, as capable of continuously transforming itself by generating innovatory conceptions of the educational process. A vision of educational change as a bottom-up process of action research is grounded in this view, and it is currently under challenge, as I shall indicate shortly. Such a vision implies that quality in education cannot be described independently of educational processes and is a dynamic rather than static concept, inasmuch as new meanings are being continually generated from within the professional culture of teachers.

The two paradigms of democratic evaluation and action research were, however, complementary rather than conflicting. Both endorsed the desirability of bottom-up educational change. The former emphasized the public's need for quality assurance and their right to a knowledge and understanding of educational change processes. The latter emphasized the information requirements of the central agents of change, the teachers. Moreover, both paradigms could utilize data generated by the other. The action research accounts of practitioners could be used by evaluators to explain their activities to stakeholders, while their own case studies could be used by practitioners to deepen their understanding of the contextual factors which shape and influence their practices. Both paradigms have employed qualitative case study methods to meet the information needs of stakeholders and practitioners respectively, e.g., methods such as unstructured and semi-structured interviewing, participant observation, the use of logs, journals, diaries, audio/video recordings and photography, to record situations and events, the gathering of biographical data from key participants, and the depiction of events and situations from a number of different perspectives (triangulation).

Action research cannot be paradigmatically distinguished from other forms of research in terms of data gathering methods. It need not even exclusively employ qualitative as opposed to quantitative methods when quantitative data serves the purposes of the research. What distinguishes action research from other forms of educational enquiry are its transformative intentions and the methodological principles (not methods) such intentions imply. The methodology of educational action research might be briefly summarized as follows:

- it is directed towards the realization of an educational ideal, e.g., as represented by a pedagogical aim;
- it focuses on changing practice to make it more consistent with the ideal;
- it gathers evidence of the extent to which the practice is consistent/inconsistent with the ideal and seeks explanations for inconsistencies by gathering evidence about the operation of contextual factors;
- it problematizes some of the tacit theories which underpin and shape practice, i.e., taken-for-granted beliefs and norms;
- it involves practitioners in generating and testing action-hypotheses about how to effect worthwhile educational change.

From the mid-1970s and through most of the 80s, government became increasingly interventive on curriculum matters, targeting resources on particular priorities linked to enhancing the economic competitiveness of the nation, such as an emphasis on science and technology in the curriculum, school-industry links, technical-vocational education, and the development of a common core curriculum through whole-school curriculum planning. These resources were administered by local government and coordinated through their advisory services. Schools and teachers retained responsibility for curriculum development but within nationally defined priority areas and guidelines. Built into the specification for many of these initiatives was an evaluation requirement, sponsored either at the national level by central government or at the local level by local education authorities. In addition, schools were expected to develop procedures for self-evaluating their performance. The inservice training of teachers was increasingly reshaped and resourced in the light of national policy priorities.

Within departments of education in higher education institutes, curriculum specialists carried out evaluations for central and local government which focused on 'policy implementation' in schools. Those who claimed allegiance to 'democratic evaluation' came into frequent conflict with their bureacratic sponsors who felt that they had a right to control the focus of the evaluation (a focus on policy-making processes and decisions about resources was usually not welcomed) and the right to own the final report and control its distribution (Simons, 1987 Chapter 6). Bureacratic evaluations became the norm and democratic evaluators found it increasingly difficult to secure contracts. Some of them found a niche in post-graduate inservice courses which supported the development of democratic self-evaluation procedures in schools (Simons, 1987 Chapters 8–10). However, following the devolvement of financial management to schools and the establishment of a highly prescriptive national curriculum in 1989, school self-evaluation became an instrument of school managers charged with responsibility for implementing standards-driven national curriculum and assessment requirements in a cost-efficient manner. It became the servant of mandatory top-down 'development planning' in schools, and lost its promise as a form of quality assurance for bottom-up educational change initiated by teachers from within their schools. Democratic evaluators turned away from schooling and found opportunities for their paradigm in other educational change settings, such as the police, medicine and nursing.

What of action research in schools? Over the last two decades the curriculum development specialists in academia were increasingly marginalized as agents of educational change in schools. They were ideologically branded by government as '60's' types responsible for contaminating the teaching profession with 'trendy progressive theories' of education. Resources to support collaborative action research in schools dried up and the curriculum specialists retreated to the beach-head of inservice teacher education (MacDonald, 1991) where higher education still retained some influence, albeit indirectly, over the professional practices of teachers. They began to increasingly cast themselves in the role of facilitators of, rather than collaborators in, school-based action research, in which context they designed courses to promote the professional development of teachers through action research. They became professional developers rather than curriculum developers and created a new specialism called 'Action Research', open to academics without specific expertise in the study of curriculum change.

Curriculum Studies departments went into decline and action research was reconstructed as a personal professional development process. This had always been a dimension of action research, a spin-off from teachers' attempts to realize their educational ideals through changing the curriculum and its associated pedagogy. In this context, professional development took on a particular meaning. Detached from this context, and in a context where the teacher was increasingly viewed as an instrument of externally driven curriculum reforms, 'professional development through action research' took on new meanings. A recent study of action research based post-graduate courses in six UK 'centres of excellence' (Elliott, 1996) suggests that action research is being merchandised in some courses as a professional development process which optimizes teachers' performance in schools in terms of their technical efficiency. This construction of action research matches the trend towards assessing teachers' performance against occupational standards defined as functional competencies. The 'improvement of practice' as the aim of action research becomes reinterpreted as the development of functional competence. The teacher as an educational innovator is replaced by the teacher as a functionary. However, the study cited above suggests that in some other courses action research is being merchandised as a form of spiritual development. Its primary aim is to promote self-knowledge and self-discovery in relation to the teacher's values and where he or she stands professionally in relation to them. Such a process may construct a professional self which views itself to be in an alienated condition and in need of salvation. What is not clear is how such courses enable teachers to resolve the internal contradiction between the ideal self and the self in action in their schools. What such courses appear to offer teachers is a kind of therapeutic relief from their experience in schools, a world in which they can have the ideal self confirmed as the 'real me' and the 'self in action' at school as 'not really me' but something I must continue to pretend to be because it pays the money. These two views of professional development through action research represent a split between the professional role and the person performing it. It is a split which is perfectly explicable in the context of externally driven reforms in schools which give little space for the expression of the generative capacities of teachers. In marketing professional development courses and packages to teachers, academics appear to be caught between merchandising action research as a form of personal salvation from the woes of life in schools and merchandising it as a way of optimizing performance in a functional role.

Conclusion

I am aware that this chapter reads like a pathology of action research in the UK. However, I remain optimistic. The tide will turn, and I believe it is already beginning to do so. Teachers are starting to articulate the educational costs of externally driven school reforms. One of these costs takes us back to the original problem that provided the context for the emergence of school-based action research in the UK; namely, the widespread disaffection of students in schools. This is rapidly emerging as a major social issue once more. Currently, the decline of authority in the family and society is being blamed and people are looking outside schools for explanations and solutions. However, some teachers and schools are aware that the problem has a curriculum and pedagogical dimension which they will need to address with public support. Spaces for teachers to engage in bottom-up curriculum and pedagogical change to stem the rising tide of student disaffection, will need to be constructed and sanctioned by policy. In the UK we may shortly see the day again when collaborative action research between teachers and academics re-emerges as an educational change strategy. In the meantime the strategy is operating in many countries across the world who have devolved more responsibility for initiating educational change back to the schools and their local communities.

References

ELLIOTT, J. (1991) *Action Research for Educational Change*, Open University Press, Milton Keynes and Philadelphia.

ELLIOTT, J. (1996) 'Bringing Action Research Home: The Experiences of Teachers who have Followed Award Bearing Courses', paper presented to the Annual Meeting of The American Educational Research Association, New York. East Anglia, Centre for Applied Research in Education.

HOUSE, E.R. (1986) 'Participatory Evaluation: The Stakeholder Approach', Introduction in HOUSE, E.R. (Ed.) *New Directions in Educational Evaluation*, Lewes, Falmer Press.

MACDONALD, B. (1976) 'Evaluation and the Control of Education', in TAWNEY, D. (Ed.), *Curriculum Evaluation To-day: Trends and Implications*, London, Schools Council Research Studies, Macmillan Educational.

MACDONALD, B. (1991) 'From Innovation to Reform — A Framework for Analysing Change', *Critical Introduction to Ruddock, J. Innovation and Change*, Milton Keynes and Philadelphia, Open University Press.

PARLETT, M. and HAMILTON, D. (1981) 'Illuminative Evaluation', in REASON, P. and ROWAN, J. (Eds), *Human Inquiry: A Sourcebook of New Paradigm Research*, London, Wiley.

SCHOOLS COUNCIL (1968) *Enquiry 1. Young School Leavers*, London, Her Majesty's Stationery Office.

SIMONS, H. (1987) *Getting to Know Schools in a Democracy: The Politics and Process of Evaluation*, Lewes, Falmer Press.

STENHOUSE, L. (1967) *Culture and Education*, London, Nelson.

STENHOUSE, L. (1968) 'The Humanities Curriculum Project', *Journal of Curriculum Studies*, 1, pp. 26–33.

STENHOUSE, L. (1970) 'Some Limitations of the Use of Objectives in Curriculum Research and Planning', *Pedagogica Europaea*, 6, pp. 73–83.

3 Practitioners, Higher Education and Government Initiatives in the Development of Action Research: The Case of Austria

Herbert Altrichter (Austria)

Introduction

Austria has seen an amazing growth of interest in action research during the last decade. Comparatively few years have brought about a surprisingly wide range of publications, inservice courses, research and development projects in Austria. To develop a more thorough understanding of the origins, development conditions and present problems of this action research movement, a small study was conducted in 1995 which comprised of literature research and of a postal survey.

In the latter part of the study fifty-six action researchers or people sympathetic to action research were invited to evaluate the state and the development of Austrian action research using a very open set of questions. Three letters turned out to be undeliverable and twenty-two people provided us with letters or tapes in which they discussed our questions and gave hints to further action researchers. Within the respondent group, middle-aged, comparatively established persons are over-represented: Two-thirds are on tenured positions. The majority are employed at universities, and about a third in schools or regional inservice institutions.

The material provided by our respondents was used to cross-check and modify our own analysis of literature published on Austrian action research work. Extracts from the letters and tapes are quoted in the following sections to present original views and voices from our respondents[1]. The German version of the paper was presented for discussion to a conference of Austrian action researchers in 1995 and rewritten in the light of the reactions provided (see Altrichter and Thaler, forthcoming). While the results are certainly not to be generalized to other national contexts with different educational histories and politics, they might offer a useful set of hypotheses for the analysis of the development of non-traditional research and development approaches under different societal conditions.

Conditions for Development

What factors have been influential in the development of action research in Austria? Judging from the data of our survey and from literature analysis, the following conditions may be considered essential:

Good Standing at Universities in a Context of a Rather Disintegrated Academic Discipline of Education

German speaking social research saw a rise of action research (*Handlungsforschung*) between 1972 and 1982 (see Deakin University, 1988, pp. 235–65). While this 'first wave' of action research had virtually vanished from the scene by the middle of the 80s (see Altrichter and Gstettner, 1993), a new interest in school-based action research developed particularly in Austria. Rather than continuing or reviving earlier German traditions, this 'second wave' of Austrian action research was stimulated by English influences, in particular by *workshops* at Klagenfurt University which were held since 1982 by John Elliott and other action researchers from the Cambridge Institute of Education and University of East Anglia.

The venue of these early workshops indicates a more general feature: Universities have played a decisive role in establishing this type of action research in Austria. The next step was the development of a two-year national course of further studies for teachers by Klagenfurt University in 1985 (see Altrichter, 1986). These inservice courses turned out to be attractive to a number of very innovative teachers from all over the country who became supporters of action research in their respective regions. Thus, a first major power base of action research evolved.

During the second half of the 1980s, research and development projects were initiated, e.g., in initial teacher education (Altrichter, 1988), and in school development programmes (see Hackl, 1994; Messner and Rauch, 1995; Altrichter and Posch 1996). Most influential among these projects was *Environment and School Initiatives*: It introduced action research into OECD research programmes which until then had concentrated on traditional large scale methodology (OECD, 1991; Posch, 1993). While early initiatives mostly originated from Peter Posch's group at Klagenfurt University, other action research groups evolved at the University of Vienna (Hackl, 1994) and at the University of Innsbruck (Kroath, 1989, 1991; Schratz, 1990).

International links which are rather poorly developed in the academic field of education in Austria seem to be a real strength of Austrian action research. International connections of some action researchers, and involvement in international high-status projects (e.g., OECD or EC), meant recognition for Austrian action research[2], made it a little more independent of the imponderabilities of the rather narrow local scene, and strengthened its stance in bidding for new projects. Initially, international contacts were rather unilateral from England to Austria. By the end of the 1980s, linkages to Australian and North American universities had also been established, particularly through the Project 'Environment and School Initiatives' through which Austrian action research received some recognition in other

European countries, such as Italy, Slovenia, and also the UK (see Altrichter, *et al.*, 1993).

The important role of university teachers in promoting action research (and the academics' inclination to publish) has resulted in an extensive number of publications both on theoretical and methodological issues, as well as on findings from research and development work (see list of references). The survey does not allow a systematic examination of the type and number of publications on action research, however, from my experience of editorial or recuitment boards it may be said that Austrian action researchers tend to publish their work in school-focused national and regional journals and in collections of papers. Rarely would they turn to one of the major academic educational journals in the German language; however, some publish in major journals in the fields of Mathematics Education and Teaching English as a Second Language. On the other hand, the number of action research papers published in journals or in English language publications is far above the average of Austrian academics in the field of education. The number and range of publications have provided action research with a visibility in the educational scene which, in turn, has been helpful for its further expansion. 'Action research is being taken seriously — there is a public discourse which is, e.g., quite different from the situation in Germany' (B12, 3^3). On the other hand, it may be, as the same respondent suspects, that 'there is more resonance in the "charts" than real substance' (*ibid.*).

What is the scope of action research activities? Is action research a marginal activity or has it acquired a firm place in the Austrian educational scene? Let us discuss some indicators: Twenty-two letters of our survey mentioned thirty-three projects with external funding. Particularly, the Ministry for Education and the Arts, some Regional Inservice Institutions and Regional Education Authorities are prepared to support action research projects. Three projects won financial support from the most prestigious Austrian research foundation — which means that one sixth of all educational research projects funded by this foundation in the period of 1986– 1995 operate on an action research basis. Also European Union and the OECD funding was acquired for one project each. MA-theses using action research are being written at four of the five Austrian universities offering MA-programmes in Education. PhD-theses in action research have been submitted to the universities of Vienna and Innsbruck. Two post-doctoral theses were accepted at the universities of Innsbruck and Klagenfurt. Thus, action research work is by no means impossible or marginalized in Austrian universities.

Given the heavy involvement of university-based action researchers in inservice training of teachers and development projects, it is, at first sight, surprising that action research plays only a peripheral role in university courses. At four universities, students may opt for some rather isolated action research course elements (in MA^4-courses in education and business education as well as in initial teacher education programmes), however, there is no single course of studies which is fully or largely organized on an action research basis. There have been some attempts at Klagenfurt University to reorganize the core courses of the teacher education programme (Altrichter, 1988; Altrichter *et al.*, 1989) and the special option on 'education in schools' in the MA-programme without, however, any lasting effect. What are the reasons for this situation?

- Firstly, Austrian university teachers tend to interpret their historic academic autonomy (*Freiheit der Lehre und Forschung*) in a rather individualistie way and usually resent attempts to coordinate individual courses in a programme of studies.
- Secondly, the university system in German-speaking countries is different from many other systems in that award bearing university courses do not have any significant career implications for teachers.
- Thirdly, the concept of professionality based on practical knowledge (inherent in action research approaches) may be in some conflict with the university teachers' claim to 'expert knowledge'; the appreciation of practical experience may disturb the traditional sequence and relative weight of practicum phases, practical courses, and theoretical lectures; the idea of continuous, long-term development contradicts the prevailing 'atomism' of uncoordinated mini-courses (see Altrichter and Gorbach, 1993).

To sum up: Although only a small number of university teachers in the field of education — concentrated in three of the six Austrian universities offering education courses: Klagenfurt, Innsbruck, and Vienna — would consider themselves action researchers or sympathize with action research, they have managed to gain a quite distinctive and high profile in the public perception by virtue of their involvement in inservice courses for teachers, development projects, publications, and expert opinions on educational matters. Through these activities they built a network which was obviously also attractive for educational practitioners. This is even more remarkable since academic faculties of education traditionally did not have a reputation with practitioners for doing practical, relevant work. Thus, the rise of action research also indicates the rise of a new generation of university teachers who were both interested in research *and* in practical educational development, and who were also prepared to collaborate with practitioners on more equal terms.

It must be seen that the establishment of action research has been facilitated by the heavily fragmented nature of academic educational research at Austrian universities. Until the mid-1960s, the discipline of education at Austrian universities consisted of a small number of chairs filled by philosophers of different allegiances (or deserving school practitioners with a philosophical vein). The 'realistic turn' in the second half of the sixties introduced empirical-quantitative research to education departments. After initial successes in filling newly created positions at the beginning of the seventies, the proportion of 'quantitative-empiricists' has stagnated at about 20 per cent of all university staff in education (Thonhauser, 1992, p. 13). Consequently, no research paradigm is dominant in the academic scene. Additionally, exchange of ideas between the different camps seems to be scarce. Most research teams rather seem to invest in contacts with foreign (in particular German) research groups of their own denomination rather than developing links to different research traditions within the country. In the niches of such a rugged landscape it might have been easier for action research to secure some relatively uncontested place and to acquire some critical mass, since no counter-pressure from 'dominant paradigms' was to be overcome.

Although the involvement of university teachers was most likely a highly conducive condition for the establishment of action research, too strong a dependence on universities may impede future development. Firstly, it will be difficult to appoint additional action researchers at university level because of the present financial constraints in the university sector. Secondly, the teacher college sector[5] has been neglected so far by action researchers. As a result the majority of teachers do not get a chance to experience this type of reflected professionalism which action research aims to promote. Thirdly, the concept of innovation embraced by action research asks for practitioners to be the leading persons in educational reform; eventually, action research does need more teacher researchers in schools than 'critical friends' at universities.

The Role of School Administration and Regional Inservice Institutions and the Societal Trend towards Decentralisation and School-based Development

Austria is a country with a long-standing tradition of centralist government of education[6]. Originally, some commentators were rather sceptical whether the action research concept, freshly imported from England, could take roots in such a different habitat. The following system features have been regarded as inimical to the establishment of action research (Kroath, 1991, p. 231):

- Regulation was very tight in the school sector and autonomy of schools was lacking. Thus, the room for manoeuvre was rather narrow for schools and limited their need for reflective research-based development.
- In Austria a zest for development was not deeply rooted in the professional ethics of teachers, and further qualifications were usually no asset for careers in the teaching profession. Thus, inservice training usually was discontinuous and often seen as a relief from professional stress.
- Since no tradition of collaboration between universities and schools with respect to inservice training had been established, there was no power base for research-oriented training programmes and no support system for the ambitious teacher-as-researcher concept.

The highly centralist education system tends to monitor the functioning of the system through input control: an elaborate legislation and ministerial circulars predefine the operation of all educational establishments to a large degree. Such a system does not have much need for process development because legislation — at least in theory — does not leave much space for discretion; and it does not create a need for reflection on the results ('output') which are thought to be defined by the 'input'. Discrepancies between regulations and educational practice are generally disregarded. If people point at them, the system would feel challenged and would react with even more elaborate input regulation.

In fact, educational administration was rather sceptical about university educational research until the beginning of the eighties. Contact between school practitioners and university teachers was rare and was impeded by a sense of hierarchy between 'practice and research' and by exclusive conditions of mutual access. However, the situation seems to have changed in the course of the eighties. Universities have become more open and more interested in practical affairs. On the other hand, many letters in our survey mention 'an increasing potential for support in the education ministry' (B9, 2) and indicate that there has been 'a shift from scepticism to cautious support' (B10, 4) on the part of the Regional Education Authorities[7] which has led to a 'comparatively strong interest from the Regional Inservice Training Institutions and from school administration' (B7, 2). For some observers the role of school administration still is 'not quite clear' (T2, 2), and 'conflicts with Regional Inservice Training Institutions which experience university initiatives as competition' (B10, 4) still persist.

Some letters attribute these attitudinal changes of school administration to gradual changes in the composition of the workforce in the ministries. The traditional image of an Austrian education ministry was as follows: Hierarchical relationships with schools — exclusion of research from schools — leading civil servant positions filled with persons with a law background. While this pattern was valid until the 1980s, in the following years a new generation of civil servants with academic qualifications (often in education or social sciences) and without any anxiety about contacting universities gained grounds, thus, increasing the intellectual breadth and the range of ideas in school administration. Now, there is both 'a progressive, innovative faction with a long-term perspective and a very conservative, defensive faction' (B12, 3).

For other commentators this shift of attitude is a side-effect of the growing problems of the centralist model of governance: The awareness is rising that local quality cannot be achieved through central regulation, but must build on the collaboration and responsibility of the people working in schools who, in turn, need (and wish) some room for manoeuvre in the face of specific local conditions. In the eighties the traditional concept of school development as 'macro-development' was challenged nearly all over Europe. Also Austrian teachers increasingly resented the centralist 'school experiments', however, there was little space left for new policy issues to emerge, since the two main political parties were entrenched in their antagonistic views about the development of secondary schools (for students of 10–14 years). A period of stagnation followed (Gruber, 1990).

Gradually however, groups of parents and teachers emerged who aimed at educational development beyond the traditional lines of dispute. In such a climate a number of topics gained prominence, such as autonomy of schools, school-based inservice training, school-based development, integration of handicapped students, or new forms of active student learning. For school administration, this increasingly 'messy' situation might have indicated the danger of a relative loss of control but it also offered a chance to free itself from the traditional patterns of macro-development of systems, to take up tendencies already emerging at the grassroot level and, thus, retain influence. For innovative practitioners, this state of affairs offered some hope to embark on innovations without head winds from the administrative system.

The consequences of this 'crisis of regulation' in the educational sector offered some chances for action researchers which had a lot to offer: Models for collaboration with practitioners beyond command structures had already been developed in action research projects. Innovative teachers found it to be much easier to identify with such projects than with state institutions. 'The action research approach was flexibile enough to adapt to local needs' (B7, 2). Its small-scale approach with much collaboration from the people concerned was 'comparatively moderate in price' (*ibid.*) Its insistence on self-reflective development nourished hopes that there would be self-control where external control was not easy or was ineffective. Given this background it is not surprising that action researchers increased their collaboration with Regional Inservice Training Institutions and were involved in virtually all the main reform projects at the end of the eighties and the beginning of the nineties — such as autonomy of schools, project work in classrooms, environmental education, alternative modes of learning, school-based development etc.

Pragmatic Approaches to Development and Success in Teacher Education and School Development

Through some early success in inservice courses and development projects (see pp. 30–3) action researchers gained appreciation from school administration and developed some attraction for innovative teachers. Also the 'very pragmatic and reformist outfit of the Austrian action research' and 'pragmatic toughness' (B12, 3) of some important advocates of action research were named as conducive factors: They invested in producing 'good examples' in collaboration with various partner institutions (plenty of which were available after the turn to greater openness in both central and regional administration) rather than doing missionary work for uninterested and reluctant groups or wearing out their energies by debates of principle. This inclusive, associative (rather than exclusive, differentiating) style of work seems to have attracted people who were interested in innovation and development of the education system but, on the other hand, did not want to fully subscribe to one of the political and institutional factions (which were the main agents of educational development until that time) and rather wanted to cultivate a 'professional' attitude open to different options of development:

> There is a network of action researchers in schools who work continuously and relatively independently from the current political tendencies, school experiments, educational fads, etc. The network has a polycentric structure (with a link to academic action research) and does not depend on the state structures for innovation of schools. (B1, 5)

On the other hand, some letters emphasize that 'comparatively many opportunities were missed': Conflicts in some projects caused a decline in energy and commitment. 'The Mittelschulbereich (the issue of integrating the bipartite system of secondary schools for 10–14 year old students) would have been a field of activity for action researchers', however, no project was started in this — politically contentious — field (T1, 5).

The pragmatic approach to action research was obviously successful in the past, however, it may be dangerous for the future: The project-type organization of most initiatives created an impression of bustling activity in public, however, it is highly uncertain how durable, comprehensive and thorough these developments will turn out to be in the long range: These small-scale projects 'are . . . little spearheads — but there is no particular broad effect' (T1, 5). The pragmatic approach which avoids debates of principles may have lead to a varied scene, but also to a scene which is diverse and disintegrated with respect to its convictions and patterns of work. There are obviously contacts between the different groups of action researchers and references to each other's work, however, one does not get the impression that a coherent discourse of action research has evolved, nor that earlier work is thoroughly discussed, challenged or used as a stepping stone for new projects. Thus, the image emerges that action research itself is repeating the pattern of incoherence which has been used to characterize the discipline of education in Austria in pp. 30–3.

The Orientation Towards Professionality, the Work Situation of Teachers and the Lack of Support Systems

Even if some letters mention that 'the number of teachers is comparatively high' (B10, 3) nobody would call action research a mass movement in Austrian education. On the contrary, it is an avant-garde group of teachers who feel attracted to action research — a group which is special and attractive because of its innovative energy and its roots in inservice institutions and projects, but still rather small. To be sure, action research in Austria has not yet reached its goal that practitioners themselves are the prime agents in initiating, conducting and publishing action research:

> Generally, action research is still an initiative originating from universities
> — i.e., university people 'want something' from practitioners. The approach
> will only be firmly rooted if circumstances are reversed and practitioners
> or schools are looking for support for action research processes from uni-
> versity people. (B10, 3)

On the other hand, some letters complain that action research is a demanding task because it is time consuming and because teachers are usually 'oriented towards action rather than towards research' (B7, 2). For some commentators these problems are an expression of the 'excessive demands (put) on practitioners' (B5, 4) by action research; for others they represent the self-made frictions of a reform initiative. Action research aims at a different image of the teaching profession where reflective practitioners collaborate with their colleagues and clients in order responsibly to develop their practice and their competencies. This type of professional practice also implies transformed conditions of work, e.g., time for reflection, conversation, and coordination during the school day; readiness to give up the comfortable aspects of the 'single combat'-mentality of the classroom teacher etc. These conditions are presently lacking (otherwise action research need not fight for 'professionalization'). The result is that those who — by practising a 'future image of the teaching profession' — want to make it a 'present one', work in a particularly stressful situation (Kroath, 1991, p. 232). Thus, a practitioner comments:

> The fact that media for distributing teacher knowledge were virtually non-existent and that I had my normal teaching load were a big impediment between 1980 and 1985. Even if the situation has somewhat improved in the meantime there is no sufficient support network which may be used individually and decentrally without having to link into the academic project network. (B1, 5)

Frequently, letters regret that there is 'no institutional framework for action research in Austria . . . [and] no network like CARN' (B9, 2): 'Institutionalisation through conferences is lacking due to a ponderous inservice training system and because professional development is not really rooted in the self-image of teachers' (T2, 3).

There have been attempts to improve the situation, but these initiatives have largely remained uncoordinated or were linked to projects with a limited life-span, e.g.: Consultation and support by external facilitators or collegial intervision groups have been provided by various projects (Kroath, 1991, p. 236). However, an attempt to institutionalize external facilitation in the field of environmental education through an 'academy of environmental education' has not yet been successful. Network journals have been (and in one case still are) published for teachers interested in research and development. A national conference on 'Teachers developing schools' hosted by the University of Klagenfurt in 1991 brought practitioners interested in reflective development together (Krainer and Tietze, 1992). In spite of its apparent success, no consecutive conference was staged until 1995 because no institution (other than the University of Klagenfurt) volunteered to organize it. However, some regional conferences, in particular in the province of Styria, have offered a forum for presenting and discussing practitioners' development work (see e.g., Krall, *et al.*, 1996, Posch 1996). Some research projects put heavy emphasis on making the development work of teachers known to the public. In some instances the development work of teachers was also published in books and journals (Schindler, 1993; Schweitzer, 1991; Altrichter, *et al.*, 1989), and several series of case studies have been edited. However, effective and easily accessible support systems for teacher researchers seem to be still highly necessary for sustaining the level of teacher research in Austria, and this is particularly true in times of transformation, of new demands and increasing pressure on the teaching profession.

Notes

1 Note, however, that the excerpts, originally in German, have been translated by the author. Therefore, no longer extracts — like in the German version of the paper (see Altrichter and Thaler forthcoming) — are reproduced.

2 E.g., the survey paper on the development of qualitative educational research in Europe published by *Qualitative Studies in Education* gives prominent coverage to the project 'Environment and School Initiatives' (see Kelchtermans, *et al.*, 1994, p. 244).

3 Quotations taken from letters are referred to by 'B', number of the letter and page number. Quotations taken from tapes sent by our respondents are referred to by 'T', number of the tape and page number of the transcript.

4 i.e., first-degree courses (of a minimal duration of 4 or 4.5 years) in Austria.

5 In Austria, teachers of *Gymnasium*-type secondary scools are educated at universities, all other secondary and primary school teachers are educated at post-secondary non-university teacher training colleges (*Paedagogische Akademien*).

6 See Altrichter and Posch (1994) for an overview of the Austrian system of education.

7 i.e., the semi-autonomous school administration in the Austrian provinces.

References

ALTRICHTER, H. (1986) 'The Austrian INSET-Project PFL: Establishing a Framework for Self-directed Learning', *British Journal of In-Service Education*, **12**, 3, pp. 170–77.

ALTRICHTER, H. (1988) 'Enquiry-based learning in initial teacher education', in NIAS, J. and GROUNDWATER-SMITH, S. (Eds), *The Enquiring Teacher*, Lewes, Falmer, pp. 121–34.

ALTRICHTER, H. (1990) *Ist das noch Wissenschaft?* Munich, Profil.

ALTRICHTER, H. (1991) 'Do we need an alternative methodology for doing alternative research?' in ZUBER-SKERRITT O. (Ed.), *Action Research for Change and Development*, Aldershot/Brookfield, Avebury, pp. 79–92.

ALTRICHTER, H. (1993a) 'The Concept of Quality in Action Research: Giving Practitioners a Voice in Educational Research', in SCHRATZ, M. (Ed.), *Qualitative Voices in Educational Research*, London, Falmer, pp. 40–55.

ALTRICHTER, H. (1993b) 'Verso una teoria dell'insegnamento della ricerca-azione', in SCURATI, C. and ZANNIELLO, G. (Eds), *La Ricerca Azione. Contributi per lo sviluppo educativo*, Tecnodid, Naples, pp. 103–20.

ALTRICHTER, H. and GORBACH, S. (1993) 'Professionalitaet im Wandel'. *Zeitschrift fuer Personalforschung*, **7**, 1, pp. 77–95.

ALTRICHTER, H. and GSTETTNER, P. (1993) 'Action Research: A closed chapter in the history of German social science?' *Educational Action Research*, **1**, 3, pp. 329–60.

ALTRICHTER, H., KEMMIS, S., MCTAGGART, R. and ZUBER-SKERRITT, O. (1991) 'Defining, Confining or Refining Action Research?' in ZUBER-SKERRITT, O. (Ed.), *Action Research for Change and Development*, Aldershot/Brookfield, Avebury, pp. 3–9.

ALTRICHTER, H. and POSCH, P. (1989) 'Does the Grounded Theory Approach offer a Guiding Paradigm for Teacher Research?' *Cambridge Journal of Education*, **19**, 1, pp. 21–31.

ALTRICHTER, H. and POSCH, P. (1991) 'Ucitelji raziskujejo svoj pouk', *Vzgoja in izobrazevanje*, **22**, 2, pp. 12–22.

ALTRICHTER, H. and POSCH, P. (1994) 'Austria: System of Education', in HUSEN, T. and POSTLETHWAITE, T.N. (Eds), *International Encyclopedia of Education*, 2nd edition. Pergamon, Oxford, pp. 423–32.

ALTRICHTER, H. and POSCH, P. (Eds) (1996) *Mikropolitik der Schulentwicklung*, Innsbruck, Studien Verlag.

ALTRICHTER, H., POSCH, P. and SOMEKH, B. (1993) *Teachers Investigate Their Work: An Introduction to the Methods of Action Research*, London, Routledge.

ALTRICHTER, H. & THALER, M. (forthcoming) 'Aktionsforschung in Oesterreich: Entwicklungsbedingungen und Perspektiven', paper to be published in the proceedings of the conference 'Schule veraendern durch Aktionsforschung', Vienna.

ALTRICHTER, H., WILHELMER, H., SORGER, H. and MOROCUTTI, I. (Eds) (1989) *Schule gestalten: Lehrer als Forscher*, Klagenfurt, Hermagoras.

DEAKIN UNIVERSITY (1988), *The Action Research Reader*, Geelong, Deakin University Press.

DICK, A. (1994) *Vom unterrichtlichen Wissen zur Praxisreflexion*, Bad Heilbrunn, Klinkhardt.

GRUBER, K.H. (1990) 'School reform and curriculum development: the Austrian experience,' *The Curriculum Journal*, **2**, 3, pp. 315–22.

HACKL, B. (1994) *Forschung fuer die paedagogische Praxis*, Innsbruck, Studien Verlag.

KELCHTERMANS, G., VANDENBERGHE, R. and SCHRATZ, M. (1994) 'The development of qualitative research: efforts and experiences from continental Europe', *Qualitative Studies in Education*, **7**, 3, pp. 239–55.

KRAINER, K. and TIETZE, W. (Eds) (1992) *Schulentwicklung an der Basis*, Boehlau, Wien.

KRALL. H., MESSNER, E. & RAUCH, F. (Eds) (1996) *Schulen beraten und begleiten*, Studien Verlag, Innsbruck.

KROATH, F. (1989) How do Teachers Change their Practical Theories? *Cambridge Journal of Education*, **19**, 1, pp. 59–69.

KROATH, F. (1991) *Der Lehrer als Forscher*, Munich, Profil.

LEGUTKE, M. (1992) 'Teachers as Researchers and Learners', paper given at the RELC Regional Seminar, Singapore.

MESSNER, E. and RAUCH, F. (1995) 'Dilemmas of Facilitating Action Research', *Educational Action Research*, **3**, 1, pp. 41–53.

LAKATOS, I. (1974) 'Falsifikation und die Methodologie wissenschaftlicher Forschungsprogramme', in LAKATOS, I. and MUSGRAVE, A. (Eds), *Kritik und Erkenntnisfortschritt*, Vieweg, Brunswick, pp. 89–189.

OECD (1991) *Environment, Schools and Active Learning*, Paris, OECD/CERI.

POSCH, P. (1993) 'The Environment and School Initiatives (ENSI). I: Action Research in Environmental Education', *Educational Action Research*, **1**, 3, pp. 447–55.

POSCH, P. (1994) 'Changes in the Culture of Teaching and Learning and Implications for Action Research', *Educational Action Research*, **2**, 2, pp. 153–61.

POSCH, P. (1996) 'Rahmenbedingungen fuer Innovationen an der Schule', in ALTRICHTER, H. and POSCH, P. (Eds), *Mikropolitik der Schulentwicklung*, Studienverlag, Innsbruck, pp. 170–206.

SCHINDLER, G. (1993) 'The Environment and School Initiatives (ENSI). II: The Conflict', *Educational Action Research*, **1**, 3, pp. 457–68.

SCHRATZ, M. (1990) 'Researching While Teaching: A Collaborative Action Research Model to Improve College Teaching', *Journal on Excellence in College Teaching*, 1, pp. 98–108.

SCHRATZ, M. and STEINER-LOEFFLER, U. (1994) 'Im Dschungel der Gefuehle', *Medien. Impulse*, 10, pp. 66–76.

SCHWEITZER, K. (1991) 'An example: "Waste Project-Oberwart District": Emancipation through Environmental Projects', in OECD: *Environment, Schools and Active Learning*, Paris, OECD/CERI, pp. 88–93.

THONHAUSER, J. (1992) 'Empirisch-paedagogische Forschung in Oesterreich', *Empirische Paedagogik*, **6**, 1, pp. 5–17.

4 Educational Action Research in Australia: Organizations and Practice

Steven Kemmis and Shirley Grundy (Australia)

Australian educational action research has developed a community of practitioners through initiatives in school-based curriculum development, school-level evaluation, in-service education and participatory decision-making in schools. It has also developed as a disciplinary area in its own right (Brown, 1981). It has also developed an epistemology, rooted in critical social science (Kemmis, 1983; Grundy and Kemmis, 1981), with a characteristic set of research problems of other approaches to educational research and educational theory. These research problems are actively being pursued by a widening community of action researchers and action research facilitators around Australia.

It is important to note that Australian educational action research emerged as distinct from its counterparts in Britain, continental Europe and the United States of America. British action research in the 1970s shared with Australian action research the participatory and collaborative style of work, but was less strategically-oriented and probably less politically aware. It emphasized interpretive inquiry where Australian action research was more critical. Continental European action research shared a similar critical perspective with Australian action research, but did not appear to have developed the same practical thrust of the Australian work, and American action research developed as more teacher-oriented and teacher-controlled. (For characteristic statements of action researchers in the 1970s, see Elliott, 1978, for a British perspective; Brock-Utne, 1980 for a continental European perspective; and, for an American perspective, Tikunoff, Ward and Griffin, 1979.)

In some ways, the development of educational action research in Australia shared features with the beginnings of action research in the middle 1940s in America. It provided a form through which essentially democratic ideals about the conduct of social research could be expressed and manifested; it provided a focusing idea for practitioners involved in school and curriculum change at a time when 'grass roots' developments were beginning throughout an educational system. But there were differences too; the methodological perspective among research specialists in social science leaned much more towards interpretive methods, and there was a possibility that action research might become swept up in methodological developments in interpretive social science, like the 'new wave' evaluation (see Kemmis, 1983, for a discussion of action research in relation to methodological perspectives in social science).

To emphasize these epistemological issues, however, is to mistake the development of the rationale for action research with its development as a practical way of working for educational researchers and practitioners. The rise of educational action in Australia was the rise of a practical activity through which Australian teachers have become researchers into educational practices. The epistemological developments have merely located these practical developments in a contemporary epistemological framework. To some extent, they have helped to legitimate the practical developments, but are, from the perspective of most action researchers, esoteric issues which do not contribute immediately to the improvement of action research practice. It is our belief, of course, that the developing epistemological and theoretical framework has contributed to the development of more consistent and coherent practice in action research, but the fruits of action research are to be judged in improvements to teaching and learning in schools (and curriculum and school organization), not in purely theoretical advances.

Action Research in Australia: Its Collective Potential

There can be no doubt that there is growing interest in action research in Australia. Many projects, however, do not style themselves 'action research', and many are flying under other banners: school-based curriculum development, participatory decision making, school-level evaluation, school-based innovations, or school-based in-service education. In the Innovative Links Project, for example, teachers from groups of schools across Australia, together with academic associates from a nearby university, are learning about the problems and potential of developing their teaching practices under changing systemic conditions of the organization of educational work. They are developing organizations that learn — within schools, across school clusters in 'Roundtables', and across the Project's national network. What they are learning deserves to be widely known and understood.

The project's newsletter, *The Big Link*, already carries substantial evidence of the kinds of learnings emerging from the work of Roundtables. Project schools and Roundtables are documenting their work for wider circulation; it is likely that case studies of what is being learned will also be produced and written for schools and teachers in the form of stories from the field to the field. Participants in the project have also begun to consider how they might distil some of their learnings in the form of lessons from the field to education systems. They recognize that, through policy and the provision of different kinds of resources, systems people play significant roles in changing the conditions and organization of educational work, and thus in changing the conditions of teaching practice. Working together in schools, in the clusters of schools that form the Roundtables, and in the project's national network, Innovative Links Project participants are in a position to synthesize perspectives on how contemporary changes to educational policy and resourcing are working out at the 'sharp end' of education — at the school and classroom level.

On the basis of their experience, project participants can already show, for example, how practices of curriculum and pedagogy are helped and hindered under changing systemic conditions. The project can already give considered feedback to state and national education agencies about problems and possibilities associated with such matters as

- the implementation of statements and profiles;

- improving social justice in and through schooling;

- improving education in the middle school years;

- improving teaching and learning in literacy and mathematics; and

- changing patterns of work organization to support collaborative planning.

The advice the Project can offer is not simply anecdotal. It is in a position to offer some well-founded advice to education systems, based on evidence of trends across the country — evidence which has survived critical and self-critical examination. In this process, teachers and their colleagues are advancing educational knowledge, and they are inviting others to join them in the communicative process that constitutes research — defined by Lawrence Stenhouse (1984) as 'systematic enquiry made public' (p. 77). Their work has important implications for the work of education systems at several levels of organization, including:

(a)   school curricula and pedagogies,

(b)   educational administration,

(c)   teacher education curriculum and the continuing professional development of teachers, and

(d)   the conduct of educational research and evaluation.

It is to be hoped that Innovative Links Project participants, the project's formative evaluators (Professor Anna Yeatman and Associate Professor Judyth Sachs), and the Project's co-workers in the administration of the National Schools Network, will be able to bring such information and the recommendations they imply to the attention of school systems across Australia. Recommendations from this work could make a useful contribution to the formation of educational policy nationally.

Changing school systems is not just a matter of changing policies, however. Governments have no shortage of advice, all well-intentioned, no doubt, about how educational policies should change. What they lack is a secure basis of well-founded advice which has its roots in the actual and the possible — not just in aspirations and ideals. Well-founded advice — of the kind the Innovative Links Project is in a position to offer — will be based in knowledge about what education systems (as functioning organizations) can and cannot achieve, and knowledge about the practical experience and educational commitments of those who inhabit the lifeworlds of education (teachers and students in schools, administrators in education systems, teacher educators, and educational researchers and evaluators, for example). But what it means to have knowledge of this kind turns out to be highly problematic. Among other things, it requires having a developed perspective about the nature of educational systems and lifeworlds — which in turn requires a particular kind of social and educational theorizing.

This section of Chapter 4 aims to make a small contribution to the development of such theorising, with a focus on the experience of modernity. The notions of system and lifeworld provide a way of understanding some of the tensions, connections and contradictions of our contemporary experience of institutional life — including life in the institutions of education. Drawing on examples from the Innovative Links Project, some tentative conclusions are drawn about teaching practices and the lifeworld, and about work organization and the system.

System and Lifeworld: A Way of Understanding the Tensions in our Working Lives

The German social theorist Jurgen Habermas believes that the tension between system and lifeworld is one of the fundamental tensions of our era (Giddens, 1991; Habermas, 1984; Habermas, 1987a; Habermas, 1987b). Some take the view that the tension between plans and policies, on the one side, and the risks and uncertainties of our lived realities, on the other, is a tension between the public and private realms. In this view, duty and obligation require that each of us works harder and 'smarter'. It might mean working a few extra hours on the weekend, for example — putting in a bit more time to meet our public obligations, even if the corollary is taking out a bit more time from our private lives. The personal cost of supporting systems in chronic revision is regarded as a private matter, even when — in a Faustian contract — extra salary is offered in compensation. Habermas rejects this view as an over-simplification.

He rejects the simple identification of the public realm with the realm of the system and the private realm with the realm of the lifeworld. His theory of the *relationships* between system and lifeworld is an attempt to break down the facile dichotomy according to which the system is regarded as public, impersonal and oppressive, and the lifeworld as private, personal and subjugated. By rejecting the dichotomized perspective (and politics) in which the system is 'Them' (or 'It'), in opposition to 'Us', Habermas offers new ways to understand ourselves and our circumstances, and new ways to engage in the processes of change and reconstruction which modernity thrusts upon us. He replaces an image of polarization with an image of interconnection between system and lifeworld.

According to Habermas, we need to avoid slipping into ways of understanding our social reality that privilege either the 'system' perspective or the 'lifeworld' perspective. As he sees it, most forms of contemporary social theory make precisely this mistake, giving one pride of place and ignoring or obscuring the other. The more complex, but better justified, perspective understands them in relation to each other. The trick is to see them not as distinct concrete realms (as 'reified', or to be treated as if they were real entities) but as different aspects or dimensions of social life, jointly present in most real settings. We can make a start on understanding Habermas' theory about the relationship between system and lifeworld by considering not the distinction between these concepts but the relationship between them. That is, the relationship between what some social theorists (for example Giddens, 1979, pp. 76–85) call 'system integration' and 'social integration'.

When we participate in the institutional life of society (becoming a teacher in an education system, for example), our lives become shaped by the organizational structures, the institutional functions and the roles and rules which operate within the particular institution. That is, we are integrated into the systems in which we participate as part of our public life in society. We are well integrated into a social system (e.g., an educational system) when we know the way the system operates, how the organizational structures work, what the role expectations are and what rules, regulations and policies we need to follow to operate effectively.

Being integrated into the social systems in which we participate does not mean, however, simply being 'absorbed' into them. Rather, systems integration involves relationships between groups of people in the organization and in the society as a whole. For instance, 'students' and 'teachers' are placed in reciprocal relationships of dependence and authority, while 'teachers' and 'administrators' similarly experience reciprocal relationships of dependence and authority.

The process of systems integration is different from the process that occurs when we interact with other unique individuals with whom we affiliate in interpersonal rather than institutional terms. The sorts of interpersonal affiliations which we have in mind here are friendships between people, the interpersonal aspects of family life (as distinct from the family regarded as a 'social institution'), neighbourhoods and community groups which are spontaneously formed around shared interests and issues (but not institutionalized 'pressure groups' or political parties).

We saw above that systems integration involved orderliness and predictability based upon knowledge of structures, functions, roles and rules. When we consider other forms of affiliation among people which are based upon interpersonal interaction rather than systemic role definition, there is also some degree of 'orderliness' and dependability about these affiliations. But it is not dependability that is grounded in rule following or role expectation fulfilment. In these cases, social life is structured on the basis of developing shared understandings with others, drawing on and developing the resources of a shared (or potentially shared) culture; we form affiliations and solidarity with one another; we develop shared norms and values; and we establish a sense of our own identity in relation to the others who also inhabit the social settings in which we find ourselves. We, thus, become integrated into various forms of interpersonal social life through establishing or accepting shared understandings, values, expectations, traditions and actions. Thus, when we are integrated into these social systems that are characteristic of the lived experiences of people, that integration takes place through processes of understanding meaning making and communication. This form of social life has been called the 'lifeworld'.

System and lifeworld perspectives are not mutually exclusive. Both perspectives are simultaneously present in most social settings. When we go into our classrooms, one set of processes is at work as we integrate into our institutional role of 'teacher' *vis-a-vis* those who take up other roles ('student' or 'principal', for example). In this process we daily constitute and reconstitute our role as a functionary of the system, one might say, and of course we also constitute and reconstitute our relationships with those in other system roles, even though these others may be distant from the immediate classroom setting (like pay clerks, curriculum development officers, or the Minister of Education). So every day, as we take up our assigned roles in the system of 'teacher' and fulfil the expectations of that role and its relations with other roles, we consolidate our integration into the 'education system'.

At the same time, another set of processes is at work as we integrate into the interpersonal relationships we form with the other people actually present in the classroom, for example, as we establish or re-establish interpersonal relationships with the children in our classes and with our colleagues, and also, through them, with parents and other people in the community. In this aspect of our work we are experiencing social integration.

Teaching Practices and the Lifeworld: Work Organization and the System

It is clear from reports coming from schools and Roundtables in the Innovative Links Project, that people working in education today experience it in terms like those Giddens uses to describe the experience of Late Modernity: 'riding the Juggernaut' of change, experiencing 'chronic revision' in the institutions, and feeling the kind of heightened uncertainty and risk that goes with preserving a professional identity at a time of rapid change in the profession and its institutions. The theoretical framework of system and lifeworld may offer a discourse in which some contemporary concerns can be articulated. The system-lifeworld framework may assist us further in understanding these tensions, in particular, it may help us to explore connections and tensions between the improvement of *learning practices* and the improvement of *work organization*. These are of central importance in the Innovative Links Project.

Arguably, the relationship between teaching practices and work organization can be understood as a relationship between lifeworld and system aspects of school settings. On the one side, participants are aware that they need certain conditions to connect with one another in the practices of teaching and learning — conditions which could be described in terms of the lifeworld dynamics of cultural reproduction, social interaction and socialization. On the other side, they are aware that organizational structures and constraints (system structures and functioning) sometimes impede these lifeworld requirements, though they can also be arranged or restructured in ways that strengthen and improve these lifeworld processes.

One of the National Coordinators of the Innovative Links Project describes a number of initiatives where teachers realized they needed to change existing patterns of work organization if schools were to become learning organizations in which practices of *research* and *peer learning* are not impeded by forms of organization which exclude teacher reflection and collaboration (Moore, 1995). Hincks

Avenue Primary School, for example, has approached the problem of finding time (to become a learning organization where action research is built into daily routines) by coupling it with its corollary: the proper use of time. In attempting to develop a 'critically reflective learning community', teacher teams have been established: 'we work and learn in teams and we need to set times for this to happen' (Moore, 1995, p. 19).

Clearly, then, participants in the Roundtables are experiencing connections and tensions between patterns of organization and teaching practices. There is a growing recognition that the two different modes of action and reason associated with system functioning and lifeworld processes may compete, conflict, or be in contradiction with one another, and that they may be brought into more harmonious and mutually-supportive relationships.

In other words, the Innovative Links Project has shown that tensions between system and lifeworld processes arise when either:

(a) patterns of work organization (and teaching practices) based on unrealistic requirements of system functioning impede the lifeworld processes of cultural reproduction, social integration and socialization necessary to sustain lifeworld relationships in schools and universities, or

(b) when teaching practices (and patterns of work organization) based on unrealistic requirements of lifeworld functioning impede systems functioning and goal achievement.

Conclusion: Research Problems and Political Prospects for Action Research in Australia

The rise of action research itself in Australia has been as a systematic and self-critical response to the system failures of provision in support of professional development, curriculum development, and school improvement. Federal initiatives under these banners have sometimes spawned very poor practices; action research theory, organization and practice have developed as a constructive response to the failures of previous provisions, and action research in these areas has provided models of exemplary practice.

The political prospects for action research must be regarded as poor, however. There are growing numbers of action researchers in Australian education, and new structures could emerge to support them, but there is evidence to suggest that a new centralism is emerging in Australian educational planning and administration which is rooted in opposition to the kind of collaborative, devolved processes characteristic of action research. A climate of managerialism is emerging; the education systems of Australia are regarded by many politicians as in a state of crisis; unprecedented forms of executive control of educational policy by politicians are developing.

But there is another dimension of political prospects of action research deserving comment. It concerns the lifeworld of the community of action researchers itself. History has taught us that the development of action research in the 1940s and 1950s was thwarted when academic researchers appropriated the developments and reinterpreted them in terms of the methodological commitments of contemporary specialist educational research (positivist research). There is a danger that the same thwarting of development may take place in Australia today, as research specialists from tertiary institutions become involved in action research projects as facilitators. If action research in Australia is to avoid being 'facilitated to death', then those who preach and teach it must first of all prove their bona fides by undertaking action research into their own teaching (and their work as facilitators). They must not only help to create the conditions under which they will become unnecessary to the practitioners whose work they support, they must create conditions which guarantee that they will become unnecessary.

Note

The first and last sections of this paper were taken from S. Grundy and S. Kemmis (1988) 'Educational Action Research in Australia: The State of the Art (An Overview)' in S. Kemmis and R. McTaggart (Eds); *The Action Research Reader* (3rd Ed.) Geelong, Victoria, Australia: Deakin University Press, pp. 321–35. The middle section was taken from 'Action Research and Communicative Action: Changing Teaching Practices and the Organization of Educational Work, (May, 1995), paper presented to the National Forum of the Innovative Links Project, Melbourne.

References

BROCK-UTNE, B. (Summer, 1980) 'What is Educational Action Research?', *Classroom Action Research Network Bulletin*, No. 4.

BROWN, L. (May, 1981) 'Action Research: Techniques and Implications for In-Service Teacher Development', paper presented at the National Invitational Seminar on Action Research, Deakin University.

ELLIOTT, J. (1978) 'What is Action Research in Schools?', *Journal of Curriculum Studies*, 10, pp. 355–57.

GIDDENS, A. (1979) *Central Problems in Social Theory: Action, Structure and Contradiction in Social Analysis*, London, Macmillan.

GIDDENS, A. (1991) *Modernity and Self-Identity: Self and Society in the Late Modern Age*, Stanford, CA, Stanford University Press.

GRUNDY, S. and KEMMIS, S. (July, 1981) Social Theory, Group Dynamics and Action Research, paper presented at the 11th Annual Meeting of the South Pacific Association for Teacher Education, Adelaide.

HABERMAS, J. (1984) *Theory of Communicative Action. Vol. 1: Reason and the Rationalization of Society* (Thomas McCarthy. Trans.), Boston, MA, Beacon.

HABERMAS, J. (1987a) *The Philosophical Discourse of Modernity: Twelve Lectures* (Frederick G. Lawrence. Trans.), Cambridge, MA, MIT Press.

HABERMAS, J. (1987b) *Theory of Communicative Action, Vol. 2: Lifeworld and System: A Critique of Functionalist Reason* (Thomas McCarthy. Trans.), Boston, MA, Beacon.

JASMAN, A. (1995) 'News from the Murdoch University [Roundtable]. South Freemantle Senior High School', *The Big Link* (2 April), p. 16.

KEMMIS, S. (1983) 'Research Approaches and Methods: Action Research', in ANDERSON, D. and BLAKERS, C., *Youth, Transition, and Social Research*, Canberra, New South Wales, Australian National University Press.

MOORE, R. (1995) 'Time to talk — An issue for learning organizations', *The Big Link* (2 April), pp. 17–21.

STENHOUSE, L.A. (1984) 'Evaluating Curriculum Evaluation', in ADELMAN C. (Ed.), *The Politics and Ethics of Evaluation*, London, Croom Helm.

TIKUNOFF, W.J., WARD, B.A. and GRIFFIN, G.A. (1979) *Interactive Research and Development on Teaching Study: Final Report*, San Francisco, CA, Far West Laboratory for Educational Research and Development.

5 The Examined Experience of Action Research: The Person Within the Process

Sandra Hollingsworth (United States), Marion Dadds (United Kingdom) and Janet Miller (United States)

Introduction

Sam: In the chapter which follows, the three of us (Sandra — Sam — Hollingsworth, Marion Dadds and Janet Miller) explore self examination and personal change as salient outcomes of action research-outcomes that broach varying cultures and contexts of action research. We attempt to capture the complexities between the experiences of engaging in action research, the shifting results of those experiences and appropriate means of representing them. We initially explored this topic from our individual biographical and cultural perspectives as letters to friends interested in action research, but as we collaborated internationally in the redrafting process, common themes emerged across our letters. Thus, in a genre which lingers between the cracks between an academic essay and a personal letter (Bell-Scott, 1994), we raise questions about:

(1) The Difficulty of Collaboration in Action Research

Marion: I struggle to understand what 'collaboration' might mean for each of us in action research, for it is a word I have often used superficially and in an overly romantic way (a tendency I share with other academics, I suspect). Even in its more positive forms, collaboration pulls on the strings of our emotional lives as we challenge together our sense of professional identity, as we ask questions about the purposes of our work, as we critique its effectiveness in changing educational practices for the better.

(2) The Silencing Power of 'Appropriate' Academic Discourse

Janet: I enjoy the exchange of letters among us as a form of inquiry into issues of 'personal change' and action research . . . here we're challenging the separation of personal from public (a separation, a dualism which historically has perpetuated the devaluing of the personal) by using a traditionally private and personal genre to construct and conduct 'public' academic inquiry. And by so doing, I think that we are arguing, along with others, that 'the personal' is indeed social and relational rather than isolated and idiosyncratic, and that 'no act of reading or writing is completely personal or private' (Hill-Collins, 1990; hooks, 1989).

(3) The Tensions (and Complexities) of Personal Change

Janet: The notion of 'personal change' that I'm working with here, then, could alert all of us teacher researchers to the difficult and complex ways in which ideas and perceptions about individual change are deeply connected to and influenced by dominant constructions of how we should and can 'be' in the world as educators, as researchers, as women and men, as students. 'Personal change' and the stories that we narrate about those changes as part of our action research are relational, not only in terms of the individuals with whom we collaborate, but also in terms of the language available to us to conceptualize and to describe those changes.

Sam's Letter

Dear Marion and Janet:

Thank you for agreeing to take professional risks and compose a chapter with me in an academic anthology as a series of essay-letters among friends! I am thinking of you both on this bright later autumn morning near the coast of California — half a continent away from the snowy cold of your home in the midwest, Janet, and a quarter of the world away from your rainy home in England, Marion. The acute awareness of the physical and cultural space among us makes me wonder about what lived experiences influence our work as action researchers.

Marion, in your lovely recent book, you wrote, 'By its nature, definition and purpose, action research is oriented towards change, towards doing something useful with the knowledge gained through the research process' (Dadds, 1995, p. 135). The quest for understanding and change, certainly, is what connects our work as action researchers. Yet what is it that shapes one's trust in particular models and methods of research? What directs some of us to an interest in organizational and institutional issues in action research and others to pedagogical and curricular interests? What compels some of us to look within and across various approaches and topics in action research and decide on a core of personal understanding as the most salient feature of the work? Not only your book, Marion, but Janet's ground-breaking book on this topic (Miller, 1990) are brilliant examples of the latter theme. My hunch is that it is not only geography and anthropological or primary culture that creates categorical and shifting spaces among action researchers, but the influence of examined perceptions as we change our lives and social positions within particular educational cultures. At least it seems to be so with my own life.

As you both know, I was born and partially raised on the cusp of the Civil Rights era in the 'deep South' of the United States, but spent an equal part of my childhood in Europe with my father-musician and my mother-ecumenical. Thus sensitivity to geographical and cultural relocations, and perhaps a related need to both take concrete action and theorize meaningfulness toward change *at the same time*, served as background to my trust in action research as a means of understanding complex and conservative educational issues. By the time I'd reached graduate school, the stillness and cleanness of experimental research, separate from the chaos of practice, became a method of inquiry I could *learn* as a student, but not one I could honestly employ in my life's work. Eventually I would seek the lived praxis of action research.

At first, however, greatly influenced by my graduate school training, I engaged in action research as a teacher-educator-expert, establishing and evaluating specified research procedures and resulting changes I practice as separate from changes in self. My interest in the personal core of action research came when I found it necessary to reposition myself from teacher-educator-expert to collaborative action researcher in order to build enough trust to ask 'real' questions about how and why people from races, classes, cultures and genders — different from my own — can experience and influence education and change differently. It was in trusting relationships with mixed heritage teachers like Jennifer Davis-Smallwood (who is African-American, Native-American and French-American) that I discovered the importance of self with/in action research. I did so by struggling with ways to construct a 'we' in collaborative action research without the judgmental and distancing 'they'. As Patricia Hill-Collins wrote

> Using the distancing terms 'they' and 'their' when describing my own group and our experiences might enhance both my credentials as a scholar and the credibility of my arguments in some academic settings. But by taking this epistemological stance that reflects my disciplinary training as a sociologist, I invoke standards of certifying truth about which I remain ambivalent. (Hill-Collins, 1990, p. 17)

Similar to your own experiences, Janet and Marion, I often stand in awe of the personal manifestations which emerge from this work. I have experienced the joy of watching teachers — like Leslie Minarik — discover the personal power to generate educational knowledge. And very much in the way you both have written, I have also struggled with the moral issues concerning the awakening of changing selves that action research seems to foster. I am troubled that the discovery of personal power often occurs simultaneously with an awakening to the basic political nature of educational agendas — and a frustrating sense that even the best 'knowledge' and the 'best' research approaches at the classroom level are not powerful enough to affect educational change. I do not want to sponsor action research if it leads to despair. Yet I continue.

Jennifer, Leslie, Mary Dybdahl, Anthony Cody and Karen Teel taught me that it is the relationships which develop between the participants of action research which are the lasting elements of this work — as well as the key to promoting transformational change. Nine years after our initial collaborative action research project, we still meet once a month to plan and work over pot-luck dinners. Because of my long-term participation in such groups, I have been challenged by teacher-colleagues to becomes as personally vulnerable in print as they are. To get at the heart of meaning in this work, I've had to give up the personal and political safety of anonymity which accompanies a more empiricist position on research to stand shoulder to shoulder with teacher-colleagues and tell the stories of our lives together. I have written extensively about the personal changes in myself as a teacher and researcher which occurred as a result of those relationships (Hollingsworth, *et al.*, 1994). My understanding of pedagogy and my action as a pedagogue, for example, have undergone a radical transformation following action research collaboration. And that change has not always been comfortable.

I remember discovering and questioning my own power as an academic positioned at the university, in my relationships with teacher-students in my action research classes. I've had to question my power to 'convince' them that the discipline of self-reflection in action research can lead to personal change and social justice. Similar to Jennifer Gore's experiences, I've been brought up short when the teacher-researchers in my classes confess: 'I'm not into this regimented reflective stuff' (Gore, 1993, p. 1).

I struggle when I work with action researchers in universities and schools who personally view action research less as social change and more as cultural maintenance. The same thing happens when I work with groups who do not see ongoing relationship as necessary to action research efforts. I wonder how I can situate the personal-ness of my work with and in relation to those groups as a 'we'? By joining with them in action research projects into who we are as a group? To understand the complexities of why my colleagues see action research in ways other than personal, I know I must do so. Yet, in fully doing so, I live the risk of transforming again my personal beliefs and behaviors.

Why do I risk in this way? Because I currently believe that the power of the self in action research is its key benefit. Becoming aware of the processes of self change is a way of living an examined life. I do not believe that the hierarchies of schooling institutions will shift enough in my lifetime to put teachers-as-researchers at the center of educational reform. However, the personal changes which accompany discovery of self in relationship with others do seem to last. And, for now, that's enough for me. What about you?

With love and respect,
Sam

Marion's Letter

Dear Janet and Sam:
Here are lights coming on in houses around me as I gaze out, wondering what to write. I try to imagine you in your homes across the world, probably just receiving the dawn. And I try to imagine teachers here with whom I have worked on action

research over the years. I invent scenarios. Hasty family kitchens. Traffic phobias. Television rituals. Paper-laden worries. Sleep bedtime stories. Will experiences of action research be anywhere near the top of consciousness as lights appear and roads are negotiated? How are we different parents, partners, neighbours as a result of our action research endeavours? Has our interior life been illuminated in any enduring way through our reflective professional journeys?

To write personally about action research as a teacher educator is to tell of the heart as well as the mind. It is to risk revealing an inner life containing illumination as well as illusion; visions as well as spectres. It demands that we tell of the bright joy and clear delight, for example, crowning the many hard won improvements of rigorous action research. A vibrant, creative play area where dereliction used to stand. A teacher with deeper understanding of a child. The release of children's voices in democracy-seeking classrooms. Reconstruction of partnerships between schools and the academy as we evolve new notions of expertise. Writing personally also requires us to be honest when equal measures of light and gloom prevail; delight with regret, for example, when the discovery of personal powers through self-study breaks a seemingly stable marriage for a friend, or raises overwhelming problems of identity for a colleague. To write personally obligates us to speak of discomfort, when self-study eclipses the certainty upon which our daily practices lean. Also, in the public experience of action research lies much dichotomy. There is personal risk in these open spaces; fear of exposure, of being judged, hurt, of losing confidence in one's ideas, of retaliating. Here is the dust and debris in the dark shadows of our corporate lives. But there is also rejuvenation here as new kinship is found. We are richer for the inheritance of hopes and ideas which our new friends bring to our old views of the world.

Your question about collaboration, therefore, interested me, Sam. The positive forms of collaboration of which you speak, and which are so evident in your hopeful book (Hollingsworth, *et al.*, 1994), help to light pathways through the new territory of change. Knowing this makes it hard to understand why, as you suggest, some embrace collaboration in action research whilst others do not. Micropolitics can be reason enough for shunning the collective were they all that collaboration offered. But there are those of us who seek friendship in action research 'to know we are not alone' (a phrase I have recently gleaned from the film *Shadowlands* about the life of C.S. Lewis). When collaboration works well, we may come to know that others experience the doubts of their work as we do, and in this there is often great comfort and stimulus to reflection. Our friends can be mirrors in which we examine and evaluate our own images. We may come, too, to see the need for change more clearly by talking together. And if we are fortunate, we sustain self-regard and confidence under the glare of self-evaluation by virtue of the confirming relationships which our friends provide. We can challenge ourselves with safety here. This is 'connected knowing' (Belenky, Clinchy, Goldberger and Tarule, 1986) at its most humane and productive.

Many's the time, however, when the yearning for private communion outweighs the requirement for public exchange, as we face the 'I' alone. For this, we have to rouse the courage to glimpse our own mirror, though it is usually impossible to separate the 'self' in this reflection from light which we absorb from others. Sweet solitude is needed: and a room of one's own, where the echoes of our friends' humane voices help to retune the sounds of our own minds and hearts.

Your biographical question also promoted thought, Sam. You asked what shapes our interest in particular models and aspects of action research. As for me — who is the person finding congruence here? For one thing, I have a preference for research which is 'useful'. My working-class upbringing taught me a keen attitude to 'waste'. In respectable poverty, things have to be used, used and used again, so educational research which helps children and teachers is preferable to research which cannot, or does not, help. It is research not wasted.

When I see action research in clear daylight, people and scenes flood my mind. I see children in classrooms, struggling to read, obey, live together, worship. I also see children whose needs and rights are not represented by the dominant structures of schooling. Here, too, are exploited teachers in difficult schools, working against their values with imposed government systems designed to extinguish professional voice. These are teachers whose deeply held beliefs and feelings about children are scorned by the quick-scoring politician and slick journalist. Action research allows these teachers to reconstruct some control over their examined practices through a carefully intellectualized and shared process. For me, the social, cultural and political all reside here. This is where I must try to discover the shifting meaning and 'usefulness' of action research as a form of educational transformation.

As we commit our examined work in action research to the written word we capture a brief sense of control over thought and action in a theoretically contingent, politically volatile world. Writing gives birth to new rays of insight. Even though it is often tortuous, writing becomes a way of clarifying the current meaning of practice, using one's own situated vocabularies, not authorized tongues that cannot speak our work. In our writing, we may hear our voice for the first time and, thus, come to know our practice in a new way. For this, we may need texts that allow us to speak authentically; that acknowledge the flickering nature of growth as the outer world kindles the inner; that allows the 'human' to warm the cool lustre of the 'academic' or melt the chilling logic of the 'bureaucratic'. What literary challenges and opportunities will our letter-essays allow, for example? Can theories of the 'personal' in action research be narrated more sharply or deeply through personal literary forms?

Something you said, Sam, went round and round my head on the train yesterday as I read and reread your letter. 'Becoming aware of the process of self change is a way of living an examined life', you wrote. Should we write our action research to know how we are living an examined life in relation to the children and teachers for whom we are researching? Should we write to bring our practices to account and to name publicly, the many selves we are, leave, become? This does, as you say, require us to be vulnerable in print, not an easy challenge to meet. Action research requires us to be visible as researchers. But how, thus made public, will our personal words be used or abused, treasured or scorned? How will those who deny personhood in research respond to the central and re-current 'I' under the spotlight of action research texts?

Central, the 'I' has to be. Action research is unlikely to touch political power structures, but it challenges us to confront the power invested in our own practices. This power cannot be veiled nor dissolved. Our actions impinge on others' experiences, their ideas, beliefs, feelings, their sense of self-worth and value. Action research should help us to understand and use that power more wisely than before. But does it? Does the examined life become a more committed and caring life, more articulate, understood — more useful? Are we better teachers, voters, friends? And our visions more radiant?

None of this is bothering the cat, however. He has been sprawled over cushions all afternoon, basking in the low wintering sun. Now he's furring around for food and affection. Before he comes to explore the keyboard I'd better take my leave.

With love and friendship to you both,

Marion

Janet's Letter

Dear Sam and Marion,

It's snowing in Wisconsin in early April (again, always) as I ready your words, words so filled with commitment and so embodied in the processes and relationships that comprise teacher action research. Even as I hope for spring, snow is caught in pine tree branches outside my study window, and I'm reminded of how often the weather here, just like action research, does not conform to any predictable pattern.

Weather does whatever it does, of course, regardless of humans' intentions or desires. And each of us, in different and often unanticipated ways, shapes and is shaped by educational contexts, discourses, and practices that frame action research. This is where conceptions of 'the personal' and 'the self' in relation to educational and social change become complicated and complicating, swirling, like the unanticipated snow outside my study window, in unpredictable and uncontrollable ways.

For example, I often do not anticipate the extent to which tensions around how and what I 'should be' researching can affect my own as well as others' constructions of my 'self' as an academic. It's your point, Sam. Teacher-research (and by association, those of us in academe who work as and with teacher-researchers) still is considered by some to be 'outside' mainstream educational research. My own 'personal' desire to work in ways by which I think can promote social justice in educational research and practice, comes into conflict with institutional and institutionalized forces that often call into question or demean my choices to research with teachers and within schools. And 'personal change' within such tensions becomes more complex, for,

> . . . the discourses and practices through which we are constituted are . . . often in tension, one with another, providing the human subject with multiple layers of contradictory meanings which are inscribed in their bodies and in their conscious and unconscious minds. (Davies, 1993, p. 11)

What I'm working toward here, then, is a notion of 'personal change' in action research that certainly acknowledges specific educational situations and individuals' varying intentions and desires. But I'm also urging that our conceptualizations of 'personal change and transformation' as one goal and benefit of action research acknowledge as well the dominant discourses about research, teaching, and learning. These discourses continue to exert great influence on our conceptions of action research, and can impose normalizing and controlling versions of how we should 'be' as teachers and researchers.

I want to consider more closely what we as academics, as women, as teacher-researchers, might mean when we talk about personal change — about 'the power of the self in action research', as you say, Sam. For example, each of us has been involved in long-term collaborative teacher action research relationships. And, like you both, I have valued above all else the personal relationships and interactions that this collaboration afforded.

Yet, those very relationships, interactions, and intentions within the six-member collaborative of which I was a member constantly changed as we worked together for six years. Each of us was changed by our inquiries as well as by the social and cultural contexts in which we conducted our research. Thus, collaboration was not the easy, stable, and unitary collection of relationships often portrayed in educational research and policy mandates. Rather, it was a complex and unpredictable swirl of power relations, and of constantly changing 'selves'.

Our work together, then, became a research context, a place to examine the very complex processes of collaboration as well as of teacher action research. Just like the weather in Wisconsin, we could neither prescribe nor predict the shifts in our own perspectives or in our relationships during the six-year collaboration. But, through our connectedness, where, as Marion says, 'the social, cultural and political all reside', we *could* consider degrees to which collaborative forums for action research, for example, do *not* always guarantee contexts for equitable and reciprocal relationships and research processes. And through our connectedness, we also could consider ways in which even collaborative 'selves' are not always predictable, autonomous, rational, and fully self-aware, but rather relational, erratic, and changing. Through our collaboration, then, we began to consider ways in which 'personal change' is a social construct, formed by and through language and relationships, rather than a solely individual, fully conscious, and inevitably developmental enterprise.

During the six years of our research collaborative's work together (Miller, 1990), I continued to worry about my potentially impositional role as 'expert' or even 'leader' in the group. But at the same time, by making 'removal of imposition' my goal within our collaborative, I remained stuck in the traditionally constructed role of 'professor' and in its associated discourses. Those discourses positioned me as someone who could rectify 'imposition' as an issue, who could negate the power relations swirling among us, and who could make totally and forever equal the relationships within this collaborative. And so, ironically, in many ways, I simultaneously constructed and was constructed as still the one in charge. Obviously, it took a while for me to catch up with the other members of our group on this issue.

What might be seen as 'personal change' through teacher research, then, involves not only my possible altered perceptions and enactments of my 'self' as researcher, for example. That notion of 'personal change' also involves awareness of ways in which *the meanings* of my research practices and relationships are variable, changing, contingent and caught up in the languages that are available to me to construct those meanings. The meanings that I construct out of my research relationships, then, are created not just by me and my desires but also by the discursive practices that contribute to the construction of those desires and to which I have access in my daily life as an academic (Miller, 1990). As Shoshana Felman notes

> We can . . . 'get personal' with a borrowed voice — and might not even know from whom we borrow that voice. 'Getting personal' does not guarantee that the story we narrate is wholly ours or that it is narrated in our own voice. (1993, pp. 13–14)

Like you both, I believe that action research, as Marion says, 'can help us to confront and understand the power which is invested in our own practices'. Like you both, I too think that confronting the ways in which power is insinuated throughout our lives provides both awareness and disruption of any fixed and stable notion of our 'selves' in relation to what, how, and with whom we work. And I agree that, as Sam points out, the moral implications of these aspects of action research must remain at the forefront of our deliberations, collaborations and research with teachers who also often work in institutions that don't always welcome 'change'.

What I want to add to all these concerns is an awareness of how conceptions of 'the self' and 'personal change' in action research are constituted, in part, through social structures and language. 'Personal change' in teacher research can become part of a normalizing discourse that begins to construct 'acceptable' versions of how action research will and 'should' affect individuals. What about those teachers who engage in research and seemingly experience no 'personal changes', let alone any social change in their particular teaching contexts? Or what about teachers who, as a result of simplistic 'reflective practitioner' conceptualizations that frame some versions of action research, just re-inscribe previous versions of themselves as teachers? Or what of us teachers who refuse outright the notion of reflection on experience as unmediated by language, values, social and cultural contexts? Should any of us be regarded as either 'successful' or 'failed' teacher-researchers as a result of the ways in which the discourses of action research construct its promised benefits?

I raise such questions in the context of our discussions about the power of action research in order to call attention to some of the ways in which language, especially, constructs versions of our teacher-researcher 'selves'. Of course, at the same time, I do believe in the potential of teacher action research to promote personal and social change. But I want to encourage a notion of 'personal change' that does not predetermine how each of us 'should' or 'could' be, but rather acknowledges the potential in all human beings to '. . . invent, invert, and break old structures and patterns and discourses and thus speak/write into existence other ways of being' (Davies, 1993, p. xviii).

And so I continue to struggle with these tensions, just as I constantly envision spring amidst the snow covered pine boughs. Spring will come, tulips will bloom in our front yard, breaking the swirling snow patterns of winter in this frozen countryside. But unlike the inevitable melting of winter into spring, our work to speak and write and research into existence other ways of being requires a daily renewal of commitment and awareness. Our connectedness encourages those daily renewals.

With affection and hope,

Janet

Postscript

Sam: The letters, read to an audience at an American Educational Research Association presentation in New York, prompted these critical responses from the audience. They reiterate, in turn, our concerns with

(1) The Difficulty of Collaboration

Dear Sandra, Marion, and Janet:

I'm writing you this letter in the big block letters of a beginner when just entering the kindergarten of action research. I was so comforted by your sharing of your self conscious awareness of the 'we' and 'they'. As a graduate student, I feel the double whammy of the 'we' and 'they'. Academic professors are willing to work with me in collaborative action research projects, then there is a different relationship when I sit enrolled in their courses. . . . I want to come to action research with a common sense of 'I can do this work; I'm entitled to do this work' and realize the emancipatory nature of action research . . . So is there a place for this discourse?

Lovingly, respectfully signed:

Deborah Floyd (The Netherlands)

(2) The Nature of Change

Dear Sandra, Janet, Marion,

I found that your correspondence is very interesting, particularly in the way you are seeing change . . . I think it's very important because we're looking at interactions between changing the self and changing the practice. . . . Recently, I heard a very prominent educational researcher talk about the future of educational research as a bridge over troubled waters. And I found myself emotionally reacting against that and saying 'I cannot imagine any form of research, let alone action research, ever being a bridge over troubled waters'. In other words, here we have a situation that is unsatisfactory and somehow we can then reflectively act upon that situation, transform it, and therefore cross the troubled waters, then we're on the other side. And we've got a nice, stable, heavenly situation where we rest a while before the next time a set of problems emerges. I think I was trying to say action research is learning to sail skillfully on an eternally troubled sea.

Signing off:
John Elliot (UK)

(3) and the Variations in Academic Discourse

Sandra, Janet, Marion:
As a novice in action research, I hope the following comment is not horribly naive. I think of it as a missing piece of your discussion. My concern comes about the animosity and apparent 'enemy-making' I see in our profession and our society. We seem to make enemies of 'them' that use other discourses, methods and paradigms and political systems. What are the relationships between action researchers and people outside of this field? What are some positive ways of working with other types of research, administrators, structures we dislike and ourselves? I think Janet begins to do this by suggesting we should value and use tensions among us. Thanks, I appreciate your work and look forward to learning more from all of you.

Terry Buchanan (US)

Sam: And the three of us — Janet, Marion and Sandra, look forward to continuing this international conversation about the examined experiences of action research.

References

BELENKY, M.F., CLINCHY, B.V., GOLDBERGER, N.R. and TARULE, J.M. (1986) *Women's Ways of Knowing*, New York, Basic Books.

BELL-SCOTT, P. (1994) *Life Notes: Personal Writings by Contemporary Black Women*, New York, W.W. Norton & Company.

DADDS, M. (1995) *Passionate Enquiry and School Development: A Story about Teacher Action Research*, London, Falmer Press.

DAVIES, B. (1993) *Shards of Glass: Children Reading and Writing Beyond Gendered Identities*, Cresskill, NJ, Hampton Press.

FELMAN, S. (1993) *What Does a Woman Want? Reading and Sexual Difference*, Baltimore, MD, Johns Hopkins University Press.

GORE, J. (1993) *The Struggle for Pedagogies: Critical and Feminist Discourses as Regimes of Truth*, New York, Routledge.

HILL-COLLINS, P. (1990) *Black Feminist Thought: Knowledge, Consciousness and the Politics of Empowerment*, New York, Routledge.

HOLLINGSWORTH, S., CODY, A., DAVIS-SMALLWOOD, J., DYBDAHL, M., GALLAGHER, P., GALLEGO, M., MAESTRE, T., MINARIK, L., RAFFEL, L., STANDERFORD, N.S. and TEEL, K. (1994) *Teacher Research and Urban Literacy Education, Lessons and Conversations in a Feminist Key*, New York, Teachers College Press.

hooks, b. (1989) *Talking back: Thinking Feminist, Thinking Black*, Boston, MA, South End Press.

MILLER, J. (1990) *Creating Spaces and Finding Voices: Teachers Collaborating for Empowerment*, Albany, NY, State University of New York Press.

Section II

Political/Epistemological Perspectives on Action Research

Section Editor: Susan E. Noffke

The six chapters in this section explore the various ways in which action research efforts are constructed along political and epistemological lines of thought and action. The importance of context to political possibility is a theme which permeates each chapter. In Chapter 6, Susan Noffke and Marie Brennan set the stage by taking on part of the task of examining the meaning of politics in the practice of action research. The questioning of structure as well as the importance of local, classroom-based teaching are highlighted as a way to move debates beyond dichotomies to strategic action across arenas or contexts of action.

Andrew Gitlin and Johanna Hadden, in Chapter 7, examine their work with educative research to foster change addressing power relations in the classroom. In this chapter, the context for educational change and the personal learning needed for teacher-initiated change are highlighted. Both inward-looking attention to the practices of teaching as well as outward-looking examinations of the processes of schooling may be necessary elements of creating more caring, socially just education.

These themes are well complemented in the study in Chapter 8 outlined by Eileen Adams, Rosaleen McGonagle, Pauline Watts, and Gaby Weiner. In this chapter, the overall socio-political context is visible, as well as the interplay between university tutors and classrooms teachers over issues of equity in education. The work in schools that the authors describe focuses attention on the many ways in which national politics intersect with the politics of social relations in schools.

Sue Davidoff, Chapter 9, in describing her work with organizational development within a South African context, adds much to understanding action research as a change methodology aimed at interjecting transformative norms within a historically enforced context of compliance. Her description helps greatly in understanding the importance of history in assessing the practical, contextual considerations involved in social justice efforts in education.

Michela Mayer, in Chapter 10, describes her work in environmental education which includes engagement with teachers over issues of pedagogy as well as curriculum. The complexity of considering local contextual factors as well as overall theoretical structures are highlighted. In this work, an alternative epistemology, one in which uncertainty and community play major roles is a focal point.

As in the Mayer chapter, the action research David Hursh describes in Chapter

11 takes place with a framework for understanding that contemporary knowledge forms, as well as the political agendas they embody, are highly contested. Both students and teachers examine various educational programs in terms of what will make for more just educational theory and practice.

While most of the chapters deal with seemingly overtly political rather than epistemological issues, the bases for knowledge claims are nonetheless evident. What counts as legitimate academic knowledge is here seen as inextricable from the political agendas the various forms of action research seek to promote. Knowledge claims within action research, as explored in this section, are thus intertwined with the agenda for action the chapters seek to promote.

6 Reconstructing the Politics of Action in Action Research

Susan E. Noffke (United States) and
Marie Brennan (Australia)

In the emerging and historical literature reporting action research projects and theory, there are and continue to be many different versions of action research. They vary in process as well as purpose according to the history and possibilities of the different sites and according to the interests, ethics, and commitments of those involved (Noffke, 1997). Among some advocates of action research, one seeming tension emerges (albeit somewhat onesided as the published voices have been primarily on only one side of the 'argument') between those who argue for a social justice or emancipatory focus and those whose primary interests appear to lie more in the areas of personal and professional growth and development (Weiner, 1989; Zeichner, 1993).

We see this debate as an important one for the field of action research and for social research in general. However, it is important not to frame the issue as an either/or, a dichotomy in which the object is to produce convincing arguments for one or the other. Rather, there is a need for a wider conceptual base, built from a recognition that all forms of action research are political. The seeming differences between intentions are apparent not only because of differences in context, but because terms such as 'politics' are constructed in ways that eclipse other meanings. What is needed is to recognize this, and not subsume everything under an unreconstructed 'politics', especially one which assumes an unproblematized 'democracy' as its goal.

In this chapter, we will focus on one dimension of those differences in orientations to politics: the scope of the 'action' that is seen as being researched and changed, and how that action is interpreted and treated as connected to the action of others outside the immediate participant(s) in the research. To draw out some of the issues we see as involved, we use the concepts 'personal' and 'professional' as organizers to work through narrower and broader versions of politics and action when analyzing action research. In working through the personal and professional dimensions of understanding action in action research, we are not attempting to be pejorative about one or the other emphasis. As teachers as well as academics, the personal and professional dimensions to our work are important arenas for our political efforts. Rather, we use these terms to better see the range of ways in which changing action as part of action research can be an indicator of particular politics

— both of action research itself as a field of research and also of its various definitions-in-use in fields other than academic.

Restricted or Strategic? The Personal within the Professional

A range of action arenas exists for those working in and writing about action research. Certainly the examples presented in this book demonstrate concerns ranging from social justice in inner city schools, teacher development in South Africa, to work with children in a single classroom. We argue here that the apparent 'choice' of the kind of action undertaken in specific projects of action research is not merely a surface epiphenomenon arising from the internal dynamics of a site. For all action research projects, the context in which they operate has been carefully 'read' and judgments have been made about the scope as well as the practical limits of the action that is and can be taken at any particular time arising from the internal dynamics of a site. This 'reading', or awareness, is, in fact, central to the participants' own sense of the need for their projects. Thus, the participants' 'reading' of the context helps to shape not only the initial or ostensible topic area of focus (whether it is concerned with environmental education, school reform, or the evaluation of innovatory practices) but also the scope of what is seen as possible to achieve through the project. The specific outcomes are clearly not going to be foretold, but the field in which those outcomes are to be taken is set before and during the course of the action research projects, as their initiators get them underway.

When undertaking action research with a relatively narrow view of the personal as well as the political, the scope of the action being researched and changed tends to appear as a carefully bounded space within current power structures. That is, the political dimensions of the focus are more or less restricted to what the individual person sees as within their levels of control. An example of this might be 'my classroom's whole language program'. The focus is on changing their own perspectives and their own practices or actions there and will not usually challenge the existing power structures and boundaries of the institution in which it takes place. Often when such projects are described by theorists or academics concerned with understanding the dimensions of action research and its current incarnations, they are dismissed as 'arrested' forms of 'proper' action research; or patronized as not fully politically enacted. While such criticisms may in fact have an element of truth in them, it is also possible that there are other reasons for keeping a project bounded in this way, other than a lack of political insight or 'will' to change.

Leaving aside for a bit the question of whether such changes in the personal arena are, in fact, significant political actions (and that is definitely a point to which we'll return), what might be some reasons for keeping a project bounded that do not necessarily imply a lack of interest in or vision of significant political change? One reason might be that the work of teachers has intensified, and has become ever more open to scrutiny (Apple, 1986). Under some circumstances, action research fostered by those outside of classrooms can be interpreted as a means of surveillance or cooption to others' agendas (Noffke, 1989; Johnston and Proudford, 1994).

Another, related issue could be that many teachers are women with major responsibilities for children and home-work in addition to their full-time teaching jobs. The politics of changing their own practice must necessarily be focused on their own classrooms, sandwiched in among the many other activities aimed at providing a quality education for (their own and) other people's children.

A third kind of reason might be a reflection of a very accurate 'reading' of the political and educational context in which they work, for example, an understanding that most state and federal initiatives, as well as those from university personnel, are not organized with the best interests of teachers and their students as the forefront of the agenda. What we mean here, are those teachers whose conceptions of themselves and their students go beyond individualistic notions of the 'personal', the 'self'. Many African American or Aboriginal teachers, for example, may appear to confine their activities to the classroom, because that is clearly the arena of political struggle that they have chosen. Others, with differing conceptions of the child in society, may choose to emphasize particular pedagogical orientations out of conceptions of the child in the society which represent very different assessments of the social order and education's role in it.

It is important not to romanticize teachers as those who necessarily have clear understandings of the context in which schools operate. Projects using the rubric of action research are potentially iconoclastic, oriented to self-promotion, and can reinvent poor practices already rejected elsewhere. They can also be so focused on individual self-development that they do not see the relationship between their own identities and the curriculum enacted with their students, for example. Yet it is equally important to recognize that the two positions are not mutually exclusive.

The problem, for those for whom this approach to educational action research is not broad enough, is that the consequence for teachers (or academic practitioners, for that matter) who undertake action research in this way, is that it leaves little space for collective action of any kind. Indeed, the version of 'professional' arising from such a position about teaching is that the profession is merely an abstract aggregation of individual teachers holding similar qualifications and possessing similar degrees of authority over their practice. It restricts practitioners to changing action only within their classrooms, thus removing an important source of support and strength, as well as alternative lenses. And yet, as the sophisticated readings of context represented in this book and as our experiences with many teachers and action researchers suggest, if significant change (and what counts as 'significant' in political actions is clearly what is at stake) is to occur in education, it cannot only be restricted to fields of action which support narrow understandings of the personal. 'Large scale', often structural as well as cultural, readings of the context must become visible aspects to our definitions of personal as well as professional practice.

Politics and 'Practice'

Some of the difficulties around understanding the political within projects in educational action research, may derive from conflating 'action' with 'activities'. Put another way, a problem area lies in seeing all activities as adding up to a social practice. We want to argue here that 'practice' and changing practice need to be seen as including the altering of activities which make up aspects of one person's work, but that this is not a sufficient explanation for achieving significant change. Activities undertaken by one person need to be seen in their institutional context, as part of a social practice that has developed historically and continues to be 'produced' in different ways by a myriad of practitioners.

A broader understanding of the personal as well as the professional, would see the links between the different types of practice in a field of action such as education. The personal and the professional are thus not defined only in contradistinction to others, or 'outside' persons or groups, but as inextricably linked to them. Similar kinds of projects might occur as a starting point — such as a concern with 'whole language' or eradicating the racist pedagogical practices in social studies teaching. However, because the links would be seen between the individual classroom and the actions of others — in that school, by the local school board, one's church group, etc., and the textbooks approved for usage — some level of action in the action research might well address those connections and alliances. This could manifest itself in actions with professional associations, for example, or through a teachers' union, or through writing and publishing alternative materials for use. It could also be connected to community organizations, especially those also concerned with the well-being of children. The project itself, taken only as a published document, might not be grandiose; however the connections with other types of practice may well make important strides towards social change.

How contexts are 'read' is a potential focal point for working with a group of people in thinking through their action research. However, it is rarely evident in works dealing with action research (Bunbury, *et al.*, 1991; Krater, *at al.*, 1994, are notable exceptions). Some of this has to do with the political economy of academic publishing (narrow, short terms works are more likely to appear in print). Yet other issues have to do with who sees published reports of action research as part of their professional arena (Noffke, *et al.*, 1996).

Politics in Personal Practice

The question is whether the focus on the personal arena, one's own classroom, can, in fact, be seen as helping in efforts to reconstruct the political in educational thought and practice. We do not need to 'debunk' the criticism of action research efforts by teachers as seemingly devoid of 'larger' issues. Classroom action research is a political activity. It focuses on children and their experiences in schooling and the resultant deepening of awareness of what's involved in the complex process of teaching and learning may sustain teachers in their frequently socially-devalued work. Yet, it matters what and who is 'cared about'. Many urban teachers, for example, who work toward change in their classrooms, see their work as in the interests of children they see as 'dying in the streets'. The focus on children cannot be lost in a definition of 'political' which see as relevant action only in terms of public, social movements. Yet it also must not lose sight of them. What is reflected in action research, as in other forms of research is the identity, multifaceted and emergent, of the participants. That leads, for us, to a focus on the kinds of 'personal' represented, not on the published 'scope' of the arena. That which guides the social practice, both initially and as it emerges, is an important area, one thus far only examined from the perspective of those most privileged within academic arenas of education. Efforts with children and within classrooms are legitimate ways to spend one's energies, but they are also connected, through the notion of practice, to other areas.

How can we Reconstruct the Political in Action Research?

The dichotomy between the personal and the professional can be used as a basis for maintaining privilege through exclusion. However, this need not be the case. A broader conception of action may well be possible, even if sometimes rejected for strategic reasons after careful analysis of the situation, the people involved, and possible consequences. The context for innovative work is not strong, nor is there much state interest in things other than compliance from the teaching force. New forms of sanctions with which to back up the directions of policies, e.g., appraisal and promotion systems, continued testing in relation to 'standards' have emerged virtually unquestioned. Yet there has been a burgeoning of interest which explicitly acknowledges its politics in educational terms. The machinery of the state isn't conducive to the production of critique, nor does it promulgate teacher research in any but isolated circumstances. Mainly, the rhetoric of action research is used under conditions more likely to lead to cooption of serious social analysis and action.

Education, at least in the US context, is embedded with practices of 'miseducation' (Woodson, 1933) and full of fear of what a genuine education might produce (Baldwin, 1963/1996). For action research, what should come out of the deliberations represented in this chapter is not a new, improved version or definition of action research. Rather, what might emerge is a recognition of the partiality, the need for attention to circumstances, the specifics of history, without getting lost in globalized concerns that are constructed as separated from the local. Some feminist, postcolonialist theorists have explored a range of issues relevant here (Spivak, 1993). These include the identification of sites and their connection to one another, the need to explore identities and the need to look for the most marginalized to speak. These positions all have relevance for educational action research. They should make it possible to read the context more carefully, to analyze the connections between arenas of practice so that local is not seen as separate from global. This does not mean that we think that all that is necessary is that teachers should just read different theory in teacher education than they do, although that is important. In the US at least, the dominance of a view of education and educational research as 'objective', apart from issues of identity and politics, has had a deleterious effect. Rather, the collective dialogue over teaching should enhance the questions arriving from practice as well as from multiple theoretical bases.

Folks KNOW that African American students (and here one can 'read in' a host of groups) don't do as well in schools. They also, often KNOW that it isn't because there's something wrong with the kids or the culture from which they come. The questioning of structures, the furthering of global perspectives is not enhanced in our daily popular cultured lives. The connections between sites may be horizontal, such as across countries' borders using the Internet to bring together teachers or students on a project. Or the connections may be across fields such as government, welfare and schooling agencies in a given local community. But the issue may also be taken vertically throughout the range of those involved, from a local grade in one classroom through to business groups, parent associations, the government and teachers' groups.

What remains for reconstructing the political within action research is much more than defining legitimate arenas for research by teachers. Education must come to grips with the ways in which its own construction and the institutions which uphold it have systematically excluded or marginalized particular groups of people and their issues. That means that democracy in its methodological as well as epistemological forms must be critiqued and transformed. Innovation in education, grounded in social justice issues, must take into account both identity as well as workplace considerations. While social justice issues seem, at times, far afield from issues of the techniques of classroom practice, forms of privilege and domination (including those of academics) must be considered as part of the work of educational action research. Only by considering both can the politics of action research be reconstructed.

References

APPLE, M.W. (1986) *Teacher and Texts: A Political Economy of Class and Gender Relations in Education*, New York, Routledge & Kegan Paul.

BALDWIN, J. (1963/1996) 'A talk with teachers', in AYERS, W. and FORD, P. (Eds), *City Kids, City Teachers: Reports from the Front Row* (pp. 219–27), New York, The New Press.

BUNBURY, R., HASTINGS, W., HENRY, J. and McTAGGART, R. (1991) *Aboriginal Pedagogy: Aboriginal Teachers Speak Out*, Geelong, Victoria, Deakin University Press.

JOHNSTON, S. and PROUDFORD, C. (1994) 'Action research — Who owns the process?', *Educational Review*, **46**, 1, pp. 3–14.

KRATER, J., ZENI, J. and CASON, N. (1994) *Mirror Images: Teaching Writing in Black and White*, Portsmouth, NH, Heinemann.

NOFFKE, S.E. (1989) 'The social context of action research', paper presented at the Annual Meeting of the American Educational Research Association, San Francisco.

NOFFKE, S.E. (1997) 'Professional, personal, and political dimensions of action research', in APPLE, M.W. (Ed.), *Review of Research in Education, 22*, pp. 299–337.

NOFFKE, S.E., CLARK, B., PALMERI-SANTIAGO, J., SADLER, J. and SHUJAA, M. (1996) 'Conflict, learning and change in a school — university partnership: Different worlds of sharing', *Theory into Practice*, **35**, 3, pp. 165–72.

SPIVAK, G.C. (1993) *Outside in the Teaching Machine*, New York, Routledge.

WEINER, G. (1989) 'Professional self-knowledge versus social justice: A critical analysis of the teacher-researcher movement', *British Educational Research Journal*, **15**, 1, pp. 41–51.

WOODSON, C.G. (1933/1977) *The Mis-education of the Negro*, Washington, DC, The Associated Publishers.

ZEICHNER, K.M. (1993) 'Action research: Personal renewal and social reconstruction', *Educational Action Research*, **1**, 2, pp. 199–219.

Educative Research: Acting on Power Relations in the Classroom

Andrew Gitlin (United States) and Johanna Hadden (United States)

Action research, in recent years, has become an important part of reform efforts that challenge many of the assumptions embedded in what is often referred to as the excellence reports (e.g., NCEE, 1983). As opposed to fostering change by setting new standards, imposing nation-wide core curricula, or developing more comprehensive supervisory techniques that will help assure that teachers do the right thing, action researchers urge reformers to give teachers the opportunity to utilize inquiry to reflect and act on school practices.[1] In this sense, action research turns conventional wisdom on its head by assuming that the limits of reform are not due to ineffective control/accountability mechanisms but rather the lack of opportunities teachers have to make considered and informed classroom decisions.

In this chapter we want to explore the possibilities of using a form of inquiry, which we call educative research, that shares much with the reconstructed wisdom of action research. We present a case report of the use of educative research to foster a type of teacher initiated change that acts on overly narrow and authoritarian types of power relations in the classroom. Before doing so, however, it is important to clarify the assumptions and values that guide educative research, if for no other reason than that all approaches to action research are not cut from the same cloth. To do so, the following section provides an overview of two of the more political approaches to action research and then places educative research within these differing visions.[2]

Types of Political Action Research

Political Approach

In the political approach, the action research method is a small part of a larger political project. Carr and Kemmis's work on action research best illustrates this approach. For Carr and Kemmis (1986), the larger political project is the development of a critical social science; an approach to inquiry that not only investigates the practical as a way to make prudent decisions, 'because the practical experience of teachers is the source of the problems under consideration' (p. 126), but adds to this view the notion that prudent decision-making may be distorted by ideological forces and institutional structures. A critical social science, therefore, 'must provide ways of distinguishing ideologically distorted interpretations from those that are not' (p. 129). In doing so, critical social science enables teachers to become more enlightened about the ways in which their own self-understandings may prevent them from examining the social and political forces which distort and limit their educational conduct (pp. 31–2). This corrective in understanding allows practitioners and others to act on schooling in ways that go beyond an improvement orientation and work toward a transformation of education and educational institutions (p. 160).

An academic operating within this framework becomes a 'critical friend helping "insiders" to act more wisely, prudently and critically in the process of transforming education' (Carr and Kemmis, p. 161). The success of critical friends is measured by the extent to which they 'can help those involved in the educational process to improve their own educational practices, their own understandings, and the situations and institutions in which they work' (p. 161). In particular, the critical friend needs to find ways to point to the political dimensions of schooling that sometimes become hidden within more technical discussions of educational practice.

Political/Humanist Approach

In the political/humanist model, politics are important, but they do not determine the nature of the project that teachers/students undertake. Politics may be expressed in various ways, such as in terms of social justice, but in each case the political orientation is tempered by a form of humanism in that a caring relation is established that allows practitioners or certification students to have the ultimate say as to how and whether the political arguments to which they have been exposed inform their own self-reflective process. The work of Gore and Zeichner (1991) fits most easily within this category.

Gore and Zeichner are quite insistent that action research should not stop with the encouragement of reflectivity. Instead, the aim is political — it is about furthering and illuminating issues of social justice (1991, p. 121). This approach differs somewhat from the political approach Carr and Kemmis take, in that politics are moderated by a strong sense of humanism. In Gore and Zeichner's work this humanism is expressed as the need to establish relationships within the program that are based on the 'fidelity to persons' (p. 122). In practical terms, this translates into a commitment to respect the focus of the questions teacher education students ask in their action research projects. The difference between the political approach of Carr and Kemmis and political/humanist approach of Gore and Zeichner, is that the latter group is less comfortable being a 'critical friend'. While the initial interactions may be critical and suggestive of many of the ideas found in the work of Carr and Kemmis, in the final analysis those doing action research must decide if the project is to have a political focus. For Carr and Kemmis it is important, and maybe even essential, that the 'other' maintains a critical focus that pushes projects in a political direction. A fundamental aspect of a critical social science is to distinguish distorted ideological interpretations from those that are not and it is likely that technocratic views of schooling (including non-political action research projects) would be considered ideological distortions.

Educative Research and Action Research

Educative research is most closely associated with the political/humanist tradition of action research methodologies. As is true of those methodologies within this tradition, educative research focuses on a political understanding of schooling — relations of power within the research relationship and those found between teachers, students, administrators, parents, etc. In particular, educative research is a process that enables practitioners and others to develop 'voice as a form of protest' (Gitlin, *et al.*, 1992):

> The notion of voice can go beyond the exploration of issues and the opportunities to speak; it can be about protest. Understood in this way, voice is inherently political; its aim is to question what is taken for granted, to act on what is seen to be unjust in an attempt to shape and guide future educational decisions. (p. 23)

In this sense, educative research enables participants to look outward at students, parents, and any number of school issues, and inward at self to determine the ways teacher beliefs and practices may help shape power relations and roles which are overly authoritarian and/or undemocratic.

Educative research also tries to combine an ethic of care with a political stance by arguing for the establishment of a dialogical relationship between those engaging in this research methodology.

> One way Educative Research attempts to restructure the relationship between researcher and 'subject' is to alter research from a one-way process where researchers extract data from 'subjects' to a dialogical process where participants negotiate meaning at the level of question posing, data collection and analysis. (Gitlin, *et al.*, 1992, p. 20)

Given the importance of this dialogical process, insisting on a political project would be inappropriate. On the other hand, viewing politics as totally optional as humanists do runs counter to the social reconstructionist tradition that informs educative research as well as many political humanist approaches to action research. As Gore and Zeichner (1991) state:

> We see our work in the elementary teacher education program at the University of Wisconsin-Madison as located within the social reconstructionist tradition in US teacher education. This tradition is the only one that brings the social and political context into focus and considers whether our work

in teacher education is contributing toward the elimination of inequalities and injustices in schooling and society. (p. 121)

Finally, educative research is a continuous process, a collective struggle, that enables educational groups of actors to identify and act on some of the most persistent problems found within schooling such as those associated with race, class, and gender. Educative research does so, not by having those involved link their analysis to an a priori political theory but rather by having practitioners and others within the educational community develop texts about self, school context, and classroom practice and aims that when viewed relationally can point to the political dimensions of schooling. (Both those imposed by context and those furthered by practices and beliefs.) What follows describes in broad strokes how this process of political theory building through inquiry enabled one practitioner to see and act on power relations within the classroom. This case report begins with an account of the school context — how the excellence platform influenced the classroom of one participant in an educative research project and then describes how educative research enabled some movement away from the authoritarian teacher/student relations that had become a dominant theme within this teacher's practice.

Naming and Acting on Power Relations in the Classroom: The Case Report

At the time I began the educative research project, I had been a public school teacher for thirteen years.[3] Although always aware of the hierarchy in education, the project forced me to critically evaluate the power relations in schooling and to examine my own teaching as part of the power structure. This examination of self and school resulted in a change in my pedagogical style that allowed for alternative and less hierarchical relations in the classroom.

The educative research project coincided with the implementation of the 'excellence' platform in my school which had created significant changes in the practice of many teachers. Concentration on rote learning of the 'basics' encouraged many of us to narrowly focus on worksheets that drilled the mandated objectives to the exclusion of more innovative approaches to learning. Teachers in my school now had a curriculum that had to be completed by the end of the year because students would be tested on the concepts, results would be published and discussed in faculty meetings, and the state-mandated, fifth grade Stanford Achievement Test (SAT) scores in math would be used to eliminate specific students from the more academic tracks when they entered junior high. This emphasis on testing predetermined outcomes also led many of us to dismantle emergent types of learning activities, such as learning centers, and abandon attempts to create a more democratic culture in the classroom, if for no other reason than the results of these efforts could never be captured on a multiple-choice test item. This was surely the case of one beginning teacher in the school where I taught.

It is disheartening to watch beginning teachers change. So often they enter their first assignment with such enthusiasm and optimism. They expect the best from their students and themselves. They delight in decorating bulletin boards, designing games, and constructing activities. They relish inventing elaborate lesson plans and creative science experiments. First year teachers often envision positive relationships unfolding between them and their students. They imagine students developing congenial interdependencies and vigorous attitudes towards school work.

Several years later, however, they sometimes find themselves discouraged with their students, resenting the time it takes to decorate a new bulletin board, and discarding batches of student work that they simply do not have time to read or grade. They have become isolated from the rest of the faculty, feel annoyed when approached by concerned parents, and are distrustful of administration. The years fold into each other and innovation disappears. Experience often carries with it embitterment and disillusionment.

I watched a beginning teacher change. At first, Karen was fascinated with creative lesson ideas and ornamental room decorations. She trusted that each of her fifth graders would do his or her best and that she could make their lives better by caring and sympathizing. She worked to acquaint herself with every facet of their lives and personalities. She deliberately wore casual clothes so that she could get on the floor to teach if necessary. She hugged them when they seemed to need it, and related to them on a personal level at all times.

The transformation was slow, not sudden. Her first year, Karen and I joined our fifth grade classes in an elaborate art project. Students spent weeks building creatures out of paper, glue, cloth and wire. They constructed some of the most outlandish beasts. The number of eyes and limbs varied with each creature and the colors and patterns on their bodies were diverse. Students laughed and giggled at each other's creations. They were proud of their creatures. They named them and ascribed personality traits and eccentric characteristics to them. Students got messy and noisy and looked forward each day to working on their ornate creations.

When they were completed, students wrote poetry about their creatures. For a language arts lesson they wrote short stories that situated their creatures in imaginary lands, and for social studies they placed their creatures in the role of historic individuals within a specific period of time. For mathematics, students constructed story problems around their creatures and gave the problems to other students to solve. Math activities included averaging the numbers of eyes on the creatures or estimating the yards of fabric necessary to make blankets for all of them. Science involved the study of animal and plant characteristics that resembled the creatures, and students constructed artificial ecological zones for them. Throughout the year many activities evolved around the creatures, and at the end of the year students related that it was the most memorable part of their fifth grade year.

Karen and I did not build the creatures with our students again. We found many reasons not to do the project the following year. A lot of masking tape was used with the creatures and supplies were short. Glue was rationed that year along with paint, wall-paper paste, and marking pens. The custodial staff did not appreciate droplets of spilled paint on the counter that had to be removed with turpentine. That first year, Karen and I thought that the exuberance our students felt working on their creatures made any extra cleaning effort worth the time. However, it was simply too much trouble to acquire the supplies in the face of shortages, and too difficult to deal with the custodian over temporary spills and messes. Besides, there were district end-of-level tests to be passed, SAT tests to administer, and a new computer grading system to learn. Creatures take a lot of class time to build.

I did not notice the change in my teaching until after I noticed it happening to Karen. This was not my first year, so it was like a breath of fresh air to work with Karen. I wanted to see her keep her enthusiasm and optimistic presence in the classroom. Mine was deteriorating and I intuitively knew it, although I could not articulate it at the time. I suppose that is why it was so poignant and painful to watch it happen to her.

I can offer insights into those experiences now. I am able to conceptualize the factors that evoked a sense of alienation; a perspective whereby the intention is to get through the work with the least problems and move on. My purpose for each day was to complete the lesson plan and proceed to the next one so that the curriculum got covered or the textbook completed by the end of the year. The final grade for each student became the object of my focus rather than the experience of learning. Teaching became an act of production rather than a process or journey.

Numerous structural adjustments took place that contributed to my alienation. Our work became concentrated and exhaustive. Regulated time schedules were strictly administered. Schedules were so tight that if we veered from the dictated time frame by five minutes, some other class would be late getting their physical education or music classes. During the next two years, the schedule became even tighter. Library, computer, physical education, music, and social skills classes, taught by 'specialists', interrupted classroom learning situations. Chapter One math students (those viewed as 'at-risk') went at specified times that could not vary with classroom activities. English as a second language (ESL) classes and resource classes were simply missed if the student did not come during the appointed time. The day was broken up and scheduled so tightly that it seemed a rare occurrence to have the class all together at the same time for longer than 30 minutes. With the newly district-mandated grading system, report cards now took hours of work each week instead of a few hours at the end of the term. Supply closets were locked that year and supplies had to be requisitioned from the secretary. Each teacher was allotted $5.00 per student for supplies for the year.

Rationalization of teaching, dividing the entire act into separate segments, was another structural factor that contributed to my alienation. Our new grading system required that we justify every learning activity with the objectives specified in the state core curriculum. School subjects that were once integrated now had to be taught separately and in isolation in order to follow district grading outlines. Lunches and recesses were split up even more on the pretense of keeping grade levels separate on the playground. The new plan coincidentally split up teachers who had for years eaten lunch together and spent recess in the faculty lounge together. Teachers associated less and less in larger groups with each other. Small 'lunch bunches' developed. The principal had her teacher friends meet for lunch each day in her office with her, and the rest of the faculty ate in groups in their classrooms, library, or lounge.

Isolation was also a part of my increasing alienation. Teachers taught for the day and often went home in the evening, rarely seeking contact with each other for advice or help. It became a sign of weakness if one had difficulty with a student. The problem with the student came to be seen as one of discipline rather than motivation. Once the question we asked *each other* was: 'How can we design something interesting so that he will want to do that?' Now the question was replaced by one we asked *ourselves*: 'How can I get him to do that?'

The school-wide concentration on self-esteem building of Karen's first year gave way to a concentration on building skills with basic math facts. Teachers drilled students daily and the computer lab was devoted almost entirely to math drill and teacher grading procedures. Several committees were formed to deal with teacher suggestions and complaints, and many new proposals from the faculty were conveniently forgotten or discarded before implementation. Some concerns broached by the faculty were made light of in principal-directed committee meetings. For example, one anonymous suggestion was criticized for a spelling error and summarily dismissed, and the principal made derogatory remarks about another suggestion because in her view whoever wrote it was obviously 'stressed out'.

The aims of education were dictated through end-of-level tests, achievement tests, prescribed texts, and district-recommended classroom management plans. The state-developed core curriculum that was originally viewed as a 'suggested framework', eventually became obligatory through testing procedures and program implementation based on the specified objectives. As the teacher, I was expected only to find ways to facilitate the prescribed curricula, school schedule, and administrative discipline plans. I felt like a robot or puppet; alienated, isolated, and powerless.

Teachers were not trusted to design their own science lessons. The science lessons were planned in advance by the school district and students were tested on those at the end of the year. The math lessons and worksheets were from the accepted district textbook. The reading program was dictated by the district and included specific skill lessons from the basal reader. I rarely altered the spelling lists recommended in the adopted text. There was no time for class discussions regarding student concerns. Teaching was so intensified that there was no time for art projects and science experiments that consumed more than their allotted 30 minutes. Flexibility was nowhere to be seen and creativity was next to impossible. Emergent teaching decisions and impulsive lesson ideas simply could not take place within the district and school dictates on my time and curricula.

The structural constraints that led to alienation also led to changes in the way I dealt with students. I used token economy systems as rewards and punishments. I walked my classes single file through the halls and stressed individual academic achievement through what we called 'cooperative groups'. I fooled myself into thinking that pre-packaged commercial materials were better than teacher-constructed ones. I increased the number of worksheets required and decreased the amount of discussion in the classroom. There seemed to be no time for the 'frills'. We needed to improve our scores in the 'basics' because that was what was recommended by the excellence platform supported by the district.

Administrative dictates became harsher and occurred more often. Faculty meetings were held each week instead of once a month, and they were punitive rather than informative. We were scolded at each faculty meeting for 'resisting' the computer grading program, or hoarding supplies in our closets. Student discipline became a major topic, and teachers began to criticize each other for having noisy classes. The faculty was divided and alienated from the process of teaching.

These factors also influenced student/teacher relations in other ways. For years I wanted to establish a democratic culture in my classroom where students were involved in decision-making, where discussions and group interaction superseded traditional autocratic learning situations, and where my role was to facilitate student-constructed knowledge rather than merely deliver the predetermined set of expert-produced knowledge. Although I had envisioned a democratic culture, I had become an authoritarian. I did not tolerate laughter in class unless it was at my discretion. I instituted a privilege for Friday afternoon with the intention of removing it if the class misbehaved. Noise levels were kept to a minimum so that no one could accuse me of not having control of my class. Following administrative directions, students were assigned to supervise each other in the restroom in order to curb horseplay and mess-making. Power relations in the classroom consisted of strictly top-down dictates from me to my students. Every part of every day was rigidly controlled. No student-initiated discussion or activity was accepted. I had my lesson plans and we were going to follow them! Each teaching day started to look exactly like the next. Although I did not recognize that my teaching practice had become stagnant, I did know that I was unhappy.

Winds of Change

In 1992, I decided to pursue my master's degree and entered a graduate program sponsored by the University of Utah. As part of the program we were expected to examine and evaluate our teaching practice. The educative research project in which I participated focused on the development of voice as a form of protest (Gitlin, *et al.*, 1992), and suggested the development of a question that challenged the constraining features of schooling. As I entered this inquiry process it became clear that there were significant contradictions between my personal aims and the actual results of my practice.

The analysis of my personal history in conjunction with the construction of a thick description of the school context led me to identify how the regulated curriculum fostered subordination and helped repress my aim for a democratic culture in my classroom. I began to ask myself whose interests were served by some teaching practices. Did students flourish or flounder within this authoritarian school environment? Was I really helping my students to develop into self-actualized individuals willing and able to cooperate with others in order to learn? Was I fostering interdependence or denying it?

Based on the analysis of self and the school context as well as observations by a peer that enabled me to compare my intentions to my teaching practices, I decided to investigate the possibilities of altering my pedagogy — of putting into place a critical pedagogy that might further democratic relations in my classroom (Freire, 1993; Shor, 1980, 1986, 1987, 1992; Shor and Freire, 1987). In the section that follows I will describe in some detail how the implementation of this critical pedagogy influenced the authoritarian power relations that had over time become a dominant aspect of my classroom ethos.

The Whisper of a Democratic Culture

One important aspect of the critical pedagogy implemented in my fifth and sixth grade classroom was to ask students to consider who benefits from school and classroom programs. We began by examining the pre-packaged state approved curriculum in economics and determined that it served corporate interests. We talked about the meaning of subordination and asked about the interests served when a curriculum is divided into sequential parts with a specified learning objective attached to each part (a rationalized core curriculum), and how the intensified school schedule influenced student learning as well as teacher/student and student/student relations. Discussing these questions led students to pose a number of additional questions. We began to talk about school dress codes and realized they sometimes helped focus disdain on those who could not afford to dress in a specific manner. We discussed the many and varied meanings of 'democracy' and the possibilities of building a democratic culture in the classroom. We examined school and district discipline plans in order to identify whose interests were served by demanding compliance to rules and regulations designed without input from parents or students. We examined the school concentration on 'The Social Skill of the Week' and discussed why specific behaviors were required and monitored. We discussed the junior high tracking program and how schools determined placement on the tracks. We also discussed the difficulties of switching tracks once placed and what that would mean to the future of each student. Students were not only posing questions but becoming critically conscious of the restraints that work upon them. Marshall, a student in the class, summarized what many students were feeling when he remarked 'It's as if they already have your future planned for you'.

I began to encourage rather than discourage dialogue (Freire, 1993) on a variety of issues. Students began to express themselves more freely. They were not hesitant to show anger in their journals, especially when they felt I was not being reasonable. James, for example, wrote, 'I got really mad because you Mrs. Hadden I thought was being pretty darn picky ... it really made me mad ... how picky can you get'. Students had never been this honest with me before. A trusting relationship was obviously beginning to develop. Students were also gaining some enthusiasm for the democratic project that was beginning to emerge. The following student statements reflect this enthusiasm.

This might be one of the funnest weeks I've had in sixth grade (Ellen).
I love the way you teach us. I have never had this much fun learning before (Gary). Now you can even tell that everyone is happier now ... this

is the best system that I know of and plus it is one of the most fairest things (Mark). You get more freedom . . . Everybody's interests are served. (Marshall)

Students seemed eager to come to school, and I was excited to begin each new day. The educative research project was enhancing involvement in the lessons, and it was particularly noticeable in class discussions.

As an essential part of the critical pedagogy, students engaged in moral discourse about social injustice. For example, Susan, a female fifth grader, remarked one day that women were often relegated to subordinate positions in the work force. She referred to a restaurant where the waiting staff were female and the manager was male. Susan said, 'It is something you always see in our society'. James once stated that he believed cooperative learning techniques favored white students over black because 'white kids have the power. They wear Nikes and designer jeans. Kids listen more to kids in Nikes. The kid who wears the Nikes will boss the group. That's just how it is'.

Frequently, students who were passive became active participants in our class discussions. The problem of motivating fifth and sixth graders dissolved. It seemed that schooling had finally become relevant to them. They could see that they had something to contribute and I was asking for their opinions. As I started to write up the educative research project, I shared it with the students in my class. They offered important insights about both teaching and learning. James said: '[I]t was cool how you could learn from us. It was like we are the teacher and you are the student. It was cool how you changed your paper when we told you. It was cool'.

Students helped design curricula. We experimented with the objectives in the core curriculum in an attempt to identify meaningful ways of presenting material. Students talked extensively about what they liked about the core and what they disliked, which objectives they thought were important and which were not, what they wanted to learn more about and what they wanted to delete from the core. We built an economics curriculum around their suggestions and worked within it to determine its relevance.

Importantly, I began involving my students in everything from field trip and lesson planning to evaluating my use of the 'hidden curriculum' of the classroom (McCutcheon, 1988). As a result of the skepticism James expressed regarding cooperative learning, I shared some research on it with the students, specifically brief summaries of the work of Johnson and Johnson, Slavin, and Kagen (*Instructor*, 1992). We discussed the pros and cons of that way of conducting a class. We discussed the meaning of the 'null curriculum' and why certain subjects, such as the legal system, are ignored or resolutely excluded from the core objectives (Eisner, 1979). Marshall was particularly interested in law and suggested adding the legal system to our social studies plans. We eagerly adopted his suggestion, and conducted several mock trials where students practiced being plaintiffs, defendants, judge, jury and witnesses.

The benefits of engaging in this educative form of action research were significant for me as well. I began to feel less alienated and to see myself as a part of the learning process again. Student achievement skyrocketed and enthusiasm for learning seemed to be at an all-time high. James said that he never knew work could be fun and genuinely wanted to be involved in the learning process.

I was listening to my students now rather than always talking at them. James remarked in class, 'I never had a teacher that could learn from me'. At any moment we might shift lessons or activities in order to follow the direction of their discussion or their interests. The students designed the bulletin boards and made the decision as to what science topic would be explored next. After identifying some of their own math anxieties, students constructed games to play that concentrated on reviewing difficult skills with each other. We experimented with different kinds of dance in the classroom and listened to each others' favorite music during recess times. I read some of my writing to them and asked for their comments. I was continually amazed at their ability to grasp difficult concepts and suggest alternative ways of expressing an idea. Power relations in the classroom were changing.

The alienation I felt began to diminish. As we moved toward more democratic relations in the classroom, my resistance to structures that rationalized the act of teaching increased. I placed less emphasis on testing and began to stress the communication and the development of ideas as well as the ability to defend those ideas. As a class we opposed the separation of aims and means by conceiving of our own lessons and employing self-evaluation rather than teacher evaluative methods. We began to ignore time schedules and sometimes spent two hours of uninterrupted learning time in class. My evaluation of the critical pedagogy, which became the centerpiece of the educative research project, revealed to us the social and political nature of the regulated curriculum, but that is not all. It also led us to systematically analyze the power relations in class, in school and in society. Educative research, as a form of inquiry, enabled both myself and the students to question power and act for change. It led us toward a process of building more democratic relations.

These findings do not suggest, however, that the process of moving from authoritarian to democratic school relations was either straight forward or without contradictions. A couple of students did not actively engage with my efforts to use schooling as a forum to raise questions about power. A few wanted me to remain as the authority figure in the classroom. Several students found it difficult to maintain this active critical stance over time. Marshall, for example, began the educative research project with the attitude that poverty was a condition of choice. In the initial student survey, he wrote that, 'poor people have a better chance than rich people . . . I think people are poor because they sit on their butt drinking booze'. During the course of the study, however, Marshall demonstrated what appeared to be a shift in his thinking. He began to speak out against one group having more than another, 'if you were born in the upper class, you have a lot better chance of going to Stanford or Harvard, than if you were born in the lower class, you have almost no chance at all'.

Unfortunately, as the educative research project neared completion Marshall's everyday comments indicated that his initial beliefs were still firmly entrenched. He noted, 'People on welfare do not want to work' and 'Wealthy people worked harder and were smarter'. Marshall's return to his initial stereotypic perspective is indicative of the uneven process that occurred in my classroom. Pedagogical gains, in terms of understanding the underbelly of what is seen as commonsense, were consistently mediated by school structures and widely held ideological beliefs expressed in the local community and the media. It is not as if the excellence platform had disappeared. Standardized testing still shaped expectations and influenced perceptions about what students learned and how well I taught. Further, I didn't always receive a great deal of support from the school administration (they viewed my newly found resistant style out of line with the objectives and goals of the district). I often felt under attack, on the defensive, and concerned about the possibilities of continuing the use of a critical pedagogy in my classroom. Nevertheless, there can be little doubt that my inquiry about self and the school context led to a rethinking of my pedagogical style which in turn allowed for the possibility of alternative and more democratic relations in the classroom. The going wasn't easy but at the least I was now teaching again, working on my educational vision, and relating to students in ways that made my practice meaningful and less alienating.

Conclusion

This case report has several implications for understanding the limits and possibilities of educative research, a political/humanist approach to action research. It is clear that the excellence platform has significantly altered the context of schooling. Teachers, such as the one in this study, have fewer opportunities to become critical subjects who put into place their vision of good teaching and schooling. Instead, they often find themselves responding to institutional structures — coping with those structures — in an attempt to survive. This survival mode not only places teachers, in many cases, at odds with their own instincts and theorizing about the nature and import of what should occur in classrooms, but importantly limits their possible resistance to wider structures that shape educational priorities in narrow and limiting ways. It seems important, therefore, that action research projects allow teachers to interrogate the context in which they live and work. While the results of such scrutiny can not be predetermined, it is possible that such inquiry will illuminate the relation between school structures, teachers' articulated vision for schooling and everyday teaching practices. If action research is to result in progressive forms of school change that don't simply reproduce the schools' role in furthering class, race and gender divides, such an analysis is essential because it puts into relief the influence of contextual factors on teachers' role and practices, and importantly provides a foundation for actions — resistance — that actively challenge the distorting influence (in this case authoritarian power relations) of these structures.

It is also apparent that teachers' inquiry about self can illuminate contradictions between desired intentions and teaching practices thereby forming a basis for 'voice as a form of protest'. Such an analysis, as this case study points out, enables practitioners to both consider what should be the nature of power relations in the classroom and how current teaching practices are shaping these relations in particular ways. Action research projects that only look outward, at students, parents and administrators for example, may miss this potentially important part of the inquiry process and not take into account how teaching practices, in part shaped by contextual factors including school structures and ideological assumptions, help reproduce an alienated student role that views students as commodities to be processed. Ironically, this is the same type of role that teachers often resist when they find themselves treated as objects shaped by outside forces (Gitlin and Margonis, 1995).

This case report also illustrates that the politics of schooling, often obscured in more technical explanations, can *emerge* from a relational analysis that looks at self, context and the relation between classroom practices and teacher intentions. While this is an encouraging result for those who adopt a political/humanist approach to action research, it is also the case that more than half the teachers in the masters program who engaged in educative research did projects that not only operated within the normative assumptions of schooling and focused on ways to simply improve that process, but separated out the political aspects of schooling, the relations of power, from what might be referred to as technical issues of instruction. In this sense, political/humanist approaches to action research, live on the border between believing that schooling is inherently a political process and the need to construct power relations between action research participants that reflect the democratic aspirations desired for the classroom. One of the limits of residing on the border is that some action research projects will do little to further the social reconstructivist aim that informs this methodology. Another limit, which clearly is illustrated in the case report, is that while inquiry of this sort can lead to political theorizing and resistance, if that resistance is individualistic, the potential positive results may be short-lived as structures continue to put teachers on the defensive in terms of justifying their roles, relations and practices. What this suggests is that action research approaches that adopt a social reconstructivist perspective aimed at creating a socially just society, need to foster collective relations. Teachers and other like-minded educators may join together to act on, and in some situations transform, school structures that limit and constrain teaching and learning, while furthering the sorting function that allows dominant groups to reassert their position of dominance.

While these limits are important, this case report also points to a somewhat hidden advantage of a political/humanist approach to action research — the politics of the methodology, which is in large measure informed by the importance of establishing dialogical relations between 'researcher' and those traditionally seen as 'subjects', is likely to encourage the same type of pedagogical power relations in the classroom. Put simply, as teachers see the benefits of posing questions (not having those questions imposed on them) and producing knowledge, they are likely to at least consider exploring these same issues with students. For those interested in fostering more democratic relations, it could be that the more uncertain politics that emerges from a political/humanist approach to action research may be better suited to altering constructed power relations in the classroom than other approaches that insist on a political agenda.

In sum, this case report suggests that political/humanist approaches to action research can lead to emergent political theories. This political understanding, in turn, can foster resistance to contextual constraints and more democratic relations in the classroom. However, if action research is to play a significant role in school change, especially views of school change informed by a social reconstructivist agenda, it might be prudent to direct the inquiry process both outward at the process of schooling and inward at the intentions and practices of teachers. It is important, in our view, to offer the possibility of collective forms of inquiry and action. For our goals, action research may enable resistance and encourage significant alteration of structures which limit teachers and students to commodities to be processed and sorted.

Notes

1 For a description of this federalist position, see *America 2000*, US Department of Education (1991), Washington, DC.
2 It is important to note that this brief review focuses only on a few of the prominent approaches to action research and is not meant to be a comprehensive review of the literature. Furthermore, while the categories developed help distinguish types of action research, these categories do not necessarily have opaque boundaries — there is overlap between the various types of action research. Finally, for a more extensive account of these categories, see Gitlin, A. and Thompson, A. (1995), *McGill Journal of Teacher Education*, **30**, 2, pp. 131–47.
3 The educative research project was undertaken as part of the requirements for a graduate degree, see Hadden, J. (1995), *Critical consciousness through curricula analysis: Success and failure in an elementary classroom* (University of Utah: unpublished master's thesis).

References

CARR, W. and KEMMIS, S. (1986) *Becoming Critical: Education, Knowledge and Action Research*, Lewes, Falmer Press.
EISNER, E. (1979) *The Educational Imagination: On the Design and Evaluation of School Programs*, New York, Macmillan.
FREIRE, P. (1993) *Pedagogy of the Oppressed*, New York, Continuum.
GITLIN, A. and MARGONIS, F. (1995) 'The Political Aspect of Reform: Teacher Resistance as Good Sense', *American Journal of Education*, **103**, 4, pp. 377–405.
GITLIN, A. and THOMPSON, A. (1995) 'Foregrounding Politics in Action Research', *McGill Journal of Teacher Education*, **30**, 2, pp. 131–47.
GITLIN, A., BRINGHURST, K., BURNS, M., COOLEY, V., MYERS, B., PRICE, K., RUSSELL, R. and TIESS, P. (1992) *Teachers' Voices for School Change: An Introduction to Educative Research*, New York, Teachers College Press.
GORE, J. and ZEICHNER, K. (1991) 'Action Research and Reflective Teaching in Preservice Teacher Education: A Case Study from the US', *Teaching and Teacher Education*, **7**, 2, pp. 119–36.
HADDEN, J. (1995) *Critical Consciousness through Curricula Analysis: Success and Failure in an Elementary Classroom* (University of Utah: unpublished master's thesis).
INSTRUCTOR EDITOR. (1992, September) 'Putting Research to Work: Cooperative Learning', *Instructor*, pp. 46–7.
MCCUTCHEON, G. (1988) 'Curriculum and the Work of Teachers', BEYER, L. and APPLE, M.

(Eds), *The Curriculum: Problems, Politics, and Possibilities* (pp. 191–203), Albany, State University of New York.

NATIONAL COMMISSION ON EXCELLENCE IN EDUCATION (1983) *A Nation at Risk*, Washington, DC, US Government Printing Office.

SHOR, I. (1980) *Critical Teaching and Everyday Life*, Chicago: University of Chicago Press.

SHOR, I. (1986) *Culture Wars: School and Society in the Conservative Restoration, 1969–1984*, Boston, Routledge & Kegan Paul.

SHOR, I. (1987) *Freire for the Classroom: A Sourcebook for Liberatory Teaching*, Portsmouth, NH, Boynton/Cook.

SHOR, I. (1992) *Empowering Education: Critical Teaching for Social Change*, Chicago, Chicago University Press.

SHOR, I. and FREIRE, P. (1987) *A Pedagogy for Liberation: Dialogues on Transforming Education*, South Hadley, MA, Bergin & Garvey Publishers.

US DEPARTMENT OF EDUCATION (September 1, 1991) *America 2000 No. 10*, Washington. DC, US Department of Education.

8   Action Research and Social Justice: Some Experiences of Schools in the Inner City

Eileen Adams, Rosaleen McGonagle, Pauline Watts and Gaby Weiner (United Kingdom)

This chapter reports on recent collaborative work which attempted to link action research to social justice and school improvement. The main aim of the work was to enable teachers to take more control over their professional practice. However, those involved have had to contend with teacher burn-out because of the recent period of rapid educational reform in the UK and the increasing use of inspection as a means monitoring policy implementation. Both of these factors have dramatically changed what it is like to teach in the inner city in Britain in the late 1990s. In this chapter we reflect on the social justice issues that confront such teachers in an increasingly bureaucratized, competitive and inequitable climate.

We focus first on how the School Partnership Project got started and the theoretical frameworks used in the research, and then consider the range of work undertaken in the four project schools and how each was affected by both the school context and government policy. The article ends with a discussion of the project's impact on all those involved.

The 'we' in this article are four members of staff in the Division of Education at South Bank University, which is a 'new' university located in the centre of London. Each of us is involved to varying degrees in teacher training and/or in educational research. The motivation to enter into closer relationships with local primary (or elementary) schools arose as a consequence of a number of factors coming together at the same time to provide a conjunction or 'moment' for action. Factors that contributed to the moment included: government pressure for initial teacher training to be more school based; a so-called crisis in the quality of schooling offered by inner-city institutions, including our own; the education reforms in the UK between 1988 and 1994 which dramatically changed the social relations and conditions of schooling nationally and the demise in 1990 of the Inner London Education Authority (ILEA) which had, hitherto, governed London's school system and been the major provider of teacher support and professional development in the London area.

The social justice issues we seek to address in this chapter, then, are the apparent pathologizing of inner city education (both at school and university level), the implications of current regulatory educational discourses for the progress of students and teachers in urban areas, and the struggle over who owns teachers' practice.

The Launch Pad Conference

The specific impetus for the research was derived from a conference entitled *Extending Professional Boundaries Through Action Research* organized by the South Bank University in London in February 1995, which was attended by one hundred and fifty teachers from thirteen local primary schools, planned and organized by tutors from the university together with local headteachers (or principals). At the conference, a local headteacher, Joe, set out the agenda for change. He suggested that there were new forms of control over teachers' professional work which had developed around what he believed were narrow performance indicators and that teachers' work needed to be more valued as their relationships with children were ultimately responsible for improving schools. He identified as potentially significant: teachers' career expectations, their biographies, the context in which they worked and the culture within which they operated. He suggested that with the demise of the ILEA, a vacuum had appeared where previously there had been extensive support for teachers, and the research and curriculum expertise in higher education could be an alternative means of support.

University tutors, at the conference, argued for the benefits of teacher involvement in action research, referring to examples of work in schools where teachers had used action research as an opportunity to transform their practice. Here, teachers had been the prime movers in bringing about change, showing themselves willing to experiment, initiate changes, report on developments and take a reflective and critical stance towards their efforts. This had resulted, it was claimed, in improved practice both for the teachers involved and other colleagues. Later in the conference, university tutors acted as facilitators in seminars with teachers, aimed at discussing what might be involved in research activity and what possibilities were available for work in schools.

The conference, thus, acted as a launch pad to establish the School Partnership Project, which aimed to create effective school-university partnerships in order, through action research, to improve professional practice and empower teachers and tutors. Teachers in four schools chose to embark on a programme of action research and meetings were held in each school to outline a framework and research programme. The intention was that the school teachers would set their own research agenda and that university tutors[1] would support them in their efforts to reflect on, evaluate and make changes, where necessary, in their practice. In the context of high profile national policymaking, it was seen by those involved as particularly important that teachers should find a voice and feel less isolated and powerless. The value of the work for tutors was closer links with local schools and reflection on, and improvements in, their own pedagogies.

Context

In the UK and elsewhere, the work of inner city schools has become the object of criticism and concern with an increasing tendency to perceive urban contexts as synonymous with high levels of social deprivation. A UK government report,

Performance in City Schools, defines the inner-city as an area where a large pro-portion of population has low socio-economic status, housing and health are poor, where educational qualifications among adults are low and there are a large number of minority ethnic groups (House of Commons Education Committee, 1995). Sig-nificantly, the publication of inspectors' reports (e.g., OFSTED, 1996) and results of national Standard Assessment Tasks (SATs) confirmed London schools' relatively poor performance compared with other parts of the country.

An additional pressure on local schools has been the growing influence of the school effectiveness movement in the UK, originally initiated by researchers (e.g., Rutter, *et al.*, 1979; Mortimore, *et al.*, 1988) but increasingly incorporated into government policy-making (Sammons, *et al.*, 1995). School effectiveness and school improvement research emphasizes the relationship between teaching, school ethos and differential outcomes of schooling as measured by examination and other forms of assessment. This in turn has produced a new vocabulary (e.g., performance/process indicators, value-added) within a bureaucratic discursive framework which places the responsibility directly on schools, rather than local or central government, for enhancing and improving the quality of education for the children in their care (e.g., Pennel and Cuttance, 1992; Gray and Wilcox, 1995).

At the same time, UK government policy has increasingly required teacher training to be more vocationally relevant by basing substantial components of train-ing in schools. This has led to the creation of new partnership relationships between universities and schools, including joint involvement in the organization and plan-ning of university training courses.

London schools, then, have experienced a three-fold attack: the loss of ILEA and its replacement by smaller, less powerful local authorities; spiralling concern about performance levels in inner-city schools; and direct blame for student 'under-performance'. Engagement in action research was seen by those involved as an innovative and potentially rewarding development arising from burgeoning school-university partnership relationships, and, for some, as a self-defence strategy to counter potential criticism from inspectors.

Social Justice, Teachers' Work and Action Research

The focus for the work thus derived from three main concerns: a commitment of all involved to work for increased social justice and opportunities in education in London; the need for teachers' work to be more highly valued in the face of increased government control over schools; and involvement in action research as a practitioner empowering research paradigm.

Social Justice

Whilst interest in social justice has covered a wide range of issues, the main con-cern in this instance was to help teachers and schools with diverse student populations to provide them with better life-chances and educational opportunities; in particular, students from working-class, black and minority ethnic groups, and those whose first language is not English. For these students, home and school environment is often grim, as the legacy of the seventeen-year Thatcher/Major years has been increasing poverty for many, and a widening gap between the rich and the poor, most sharply visible in the big cities.

While working-class and black under-achievement has been a focus of UK education since the 1950s (see, for example, Halsey, *et al.*, 1980), recent government inspection and regulatory policies have once again accorded such so-called disadvantage a high profile. In particular, attention has been drawn to poor performance of working class and/or black male students in London and other metropolitan areas (e.g., OFSTED, 1996). The question for the project was to what extent might schools intervene in this potentially downward spiral, and how might action research inform such interventions.

Teachers' Work

UK education legislation of the late 1980s and early 1990s sought to centralize power by the introduction of the national curriculum, and increasing the role of assessment and inspection while decreasing powers of local education authorities. What became increasingly clear, also, was the government's determination to break with the past and exclude educational professionals from active participation in the new curriculum formulations. School teachers' work spiralled out of their control, changing dramatically during and after the 1988–93 period of education legislation.

The form of national curriculum which emerged was heavily prescriptive and regulatory, accompanied by extensive mechanisms of control and accountability, one of which was regular inspection of schools. New agencies (all quangos: quasi non-governmental organisations[2]) were established to oversee and monitor the changes, the most important of which were School Curriculum and Assessment Authority (SCAA), Office for Standards in Education (OFSTED) and the Teaching Training Authority (TTA). As a consequence, the teachers involved in the project had or were experiencing enforced changes to previous practice, increased workloads, decreasing autonomy as professionals, and expanded systems of surveillance and inspection.

Throughout the project, all the schools involved were preparing for an inspection visit. The Education Act of 1993 requires schools to be inspected fully every four years and the results published with the aim, in particular, of creating school 'league tables' of performance and identifying 'failing' schools. Some London boroughs were targeted for extra inspection and for the schools involved, stress levels arising from this often gruelling process were particularly high.

Action Research

Much has been written on how action research can contribute to the professional development of teachers but relatively few writers have focused on its explicit commitment to challenging social and educational inequality (Weiner, 1989). An exception to this is Kemmis (1988) who identifies four action research elements: a strong interest among educational researchers in helping practitioners deal with problems of practice; a broad methodological interest in interpretive methods; a growth of collaborative work in curriculum development and evaluation; and an explicit ideological commitment to addressing social and political problems of education through participatory research carried out by practitioners. In his view, teachers are constantly involved in monitoring and evaluating their work and seeking to improve on their practice, a process of (practitioner) research in which data is systematically gathered and analyzed in order to inform and improve practice. Action research, according to Kemmis, requires practitioners with a commitment to enhancing social justice, to consciously engage in developing a fuller understanding of their work through systematic enquiry, careful evaluation and testing out of possibilities as a basis for action.

Moreover, as Uzzell points out, practitioner researcher does not merely record the impact of change, but is itself an agent of change:

> the researcher plans an active role in becoming a change agent by informing, encouraging and supporting the community group and studying and interpreting their actions in the light of his own interventions. (Uzzell, 1979, p. 65)

Change might involve generating different ways of thinking and working or it might involve modifying attitudes, management practices or working relationships within the school. However, not all change is successful. It is also, we suggest, important to acknowledge that 'failure' to achieve the desired outcomes of an action research initiative need not necessarily be seen as a negative experience, so long as those involved are able to learn from it and re-invest that understanding in further development. Action research was thus used by the project because of its two-fold capability: to expand the professional space and autonomy of teachers, and as a means by which educational inequalities could be addressed.

Setting up the School Partnership Project

In initial whole-school meetings, tutors and teachers discussed their respective roles. It was agreed, for example, that evidence needed to be collected systematically and that most of that evidence would come from the teachers. Background reading, frameworks of understanding and general information, help with choice of research method, and skill in analysis of documentation would come from the tutors. Thus, the role developed by university tutors (Eileen, Pauline, Rosaleen and Gaby) within the School Partnership Project, was that of critical friends, able to provide information, support and encouragement to busy practitioners. Significantly, a potential problem was identified, of conflict between the roles of teacher/researcher and tutor/ critical friend, each having different requirements from the research.

Working with the Schools

Four schools chose to participate in the School Partnership Project, all in predominantly working class, inner city locations. Each school had between 300 and 700 students, aged between three and eleven, from a range of different ethnic and cultural backgrounds. Significantly, all the schools were preparing for or had recently experienced a government inspection, and indeed, headteachers tended to prioritize the need for staff to develop skills for facilitating school improvement in the light of any such inspection. In contrast, teachers had individual concerns related to learning and teaching in the classroom, and also relating to whole school issues, such student behaviour, reading or how to support children with special educational needs.

Each school developed its own research programme, with initial discussions and information gathering, followed by data gathering, reflection and further discussion, and then formulation of proposals for change. The project began in late 1995 and continued throughout 1996. We consider the work of each school in turn: City Primary School, Borough Primary School, Eden Primary School and Gateway Primary School (all pseudonyms), all in one South London neighborhood.

City Primary School

City School is a small primary school with a shifting population of students and a recent relatively high turnover of staff. For some time, the headteacher and the school staff had been concerned about two specific aspects of the school: the management of pupils' behaviour and the standards of reading achieved by pupils. Initiated by the headteacher, the research initiative began when meetings were arranged between members of staff and two tutors (Rosaleen and Gaby) to agree on a programme of action research which would generate a range of strategies addressing the two issues. Over an informal lunch, staff and tutors introduced themselves and talked about their aspirations for the work, creating, it was hoped, the basis for a sound working partnership. Various points of view regarding perceived problems and possible solutions were aired with the aim of establishing a positive, collaborative atmosphere. However, it soon became clear that the headteacher himself was under considerable pressure, and in fact, later in the year he went on extended period of sick leave (which eventually led to early retirement), with stress cited as the main cause.

Teachers further suggested that it was important for tutors to have some understanding of the problems of the school. Whereas in general, student behaviour appeared 'reasonable', approximately a third of the children in each class were, it seems, responsible for creating difficulties of some kind which inhibited their own and others' learning. Attempts to gain parental support to combat behavioural problems had been largely unsuccessful and while a number of strategies had been tried in the past, the imminence of a government inspection provided a particular incentive to move things forward more speedily.

Thus, while other concerns were expressed, say about standards of reading (test results had been poor), it was decided to focus on behaviour, with the view, as expressed by the headteacher, that if students' behaviour improved, learning overall (including that of reading) would also show improvement. The focus, for the first year of the research at least, was therefore on developing an effective behaviour management-policy in the school, emphasizing, in particular, patterns of misbehaviour in the playground — in the belief that many incidents which started in the playground also had an impact on work in the classroom.

After several sessions led by the tutors which introduced and discussed aspects of behaviour management and research possibilities, it was proposed to undertake two separate week-long blocks of observation of students' behaviour in the playground, where, it was felt, much of the poor behaviour in the classroom originated. Observation sheets of critical incidents (Tripp, 1994) were piloted and agreed, involving documentation of date, time and place of incidents, and the perpetrators and victims involved and subsequent actions taken. Tutors collated and analyzed the outcome of the questionnaires, providing reports to staff on the basis of which a new and more effective school behaviour policy would be drafted and piloted. The action research cycle would then be repeated to see whether the policy could intervene and interrupt previous undesirable behaviour patterns. At the time of writing, a behaviour policy was being developed from the findings of the research thus far, which was to be evaluated and revised in a further action research cycle. Significantly, the school had also been informed that it was to be inspected in the forthcoming academic year.

Borough Primary School

Borough School is a small school, located in a quiet road in a commuter area of South London. The school is bounded by playgrounds, playing fields and houses with gardens. Four teachers became involved in Borough School's action research initiative. One was keen to gain further professional qualifications, while the others had been 'advised' by the headteacher to become involved in the project. She felt that they would benefit from the experience of taking a closer look at their work, and by explaining and justifying their practice. At preliminary meetings with the tutor (Eileen), it was agreed that the research should contribute both to school policy and to practice. First, teachers were to document and appraise the existing situation as a basis for identifying possibilities for change, and these, then, would be implemented, monitored and evaluated in progressive action research cycles.

The concerns identified by teachers were: students who exhibited behavioural and work difficulties; how to work more effectively with groups of children; the relationship between self-esteem and academic performance; and the Physical Education (PE) curriculum. At first, the teachers seemed tentative and lacking confidence; nevertheless, they persevered in collecting evidence, producing documentation, and appeared to find the exercise more satisfying than first anticipated. One reason given for this was that closer scrutiny of their practice had revealed insights they would have otherwise missed. They thus felt encouraged to continue.

One teacher focused on four students who presented particular behavioural difficulties linked to problems with their school work. Notes and observations were made of the students' work and of their behaviour with the aim of finding ways of reinforcing good behaviour, creating positive learning experiences and creating strategies for encouragement and support. The teacher found that she became more aware of the blocks and frustrations which the children experienced. Later, she was able to develop and extend this work when she moved to another class at the end of the year.

A second teacher chose, through action research, to develop more effective strategies for group work. She considered a number of factors: exploring differentiation in set tasks, ways of managing differently sized groups and how to motivate students through group activities. The action research strategy eventually adopted was to experiment with various kinds of group work in Science. For example, groups were sometimes given specific assignments set by the teacher, and at other times, allowed to determine their own approaches to problem-solving and negotiating with other students about how they could best work together. Her observations of these group activities raised questions about the benefits of different kinds of group organization in the support of children's learning, the skills needed by children in order to develop through group work and the practicalities of organization.

A third teacher uncovered the fact that her students neither took pride in their work nor worked hard enough to 'do their best'. The reasons for this, she suggested, were that the students had poor self-esteem and that peer group pressure was frequently negative, resulting in bad behaviour. She had already tried ways of evaluating students' work, for example, through a yearly conference where individual students were asked to review and comment on their work. However, the teacher felt these had not been altogether successful, as students did not seem to take the conference seriously, but seemed merely to go 'through the motions' of taking part.

Discussion between the teacher and the tutor thus explored questions concerning what makes students and teachers value their work and how this might be demonstrated. It was decided to focus on several areas of the curriculum — dance and drama, written work and geography — with the aim of helping students develop a vocabulary for describing and valuing particular qualities in their work. It was hoped, in so doing, to establish a set of expectations and criteria which encouraged students to develop a self-critical stance.

Following suggestions from local inspectors that teachers should understand the requirements for Physical Education (PE) in the National Curriculum (school sport was one of Prime Minister John Major's particular interests), a fourth teacher focused on the school PE policy. She extended previous worked on assessment of gymnastics to preparation of schemes of work with differentiated tasks for different ability levels and years.

An additional task was to devise appropriate monitoring and recording of students' development, and as a contribution to this, she had investigated children's perceptions of PE, their likes and dislikes, and their views of personal strengths and weaknesses. This was achieved through the creation, by students, of 'picture profiles' of themselves in relation to achievement and enjoyment of PE. These selfportraits were then used by the teacher as a focus for discussion with the class, to help students identify their strengths and weaknesses and decide on areas where they needed to improve.

The teacher also mounted an extensive data gathering exercise involving possibilities for professional development in PE and official documentation on the PE curriculum with the aim of exploring strategies for all the school staff for implementing the statutory requirements. At the time of writing, she had produced a draft policy, evaluation sheets for which had been distributed to staff for comment. This was to be followed by a policy redraft, and an exhibition involving photographs of students engaged in various PE activities, annotated with quotes and information taken from National Curriculum documentation to inform teachers, parents and students about the PE curriculum.

Eden Primary School

Eden Primary School is an inner city school on a split site, divided by a busy road and surrounded by municipal council housing estates and extensive industrial development. Staff at the school had spent the year before the project reviewing existing school policies, and what changes might improve school management and classroom practice. Participation in the project occurred at the time when preparation was being made for a government inspection, and staff saw involvement in action research as one way of 'showing improvement'.

At this meeting to which Eileen was invited, the headteacher stressed that there was a particular need for teachers to be clear on the requirements and the implications of the National Curriculum but also suggested a number of other research possibilities including school policy for teaching and learning, the development of a special needs policy incorporating the new government code of practice, and a more standardized record-keeping system.

Prompted by the headteacher, teachers considered these and other possibilities and discussion centred, as in City School previously, on the school behaviour and discipline policy and how it was being put into effect. It was agreed that a starting point might be to consider the link between relationships and discipline in the school. Some teachers saw a need to focus on students who presented particular behavioural challenges; others suggested that emphasis should be directed to factors which might influence behaviour — for example, communication skills, special needs support, self-image in students, the outdoor environment, support networks for children and bilingualism. Given the wide range of possibilities, further meetings were held by the teachers to clarify the research agenda and with the tutor to help frame individual research questions, decide on ways of collecting evidence, and make comparisons with work elsewhere.

Although the teachers in this school appeared to take longer than others in the project to decide on research possibilities, these relatively 'small steps' had the immediate effect of raising awareness of practice issues in the school, in that because teachers were obliged to define an area of their work which posed a challenge or a problem, they also needed to explore the issue in some depth and talk about their work with colleagues. Thus, according to the headteacher, benefits from involvement in action research were already substantial as teachers began to experience a greater sense of achievement and control over their work. Teachers displayed a greater degree of confidence in interpreting government curriculum requirements and a stronger sense of ownership of the means to implement them. Importantly, the research seemed to have enabled inner-city teachers to recognize their ability to effect change rather than merely reacting to the apparently endless stream of government policy directives.

Gateway Primary School

Gateway School is the largest primary school in the area, located in the midst of a number of high rise municipal council estates. Collaboration with the school had started a few months before the conference and a working relationship established between the tutor (Pauline), the teachers and the headteacher. The aim of the research was two-fold: to enhance the professional development of all teachers involved and to improve the quality of provision within the Early Years Phase. This proved a complex task because many of the issues which arose subsequently were derived from the tension between this twin focus. At different times, the numbers of teachers involved varied from between four and ten.

The Early Years phase in Gateway School comprises two nursery (kindergarten) classes (for children aged three to five) and four reception classes (for 5-year-olds). Each class had more than thirty children from diverse cultural backgrounds. This was managed by a coordinator who, with the deputies and headteacher, made up the senior management team of the school. The early years coordinator was a young, energetic new appointment and her developing relationship with the staff was a key feature of the research. Other teachers involved included a newly qualified teacher who had completed a year of teacher training at South Bank University the previous year and four other teachers who had worked at the school for some years.

For Pauline, the role of facilitator was a new one. She had been at the university for a relatively short time, having previously worked as an infant teacher where she herself had been involved in action research as a practitioner/researcher. She was therefore convinced both of the value of action research and of her capacity to act as critical friend. Following initial discussions between Pauline, the headteacher and the Early Years Coordinator, meetings took place, first with the Early Years team and later with other teachers in the school. Other team leaders were, however, not as supportive of the research, which created the first tension.

The group discussed areas of success and concern which might become the focus for research, and emerging concerns included the teaching of reading and language development, managing limited time and space, outdoor play, and classroom organization. It was agreed initially to concentrate on language, as this area 'felt exciting' for teachers who were willing to share their concerns with each other.

Needs were being expressed publicly, perhaps for the first time, in a large school where the particular concerns of Early Years teachers were but one small element of a larger picture.

The early meetings were particularly invigorating. Teachers brought evidence of children's work, including a videotape which the group helped to analyze and evaluate. There were other equally fascinating pieces of evidence such as descriptions of classroom activities, accounts of strategies which children used when reading together and a diary of one teacher's observation of one child. In the discussion which followed, teachers tried to make sense of the complex and challenging job of educating young children in an inner city school.

Plans were made for further meetings when the tutor was to work with the teachers to prepare presentations of work in progress for the headteacher and other staff and tutors. However, the action research cycle was brought to a standstill when a government inspection intervened. Teachers were obliged to devote attention to preparation for the inspection at a time when some were increasingly valuing their involvement in the action research process. The day conference at the university occurred immediately following the inspection, and though the outcome of the inspection had proved highly satisfactory, school staff were tired and grumpy, and certainly not ready to share their work publicly with people outside the school. The momentum was lost and consequently, the next evening meeting where teachers were expected to present their work was poorly attended. At the time of writing, though there is much collaboration with the school in other areas, the action research has not restarted.

The support of the Early Years coordinator for the project was an important element of the early success of the research. She was new to the school and keen to initiate action research. However, she was viewed warily by other staff and thus was worried about sharing her ideas with colleagues for fear of damaging relationships which were still quite fragile. Additionally, even highly committed teachers, such as another new to the school, reported feeling heavily overloaded though she was used to collecting evidence about children's work (for her university course work) and was among the first to offer ideas for future development. Long-standing teachers who had been interested in the project early on found the action research initiative to be an extra burden as the inspection drew nearer.

The position of the head was also significant. He ran what was considered to be an 'effective' school by the subsequent inspection and was well thought of by the staff, showing a high degree of interest in staff development. He had taught at the university and was keen for closer links between the two, seeing the action research project as providing opportunities for the enhancement of professional development. However his position provided an additional set of tensions. Thus, though it was agreed that notes of each project meeting would be made available to him, it was notable that at the one meeting he attended, only new members of staff were willing to discuss their work openly.

The research clearly brought benefits to some of the individuals involved. The Early Years coordinator was, during the project, able to relax into working as an ordinary team member, rather than as a manager; the tutor was able to carry out research in schools; and the headteacher, to make provision for the professional development of the staff. The benefits for the teachers were that they were able to analyze and evaluate children's work and identify issues raised as a basis for considering change in their own practice. As to benefits for students, there appeared for a while to be a heightened awareness of the need to give attention to differences between students and to consider them as individuals.

The time was too short, however, for the teachers to come to see research as integral to teaching, though they appeared to appreciate the idea intellectually. Consequently, they saw the process of action research as 'taking them away' from teaching and planning, as extra to their normal workload, rather than as a way of validating their work. Because the project was funded by the school, there appeared to be an element of coercion for the teachers to work as a group and not opt out of the activity. This, according to Pauline, severely weakened the effectiveness of the project.

There were also some contradictions for the tutor. In trying to encourage the teachers to adopt a critical stance, Pauline felt compelled to put pressure on staff to share their work publicly at a time when teachers should, perhaps, have themselves taken control of the research. Nevertheless, Pauline felt she had gained much from involvement in the project, for example, concerning the importance of timing, the significance of external events, the influence of chance and the need to stand back from situations in order to make reflective, professional judgments.

Analysis and Evaluation

As we have seen, there were a number of dilemmas arising from the School Partnership Project. It was not easy to develop the action research initiative in the 'cold climate' of low teacher morale and increased stress in London schools. (It needs to be remembered that nine out of the thirteen schools which took part in the conference decided not to participate in the project.) How can the work be evaluated? What impact has been made on the teachers, schools and university tutors?

Schools

The demise of ILEA compelled schools to develop substitute self-help strategies and look to other providers for in-service education and professional development. The School Partnership Project was an expression of this, though it took different forms in each of the schools involved. During the project all the schools were experiencing pressure from the government's inspection programme, which appeared simultaneously to generate and obstruct action research activity. As we have seen from Gateway School, the inspection process could obstruct the research; on the other hand, a forthcoming inspection provided other schools with the incentive to join the project as it would look good to the inspectors. Additionally, the action research topics chosen tended to reflect and respond to emphases within government policymaking (and by inspectors), for example, on discipline, reading, planning, rather than representing wider professional issues of staff development and professional renewal.

Headteachers and Teachers

Headteachers, under pressure to do well in forthcoming inspections, were anxious to present action research as a quality indicator, as well as viewing collaboration with the university as a means of school improvement and staff development. This view was not shared by many teachers, who, at the beginning of the project, tended to see action research as yet another 'extra' to existing heavy teaching and administration duties. They were thus, understandably cautious about the amount of time they could devote to the research. For a few teachers, however, the project appeared to encourage recognition that they might be able to effect changes themselves rather than merely react to government policy. Some found the experience of action research helped them develop a more reflective and self-critical stance to their work, and to look more closely at their practice and consider alternative approaches. As the research progressed, they became more proactive, taking greater control of their work and of ways of working in the school.

Relationships between Teachers and Tutors

Teachers and tutors both reported feeling unable to give sufficient time to the research. Tutors were able to spend only short periods of time in school on project work, because their work conditions were being similarly shaped by increasingly regulatory government policies restricting the scope of initial teacher training. Working contacts between teachers and tutors were therefore primarily through meetings focusing on teachers' experiences of action research. It was certainly the case that had tutors been able to spend more time in the schools, teachers and tutors might have developed a greater degree of trust and more confidence in sharing research experiences.

University Tutors

Tutors saw their involvement in action research as an important part of their professional work although, like the teachers, it was viewed as additional to their usual workload. Changes in university funding had created added demands on university tutors, who were expected to undertake more research in addition to their teaching duties and responsibilities for supporting students in schools. The project acted as a linking mechanism between these areas of work, creating, it was felt, dynamic relationships between research, teaching in schools and teacher education. Tutors were therefore able to develop closer relationships with schools where their students were placed for school experience and, simultaneously, raise their own research profile and contribute to raising achievement levels in inner-city schools.

Overall, then, although the cold climate of British education seemed often to present huge obstacles to the progress of the project, it is nevertheless our view that action research can provide a framework for enabling complex relationships between schools and universities to develop and flourish. It can enable practitioners to extend support to each other, provide a buffer between government policymaking and school/university practice, and enhance the quality of learning and teaching through targeted professional development. It is thus an approach particularly suited to the present day needs of London's inner-city schools and one that we shall seek to develop more widely in the future.

Notes

1 Throughout this article, we differentiate between school and university staff by referring to those based in schools as teachers, and those based in the university as tutors.
2 It has been suggested that Britain is currently ruled by a 'quangocracy', that is by 'quangos' — quasi non-governmental organizations (ref.).

References

DEPARTMENT OF EDUCATION AND EMPLOYMENT (DEE) (1995) *GEST: Raising Standards in Inner City Schools 1992–95*, London, DEE.

GRAY, J. and WILCOX, B. (1995), *'Good School, Bad School': Evaluating Performance and Encouraging Improvement*, Buckingham, Open University Press.

HALSEY, A.H., HEATH, A. and RIDGE, J. (1980) *Origins and Destinations: Family, Class and Education in Modern Britain*, Oxford, Oxford University Press.

HOUSE OF COMMONS EDUCATION COMMITTEE (1995) *Performance in City Schools: 3rd Report*, London, HMSO.

KEMMIS, S. (1988) 'Action research in retrospect and prospect', in KEMMIS, S. and McTAGGART, R. (Eds), 2nd Ed. (pp. 27–39), *The Action Research Reader*, Geelong, Victoria, Deakin University Press.

MORTIMORE, P. *et al.* (1988) *School Matters: the Junior Years*, London, Open Books.

OFSTED (1993) *Access and Achievement in Urban Education*, London, HMSO.

OFSTED (1996) *The Teaching of Reading in 45 Inner London Primary Schools*, London, OFSTED.

PENNEL, D. and CUTTANCE, P. (Eds) (1992) *School Effectiveness: Research, Policy and Practice*, London, Cassell.

RUDDUCK, J. (1992) quoted in LOMAX, P. (1994) *The Narrative of an Educational Journey or Crossing the Track*, inaugural address, London, Kingston University.

RUTTER, M., MAUGHAN, B. MORTIMORE, P. and OUSTON, J. (1979) *Fifteen Thousand Hours*, London, Open Books.

SAMMONS, P., HILLMAN, J. and MORTIMORE, P. (1995) *Key Characteristics of Effective Schools: A Review of School Effectiveness Research*, London, OFSTED.

TRIPP, D. (1994) *Critical Incidents in Teaching*, London, Routledge.

UZZELL, D. (1979) 'Four roles of the community researcher', *Journal of Voluntary Action Research*, 8, pp. 1–2.

WEINER, G. (1989) 'Professional self-knowledge versus social justice: A critical analysis of the teacher-researcher movement', *British Educational Research Journal*, **15**, 1, pp. 41–51.

9   School Organization Development in a Changing Political Environment[1]

Sue Davidoff (South Africa)

In this chapter I describe a case study of an organization development intervention at a typical African school in Cape Town, South Africa. Action research is used as a methodology for change in the process. As background to this case study, information about the consulting agency — the Teacher Inservice Project — is given, as well as contextual background to apartheid (and post-apartheid) schooling in South Africa. The case study documents the process of meeting with members of the school community and assisting them in a process of identifying the concerns that lay beneath their appeal to develop a code of conduct. It is precisely in such a process (of penetrating beyond the symptoms of dysfunctionality) that action research can facilitate the deepening of understanding and the moving to action (and improvement).

Teacher Inservice Project

The Teacher Inservice Project is a school-focused project based in the Faculty of Education at the University of the Western Cape, Cape Town, South Africa. Our main focus is whole school (or institutional) organization development, where we provide inservice support in the form of organizational capacity building to schools, tertiary educational institutions and other inservice projects. The aim of the Teacher Inservice Project (TIP) is to establish a culture of ongoing personal, professional and institutional development at schools. Our approach is informed by the understanding that classrooms are part of schools and schools are part of a greater social context. Social and political movements affect the way in which schooling is conceived and constructed. Similarly, innovations in the way in which schools operate can impact on social transformation.

Action research is embedded in our praxis. Reflective processes form an essential part of our own organizational activities, by way of reflective reports (written on a monthly basis) as well as field notes and (as colleagues) ongoing reflection of our work. At the courses we offer, participants are invited to evaluate our courses. In our action research approach, we are testing the assumption that what happens in a classroom will be affected by and affect what is happening in the school as a whole — in other words, that the classroom and the school are interdependent, and cannot be looked at separately.

We believe that for significant educational reconstruction and development to occur, teachers need to own the process of change. Our experience has shown that change imposed from outside of the school setting, by people other than those who work in the schools, is unlikely to succeed. This is one of the basic assumptions of action research — that the need for change must be identified by those undergoing the change. Because it is very difficult for individual teachers to commit themselves to a process of change if the school environment is such that it does not support that change, we link individual teacher development with organization (whole school) development. We aim to facilitate a process where teachers (and schools) can identify their own goals or problems. We then assist them in developing appropriate strategies to deal with these goals (or problems), so that they are intimately involved in the process of change from the beginning of our working together.

The process of identification of issues and needs, and the development of strategies to address them is part of our broader action research strategy. We ensure that we start where teachers and schools are, by beginning every process with questions for our participants around their major concerns or issues about their school, rather than with our own agenda for a particular teacher or school. We understand that teachers have a far deeper contextual understanding of their situation than any outside consultant, and that these understandings need to be made conscious in order to actively inform the change process. However, we also recognize that consultants can and do bring critical expertise and freshness of insight into a situation. Together we can create a valuable starting point for a meaningful process of change.

In a whole school context, action research becomes a systematic way of evaluating the extent to which a school is achieving what it has set out to achieve — be it in terms of, for example, the structures, strategies or the staff development programmes which have been set up by the staff.

Our organization development interventions are informed by a particular framework for understanding schools as organizations. This framework underlines the systemic nature of organizational life, and highlights the interdependence of the various elements of an organization. It is also important as a way of providing a conceptual map for participants in our programmes, and as a diagnostic tool for ourselves (as facilitators) and participants (in organizational self-study or self-reflection).

This framework was developed by two colleagues and myself as a way of understanding and representing the various elements of organizational life. Since then we have used it extensively in the Teacher Inservice Project, as a way of facilitating understanding of seemingly disparate and often overwhelming issues to participants on our courses or involved in our school-based organization development interventions.

One of these interwoven elements of organizational life is the identity or culture of the school, where the norms, the policy, the vision, the mission, the ethos, the direction and the purpose of the school are to be found (often ill-defined, or defined by default or negatively, rather than in a positive, conscious, chosen way). Another element, that of strategy, involves goal-setting, planning and evaluation; if there is no sense of direction, no purpose or vision, planning will tend to be *ad hoc* and will

Figure 9.1: *Framework for understanding organizations: Elements of organizational life*

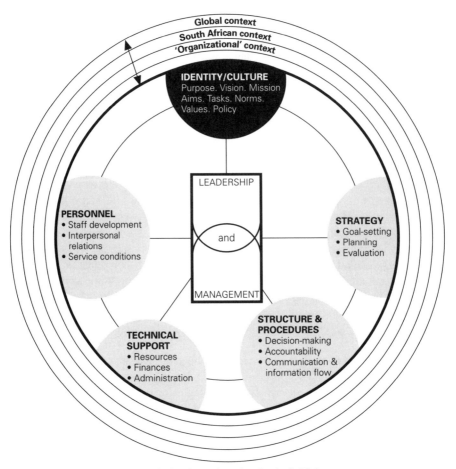

Source: Reproduced with permission from Juta Academic Publishers.

take the form of crisis management-type plans, or plans around dates for events and time-tabling. In most schools in South Africa little or no evaluation (or appraisal) takes place. Resistance to an imposed top-down form of evaluative control was rejected by teachers and unfortunately over the years nothing replaced it. This has resulted in a breakdown in accountability and support for and development of quality classroom and school (organizational) practice.

The element of structures and procedures takes into account aspects such as accountability, decision-making, and information flow. Without appropriate structures and procedures to support it, the most inspiring vision will remain lofty and unrealized. Similarly, structures and procedures reflect a particular ethos — for example a top down decision-making structure and procedure will not enable all the relevant stakeholders to participate meaningfully in shaping the life of the school and feeling an active part of that movement.

Technical support is an element which is frequently overlooked or not taken seriously enough. Here we talk about the physical resources the school has at its disposal — desks, chairs, books, classrooms, photocopy machines, science and biology equipment, TVs, computers. Also relevant here is who has access to these resources. Part of the technical support at a school is the financial management. Another aspect is the school administration: is there adequate administrative support, are there people responsible for ensuing that information flow is effective, and that teachers can get on with their important task of teaching rather than having to spend disproportionate amounts of time doing administrative work? Historically, physical resources have been spread extremely unevenly in South Africa.

Looking at the people element of an organization, we have personnel, where concerns such as interpersonal relationships, human resource (or staff) development and conditions of service are relevant. Here we are concerned with providing an environment at schools where life-long learning becomes part of the culture of the school. This means, among other things, that the developmental needs of the staff, in terms of the vision of the school as a whole and the individual needs of staff, need to be taken into account.

In the centre, and holding it all together is the leadership and management of the school: the way in which all of these interweaving elements are held together at the centre. Here leadership and management capacity is important — the ability for those in leadership positions (and potentially that means every teacher and other stakeholders in the school, including parents, students and community leaders) in the school to be creative and responsible leaders. Thus a healthy school is one in which leadership capacity is being developed in all staff members (and other constituencies) through ongoing personal development processes, designed to build the capacity of those people involved in the life of the school to participate meaningfully in its change processes. Leadership and management means directing and holding, pushing forward while maintaining a secure base, inspiring and supporting, listening, paying attention, linking theory with practice.

Another dimension of understanding schools as organizations, one which is often under-emphasized is the contextual reality of the school. No school exists in a vacuum, outside of its immediate and broader community. The micro-context of the school is understood as the location of the school within its immediate community, and the schooling and education system, while the macro-context refers to the school as seen within broader South African society. Presenting issues at the school must be analyzed and understood within the context of societal dynamics, including issues around power relations: race, class gender and other areas of potential exploitation and oppression. If an understanding of and response to school issues does not take these dynamics into account, they are unlikely to be addressed in any kind of satisfactory way. The shift from self-understandings to critical reflections needs to be mediated through and seen against the background of broader social concerns.

South Africa — Some Educational History

Although theoretically (following the elections in April 1994) we have a single department of education in South Africa, as opposed to racially segregated departments of education, conditions in schools remain vastly uneven and disparate. The apartheid regime ensured that educational provision served the interests of the white population. The most disadvantaged of all were the schools serving the African population, which fell within the then Department of Education and Training (DET). It is not uncommon, with these (ex)DET schools, even currently, to encounter conditions such as no electricity or proper toilets; no staffroom or hall; insufficient classrooms and desks within the classrooms; too few textbooks; in certain cases no proper school buildings at all; up to ninety pupils in a class; no photocopy machine; no secretarial support; no telephone; desolate wind-swept school grounds . . .

It is not hard to imagine the effect that such conditions have on the morale and commitment of the teachers working there. Often these teachers are under-qualified, and therefore on a low salary scale. As a result they spend much of their time studying to improve their qualifications, in order to improve their salaries.

The consequences of such a situation are inevitable, and the way in which the demoralization of teachers is witnessed takes many forms. Three other issues need to be mentioned here: the first is that most of the principals of these schools (and most South African schools) have not received adequate or specialized preparation for their task, and are not able to guide or manage the school appropriately. The second is that part of what made apartheid succeed for so long was that it took an extreme form of authoritarianism, which then permeated every aspect of society. Our schools have mirrored that authoritarianism, leaving teachers largely passive and lacking in professional and pedagogical assertiveness and imagination. The third issue is that there has been no history or tradition of inservice work taking place at schools. Thus engaging in any inservice activities has been left to the enthusiasm or commitment of individual teachers, since there is no policy which ensures that ongoing professional or institutional development takes place. Because of the conditions described above, relatively few teachers take up the challenge of transformation.

All of these contextual factors are crucial background knowledge to understanding the challenges of building the capacity of schools to become 'learning organizations' — schools where there is a culture of ongoing personal, professional and institutional development.

One School Among Many

One school — serving African students with an all-African staff — approached us for assistance. While the school building itself is fairly modern and large, inside it is barren. Just the bare bones of the building and very little else. The school is located within an area which has mostly 'informal' houses surrounding it: houses put together with corrugated iron, or sheets of plastic or planks of wood. This is an extremely poor community, serviced by bad roads and poor water supply and sanitation.

This is a high school, with almost 2000 students, whose ages range between 13 and 20. In any one standard there will inevitably be a wide range of ages: many students fail repeatedly, or 'drop out' of school and then return some years later. Age is not taken into account when assessing in which standard a student should be placed. There are forty-nine staff members at the school, most of them fairly young and with only a few years of teaching experience. The principal is a quiet, unassuming and also unassertive person, who does not want to put undue pressure on his staff. In most (ex)DET schools (given a particular historical context) there is a strong pressure from staff to 'democratize' the school. Often the consequence of this is that directiveness or assertiveness on the part of the principal is construed as authoritarianism and therefore rejected.

The school's presenting concern was for assistance from TIP in the development of a code of conduct. It was a very specific request, and one that could easily have been responded to by providing a structure for them to draw up such a code. If our approach were a more technicist rather than critical one, we would have responded at this symptomatic level. However, our understanding is that real transformation and healing of an organization means exploring beyond and beneath the symptoms and trying to find the roots and underlying causes of current situations. Walker (1995), drawing on the work of Horton and Freire (1990) underlines this:

> The point is to shift away from immediate problem solving to the complexity of the critical educational processes, where the latter may not necessarily solve our immediate practical problems, but are likely to generate new questions as we find out what we do not know, rather than what we know. (p. 18)

We also argue that it is not our understanding alone, but the participants' that is crucial to the process of transformation.

The First Encounter

Two colleagues from the Teacher Inservice Project were assigned to work in this particular school. We arranged to meet with a small but representative group of people initially, to explore the possibility of taking the process further. Present at this initial meeting were the principal of the school, senior staff members and a few students from the students' representative council. The principal of the school opened the conversation by telling us why they needed a code of conduct. They felt that the previous one lacked legitimacy, and needed to be rewritten to reflect the democratic ethos of the school. In passing, he mentioned that they had had problems with students at the beginning of the year, and that a legitimate code of conduct was needed. We were surprised that their code of conduct lacked legitimacy, since it had been drawn up previously by management staff, teachers, and members of the parent, teacher, student association (PTSA) — a democratically elected school committee.

During the meeting we both observed that in spite of the fact that this was a representative leadership core of the school, not many people were vocal. Participation in the articulation of their concerns came from very few of the people in the room. This obviously created some cause for concern for us: we were meeting with staff and student leadership and yet very little leadership was, in fact, being demonstrated.

I was struck by the urgency of their call, and their fixation on the code as a solution to their problems. This seemed to be a case of what Fullan (1991) refers to as 'false clarity' — that is, an oversimplified understanding of what the issues or problems were. It therefore seemed appropriate to ask them what concerns they were facing that had prompted them to want to rewrite their code of conduct. Some of these concerns were:

- a high rate of absenteeism on the part of teachers and students
- general lack of discipline at the school
- conflict and tension among staff members — staff cliques mean that groups of teachers tend to make the same decisions in support of their cliques
- decisions that are made are not carried out, and often the staff seems to be defiant
- lack of legitimate authority of the 'control staff'[2]
- with the Students' Representative Council (SRC) there is a lack of relationship between the teachers and students
- problems in the democratization of the school
- a high teacher-student ratio: forty-nine teachers for almost 2000 students
- low teacher morale
- no culture of teaching and learning at the school — teachers do not, on the whole, seem to show commitment to their responsibilities, nor to any notion of professional development, and students attend school and lessons erratically, often not completing work or homework
- no teacher evaluation taking place
- poor academic results
- a general sense of teacher passivity — a culture of 'demand' or 'entitlement' politics; teachers asserting their rights without taking responsibility or playing an active role — often teachers do not say what they are thinking.

Their urgent concern made sense. On reflection, my colleague and I felt that we needed to assist the school to reflect on its culture — the norms, patterns and habits of the school, and to help them to commit themselves to a consciously chosen, more positive identity. This could then be reflected in a new code of conduct. However, attempts to modify the behaviour of teachers and students at the school through the development of a policy document alone would surely fail if the underlying malaise of the school was not made conscious. This requires an initial (and often painful) process of reflection, of owning and acknowledging what exists at the school, and then of developing commitment to a shared vision, and a new sense of purpose and direction. How to achieve this vision then requires careful planning, and the processes of implementation require ongoing reflection and evaluation.

We felt the despair of the participants: the problems were overwhelming, the reality dismal. Ownership of a code of conduct implies active participation, critical engagement with not only the document, but also the issues giving rise to the perceived need for such a document. Even in this initial meeting, there had been such uneven participation, and this from a group of people seen, in one way or another, to be in leadership or senior positions in the school. Given the history of education in South Africa, how could it be possible to begin to turn the situation around, to provide opportunities for development to those who had systematically been disempowered and stripped of authority? Clearly their present situation was not contributing towards the building of confidence, self esteem, enthusiasm and commitment to teaching and learning. Any intervention therefore, if it was to be effective, needed to take the broader social and political context into account and not focus too strongly on the micro-issues of the school. Carr and Kemmis (1986) put it in the following way:

> . . . school communities must become, and see themselves as becoming, participants in a general social project by which education and educational institutions may be critically transformed in society at large. (pp. 159–60)

In South Africa, there has been a very particular relationship between schools and society and notably, the different schools serving different race groups and interests. Our challenge and pedagogical concern is to mediate a process which brings to consciousness the complex web of realities and constraints which keep teachers feeling helpless, despondent and uninterested.

Meeting the Whole Staff

After this initial consultation, it was agreed that we should run a workshop with the entire staff, where we could assist the staff in looking reflectively at their school, with a view to beginning a process of transformation. Our first workshop was thus intended to elicit from the staff as a whole their own feelings and perceptions about school, including its strengths and weaknesses. Institutional and individual self-reflection and self-understanding are central to our particular approach to organization development. Also central to our approach is the recognition of the importance of this first intervention with the school staff: it is not merely a data-collection process (i.e., developing a deeper and clearer picture of the school), but it is also a therapeutic intervention, where staff members have an opportunity to talk about issues in a structured and safe environment.

We asked them, therefore, individually at first and then in small groups (about six per group), to identify what aspects of the school they felt positive and enthusiastic about, and what aspects of the school they felt negative about. Groups were self-selected (in order to allow more free-flowing and open conversation). The issues from each small group were then placed on the wall and participants were given an opportunity to walk around the room and see what issues had emerged from other groups.

The power of this initial process as a way of releasing pain, anger and frustration is often enormously cathartic. It also provides an open space for teachers to acknowledge aspects of school life about which they feel positive — something which does not happen often. Our participatory methodology ensures that the picture of the school which emerges is the picture of those people working in the school, together with our own sense of it. As external consultants we see ourselves as critical facilitators of the reflective moment, relying to a large extent on our own intuitive understanding, our experience and craft wisdom, and our theoretical background and framework. If issues are clearly being avoided, if power relations are interfering with group processes, or if we feel something important has been omitted, we will pick this up during the course of the workshop. Our own values, grounded in the basic human rights and the dignity of each individual, shape the nature of our facilitation.

We decided to keep the design of the first workshop simple — an introductory workshop after which the staff could decide whether to proceed or not. Without the will to engage, to begin a process of addressing the issues facing the school, very little would be likely to take root. Thus the workshop design was to identify the perceived needs of the school and to provide a framework for whole school organization development within which participants could begin to understand and analyze the issues they were facing.

As was to be expected, in this workshop the staff identified very similar issues to those which had been highlighted in our initial meeting. What was identified particularly strongly was the lack of cohesion and trust among the staff, and lack of clear leadership and vision from the principal and other people of influence in the school. There was no contradiction, but rather strong reinforcement of what we had heard at the previous meeting. Our approach — of ensuring that the teachers take control of the process, and that they reflect on underlying issues rather than merely be given options for an appropriate code of conduct — was a crucial part of the process of enabling teachers to make meaning of their situation and to become critical agents of change.

It was clear that the process that teachers had undergone — of expressing their feelings and of having an opportunity to let out some of what they had been carrying with them — had liberated much tension, stress and energy. The atmosphere in the room had been vital and pulsating. There was also intense interest shown by the teachers to find out what their colleagues' feelings and perceptions were. Much laughter and serious discussion accompanied the walk around the room to look at the comments. After the 'walk-about', we had an open plenary discussion, where people were given an opportunity to respond to the emerging issues. Here some people commented that it was helpful to recognize and acknowledge what others were struggling with, and that they were not alone with their concerns.

We felt that a real process of development was just beginning to unfold. Yet, because of the nature of the problems, it was easy to see why the teachers felt so despondent and demoralized, and why they felt overwhelmed by the magnitude of their problems, which seemed to extend unlawfully in every direction, beyond comprehension, beyond manageability. Paralysis, lack of commitment and enthusiasm were perfectly normal responses to a highly abnormal situation.

We presented and explained our framework for understanding the elements of organizational life (see Fig. 9.1). Part of the difficulty of working with schools in South Africa has been that they have tended not to conceive of themselves organizationally. This has impinged negatively on their ability to begin meaningful processes of self-understanding and transformation, since their thinking has often been chaotic, lacking in coherence and order. Relating people's perceptions of their school to an organizational framework seems to provide a new level of insight and understanding.

This organizing framework is a dynamic tool for analysis, diagnosis (problem defining) and problem solving. Central to its effectiveness is that it is not used as a fixed model which provides uncritical and objective facts about an organization.

Strategic thinking and planning is crucial if ongoing development and critical self-understanding is to occur in schools. The activities of goal-setting, planning and evaluation should always be in the context of particular issues the school has identified which need to be addressed, or a chosen vision that needs to be realized. However, organizations are not static — they assume a life of their own, and move and shift and change as the organization development process impacts. Therefore ongoing and cyclic planning and reflection (strategic thinking and action) forms part of the action research cycle of the school as a whole. Any interventions, any attempts to improve the school which do not have built into them reflection and evaluation cycles, are unlikely to take root. Evaluation (reflection) and development cannot be separated. We had begun with a process of reflecting upon and evaluation of the school, and this provided the springboard for decisions to be made about its future development. As the school began to engage in a process of development, it would need to reflect upon the extent to which educational and whole school goals were being achieved, and find ways of adapting plans in order to ensure that development was taking place.

Linking Theory and Practice

Taking our own insights and reflections, and the perceptions of the school staff into account, we entered our next workshop, a week later. The principal indicated that the initial intervention had already begun to make a difference, and that the atmosphere in the staffroom was palpably different. An important strategy during this next process was to deepen and enhance self-reflection and critical engagement with the issues. Using our organizational framework as a basis for analysis, we asked teachers, in groups, to take the issues they had identified in the previous week, and to place them where they thought they belonged in the framework. For this exercise, each group was given a diagram of the elements of organizational life, and the issues which their particular group had identified in the previous week. The issues had been written up on small pieces of paper and so were easy to move around on the larger sheet. Every issue, without exception, found a home. Teachers became excited as they began to build a graphic picture of what their school looked like. Once all the 'pictures' had been presented to the staff as a whole, we discussed the emerging composition.

In the reflective and analytical process, lack of vision and direction and a debilitating culture were clear (Identity), but interpersonal relationships (Personnel) were also highlighted as being problematic. The presenting problem — the need for a code of conduct (Structures and Procedures) — was inextricably linked with the overall culture and identity of the school, and could not be addressed in isolation. There was a need for the school to begin to define its own direction, to sculpt a vision, to look forward by reflecting clearly on the past and present. However, from our own sense of what the staff were saying, there were too many cliques, too many divisions on the staff to begin this process. Staff members were unable to work together, and they needed to look at this more critically. Some team-building needed to take place — assumptions about a shared and common vision were still too remote. We suggested this, and the staff concurred: they needed to learn to listen to one another, to talk together, to plan, to be honest, to acknowledge differences and the strengths and weaknesses of self and other.

This process of linking theory and practice — of looking at practices within the school and understanding them within a theoretical framework, provided the springboard and confidence for the process to continue. Organization development is a step-by-step process. While it can be used to diagnose where to intervene in a crisis situation, that first intervention will inevitably form part of a longer-term developmental process. The problem of quick-fix solutions to endemic problems is highlighted here: the first process is part of a broader process of ongoing development within which all the elements of an organization need to be embraced and worked. The inter-relatedness of the elements of an organization means that we need to look at systemic change — individual teachers, the school as a whole and the broader context within which it is located — if we want to address concerns of an organizational nature.

Back to the Beginning

A code of conduct is a set of rules, a procedure which relates to the norms and reflects the identity and culture of an organization. It cannot be used to develop a new culture, nor ensure accountability of staff and students. It had not worked in the past — a new code of conduct set up without an accompanying process of attitudinal change, culture change, development of hope and commitment — did not promise to work miraculously now. A new identity needs to be forged, with conscious and transformed and active values. A shared vision, a strategy for achieving it, new structures and procedures to facilitate this, ongoing reflection on the process (and products!) . . . all these changes might well be reflected in a new code of conduct. The urgent need to have a code of conduct reflected the hope that a set of rules could create a new set of values. A set of rules, captured in a code of conduct will only be respected and abided by if it reflects those values.

In Conclusion

This chapter argues the importance of school-wide improvement initiatives (building enabling school environments for ongoing professional development) as a way of impacting on classroom practice and the quality of teaching and learning. Organization development provides a structured way of supporting and facilitating institutional self-study, providing a framework for cyclical reflection, planning and evaluation.

But what of the future of South African schools? All the schools with which we have worked have entered into this kind of process voluntarily. Many schools are stuck in patterns where a kind of paralysis has set in, and where little movement is likely. Without an enabling and supportive policy environment which ensures that all schools (and teachers) are expected to participate in ongoing development processes, very little meaningful change can be expected. School policy in the past has tended to take the form of high degrees of control, rather than supporting bottom-up, teacher-owned change. We still await policy for inservice education: the question is, will the policymakers and informers also be the practitioners, or will the divide remain, keeping practice and theory, action and research separate?

Notes

1 This chapter draws to some extent from a paper written with two colleagues, Sandy Lazarus and Allan Kaplan: 'Organization Development: An Argument for South African Schools. I would like therefore to acknowledge their contribution to this chapter.
2 Control staff is generally understood to be the principal and the deputy principals of the school.

References

CARR, W. and KEMMIS, S. (1986) *Becoming Critical: Education, Knowledge and Action Research*, Lewes, Falmer Press.

FULLAN, M. (1991) *The New Meaning of Educational Change*, London, Cassell Educational Limited.

HORTON, M. and FREIRE, P. (1990) *We Make the Road by Walking*, Philadelphia, Temple University Press.

WALKER, M. (1995) 'Context, Critique and Change: Doing Action Research in South Africa', *Educational Action Research*, **3**, 1, 1995.

10 Action Research and the Production of Knowledge: The Experience of an International Project on Environmental Education

Michela Mayer (Italy)

Introduction

One of the challenges for contemporary action research is how it deals with validity in terms of knowledge production. As Susan Noffke (1994) pointed out, the goal of action research

> has been represented as lying primarily within the areas of personal and professional development. Action research, in this way is valued less for its role in the production of knowledge about curriculum, pedagogy, and the social contexts of schools, and more for its ability to help teachers 'grow' in their self-awareness or in terms of their professional skills and dispositions. (pp. 15–16)

This situation reflects a hypothesis, often implicit, about curricular reform and educational innovation: that it is possible to change the professionality of teachers, the way they teach, without changing their implicit image of the disciplines and of knowledge in general; or conversely, that it is possible to change the contents of teaching without changing the form and the methods, the image that the teachers have of what learning and teaching are about: Forgetting in this assumption that 'Thought about curriculum is, in one of its dimensions, thought about the nature of knowledge' (Stenhouse, 1975, p. 20).

The experience I want to present has to do with knowledge consciously produced by a group of teachers-researchers and it also offers matter for reflection about the questions that such a production presents for action research projects. First, I should like to present the context in which the research took place, and how we required teachers to take care in their research of the wide theoretical debate about the complexity of knowledge. In the following sections I will present the teachers' reflections as they emerged from their final research reports, or from discussions, showing how teachers have used action research in order to produce knowledge that is not only relevant to their practice but that constitutes a contribution to a more theoretical and general process of construction of knowledge. My final reflection is about the challenge that this experience implies for action research and for the role of the 'academic researchers' involved, showing that production of really valuable and general knowledge is possible if the emphasis of the research is on such knowledge and if the researchers accept the role of 'mediators' between academic and practitioner knowledge.

The Context of the Research Project

The context within which this research possibility came about was the ENSI — *Environment and School Initiatives* — project, an international OECD-CERI proposal coordinated by Kathleen Kelley Lainé and in which other authors in this book also took part. Each participating country selected a network of schools and teachers ready to take part in an innovative educational process and to reflect on their own concrete experience. Countries contributed to the project through 'national reports' concerning the different issues proposed by the project, and one of the points internationally agreed upon was that of 'taking action research further with teachers to strengthen their research activities, especially that of producing knowledge' (OECD-CERI, 1995, p. 8). In fact, environmental issues challenge schools' practice not only because they concern 'choices based upon values' but because they ask teachers to view environmental issues in their complexity, and consequently to contribute to discussions about the way they conceive knowledge and the production of knowledge at school.

In the Italian research proposal this point was articulated as follows:

> the search for educational methods able to deal with intrinsically interdisciplinary problems, that need a systemic approach and a culture of complexity in order to grasp relations and effects on global level, without reducing the analysis to a study of components; (Losito and Mayer, 1995, p. 13)

The term 'complexity' takes on different meanings in different contexts and in different cultural environments, both nationally and internationally. In some countries the term is often used in a 'negative' way, meaning 'complicated' — too difficult to understand with current knowledge levels — while in other cases the term takes up a widespread epistemological debate on the structure, organization and limits of human knowledge and therefore on the 'culture' that informs society and schools, and that teachers themselves contribute to reproduce.

Discussion of complexity does not involve only disciplines but the *assumptions* not only of science but also, and above all, of everyday life and the culture in which we are often unconsciously immersed; assumptions which Schon calls 'technical rationality' (1983) and Cini (1994) calls 'the culture of machinism'. If complexity is something inside the knowledge process, what it effectively requires is a reflection on knowing, on the assumptions that, in our everyday world, reduce reality to combinations of machines and knowledge of reality to knowledge of the laws that govern them.

Whereas this debate has only marginally touched the world of education, the situation in environmental education is somewhat different: how can you demand action for the environment basing your arguments on the same technicist illusion of controlling and predicting that has caused so much damage? The search for quality in environmental education — the awareness that action for the environment moves in different contexts from that of technical measures to dominate the environment — requires a reflection on knowledge. The Italian teachers accepted our proposals not because they wanted to take part in a philosophical-epistemological debate, but to seek in their project instances where awareness and behaviour were consistent with a 'new culture of complexity'.

The Italian research group was composed of twenty-five teachers coming from different schools, spread all over the country, and from different schools levels, from pre-primary to high schools. Bruno Losito was titled 'pedagogical support' and I was 'national coordinator', and we both worked as facilitators of the teachers' research work. Because of the national dimension, research seminars of three or four days were carried on three times a year for three years (1990–1993) with the aims of developing action research competences, reflecting on the initiatives teachers were carrying out, and constructing knowledge upon shared issues.

The fact that teachers belonged to different types of schools and were teaching different disciplines, from humanities to chemistry, made our discussions much richer and more meaningful, although it created some language problems in the beginning. In these reflections and discussions not only was the philosophical-epistemological debate about complexity 'reconstructed' by each teacher in terms meaningful within their practice and their discipline, but new elements, often elements that connected theory with practice, were added, and the 'whole' image of environmental education came under discussion. The papers that teachers prepared for an International Seminar held in Perugia (1992) and the research reports they produced allowed me to reconstruct in the following the main elements of this discussion.

Knowing Knowledge

For many of our teachers, one of the challenging assumptions in the ENSI project was that knowledge can only be constructed through an individual process which gives meaning and value to experience and communication. If this is true, then the teacher's role must change. S/he traditionally, and at times unwittingly, is used to transmit knowledge s/he possesses, but should instead learn to construct meaningful contexts and pose 'legitimate questions' — i.e., questions which do not have readily known answers (von Foerster, 1971) — within which students can 'actively create their meanings' (Elliot, 1991).

According to this approach, the teacher is no longer a repository of knowledge, nor is the student an empty container that must be filled. The teacher
instead becomes a path facilitator in a route that is not rigidly determined
at the outset but built 'together with' the pupils. We call this joint project-
building 'co-creation' . . . (Gilberto Bonani and Carlotta Lazzarini, 1995,
p. 9)

This co-created and context-linked knowledge is significant because it is useful and
usable in real life and not because it is part of the syllabus or because it is 'objective and divorced from reality'. On the contrary, value judgments, expectations and
anything making experience important and meaningful, are part of this knowledge.
This is not only 'valid' because it is useful, but also 'valuable' in that it is seen to
be important for people. It is also exemplary knowledge, in the sense that it provides
an 'example', an experience, of how knowledge is constructed.

Along with the path of knowledge-construction, teachers discovered the path
of awareness. Environmental education also runs a risk. To talk of action for the
environment, of dynamic qualities, of development — even if sustainable — can
once again lead people to simplify, to reduce in order to quickly find those 'sure'
solutions that guarantee effective action. The culture of complexity shows this to be
an illusion: that the apparently 'static' qualities of listening and reflection must be
added to the dynamic qualities of action taking; that any solution is partial and any
action for the environment must follow 'action research' lines, aware of unexpected
events and possible mistakes, in which effectiveness is guaranteed by continuous
observation and the capacity to change direction quickly.

Another question takes us back to our initial epistemological problem: does
a different educational context also allow the construction of a different kind of
knowledge? The following was one of the common views emerging from the group
discussion:

Knowing involves a 'project' on reality, even implicit, on the part of the
knower. This project is always, at least ideally and often unconsciously,
one of modifying reality, which at the same time acts on the person,
interrelates with him and changes him. Being aware of this process, of the
limits of the observer and his interdependence with the subject observed,
not only changes the manner but also the contents of knowledge. (ENSI
group discussion, Losito and Mayer, 1995, pp. 59–60)

This is the real meaning of 'systemic approach' for the whole group. The effort that
characterized the paths of the different schools was that of keeping 'everything
together' — the system that is the object of the study, the observer and his 'project'
on reality, the relations which represent a link among themselves and with a possible outside environment that is both object and observer.

Environmental education thus puts forward a 'global', 'systemic' and 'interdisciplinary' approach, not because it deals with the problems of the planet or because

it needs contributions from different disciplines, but because it allows the focus of study to be on a real concrete problem without prior simplification. This therefore needs a working method that should never lose sight of the problem in its overall context and which allows comparison and co-operation between differing points of view, value judgments and disciplines.

Having accepted this common position in environmental education, teachers do not reject disciplines, because they do not deny its use and importance. Rather, they are aware that the problem is not solved by dividing it among disciplines: a system is not the sum of its parts and a map is not the territory. Disciplines, however,

> ..., like magnifying glasses, serve to better distinguish something specific. It is here, and not before, that we discover the educational importance of disciplines created not to build self-contained worlds, cathedrals of know-ledge in the desert, but privileged observers' posts grasping the nuances of complexity. (Gilberto Bonani and Carlotta Lazzarini, 1995, p. 29)

Reductionism is not in the disciplines themselves but in the belief that only dis-ciplines can define and solve problems. Pedagogically, all the attention devoted to problem-solving is also the result of reductionist thinking. Even if it can develop the ability to think, it forces students to concentrate on results. It makes them believe that it is right — and possible — to find quick effective solutions, whereas in fact, understanding the problem is more important than actually solving it. These are often many different solutions depending on unforseeable circumstances. In any case, there are no short-cuts for the environment or in education: lasting results may be achieved only in the long term.

Respect for complexity and long-term changes does not reduce the value of disciplines, but creates an awareness of their limits: in a world where knowledge has certainly not been able to avoid environmental disasters, a culture of complex-ity should avoid the mistakes of the many scientific and technological 'solutions' which have contributed to creating just those environmental problems we are facing today. A certain kind of environmentalism is just as limiting as the technological society it is trying to combat: nature should not be respected as an 'object' but as a 'process', and the processes via which nature finds its 'solutions' are non-linear, redundant, often random and unpredictable.

> Action is not purely cognitive but also affective and value-laden. By the end of the task children have experienced and come to know a much wider network of relationships. They realize that solutions to problems are rarely black and white and are more likely to be ambiguous ones which activate a whole set of other research questions. They understand that reality can-not be deconstructed through the language of individual disciplines or con-trolled and dominated at will but rather can be lived through experience,

personal and group relationships which extend their ability to make sense of man's position in the world. Understanding in the sense of interpreting and having a sense of being together. (Carlotta Lazzarini, Poster for the Perugia International Seminar, 1992)

Uncertainty and Sense of the Limit

Another shared element in the group was the revaluation of uncertainty, of doubt, and conflict, as an awareness that allows us to go deeper into problems, and to face them without reducing or simplifying them in any way.

'The more knowledge increases, the greater the mystery', is the reminder from Chieti Primary School absolutely consistent with the last debates on science and its limits (Ravetz and Funtovicz, 1989).

The awareness of limits must not hinder action, but requires the ability to act in uncertainty, to face risk and unpredictability in concrete situations, while maintaining control. As the Messina teachers quite rightly point out, this is because 'the passing from thought to action' demands facing a reality that suddenly 'reveals limits and disorders'. Uncertainty allows us to be flexible, and to listen and appreciate other people's opinions, to abandon known paths and seek new ones.

The ability to handle the unforeseen is not only required of students, but above all of teachers who have to abandon the certainty of rigid and detailed programming when dealing with environmental education projects.

My habit of wanting everything under control, to programme and make the students 'trot along', as well as my scientific deterministic training, were in opposition to the need to practice listening, to guide reflection, to find the way to 'observe my teaching', to accept the students' views as a fundamental element of our dialogue. (Luisa Borettini, 1995, p. 14)

Realizing that not only can we act in conditions of uncertainty, but indeed that 'we must act' in situations of uncertainty, seeing that a real situation never evolves in a completely predictable manner, allows us 'to remain on our guard'. ENSI proposed action research and reflection on action as an instrument of awareness and action in situations of uncertainty. In this way students and teachers can 'maintain control', not necessarily of the short-term results of their actions, but on the processes they are implementing.

Recognizing the limits of disciplines, above all of scientific ones, the posing of the problem of uncertainty and unpredictability to oneself means recognizing the illegitimate nature of the claim to 'objective' knowledge of reality. Stating the complexity of reality does not mean refusing to understand it, but taking on the responsibility of knowledge that wishes to connect in 'one whole story' all the information, values, feelings and interpretations.

> Increasing knowledge, having more possibilities of alternative choices is only meaningful if there is an increase in sensibility, a responsibility towards the ways in which these choices will determine future scenarios. . . . To talk of maintaining a neutral position, of remaining outside one's own context, has no meaning, since every decision we make within a project cannot but be the product of a choice and therefore marked by a definite tendency, the expression of a particular position. . . . To foster awareness and sensibility is very different to making propaganda. . . . It is certainly easy to fall into the propaganda trap, all you have to do is to point the spotlight wherever is most convenient, submerge the students with 'reliable' data, proving scientifically the truth of our claims. . . . Propaganda is order, security, predictability, certainty. It was no accident that our group was uncertain-chaotic-conflicting-unpredictable. (Franco Serra, Technical Institute of Iglesias, Comments to Perugia International Seminar, 1992)

Moreover, it is not just necessary to accept that environmental evolution and environmental problems are unpredictable, but that the results of educational processes are also intrinsically unpredictable. Education and environment are problems that require investment for the future, and therefore need long-term planning, without ever thinking of being able to master the necessary information in order to forecast their evolution. In both cases — environment and education — there is a need for awareness of values and ideologies which yield not only the answers given to the problems, but also the questions posed. Environmental and educational issues are always controversial, as a result of conflicts between different scales of values and images of the world.

> I want to give you an example: a school operates a little bit like chemical agriculture: in order to ensure a good crop of grain, and suppress anything that isn't grain, additives are introduced into the soil. A school like this works quite well, as does chemical agriculture; in fact it feeds people. The problem is that long term, this strategy is a disaster because it does not allow the earth the possibility of recovering its own productive ability. But this is what we do with the children we work with: often we drastically reduce their possibilities for choosing change and engaging with uncertainty in an active way. A return to organic farming is economically very difficult. For the school, too, reaching an educational situation that takes complexity into account is a difficult enterprise, because it challenges the times and spaces of teaching and learning and the very way we train ourselves. . . . (Franco Lorenzoni, Giove Primary School, Intervention in the Perugia Seminar debate, 1992)

The Challenge for Action Research

We can stop here, but the teachers have written much more. In the process of trying to construct theories which give meaning to their own practice, and at the same time practices which involve them in exploring theories beyond their own, they created a wider context and raised wider and more commonly shared issues than those that could have been constructed individually.

The knowledge produced by the teachers is not only relevant to their practice, to the obstacles they face and the ways they have invented to overcome them. These teachers are reflecting upon the kind of knowledge they have used until now and the kind they are trying to construct. Their reflections are a re-encounter and a subsequent process of transformation and immersion in practice of the themes within the 'complexity debate' and the critique of modernity: from the impossibility of 'objectifying', and thus of distinguishing between the observer and the observed, to the importance of keeping several points of view and of valuing the relatedness of elements of knowledge rather than just the elements in themselves. Uncertainty, risk, continual transformation, which are part of the post-modernist flag, are recognized by the teachers as day to day realities.

Moreover, the teachers are also aware of the burden that this entails: because, whereas it may be easy in theory to accept the call to abandon all certainty, including that of the self, it is impossible to act without some, albeit limited, reference points. The risk of total relativism, total uncertainty, is that of immobility. It is a classic example of 'double bind', creating the very immobility that it seeks to reject (Watzlawick, *et al.*, 1974). The strategy the teachers are proposing is that of rejecting Aristotelian dualism — true/false, right/wrong, objective/subjective, certain/uncertain — and instead of accepting the challenge of keeping an equilibrium between the necessity of certainties, even if limited in time, and the necessity of taking risks.

If we then analyze the route the teachers took to arrive at these reflections, we can see that our research proposal and the context which the ENSI project proposed to teachers turned out to be significant in many respects:

- it proposed research problems and methods but did not specify a rigid set of objectives and strategies. Teachers continued to feel owners and initiators of their own research,
- it challenged teachers' expertise and their implicit image of learning-teaching processes bringing together environmental values and educational values,
- it proposed a specific theoretical context while at the same time offering a concrete point of reference, that of the group, which allowed reflection and discussion within this context.

In the ENSI project, teachers found themselves being asked to be part of various communities: the Italian research group in the ENSI project, the international community sharing the assumptions of the ENSI project, and a wider and more diverse community that recognizes itself in a series of values that are not only environmental or educational but social too, and who in the name of these values is questioning the common sense, all that is taken for granted and that underlies a large part of disciplines, schooling and current research.

The knowledge of being part of a community, of sharing certain issues considered relevant by others, provides that security, those points of reference, without which the teachers do not have the courage to venture very far from their practice. In these conditions the teachers agreed to commit themselves to a research that explored how 'to deconstruct common sense and recostruct it as "good sense"' (Walker, 1995, p. 18) in order to contribute fully to the construction of 'knowledge' with a capital K.

This poses some questions for action research facilitators: what we are asking teachers is often to talk about themselves and their own practice without inviting them to link their own experience to a wider debate, to theories that allow them to deconstruct their common sense. In doing this, isn't educational research continuing to send an ambiguous message? It is claimed that knowledge produced in this way is valuable, yes, but to whom? Not to the academics, who in fact delegate the task of linking together the various individual stories to the researcher who then interprets them and transforms them into her/his own research. The knowledge thus constructed is not useful to other teachers either if all they have in common is a working methodology and do not share common issues and theories. The relevance of knowledge produced by action research becomes restricted to strategies of professional development with very little scope for effectively influencing the often implicit theories which condition teachers and the knowledge that is part of their profession.

In this situation, even the relationship between the academic researcher and the teacher cannot be an equal one between people who, each within their own role and competencies, can recognize shared fields of research. Instead, the relationship begins to resemble more and more that of tutor-pupil, analyst-patient, teacher-student.

The reflection on ways of knowing and on complexity also opens up a debate on the meaning of action research in the field of education on the values and the prospectives that guide it. At the moment, teachers are at one and the same time mediators for and victims of the double power game that the school claims to play, a game proposed to them by the *discipline* as an ordering of knowledge, and by the *discipline* as an ordering of people and their work (Kemmis 1989, paraphrasing Foucault, p. 18). Even if action research as a strategy for professional development succeeds in challenging the power of the structure, it will never be able to disrupt the implicit power of the discipline, in the sense of subjects of study, if it does not direct its attention to the construction of knowledge. It is through the disciplines, first and foremost, that a vision of the world, a conception of power, is transmitted which not only defines what cannot be done but also what cannot be asked.

At this moment teachers, schools and education research are at a turning point. The possibility is there to break with the myth of the conceptual predominance of technical rationality — whether it be through the discourse of complexity challenging the 'culture of machinism', Post-modernism's critique of the Enlightenment Project, or the environmental debate on sustainable or non-sustainable societies. Once the myth of technicism and of the expert are open to debate, knowledge is no longer constructed in privileged spaces, but can be subject to cross-breeding between different subjects with their different interests. Teachers could then become mediators between a kind of knowledge delegated to the experts, and as such a source of power, and a shared knowledge, which is not homogenous and neither it is objective or subjective, nor is it so different as to be beyond communication. A knowledge which can be subjected to criticism and to discussion by all those who have an interest in it.

Interest, in Latin 'inter-esse', means literally 'to be-in-between', to be a mediator, to create connections. It seems to us that what we have accomplished through our research on complexity is to have kindled an interest, and thus created connections between the practical work of the teachers and the theoretical work of the scientists and philosophers. We too, as facilitators played the role of mediation between the world of academic research and the world of practice. But not mediators in the sense of interpreters, of those who speaks for others, but mediators in the sense of being aware of the interests of both sides, thus creating links, communication networks, always different because adapted to the different contexts in which mediation takes place.

Action research could then also be seen as a 'nomadic research', just as complexity is proposed as a 'nomadic concept' (Stengers, 1987). In the same way, researchers and teachers could also be 'nomads', not only in the sense of resisting a rigid and predefined identity, but also in their ability to live in different places, to offer — without domesticating and being domesticated — different forms and possibilities of 'accessing reality', leaving it to the users to judge their relevance. Nomadic subjects and concepts defend their own ambiguity, resisting rigid categorizations, but also carrying the values of mediation and cross-breeding. Those values of objective truth and rationality, shown to be illusory, need to be replaced by other values which provide points of reference to those who choose to operate in uncertainty and to 'resist the seduction and entrapments that accompany the comforts of belonging' (McLure, 1995). It is a matter of shifting from the 'Paradise Lost' of certainty (Cini, 1994) 'to a culture of limits and responsibility', with each individual taking on their own responsibility 'for the way in which we are able to define the world, to take account of our experiences' (Stengers, 1992).

Within this culture, we need to add to the research for a rational reconstruction, the wisdom of experience — wisdom as a combination of *episteme* and *nous*, of rationality and intuition in Aristotele's words (Somekh, 1995) — to the rigor of data the charm and ambiguity of poetry. And the teachers — who by their professional nature are in between the knowledge of the experts and the knowledge their pupils must learn to construct — could produce knowledge which addresses this difficult task of mediation indicating to the researchers, operating in more academic spheres, what trails to follow.

Michela Mayer

Acknowledgments

To Ann Magyar, not only for her passionate help in translating and revising the English first version, but also for emotional support and critical discussions.

References

BONANI, G. and LAZZARINI, C. (1995) *I cannoni della neve*, ENSI research report, Frascati, CEDE.

BORETTINI, L. (1995) *A scuola nel parco: tra limiti e risorse un percorso di educazione ambientale*, ENSI research report, Frascati, CEDE.

CAIANI, C. and CIANCAGLINI, A. (1995) *Via Bosio: una scuola come laboratorio. Fare scuola fuori della scuola*, ENSI research report, Frascati, CEDE.

CINI, M. (1994) *Il Paradiso Perduto*, Milano, Feltrinelli.

ELLIOT, J. (1991) 'Environmental education in Europe: Innovation, marginalisation or assimilation', *Environment, Schools, and Active Learning*, Paris, OECD-CERI.

KEMMIS, S. (1989) 'Some ambiguities of Stenhouse's notion of "The teacher as researcher": towards a new resolution', Lawrence Stenhouse Memorial Lecture, BERA annual meeting, University of Newcastle.

LAZZARINI, C. (1992) *Poster*, Perugia International Seminar.

LORENZORI, F. (1992) Intervention in debate, Perugia International Seminar.

LOSITO, B. and MAYER, M. (1995) *Environmental Education: A Challenge for Educational Innovation*, ENSI national research report, Frascati, CEDE.

McLURE, M. (1995) 'Identity and teachers' work', CARE, University of East Anglia, unpublished paper.

NOFFKE, S. (1994) 'Action research: towards the next generation', *Educational Action Research*, **2**, 1, pp. 9–21.

OECD-CERI (1995) *Environmental Learning for the 21st Century*, Paris, OECD-CERI.

PEDDIS, L. and SERRA, F. (1995) *Jobs and Environment Reclaiming: A Challenge from the Classroom*, ENSI research report, Frascati, CEDE.

RAVETZ, J.R. and FUNTOVICZ, S.O. (1989) 'Usable knowledge, usable ignorance. A discourse on two sorts of science', proceedings of the International Conference, *The Experts are Categorical: Scientific Controversies and Political Decisions concerning the Environment*, Paris.

SCHON, D.A. (1983) *The Reflective Practitioner*, New York, Basic Books.

SERRA, F. (1992) 'Comments.' Perugia International Seminar, *Images of Society, Nature and Science through Environmental Education*, Perugia.

SOMEKH, B. (1995) 'Participatory Action Research and Learning Organisation: Problems and Possibilities', paper presented to the MOHD Symposium, ECER Conference, Bath.

STENGERS, I. (Ed.) (1987) *D'une science à l'autre. Des concepts nomades*, Paris, Editions du Seuil.

STENGERS, I. (1992) 'Progrès et complexité: tension entre deux images', proceedings of the International Seminar *Images of Society, Nature and Science through Environmental Education*, Perugia.

STENHOUSE, L. (1975) *An Introduction to Curriculum Research and Development*, London, Heinemann.

VANADIA, I. (1994) *Altolia. Dall'immaginario al territorio alla mappa* (from the ENSI research report), Messina, Pungitopo.

VON FOERSTER, H. (1971) 'Perception of the future and future of perception', *Instructional Science*, pp. 31–43.

WALKER, M. (1995), 'Context, critique and change: doing action research in South Africa', *Educational Action Research*, **3**, 1, pp. 9–27.

WATZLAWICK, P., WEAKLAND, J. and FISCH, R. (1974) *Change*, Italian Edition Roma, Astrolabio.

11   Critical, Collaborative Action Research in Politically Contested Times

David Hursh (United States)

Education is a 'contested terrain' (Edwards, 1979; Giroux, 1983) in which contrasting conceptions of what should be taught and how are struggled over, with some conceptions becoming dominant and others suppressed. Kliebard (1995), in his aptly titled *The Struggle for the American Curriculum: 1893–1956*, depicts four conflicting approaches to education that have clashed throughout the twentieth century: humanism, developmentalism, scientific or social efficiency, and social meliorism. These four conflicting approaches are underpinned by differing political, ethical, and epistemological conceptions of the aims of society, the relationship between school and work, and the nature of learning. For example, humanists are primarily concerned with passing on the accumulated, often canonical, knowledge to students. In contrast, developmentalists connect education to children's development, learning processes, and knowledge.

In the waning years of the twentieth century, social efficiency has become the dominant approach and is contested most vigorously by social meliorism or social reconstruction. Social efficiency emphasizes shaping education around the needs of business and the economy. In the early 1900s Frederick Winslow Taylor promoted scientific efficiency as a way of increasing worker productivity and the principles and techniques were quickly adopted by curriculum theorists and education policy makers, such as Franklin Bobbitt (1912) and David Snedden (1915), as a way of improving educational productivity. Major corporate, governmental, and nongovernmental policy makers currently are working to reshape education around the needs of capital. One example of these efforts was the 1996 education summit called by some governors and the heads of several major corporations. Another example, as will be described later, is the activities of the National Center for Education and the Economy.

In contrast, social reconstructionists focus on education as a means of achieving democracy, justice, and equality. Dewey, as I will later narrate, opposed Snedden's subordinating education to work. Currently, critical educational theorists and practitioners such as Apple (1993), Giroux (1983), Meier (1995) and Peters (1994) promote educating students to be democratic citizens and workers.

Therefore, if we acknowledge that education is contested and that particular educational theories and practices become dominant not because they are naturally superior, but because of shifting political, ethical, and epistemological views, then educators can and should situate their educational theories and practices within the competing educational conceptions. What and how we teach are not only significant for their classroom implications, but for how they connect to larger issues of what is worth knowing, the nature of learning, the aims of society, and the relationship between school and work. In this chapter I also want to connect education to competing conceptions of justice, conceptions that are also linked to social efficiency and social meliorism.

By linking education to conceptions of justice, we are also reminded that understanding education entails not only analyzing classrooms within the larger context of the organization of the school and the organization and practices of other institutions such as corporations, we also need to analyze education as part of the contested social discourse. For example, the discourse of multicultural education can be entirely utilitarian and functional, focusing on promoting students in 'working well with others from diverse backgrounds' (RCSD, 1994). Or the discourse of multiculturalism can be social, critical; promoting students to analyze and change cultural, political, economic, and historical patterns and structures (Sleeter, 1991) Similarly, as I will show below, conceptions of justice can promote property rights and the right of the individual to compete economically or personal rights and the rights of all to health, safety, education, and culture.

In situating education in this way I want to argue for action research that includes more than the classroom, that connects educational theory and practices to the larger social context of knowledge, learning, jobs, and justice. Therefore, I will argue that action research can be most effective if conducted collaboratively by teachers and administrators within and across settings. Lastly, I want to argue for a conception of action research that does not feign neutrality but aids educators in collaboratively engaging in a critical, political process to oppose the increasingly prevalent conception of education as preparing individuals to be economically competitive individuals. Instead, action research can be used to develop and refine theories and practices that develop critical citizens who actively engage in understanding and changing the world.

The Current Educational and Political Conflict

Education for Individual and Corporate Competitiveness or for Critical Democratic Citizens and the Broader Social Good

Since the beginning of the 1980s, conservative and corporate interests have pushed to eradicate conceptions of justice focusing on equality and personal rights, such as the right to equal education or health care, and to elevate conceptions emphasizing eliminating 'unjust and unfair regulations of private property rights' and as promoting the ability to profit within freely functioning markets. Justice is whatever the market delivers; it is situated within 'an ideology of individualism . . . which emphasizes individual responsibility within a free-market economy and, thereby, defends the notion of the minimal state on moral as well as efficiency grounds' (Peters,

1994, p. 66). David Harvey (1993) argues against property and for personal rights by examining a specific historical event: the 1991 fire at a North Carolina Imperial Food chicken processing plant that killed twenty-five workers and injured fifty-six others, many of whom died because the fire doors were either blocked or locked. Harvey examines the lack of protest by groups representing labor, minorities or women, with the marches and protests to the Triangle Shirtwaist Company fire eighty years earlier. He gives several possible explanations for the different responses, arguing that the crucial factor has been how justice has been redefined as the freedom to compete rather that the right to health, safety and equality. Industrial tragedies are seen, therefore, as the unfortunate but unavoidable outcome of corporate competition in a global economy.

Harvey (1993) decries this subjugation of human welfare to capitalist profit, warning that we need to struggle against 'exploitation, profit-making, and worker disempowerment' (p. 101). Rather than acquiescing to definitions of social justice as individual economic competition within unregulated markets, Harvey draws on Young's conceptualization of social justice as countering the oppression that operates through exploitation, marginalization, powerlessness, cultural imperialism, violence,[1] (Young, 1990) and the oppressive ecological consequences of other's actions.

Harvey locates his conception of justice not in some universal principle but in 'class struggle over the particular conception of justice and rights that shall be applied to a particular situation' (Harvey, 1993, p. 101). What is at stake is how justice is to be defined and, consequently, the ways in which we conceptualize, discuss, and implement justice. Justice, as a discourse and as a practice, is contested and conceptions that support profits and oppress workers are currently in the ascendancy.

The same struggle over how justice is to be conceptualized and practiced is occurring in education. The restoration of property over person rights (Bowles and Gintis, 1986; Brosio, 1994; Apple, 1993) underpins the theoretical rationale for redirecting education away from developing democratic citizens and toward developing individuals, now depicted as human capital, who can compete in and provide benefits to the economy. Recycled conceptions of social efficiency in which schools are to create economically competitive individuals are evident in the policies and projects of the National Center of Education and the Economy (NCEE), an educational think-tank central to educational reform efforts at the national, state and local levels. While examining the NCEE may seem irrelevant to educators undertaking action research, it is a good example of an educational organization with strong corporate and governmental links playing a central role in recent educational policy.

The NCEE aims to shift our educational goals away from Dewey's emphasis on developing 'the kind of intelligence that would lead to a command of the conditions of one's own life and ultimately to social progress' (Kliebard, 1995), and toward developing human capital. Our societal goal for education should be economic 'productivity and competitiveness', achieved through 'the skills of our people and our capacity to use highly educated and highly trained people to maximum advantage in the workplace' (Marshall and Tucker, 1992). Education should be reorganized with students educated and evaluated in light of the needs of the workplace. They propose and are in the process of carrying out through their many organizations (i.e., The New Standards Project, The National Alliance for Restructuring Education, and others) an elaborate plan in which technical competency standards are set for every imaginable occupation and 'world class standards' of mastery and performance are set for every stage of education from kindergarten through college graduation. The NCEE proposes that education be organized through a rational analysis of the needs of the workplace and 'national content standards [that] represent a *professional consensus* regarding what is worth teaching . . . Each professional group defines their standards in terms of the context and processes unique to their discipline yet when examined as a whole they speak with a common voice regarding significant themes . . .' (emphasis added, NCEE, undated 2). The NCEE assumes that setting standards and preparing students for work is unproblematic and that setting curriculum standards is an objective, neutral, apolitical process. But standards are contentious issues with groups disagreeing on what's worth knowing.

The recent process of developing the national history standards created more disagreement than agreement and the interest in US national standard setting has waned (Diegmueller and Debra, 1995). Furthermore, the difficulty of setting standards in the subject areas pales in comparison to the debates over more contentious areas such as multiculturalism. Multiple conceptions of multiculturalism have been developed, ranging from an apolitical focus on human relations to socially reconstructive views (Sleeter and Grant, 1988; Cornbleth and Waugh, 1995). The NCEE recognizes none of these differences, offering only that multiculturalism promotes 'working well with others from diverse backgrounds' (NCEE, 1994). The NCEE became a major educational player in national, state and local educational policy because its agenda complements that of those in power. The goals of the NCEE are seconded by the Clinton administration. Marshall Smith, undersecretary of education, argues that the rationale for educational reform is primarily based on the ever-present challenges of international competition and a changing workplace

> [I]ncreases in productivity and the spread of information have contributed to the growth of a more global, competitive, knowledge-intensive economy . . . As machines replace more and more manual workers, the demand for low-skilled jobs has shrunk. Higher-skill jobs not only bring high wages, they also hold more promise for stability . . . [G]overnment policies should focus on expanding opportunities, on providing Americans with sustained access to the knowledge and skills necessary to participate in the new economy. (Smith and Scoll, 1995, pp. 390–91)

The NCEE and the Clinton administration are not alone in promulgating education for developing the economy through improving individual competitiveness. Significant numbers of the corporate and governmental leaders in New Zealand, Australia, and the United Kingdom have similar aspirations. 'This approach leads', writes Michael Peters (1994) regarding New Zealand,

> to designing an educational system in which the relationship between individuals . . . is controlled through a series of mutually reinforcing steps:

Objectives should be clearly identified; performance must be monitored; incentives and sanctions should be in place to encourage managers to act to meet agreed upon objectives rather than to follow their own goals. (p. 71)

The political and educational conflicts over privileging property or personal rights and developing human capital or democratic citizens are not new, but have been waged over the last century. Sixty years ago David Snedden (1915) and John Dewey (1915) vehemently debated whether education should meet the needs of industry or whether industry should be reshaped to meet the needs of democracy. Snedden, like the NCEE, argued that schools should aid 'the economy to function as efficiently as possibly' by sorting and training students for their 'probable destinies' in the workforce. Schools should be organized so that experts would conceptualize the goals, organizational content and methods to be carried out by teachers. Teachers would need to be 'disinterested', for those not 'presenting the opinions of the controlling majority', would have to 'withdraw from teaching' (Wirth, 1970; 163–64). In contrast, Dewey was not interested in making the interests of students subservient to the interests of employers. He instead argued for the development of such intelligence, initiative, ingenuity and capacity as shall make workers, as far as possible, masters of their own industrial fate.

The kind of vocational education in which I am interested is not one which will 'adapt' workers to the existing industrial regime . . . but one which will alter the existing industrial system and ultimately transform it. (Dewey, 1915)

Over the last century the purposes of schooling, what should be taught, to whom, and how have been embedded in larger debates of how justice should be defined, the nature of work and of community. While the debates may seem abstract and irrelevant to our daily lives, as Harvey points out, changing conceptions of justice have real, and sometimes deadly, consequences for workers. Working conditions have become more precarious and competitive. Similarly, debates over how we conceptualize justice, knowledge and the purposes of schooling have real consequences for the lives of teachers and students.

Critical Collaborative Action Research for Democratic Schools

In my own work, I want to oppose the implementation of educational policies that embody the social efficiency tradition, policies that ignore the subjective and political construction of curriculum, that overlook the fact that many of the jobs for which students are being prepared do not exist, and that disregard the idea that multicultural education means more than getting along in the workplace. I want to contest the reassertion of property over personal rights and the promotion of the competitive individual over the community. I want to examine the ways in which the discourse of property rights, education for work, and competitive individualism conceals the interests of those in power.

I undertake such actions fully aware that whatever understandings I have are limited and problematic. There is no one definition of justice or democracy to which I can cling. There are no guarantees of correctness and, as Usher and Edwards remind us, 'All knowledge claims are partial, local, and specific rather than universal and ahistorical, and that they are always imbued with power and normative interests' (1994, p. 10). Given both the contested and problematic nature of knowledge, action research cannot be undertaken with the hope of finding the one right answer (Tyack, 1974) but with the goal of continually making problematic and examining all discourses, practices, and structures. As Noffke reminds us, we need to highlight

> the ways in which [we as] educators are partially correct, yet in continual need of revision, in [our] thoughts and actions. The process does not end, as with traditional notions of research, with richer understandings of education for others to implement; rather it aids in the ongoing process of identifying contradictions, which, in turn, help to locate spaces for ethically defensible, politically strategic action ... Action research, then, is about taking everyday things in the life of education and unpacking them for their historical and ideological baggage. It is similar to, but not the same as, the everyday process of improvement, in that it is public and collaborative. (Noffke, 1995, pp. 4–5)

The aim of action research becomes developing communities that engage in critically reflecting and acting on what they know and do. While I cannot claim to have cornered some version of the truth, I can argue that the social and educational community in which I live embodies the consequences of the shift towards emphasizing property over personal rights and competitive individuals over the community. I live in a metropolitan area where increasingly large numbers of children grow up in poverty, where schools have grown more rather than less 'separate and unequal', where the major industries lay off more workers than they hire, and where the city school district's goals are derived from those of the NCEE (Shannon, 1993; Hursh and Noble, 1995). As an educator I want to develop coalitions that struggle against exploitation, marginalization, powerlessness, imperialism, and violence. In the remainder of this chapter I will describe two projects in which an urban school district and the teaching and curriculum program of the Warner Graduate School of Education and Human Development are raising and responding to some of the above issues.

Rochester Educational Access Collaborative (REAC) and the Genesee Vallee Research and Reform Collaborative (GVRRC)

The two projects described below are collaborative projects within and across institutions. In both projects we aim to develop new curricula and teaching methods situated within an analysis of educational and social goals. In both projects the participants, students as well as teachers, have complex and different understandings of school and society. We do not agree about what students should learn or what and how to teach. But in both projects opportunities exist to collectively carry out activities and to learn from them.

The Rochester Educational Access Collaborative (REAC) is a Ford Foundation funded project with the specific goal of increasing the number of historically underrepresented youth graduating with baccalaureate degrees. A central focus of the project is creating and operating the Teaching and Learning Institute (TLI), a local high school magnet program on careers in education. While understandably the magnet program is the chief responsibility of the high school faculty, labor and educational activists, and university master's and doctoral students are centrally involved.

Although not explicitly planned as action research, REAC fits the action research model because we are raising what Kemmis and McTaggart (1988) call 'educational concerns', then developing, carrying out, and assessing theoretical and practical responses that are situated within a political, ethical and economic context. Our educational concern of increasing the number of historically underrepresented youth entering teaching led to questions of how to transform schools so that students experience less marginalization and powerlessness and can analyze and change cultural and political structures (Sleeter, 1991). We began the project by admitting twenty-six ninth graders into the program. A central part of the program activity is a seminar where the students can 'examine the institutional structure of education and schooling, as well as the working environment of teachers and students' (TLI, 1995, p. 1).

The seminar is the responsibility of a high school teacher who is assisted by master's and doctoral students from the teacher education program. One unit developed and led by the doctoral students focused on engaging students in analyzing questions of identity, particularly of race, class and gender. Students questioned notions of 'acting black' or 'acting white', what it means to be a Latino/a, and why students are presumed to fit certain expectations based on ethnicity, class or gender.

In another unit, developed primarily by the master's students, we wanted to encourage students to make problematic their own schooling. We presented to the students a video about Central Park East, the innovative public school in Harlem, that provides an alternative to the structure and practices of traditional high schools. Our students were presented with the possibility that they could experience class periods of ninety rather than thirty-seven minutes, assessment by portfolios rather than standardized tests, and heterogenous rather than homogeneous student grouping.

We were surprised when the students defended their own school, claiming that tracking 'works' because the stronger students aren't slowed by the less bright, that classes of ninety minutes would be incredibly oppressive, and that standardized tests are a fair measure of what they've learned. Because we wanted to better understand the students' perceptions and continue to propose alternatives, we asked the students if they would be interested in interviewing students from a local public school with many of the same characteristics of Central Park East. They were and we spent the next two weeks developing questions, interviewing students, and writing responses. The ninth graders then developed sets of questions to ask students, teachers, and administrators in their own school; interviewed them; and recorded the interviews on video.

We learned from this project that students come into school with their own 'histories' and have come to understand schooling in particular ways not easily changed. The students, who were all now in the college bound rather than general track, defended tracking. In their other classes students were primarily concerned with being taught what would be on the state's standardized final exam and less with following their own questions. As one ninth grade teacher, who is also a doctoral student protested, echoing Freire: 'All my students want me to do is bank them'. The students understood high school as a place where individuals competed for admission to college (often quite literally as students competed for athletic scholarships), and college as a ticket to a job.

But through a variety of activities students also began to realize that they could ask questions and generate knowledge. Not only did they develop all the questions for their project studying their school, they generated most of the questions for the identity unit. Furthermore, some students regularly returned to the seminar room during lunch to further discuss issues raised in the seminar and to ask even more questions. Lastly, such activities helped students to understand that they could collaborate on projects and learn from one another. So, although we never explicitly assessed whether the students were learning to place less emphasis on individual competition and to see schooling as more than the hoop-one-jumper in order to obtain a job, our interactions led us to conclude that we were changing the students and they us.

A second project, The Genesee Valley Research and Reform Collaborative (GVRRC), intentionally incorporates the action research principles of collaborative research by teachers and administrators, of coupling an analysis of teaching practices with an analysis of the organization of classrooms and schools, and of linking teaching to larger educational and political issues. The project was initiated by a group of teachers, administrators, and university faculty who were frustrated with pervious reform efforts. The founding group developed the project goals and process, including the goal of creating

> . . . learner sensitive [schools] where the student's learning is holistic rather than compartmentalized, active rather than passive, and which foster the learner's independence and responsibility for personal and group learning, growth and development. (GVRRC, 1994)

The group also developed the collaborative action research model, invited schools throughout the metropolitan area to participate, and chose four elementary schools to participate based on their commitment and understanding of the project.

Over the first several months of the project, the individual school teams of about six teachers and one or two administrators met every other week within their schools, and the four schools met as a group once every other month. Furthermore, because the New Zealand educational system appears to have many of the characteristics of the system we wanted to develop, several of us traveled to New Zealand in July, 1995 to study their educational system and presented our research to the collaborative participants.

The two primary schools with which we are collaborating (one urban with 80 per cent minority and one rural with a significant migrant population) are focusing on literacy as situated within issues of diversity and developmentally appropriate curriculum. In undertaking the research, they are discovering the value of collaborating and the ways in which our theories and practices are partially correct and partially in need of revision.

The teachers in the urban school, like all teachers, vary in their approaches to literacy and teaching. But they openly share their observations regarding their classrooms practices; they find ways to challenge each other's convictions and emerge as a stronger group than if they simply shared unanimous views. Over the current academic year, the teachers and administrators have developed specific questions around our goals that they will investigate. As they plan and implement different teaching practices, they will use several means to document and evaluate their changes, including being observed by other teachers, university faculty, and graduate students. The team has also been able to observe teachers in the other collaborating schools and to build on the research conducted in New Zealand.

Both these projects — REAC and GVRRC — are characterized by teachers and administrators collaboratively engaging in research about their practices and linking their practices to larger social issues. The REAC project has raised questions about how to develop teaching practices that help students understand themselves better as youth, particularly minority youth, entering teaching, and help students develop a critical but not cynical view of schooling. It also raises the question: Can we develop in students a desire to critically engage the world and to continue initially in their own education and later in the education of others because of a commitment to a larger social good? In the GVRRC project, we are situating literacy within larger social issues of the meaning literacy has for our minority students, primarily African-American and Latino, and how we can connect literacy to the students' understanding of themselves, school, and the world.

The two projects share some similar characteristics. Both are long term collaboratives within and across institutions developing new curricula and teaching practices. Furthermore, both are situated within analyses of their social context. We learned that what we thought would be easy — having students who are already partly disaffected with school develop a critical analysis — was not. The students, in a school district where only 40 per cent of ninth graders graduate, had difficulty connecting their own questions about what it meant to be an academically successful minority to their own educational experiences. But they did engage in discussions with the teachers and most will continue in the program throughout their high school career.

In the literacy project, we're engaged in clarifying our different conceptions of literacy and schooling as a necessary part of discussing teaching practices. In both projects, participants hold different views about education, some promoting Deweyan conceptions of critical democracy and others more inclined to see education as preparation for work. But it is in bringing to the surface our conceptions and our willingness to engage in the discussion and analysis, asking difficult questions, aware that there is no one truth or right answer, that we become active participants in the political and educational process.

Acknowledgments

These projects and this chapter would not be possible without the assistance of numerous colleagues. I want to acknowledge the following colleagues for their specific editorial assistance: Nancy Foster, Rebecca Goldstein, Derrick Griffith, Margaret Murphy, Kate Ramdin, Paul Stein, and the editors of this volume. I also want to thank the masters' students, teachers and administrators who have participated in both projects.

Note

1   These conceptions are further described as: Exploitation: The transfer of the fruits of the labor from one group to another. Marginalization: The expulsion of people from useful participation in social life. Powerlessness: The lack of that authority, status, and sense of self which would permit a person to be listened to with respect. Cultural Imperialism: Stereotyping in behaviors as well as in various forms of cultural experience. Violence: The fear and actuality of random, unprovoked attacks (Young, 1990, p. 47).

References

APPLE, M. (1993) *Official Knowledge: Democratic Education in a Conservative Age*, New York, Routledge.

BOBBITT, F. (1912) 'The elimination of waste in education', *The Elementary School Teacher*, **12**, pp. 259–71.

BOWLES, S. and GINTIS, H. (1986) *Democracy and Capitalism: Property. Community, and the Contradictions of Modern Social Thought*, New York, Basic Books.

BROSIO, R. (1994) *A Radical Democratic Critique of Capitalist Education*, New York: Lang.

CORNBLETH, C. and WAUGH, D. (1995) *The Great Speckled Bird: Multicultural Politics and Education Policymaking*, New York, St. Martin's Press.

DEWEY, J. (1915) 'Education vs. Trade-training-Dr. Dewey's Reply', *New Republic*, May 3.

DIEGMUELLER, K. and DEBRA, V. (1995) 'Playing games with history', *Education Week*, **15**, 11, Nov. 1, pp. 29–34.

EDWARDS, R. (1979) *Contested Terrain: The Transformation of the Workplace in the Twentieth Century*, New York, Basic Books.

GIROUX, H. (1983) 'Theories of reproduction and production in the new sociology of education: A critical analysis', *Harvard Educational Review*, August, **53**, 3, pp. 257–93.

GENESEE VALLEY RESEARCH AND REFORM COLLABORATIVE (1994) *Request for Proposals.*

HARVEY, D. (1993) 'Class relations, social justice, and the politics of difference', in SQUIRES J. (Ed.), *Principled positions: Postmodernism and the rediscovery of value*, London, Lawrence and Wishart, pp. 85–121.

HURSH, D. and NOBLE, D. (1995) *Social efficiency with a liberal face?: The case of the National Center for Education and the Economy*, paper presented at the annual meeting of the American Educational Research Association, San Francisco, Ca., April.

KEMMIS, S. and MCTAGGART, R. (1988) *The Action Research Planner*, 3rd Ed. Geelong, Deakin University Press.

KLIEBARD, H. (1995) *The struggle for the American curriculum: 1893–1956*, New York, Routledge.

MARSHALL, R. and TUCKER, M. (1992) *Thinking for a living: Education and the wealth of nations*, New York, Basic Books.

MEIER, D. (1995) *The power of their ideas: Lessons for America from a small school in Harlem*, Boston, Beacon.

NATIONAL CENTER FOR EDUCATION AND THE ECONOMY (undated) *The five design tasks: a framework for middle school restructuring*, Rochester, NY.

NATIONAL CENTER FOR EDUCATION AND THE ECONOMY (1994) *Design tasks/goals: For the Rochester City School District*, Rochester, NY.

NOFFKE, S. (1995) 'Action research and democratic schooling', in NOFFKE S. and STEVENSON R. (Eds), *Educational action research: Becoming practically critical*, New York, Teachers College Press.

PETERS, M. (1994) 'Individualism and community: Education and the politics of difference', *Discourse*, **14**, 2, April, pp. 65–78.

ROCHESTER CITY SCHOOL DISTRICT (1994) *Design Tasks/goals*, handout to teachers.

SHANNON, P. (1993) 'Developing democratic voices', *The Reading Teacher*, **47**, 2, October, pp. 2–10.

SLEETER, C. (Ed.) (1991) *Empowerment through multiculturala education*, Albany, NY, SUNY Press.

SLEETER, C. and GRANT, C. (1988) *Making choices for multicultural education*, Columbus, Ohio: Charles E. Merrill.

SMITH, M. and SCOLL, B. (1995) 'The Clinton human capital agenda', *Teachers college record*, **96**, 3, Spring, pp. 389–404.

SNEDDEN, D. (1915) 'Vocational education', *The New Republic*, May 3, p. 40.

TEACHING AND LEARNING INSTITUTE (1995) *Class syllabus.*

TYACK, D. (1974) *The one best system: A history of American urban education*, Cambridge, Harvard.

USHER, R. and EDWARDS, R. (1994) *Postmodernism and education*, New York, Routledge.

WIRTH, A. (1970) 'Philosophical issues in the vocational-liberal studies controversy (1900–1917): John Dewey vs. the social efficiency philosophers', in BELLACK, A. and KLIEBARD, H. (Eds), *Curriculum and evaluation*, Berkeley, McCuthan, pp. xxx–xxx.

YOUNG, I.M. (1990) *Justice and the politics of difference*, Princeton, NJ, Princeton University Press.

Personal/Pedagogical Perspectives on Action Research

Section Editor: Melanie Walker

Section III looks at the tensions between personal and pedagogical transformation and research/development/production. Each author speaks personally about the issues which underlie tensions between life/theory/work/and reform. The tensions between the lifeworld and the world of work are laid out in Chapter 12:

> 'Research', we suggest, is not a technical set of specialist skills but implicit in social action and close to the ways in which we act in everyday life, for we find increasingly that the worlds of academe and social life, theory and practice, work and family are not really so different but constantly interrupt one another, often in complex ways.

Each author in this section attempts to lay out different issues around discourse which illuminate our understanding of the differences and connection between personal and pedagogical understandings and the production of research and development. Anchelee Chayanuvat and Duangta Lukkunaprasit write about how they use classroom research to study their experiences as language teachers in Thailand, and Lesvia Rosas uses the discourse of research to study teachers' personal transformation in Mexico. Similarly, Christine O'Hanlon looks at teachers' personal discourse in professional journals as a way of helping her understand her work as a teacher educator. Ivor Goodson and Christopher Day separately examine educator's lives and working biographies to better understand the nature of action research. Finally, Robyn Lock and Leslie Minarik think about primary students' discourse around the nature of gender and play as a way for Leslie to improve her teaching and students' sense of agency in school and society.

12   Transgressing Boundaries:
Everyday/Academic Discourses

Melanie Walker (South Africa)

Research, we suggest, is not a technical set of specialist skills but implicit in social action and close to the ways in which we act in everyday life, for we find increasingly that the worlds of academe and social life, theory and practice, work and family are not really so different but constantly interrupt one another, often in complex ways. (Schratz and Walker, 1995, p. 2)

Finding Myself in Research

For a long time now I have been bothered by the divide between theory and action, between educational research and practice, and by powerful academic gatekeepers who construct hierarchies to determine what counts as research, and control what counts as educational knowledge. Thus there is a thread running through my research and writing, reaching back to my first encounters over ten years ago with a university-based education faculty and the tensions it generated for me, as a former school teacher, to work there. Why was it that within universities academic discourse seemed to be privileged as the authoritative version/s of educational life? Why was it accepted that specialized discourses restricted access to ideas? Did communities outside the academy not also have cultural resources of value in addressing social inequities?

Nor was I particularly drawn to research divorced from action and social change. Living and working in South Africa, I had a broader commitment to social and educational justice in the face of the gross disparities that marked the education system, and a belief that in some ways, however imperfectly, teachers in their professional lives could contribute to building democratic cultures. At that time I used the language of 'building now in our schools for what we want later', of 'realizing education in practice', and of exploring 'a pedagogy for a future and non-racial democratic South Africa' (Walker, 1988). Where (if at all) did these ideas fit in the academy where so much of the research seemed to support the raced, classed and gendered status quo?

It was in the context of such tensions that I first encountered action research; I was powerfully attracted by its promise ('improvement' and 'understanding') and possibility ('democratic schooling'), and the central position for the professional knowledge and insight of practitioners, both teachers and teacher educators.

Recently, I read Susan Noffke (1995, p. 5) who explains lucidly that action research means 'becoming practically critical' in and through 'a continuous process of clarification of our vision in the area of social justice, of recognizing the constraints on practice, and of developing the capabilities necessary to realize those visions, while at the same time holding all three as problematic'.

My understanding thus is that in changing my practice through action research I explore the lines of power and understanding in my own working life, and so become more critical of the power relations in which I and others are embedded. Thus might I might act as wisely as possible, with others, in my own particular social circumstances, and construct 'really useful knowledge' (Johnson, 1981) to build democratic education. For my own part, the attraction of action research still lies in the never ending spiral of action, reflection, inquiry and theorizing arising from and grounded in my practical concerns, 'a process of becoming, a time of formation and transformation, of scrutiny into what one is doing, and who one can become' (Britzman, 1991, p. 8).

In short, action research for me is exemplified in the notion of 'praxis' as a dialectical and interactive shaping of theory and practice, research and action, underpinned by a commitment to democratic social changes.

Reflexive Refrain I

Yet this is also not a storyline now victoriously concluded, or free of conflict and contradiction. Ten years on, still working in a university, albeit a different one, I wrestle in a different but related way with the seductive power of abstract discourse. It is not an easy struggle, indeed it has had extraordinarily emotional moments occasioned by presenting my profane offerings at Theory's sacred shrine, shrinking inside myself when told 'Hmmm, you need to look towards some tough theoretical engagement'; 'a rather therapeutic account'; 'very small beer theoretically'. I am silenced and excluded, and spend the next year puzzling over why I do not wish to be complicit in the construction of academic boundaries, but nonetheless desire some form of recognition that turns on those same hierarchies of research and knowledge.

Theory, Practice and Research

I used a short paper for an AERA symposium in 1995, called 'Political, Practical and Pedagogical Problems in Teaching about Action Research' as a first opportunity to publicly rehearse and share my problem. This chapter continues that discussion and should be read as an ongoing conversation rather than some final or authoritative pronouncement. My AERA paper turned on arguing for the importance of access to critical academic theory/discourse for such knowledge enables us to interrogate, understand and disrupt our everyday educational practices. My thinking was that, while the experiential learning in action research is undoubtedly powerful, is it sufficient as the sole arbiter of the knowledge we construct? How do we avoid recycling common sense, or romantically celebrating practice without facing up to the fact that experience is never unmediated but structured by particular cultures and settings (racist, sexist, classist). Often when we (academics as well as teachers) think we are producing our most true selves we are simply playing parts in some- one else's script (Silverman, 1993), playing out, not producing knowledge. Silverman (1993, p. 184) quotes Wittgenstein: 'The aspects of things that are most important for us are hidden because of their simplicity and familiarity'. It seems to me that it is academic knowledge and academic theories which provide us with frameworks and categories for thinking that enable us to recuperate the good sense in common sense (Gramsci, 1971).

The point is to shift from immediate problem solving to the complexity of educational processes, where the latter might not solve immediate practical prob- lems, but may well generate new questions. Michael Schratz and Rob Walker (1995, p. 125) explain this relationship between theory, practice and research with admir- able clarity:

> theory is not just a back-up that can be turned to when all else fails, rather it is what makes it possible to see the world differently and so be able to act in different ways ... theory is concerned with giving meaning and intent to action, and with reading meaning and intent in the actions of others. Theory extends our capacity to see alternatives, reminding us of the lost opportunities we create with every action we take and every word we speak. Its concern is not simply to say why the world is as it is but to provide us with the space to think how it could be different.

Border Crossings

All this then raises, as I see it, the problem of access to different discourses, crossing and transgressing the 'line' (Muller and Taylor, 1994) between everyday discourse (what practitioners know and do in their classrooms) and academic dis- course (the domain of university academics), between a discourse of practice and one of theory. Griffiths and Tann (1992) suggest that because teachers have only a partial view of the situations in which they work, they need access to more than one language, to be able to move from the discourse of professional practice to that of the academy. Yet they also point to the difficulties teachers experience when they try to make the connections between academic theory and personal theorizing and everyday experience.

Importantly, then, Bridget Somekh (1994) points to the need to 'inhabit each other's castles', in other words the traffic across borders should be in both direc- tions. She explores the nature of university school/teacher collaboration and argues that teachers bring to action research projects a commitment to their own profes- sional learning; academics usually bring a concern for research in its own right (even at the expense perhaps of action in the action research couplet). The academics then bring the discourse of the academy (perhaps captured by 'research') which may well alienate teachers. Yet those same terms 'give the project status in the eyes of the academy' (p. 19) where personal knowledge and practical wisdom are still not accorded the same respect as more traditional research. Somekh sees the way forward as lying in giving each group access to the discourse of the other:

> We recognized that the discourse of the academy was well honed to certain kinds of analytical thinking and we deliberately introduced some of its terminology in our discussions with our teacher-researcher partners. Although we felt the need to adapt our discourse when talking to teachers, we felt it would ultimately be patronizing to restrict it, so we attempted to compromise by learning to move from one discourse to the other, as fitted the circumstance and the individuals concerned. (p. 19)

And of course teachers must cross the border as well, although Somekh concedes that this was not easy. She learned that teachers often found academic literature on student learning inaccessible, while their working conditions did not anyway encourage research practice, not least that the press towards practical action works against the tentativeness of much academic writing. However, Somekh also stresses that it was not the case that academic discourse was more extensive than that of the school. The two were different, inescapably they implied differential status for the two user groups, but 'neither was more extensive or in its way more exclusive than the other' (p. 20).

For Somekh and her colleagues such school-university collaboration, while not overlooking the effects of power, marries Eisner's (1991) notions of 'educational connoisseurship' and 'educational criticism', both of which are essential to educational improvement: '. . . the private world of the classroom is placed in the context of other classrooms, in other schools; the patterns of practice across the education system can be explored by meta-analysis of action research in individual classrooms' (Somekh, 1994, p. 23).

Central to this is the notion of collaboration from different spaces and across different discourses, but a collaboration recognizably criss-crossed by lines of power rather than some patronizing notion of 'equality'.

Of course, teachers might as easily guard their own territory and operate their own exclusions, arguing that academics are strong on theoretical prescriptions, but thin on 'real' knowledge of schools and classrooms. Teachers then resist crossing into theory's domain. In part, at least such attitudes are the effect precisely of a faulty notion of theory engendered by academic gatekeeping! The point would seem to be that unless we learn to transgress, how are lecturers to be heard outside the academy, or teachers to be listened to seriously inside the university? The issue of access to different discourses is, however, not so easily resolved for people working under differing professional, cultural and institutional conditions. Muller and Taylor (1994, p. 5) warn of the possible danger in 'hybridizing' the boundary between different knowledge domains so that the emancipatory project 'turns against the intentions that drive it' (p. 12). They construct a useful argument, albeit one which assumes border crossings in one direction only, and a glaring absence of reflexivity as to how they and other academics come to construct those not in the academy as the Other. At any rate, they consider that the 'boundary bashers', or what McWilliam (1995, p. 6) refers to as the 'inverted intellectual snobbery' of those who insist that 'a spade should be called a spade and never as an earthmoving agricultural imple-ment', unwittingly connive at their own marginalization by those who have the power to classify where the line should be drawn. They argue for the need to theorize the boundary rather than erase it and so make different discourses more widely access-ible. They thus propose 'prudent boundary crossing of the space between exclusive domains of discursive activity' (p. 11). The correct strategy, they say, is to equip people with the 'social and cultural papers needed to cross the border safely' (p. 11). Erica McWilliam (1995), explores the issues of accessibility of texts and suggests the need to write more simply, but not simplistically in order to enable others 'to occupy the site of knowledge themselves' (p. 5) and provide access to ideas which she finds 'pleasurable, pragmatic and overdue in Education' (p. 4).

Similarly, Kramer-Dahl (1995) recognizes the need to read and write 'against the grain of academic discourse', but to do this involves knowing and entering that discourse. The tension is of course that such discourse embodies relations of power and ways of knowing so access to academic discourse (and research discourse would be part of academic discourse) can be at the same time both oppressive and the means to challenge such rules. Only by providing the patterns of research/university dis-course do we enable others to enter the dominant ways of speaking and knowing.

The kernel of the issue then seems to be one of: either assuming 'a radical equality of worlds of discourse' (Muller and Taylor, 1994, p. 12) and the logical development then of a common language about research and the dismantling of the 'line'; or learning to celebrate difference and crossing not destroying boundaries.

Reflexive Refrain II

Terry Volbrecht (1994) writes to me:

> 'It is somewhat ironic for academics to lament people being stranded at the border without their papers when they/we have been instrumental in drawing the borderlines and in appointing border police. Soon we will be saying 'This hurts us more than it hurts you!' You do not seem to think that academic knowledge is implicated in the processes of exclusion and marginalization. You assume academic knowledge to be a 'good' to which people must be given access so that they can disrupt everyday educational practices. But academic discourse has played a central role in the creation of those practices. While not wishing to demonize academic knowledge, we need to see it for what it is, which is many things both good and bad; there is nothing essentially good about being esoteric'. So, who are the border police[men]? Who has the power to decide what counts? Who establishes the hierarchies? Why is academic discourse aimed at exclusion?

Who gets excluded, why, and with what effects? Pushing the metaphor of border crossings a little further, do we cross borders to find something on the other side which we think we do not have? What then does this mean for understanding power relations?

The point surely is that knowledge is not necessarily located in an academic paper, it is constructed and lives in different spaces, and the generation of knowledge about practice is not the exclusive property of universities: 'There are valuable things to be learnt from university generated theories, but this external discourse must feed into a process of inquiry that is initiated from the ground up' (Zeichner, 1993, p. 204). While Ken Zeichner would not subscribe to some kneejerk anti-intellectual rejection of what the academy might offer, he also questions the rejection of practitioner knowledge; both need to be held in creative tension. Sadly, this respect too often is not a reciprocal one, for, he notes, the control of educational knowledge, while it may have expanded somewhat to include teachers' perspectives 'there are real limits to the degree the discourse has been widened' (p. 208). Teachers, argues Zeichner, are still conspicuously absent from the research literature. At issue surely is that we must also challenge the academy's (constructed) rules by continuing to ask for whom, by whom and how is research in/on education to be? As Schratz and Walker (1995, p. 124) say, the academy needs to be seen as 'a source of ideas not a warrant for them'. It also means that if we recognize that there are differences, then collaborative relationships between teacher educators and school teachers should be grounded in forging links across and in an acknowledgement of difference, not some romantic notion of democratizing research practice which serves only to flatten action research and erode its emancipatory potential and military when research is found to be complex not simple (Cocks, 1989).

Reflexive Refrain III

If I am to face up to my own assumptions, I would need to ask at this point what a school teacher might make of the 'acknowledgement of difference'. Does it mean that knowledge about education and action research is the expertise of the academy (where teachers must anyway go to learn about action research!). Are 'differences' hierarchically arranged so that some are taken more seriously as knowledge producers while others are patronized?

There is a further dimension to my problem: the 'academy' is by no means homogeneous in practice, and many universities still resist or refuse to register action research projects for doctoral degrees or to award tenure on the basis of action research. Moreover, not many of those same universities contain academics committed to doing their own action research and supporting that of teachers and students.

A colleague of mine has written of his own encounter with the 'border police' — an attempt to register a doctoral proposal (at a different university from that at which we both work):

> If I am to separate my educational mission and my research, what are the implications for conducting action research for Ph.D. purposes? . . . I am still disturbed by how I allowed myself to be silenced by the 'authoritative discourse' (Bakhtin, 1981) of the [Higher Degrees] committee, so that I was unable to speak as a representative of the action research discourse community or to challenge the authoritative Ph.D discourse 'that permits no play with its framing context (Holquist in Bakhtin, 1981). (Volbrecht, 1994, p. 18)

How can one both participate in practice/action and research it, some say dismissively? So action research is not defined as 'real research' by the '[academic] guardians of the "knowledge base"' (Zeichner, 1993, p. 210). At issue is the hierarchy in place even within the academy itself (not just the university and schools, or academics and teachers). As Ken Zeichner remarked in the AERA symposium: 'Teaching courses in which a lot of teacher knowledge is read and discussed does not carry as much status in my department as those in which the latest post structuralist, critical, and feminist theories are read'.

Thus Zeichner (1993, p. 210) suggests that 'action research has not managed to alter the balance of power between academics and practitioners when it comes to defining what counts as educational research'. Why should/would teachers want to be heard in the academy, especially if we can acknowledge that different forms of knowledge contribute to addressing social inequality, and people on different terrains with different perspectives contribute to making knowledge about education?

The lack of respect for different discourses is troubling. Yet, research criteria and standards in the academy have been historically constructed, and these rules mirror the relative positions of different groups in society. Teachers are then positioned as reproducers and consumers of knowledge in relation to academics, the knowledge producers; action research as not of high status. The line itself serves particular interests, and gatekeepers of more traditional research forms exhibit little reflexivity regarding their (constructed) positions and location in academic relations of power when they act as border police to turn back new immigrants.

As Jill Adler (1996) asks, when teachers working under extraordinarily difficult circumstances clearly benefit professionally from practice directed inquiry, but fail to meet 'research' criteria as a direct result of their personal and institutional circumstances, do we place them outside a teacher-as-researcher community? Surely not, she argues: 'for this would not only be detrimental to potential inquiry activity and learning experiences for such teachers, but it would subvert the movement's own political goals for voice, ownership, status and power for all teachers'.

Reinscribing the Everyday

Moreover, too often the language of research is distant from the everyday life of those human agents acting and choosing which it claims to seek to understand. This is a world of action and emotion, the sensuous and profane. Noffke (1995) reminds us that we realize our vision of social justice and democratic action in concrete everyday circumstances: the lunch queue, the history lesson, discipline, class tests. Our problem is how to find the language that can link our everyday words to the world of academic research without obliterating the ways in which the everyday is inscribed in our working lives, written onto third world squatter camps and inner city schools, and those more mundane actions of standing in classrooms, sitting through the school assembly, and longing for the lunch break to ease our tiredness. Is theory to be enriched by these encounters, or only practice to be enriched by theory?

Schratz and Walker (1995), however, do not then pose an opposition between 'theory' on the one hand and 'practice' on the other, but suggest what is at issue 'is a conflict between two different forms of theory. *One kind of theory takes its authority from the academy . . . the other kind of theory, [is] implicit in everyday life . . .*' (my emphasis, p. 112). They see theory 'as implicit in every social action . . . and rather than seeking to replace these everyday theories, we seek to explicate and understand them' (p. 105).

Whatever our questions and concerns about action research, they may well be better addressed as Terry Volbrecht comments, 'without subjugating all our knowledges to the gaze of the great Academic in the Panopticon's tower!' (personal communication), and indeed, without subscribing meekly to the constructed binary which privileges the academic over the everyday, but rather look to the integration of 'the discipline of theory with the different but equally rigorous discipline of practice' (Winter, 1993, p. 315).

Then, if we are to follow Schratz and Walker's point, the academic is to be seen as inhering in the everyday; the binary is then dismantled and reconceptualized as everyday/academic discourse/s. The central methodological task then becomes that of reflexivity, mostly absent in conventional academic texts, written with no apparent ownership, separating knower and known to obscure their own construction as socially and historically produced artefacts.

The Way We Know and Not Only What We Know

What happens too when academics try to colonize classroom work (and discourses) is highlighted by Johnston and Proudfoot (1994) as the evaluators of an action research project to explore the construction of gender in the early years of schooling. The funding proposal was externally funded and managed but the research was to be undertaken by teachers in their classrooms. Difficulties arose over competing expectations of the action research approach where the external management committee expected cutting edge research in the area of gender: 'In many respects . . . a traditional research project in which teachers would act as researchers gathering data to make new discoveries, thus informing theories of gender construction in the early years of schooling at a general level' (p. 8). These expectations were conveyed to the teachers, generating some uncertainty for them as to how they would cope: 'They were speaking a language . . . we had never considered' (p. 8), one remarked afterwards. Nor were the teachers allowed to choose issues themselves but were 'encouraged' to identify research questions which had not yet been investigated in feminist research. The key end product was also to be case study reports with a particular format and deadlines. Not surprisingly, 'to a large extent the case study reports, rather than changed practices or personal understandings, became the major focus of the teachers' efforts' (p. 9). Johnston and Proudfoot therefore characterize this project as an example of technical action research aimed more to develop the research literature than practice. They cite Carr and Kemmis (1986, p. 198) who warn against 'appropriating practitioners' self-understandings and formulating them within theoretical or interpretive frameworks shaped by the concerns and interests of outside observers'. The alternative is action research which 'involves practitioners directly in theorizing their own practice and revising their theories self critically in the light of their practical consequences' (*ibid*).

At issue here is the point that because action research involves both the construction of knowledge and its practical implementation, it must also involve a process of learning. Thus we must also consider not just what we know (for example how we might come to theoretical knowledge) but also the way we know. There seems little point in the transfer (or imposition) of academic knowledge to passive non-expert vessels in a didactic fashion, not unlike the distinction Barnes (1988) draws between 'hot' and 'cold' science teaching. We have 'cold' research when theoretical knowledge is transmitted irrespective of its relationship to our practice, or when the practical is simply coopted into the service of the theoretic. 'Hot' research, by way of contrast, would involve an active questioning curiosity, judgment and the appropriation of theory when confronted by the everyday world of children and teachers: 'transforming action on reality' (Freire, quoted in McTaggart, 1989, p. 6).

Reflexive Refrain IV

I worry still about what counts as research, simply because mine is an educational research culture and academic environment still dominated by white, mostly male, academics. This is not to say that all teachers, especially black and women teachers, aspire or would want to enter the academy, although many may wish to conduct an action research study for a masters or doctoral degree, or participate projects which are less about research production as a primary aim, more about reflective professional learning. Would it not be that teachers positioned as researchers in their own classrooms might both challenge some of the academy's exclusionary rules by producing critical and disciplined action research studies; but also start to build a climate in which their own students participate in research practices and take their view of what a teacher is from a different set of practices from that of the old authoritarian system? This seems especially important, if as numerous studies show, the way we teach is strongly determined by the way we ourselves were taught. So there are strategic/ political issues and educational issues inescapably intertwined here. How to act to tease out the threads is an ongoing conversation, shaped by where we find ourselves at different historical moments.

Still, it is also worth closing this particular circle of dialogue with a reminder to myself of the emancipatory project which initially attracted me to action research: the desire and concern for 'real instances of improving the lives of children and the people who care for them' (Noffke, 1995, p. 7). That this remains a subjugated discourse, outside the parameters of dominant constructions of what counts as research and legitimate knowledge in the western, masculinist academy ought to be the occasion for us to reflect critically on our taken for granted assumptions — about the academy and about schools. Moreover, if the theory that is denied teachers does not enter/challenge teacher's actions, the project of democratic education and pedagogical transformation is perhaps less likely to flourish; unless practitioners using their discourse of practice challenge the discourse of theory, and theorists leave their world and enter that of practice.

Acknowledgments

My special thanks to Stella Clark, Uta Lehman and Terry Volbrecht for insightful comments on earlier drafts of this chapter.

References

ADLER, J. (1996) 'Professionalism in Process: Mathematics Teacher as Researcher from a South African Perspective', unpublished paper, Faculty of Education, University of the Witwatersrand.

BARNES, D. (1988) 'Knowledge as Action', in LIGHTFOOT, M. and MARTIN, N. (Eds), *The Word for Teaching is Learning*, London, Heinemann.

BRITZMAN, D. (1991) *Practice Makes Practice: A Critical Study of Learning to Teach*, Albany, State University of New York Press.

CARR, W. and KEMMIS, S. (1986) *Becoming Critical: Education, Knowledge and Action Research*, Lewes, Falmer Press.

COCKS, J. (1989) *The Oppositional Imagination — Feminism, Critique and Political Theory*, London, Routledge.

EISNER, E. (1991) *The Enlightened Eye*, New York, MacMillan.

GRAMSCI, A. (1971) *Selections from Prison Notebooks*, London, Lawrence and Wishart.

GRIFFITHS, M. AND TANN, S. (1992) 'Using Reflective Practice to Link Personal and Public Theories', *Journal of Education for Teaching*, **18**, 1, pp. 69–84.

JOHNSON, R. (1981) 'Really Useful Knowledge', in CENTRE FOR CONTEMPORARY CULTURAL STUDIES (CCCS), *Unpopular Education: Schooling and Social Democracy in England Since 1944*, London, CCCS.

JOHNSTON, C. AND PROUDFOOT, C. (1994) 'Action Research — who owns the process?', *Educational Review*, **46**, 1, pp. 3–14.

KRAMER-DAHL, A. (1995) 'Reading and Writing Against the Grain of Academic Discourse', *Discourse*, **16**, 1, pp. 21–38.

McWilliam, E. (1994) *In Broken Images*, New York, Teachers College Press.

McWilliam, E. (1995) 'Performing the posts: Writing and speaking pono-feminism', paper presented at the annual meeting of the American Educational Research Association, San Franscisco, CA, 18–22 April, 1995.

McTaggart, R. (1989) 'Principles of Participatory Action Research', paper presented at the Third World Encounter on Participatory Research, Managua, Nicaragua, September 1989.

Muller, J. and Taylor, N. (1994) *Schooling and Everyday Life: Knowledges Sacred and Profane*, mimeo, University of Cape Town.

Noffke, S. (1995) 'Action research and democratic schooling: Problematics and potentials', in Noffke, S.E. and Stevenson, R.B. (Eds), *Educational Action Research: Becoming Practically Practical*, New York, Teachers College Press.

Rudduck, J. (1994) *Developing a Gender Policy in Secondary Schools*, Buckingham, Open University Press.

Schratz, M. and Walker, R. (1995) *Research as Social Change*, London, Routledge.

Silverman, D. (1993) *Interpreting Qualitative Data*, London, Sage.

Somekh, B. (1994) 'Inhabiting each other's castles: Towards knowledge and mutual growth through collaboration', paper presented at the annual meeting of the American Educational Association, New Orleans, April 4–8 1994.

Volbrecht, T. (1994) 'Revisioning a PhD in academic development: An exercise in narrative enquiry', in Leibowitz, B. and Volbrecht, T. (Eds), *Language in Development, AD Dialogues 4*, Bellville, South Africa, University of the Western Cape.

Walker, M. (1988) 'Thoughts on the potential of action research in South African Schools', *Cambridge Journal of Education*, **18**, 2, pp. 147–54.

Winter, R. (1993) 'Action Research, Practice and Theory', *Educational Action Research*, **1**, 2, pp. 315–16.

Zeichner, K. (1993) 'Action Research: Personal renewal and social reconstruction', *Educational Action Research*, **1**, 2, pp. 199–220.

13 Modes of Discourse for Living, Learning and Teaching

Gen Ling Chang-Wells and Gordon Wells (Canada)

Two fundamental premises underpin the work of our collaborative action research group, as we attempt to bring about change in classroom learning and teaching through a focus on discourse and activity.[1] First, we believe that learning is an integral aspect of any form of activity — a condition of living, not merely a preparation for life in the future. Second, we believe that education at all levels must be conceived in terms of dialogue: an attempt, through the use of various modes of discourse, to develop understanding of, and to act effectively and responsibly in, our shared but diverse social and physical environment. The basis for these assumptions is to be found in our reflections on our own personal and professional experiences, as these have been enriched and given focus through our reading and discussion of the works of writers in a wide variety of intellectual traditions.

Particularly important for our group, in this latter respect, has been the confluence of ideas, stemming from the work of Dewey (1938) in the United States and Vygotsky (1978, 1987) in Russia, that is currently referred to as social constructivism. A central theme in the work of both these scholars is that human beings learn in the course of participating in purposeful joint activity as, with assistance from more expert others, they master the use of the material and intellectual tools and practices that mediate the achievement of the desired outcomes of those activities. This conception challenges the assumptions on which traditional practice is based by rejecting the view of education as the transmission of decontextualized skills and items of knowledge which, having been acquired, may subsequently be put to use in 'real' activities. Instead, learning is seen as 'an integral and inseparable aspect of social practice', a concomitant of 'engaged, dilemma-driven' activity, in which 'agent, activity, and the world mutually constitute each other' (Lave and Wenger, 1991, pp. 31, 33). Rather than merely adding to the student's fund of knowledge, learning involves a 'process of transformation of participation itself', which occurs as a function of all participants 'transforming roles and understanding in the activities in which they (currently) participate' (Rogoff, 1994, p. 209).

Such a transformative view of education has far-reaching implications for the role of the teacher in the teaching-learning relationship. In particular, it makes clear that, to be effective as teachers, there must be a continuing transformation of our practice that is shaped by and shapes our developing understanding of our students, of the topics that are selected, and of how our joint engagement with these topics is affected by the nature of the activities in which they are embedded. With this transformation of practice as our motive, the major focus of our action research has been on developing modes of classroom activity that provide frequent opportunities for our students, as well as ourselves, to be transformative learners through collaborative participation in productive activities that, individually and collectively, we find interesting and relevant.

However, to base the curriculum on the criteria of interest and relevance alone would be both limited and limiting. A teacher's curricular decisions must also be informed by a critical analysis of the historical, cultural and political context in which they are taken. Adopting this larger perspective, it seems clear to us that there are many important domains of human experience and understanding that the students in our schools would be unlikely to engage with unless teachers deliberately attempt to kindle interest in them and provide guidance and assistance as students begin to participate in the relevant practices. This is particularly the case with the academic disciplines that underpin the subjects of the school curriculum. In this context, we are also conscious of our responsibility to meet the expectations of society, as these are set out in the sequence of topics for study in the *Common Curriculum* (OMET, 1993) and in the accompanying specification of 'learning outcomes'.

However, while agreeing that it is important that students should master the 'generic knowledge and skills' that form the core of the curriculum, we are convinced that, whenever possible, these should be treated, not as ends in themselves, but as means to be used in solving problems of practical and social significance. At the same time, as well as the procedural knowledge that is constructed through participation in productive 'hands-on' activity, we believe that students should also develop the understanding that is the outcome of the 'minds-on' activity in which personal experience is extended and enriched through being juxtaposed and integrated with culturally-developed knowledge and modes of interpretation and representation (Cobb, 1994; Kalantzis and Cope, 1993). In this latter respect, an important part of the teacher's responsibility is to introduce the various forms of metalanguage that enable knowledge itself to be reflected upon, and to encourage students to adopt a critical and reflective stance both to the ideas they encounter and to the actions they perform. For it is in this way that they are best enabled to participate in classroom activities as autonomous, intentional and transformational learners, not restricted to the ways of acting and thinking of their immediate communities but able to extend and change them through their own critical and creative participation (Engeström, 1991; Scardamalia and Bereiter, 1994).

Finally, we are convinced that, whatever activities are selected in the light of the above criteria, it is essential that, as a central feature of the process, students are encouraged to collaborate in 'negotiating and renegotiating meaning' (Bruner, 1990, p. 123) in a continuing attempt to construct an understanding of the material and social world that will enhance their further participation in joint activity. This brings us to our second emphasis — the transformations that are mediated through dialogue.

The Dialogic Nature of Discourse

In the historical development of human societies, as well as in the development of their individual members, the propensity for collaborative meaning-making plays a critical role. As the mediator of joint activity, language enables participants to coordinate their actions — to negotiate goals and evaluate outcomes. This is its interpersonal function. At the same time, in its ideational function, it provides a means of representing objects and events and the relationships between them; it thus constitutes a powerful tool for collaborative remembering, thinking and problem solving. In this role, as Halliday puts it, language functions as 'a theory of human experience' (1993, p. 97).

Developmentally, language appears first in the oral mode and, for most forms of activity, it is oral discourse that remains the primary mode of interpersonal interaction. However, where the activity requires the accumulation and communication of accurate information as the basis for systematic knowledge construction, the transient nature of oral discourse makes it an inadequate tool. It was primarily to serve these latter ideational functions that, historically, the written mode of language was developed (Halliday, 1985).

As a means for mediating intellectual activity, the crucial characteristic of writing is that it gives a permanent representation to meaning. Written texts can be read and re-read, silently or aloud, and — either by the writer or by subsequent readers — they can be critically interrogated and revised, with each successive version of the text providing the basis for further reflection and reformulation. Thus, as Olson puts it: 'What literacy contributes to thought is that it turns the thoughts themselves into worthy objects of contemplation' (1994, p. 277). By the same token, becoming literate can be thought of, at least in part, as appropriating this powerful tool for thinking with (Lotman, 1988), and of bringing under conscious and deliberate control meaning-making capacities that, previously, were only deployed spontaneously in oral discourse (Vygotsky, 1987). However, once literate modes of discourse have been mastered, the practices that they enable can, to a considerable degree, be carried out also in speech.

Whether in the oral or the written mode, however, discourse is essentially social in nature. Furthermore, because it is constituted of a series of contributions that are sequentially inserted into the ongoing flow of activity, it is also inherently dialogic. Intended to play a part in advancing the activity towards the goal to which participants are orienting, each contribution is a strategic act that is both responsive to the speaker/writer's interpretation of the current state of affairs and assumes, in turn, a further responsive act (Bakhtin, 1986). However, in claiming that discourse is necessarily social and dialogic, it is not being suggested that there is no place for disagreement. On the contrary, since any community includes diverse voices and points of view, argument and debate should be both expected and encouraged. Indeed, as a variety of studies have shown, advances in action and understanding are often best achieved through attempts to resolve disagreement.

Discourse is undoubtedly the most salient aspect of educational activity. In classrooms of all kinds, some form of discourse, either spoken or written, is going on for most of the time. However, focusing on its tool-like function leads to the important recognition that this discourse is not an end in itself, but a means of achieving the goals of the larger activities that constitute the object of education. Furthermore, it is not the only means. Non-verbal actions of various kinds, such as observing, experimenting, drawing, model-making and so on, are also important ways of making meaning. Together with talking, writing and reading, they make up the semiotic tool-kit that participants master through using the different tools in complementary and mutually reinforcing ways to achieve (and at the same time to develop) the goals of the activity in which they are engaged (Wells, 1994). In an important sense, therefore, all these mediational means are dialogic.

Unfortunately, however, the potential for collaborative knowledge building that is inherent in a dialogic conception of educational activity has remained largely untapped in most educational institutions. Both the transmissionary mode of curriculum delivery and the narrowly individualistic and competitive ethos that pervades most classrooms has militated against its realization. Nor, in most cases, has the current enthusiasm for 'cooperative learning' brought about a significant change. For simply having students carry out some tasks in groups does little to alter the traditional orientation, unless the nature of the overall activity is itself radically changed and the roles of the participants renegotiated. It was thus to bring about such a transformation of classroom activities and of the discourses that mediate them that several classroom and university educators came together to form our action research community. Shaped by our growing understanding over the course of a year of working together as a research community, we have come to realize that, if we want to bring about the sort of changes implied by a transformational dialogic conception of education, we also have to focus on the modes of discourse among ourselves, both as practices and as objects of investigation.

Overlapping Communities: Our Classrooms, Our Schools and Our Research Project

In the first phase of our research (1991–94), we began with a focus on oral discourse in the learning and teaching of science (Shechter, 1994; Wells, 1995; Wells and Chang-Wells, in press; Allen, *et al.*, in preparation). However, as the research proceeded, it became clear that, in order to understand as well as to intentionally provide for the sort of practices and conditions of learning implied by the conception of education outlined above, we needed to broaden our focus.

First, we needed to extend the scope of our project to include all areas of the school curriculum. While the demands of timetabling may require the sharp differentiation of 'subjects', the developmental needs of the student as a whole person do not, as is emphasized in our provincial curriculum policy (OMET, 1993). Furthermore, particularly for the elementary and intermediate school teachers in our project, it was natural to wish to extend to other areas the understandings gained in relation to science. Yet science proved to have been a well-chosen starting point, for it had led us to see the essentially collaborative nature of knowledge building, the importance of 'progressive discourse' in this process (Bereiter, 1994) and, in particular, the value of an 'inquiry' orientation in creating the sort of community in which transformational, dialogic learning and teaching can be enacted. In our current work, therefore, as we investigate the interplay between action and the different modes of discourse in classroom activity, we are exploring what these key concepts might mean when they are brought to bear on other areas of the school curriculum.

Second, with our growing understanding of the relationship between learning and participation in a community of inquiry, we have come to recognize that the changes we are attempting to bring about in classrooms are, to a considerable extent, dependent on making changes at other levels in the institution of education as a whole, most notably in the ways in which policy is developed and enacted in schools and school boards, and in the preparation and professional development of teachers, administrators and teacher educators. In our different places of work, therefore, each of us is attempting to develop a community of inquiry among the colleagues in our immediate environment, where one focus of our inquiry is to explore the nature of the practices of the school community and their relationship with those of the classroom communities formed by individual teachers with their students.

The recognition of these as two overlapping communities, whose practices have consequences for each other, makes it equally important for us to ask how transformational and dialogic is the culture of the school community wherein teachers learn as they teach. However, the search for answers to this question is beyond the scope of this chapter, as is exploration of the nature of the relationship between school and classroom communities. Rather, this chapter focuses on the third overlapping community — that of our own research team. But as we look more closely at our own practices, we undoubtedly need to consider how they relate to those of the other two.

Modes of Discourse within our Communities of Inquiry

Like any community, our research team uses both oral and written modes of discourse as tools for a variety of practices. Practices which use the oral mode of discourse include our regular meetings, our social gatherings, interviews conducted with students and members of the research team, classroom talk, and our conference presentations. Practices which rely on the written mode of discourse include our e-mail, our ethnographic notes of classroom activities, our research reports, and our published or in-progress writings. In addition, for purposes of research, many of our oral practices are recorded either in audio or video form and extracts transcribed and entered into a computer-supported database. For example significant parts of our classroom discourse and our monthly meetings are in the form of transcripts, making them more accessible for analysis.

Considered from the point of view of the different media involved, oral and written discourse may, on first examination, appear to be very different. Closer analysis of our practices, however, suggests that the medium may be less important than the practices that the discourse serves. It is this observation that the next section of our chapter will address.

A Comparison of the Practices Served by Meetings and E-mail Communication

Probably for all members of our research community, the preferred mode of discourse is some kind of face-to-face interaction. But, because we work in widely separated locations, the opportunities to meet and talk are relatively infrequent. To supplement our monthly meetings, therefore, we have had to explore the potential of other modes of discourse to pursue our collaboration in inquiry. Of particular importance, in this respect, is our use of e-mail to establish connectivity among ourselves in a way that transcends the constraints of time and space. Taken together, meetings and e-mail communication form one component of our oral and written discourse data, which have common as well as unique features.

What are these features and how do they shape our practices and learning, individually and as a community? A recurring feature is that both our e-mail communication and our face-to-face interactions are used as a means for celebrating and maintaining friendships and for providing support. They are also used to define and establish membership, since, over the course of the year, we have had several discussions as to who may or may not participate in our meetings and our e-mail network. Viewed in this manner, the line between the purposes served by our oral and written discourses, in the form of meetings, social gatherings and e-mail communication, is blurred. In our use of the two modes for such practices, we currently think that they do not differ significantly.

However, unlike our regular meetings, during which the conversations are public, e-mail accords individual members the potential to engage in private conversations. Depending on the nature of these conversations, e-mail has the potential, but not necessary, consequence of establishing exclusion and inclusion of various members, thereby affecting the culture of a particular community. These features and their consequences are not unlike the manner in which students in classrooms exploit written discourse, be it to counteract the public nature of classrooms or to establish a culture of inner and outer circles or of hierarchy amongst various groups. When the written mode is used for such practices, we would argue that writing serves as a more powerful tool than oral discourse in the maintenance of social networks and structures. It is the recognition of the existence of such distinctions between the two modes of discourse in adult practices that will enable us to discern them amongst our students in schools and their consequences for students' behaviour and learning.

Nevertheless, the establishment and maintenance of social relationships is by no means the most significant of our e-mail practices. As well as providing an informal means of communication, quite close to conversation in its spontaneity, e-mail can also function as a medium for more formal, reflective writing. In this mode, it serves as a tool for the ethnographic documentation of events, or issues of policy, as they occur in our classroom or school communities. For example, an extended discussion developed recently around the range of practices among our schools and school boards with respect to assessment, evaluation and communicating with parents about students' progress. When used to serve such a purpose, e-mail as written discourse is far more significant than the oral discourse of our meetings. This is because the act of composing brings the writer to re-visit the event or issue in a more deliberate and thoughtful manner.

This use of e-mail to document our practices in the other two communities also has the effect of changing the research practice of ethnographic note-taking, which is by and large private. E-mail, being public, changes the act of documentation; instead of writing for self as reader, one writes for the community of co-researchers as well. Added to this, the ethnography as written is often not a static or one-shot account. Rather, it has the potential of transforming from a product to an interactive and dynamic process. This happens when co-researchers respond with analogous or different accounts, resulting in a richer and more complex portrait of school practices in the wider community in which we work. This particular use of e-mail, we conjecture, changes teacher-researchers' understandings and, over time, their actions as well. Certainly, one consequential outcome for us is that, through e-mail, we have the opportunity to locate and view our own practices within larger and overlapping communities, thereby developing greater sociocultural understanding of the world of schools and classrooms and of their political ramifications.

Equally important is that, in employing e-mail in this manner, we are experimenting with its use as a joint research methodology that is of value to teacher-researchers. Any classroom ethnographer will attest that their observational notes are often successful in detailing the observable behaviour of participants. But it is a much more challenging task to ascertain and describe their thought processes and the intentions and motivations that underpin their behaviour. However, as we examine the ethnographic accounts in our e-mail communications, we realize that they provide rich vignettes of teachers' thought processes in their planning or responding to their enacted curriculum, of their visions and expectations for their students, of their beliefs and values, and of the factors that shape their current actions. When, as a group, we perceive our e-mail writings as ethnographies of teachers' thinking and analyze them for patterns, uncertainties and surprises, our efforts have transformational value both for ourselves and for the larger community of teacher-researchers.

It is this aspect of our e-mail practice to which our regular meetings are in some ways similar. We have, over the course of our first year as a research community, taken a metacognitive stance to our meetings when, at intervals, we have reflected upon how we have conducted past meetings and what purposes they have served. These reflections have gradually led us to identify various features, of which one that we particularly value is the practice of using our meetings for the development of a dialectical understanding of practice and theory. It is to such an end that we had a series of meetings during which individual members of the community both provided a qualitative account of one aspect of their practice in the other two communities and looked at it from a theoretical and interpretive perspective as well. Indeed, it is precisely on such occasions, we believe, that we are most fully engaged in transformational dialogic learning.

Linking the Practices of Overlapping Communities Through Oral and Written Research Activities

The objectives of our individual and collective research agendas also entail interviews with the students of the teacher members of our research team, video or audio recordings of units of study in classroom communities, and teachers working together as school communities. These not only provide us with data for our research agendas, but they also capture the modes of discourse in the overlapping communities of classrooms and schools.

The data we have of our modes of discourse in the two aforementioned communities are further enriched by our efforts to make permanent records of some of those research activities that are conducted orally. One example is transcripts of our interviews; another is the oral and written discourse of our joint engagement in preparing for conference presentations, or our collaborative writing of research reports as well as papers for publication. When these research activities are audio or video taped and when drafts of our writing are kept, together they provide us with added discourse data that demonstrate the complementary role of oral and written discourse in joint activity.

From our current work, we observe that when transcripts (that employ the written mode to create a paper trace of oral discourse) are examined intentionally and critically, they provide occasions for us, individually or collectively, to work within our 'zones of proximal development' (Vygotsky, 1978). This is only possible, however, if each of us exploits the dialectical juxtaposition of our actions, intentions and intertextual knowledge-base. In other words, analysis of any artifact, action or discourse is, by itself, an insufficient condition for transformational learning to occur. What is also required is the exploitation of one's theories of knowledge and expertise as lenses for meaning-making. Unless we look at our practices through the lens of a theoretical framework, and unless connections are made between our practices and other educational practices, some of which are similar and some different, our research activities will not have transformational consequences.

Working together as a community to provide a dialogic counterpart to an individual member's practice and thinking, as we explore practices captured on video or in transcripts, has also enabled us to make parallels between the learning we are experiencing as a research community and that of our students and ourselves in our classroom communities (Donoahue, 1996; Galbraith, *et al.*, in press; McGlynn-Stewart, 1996). And, in both cases, we realize, it is not so much which mode of discourse is used that is significant; rather, it is whether, in whatever mode, the discourse is progressive. Subjecting our research activities to this question is, in fact, the first step in changing our participation and practices into those that our conception of education proposes. If we are successful in this, we shall engage in learning which is transformational for us, and simultaneously we shall have profound effects on the learning that goes on in the classroom and school communities of which each of us is also a participant member. It is through such 'bottom-up' transformation of the institutions in which we work, we believe, that the reform of education can be most effectively achieved.

Conclusion

In all three communities — classroom, school and research team — discourse is an essential tool for2 collaborative activity. But, because it is taken for granted, it is rarely examined critically. In this investigation of our own modes of discourse — as practice, as research activity, and as research data — we have highlighted a possible methodology for researching into the complex links among the three communities and the consequences each has for the others. We have also sketched the potential of such an undertaking as an intentional and ongoing form of teachers' professional development. What is most significant for us about our analysis, however, is that it has led us to see that it is the dialogue about our new understandings and their implications for practice that changes the nature of our activity from research that is being done as an end in itself to research that transforms our living, learning and teaching.

Note

1   The writing of this chapter was supported by a grant from the Spencer Foundation to the Ontario Institute for Studies in Education. It is based on our presentation at the International Conference on Teacher Research, University of California, Davis, April 1995, in the preparation of which all members of the Developing Inquiring Communities in Education Project (DICEP) participated: Patrick Allen, Zoe Donoahue, Karen Hume, Monica McGlynn-Stewart, Myriam Shechter, Barbara Smith and Mary Ann Van Tassell, as well as the authors. We should like to express our gratitude to the Spencer Foundation and to the members of the DICEP team for their contributions.

References

ALLEN, W.P.B., *et al.* (in preparation) *Inquiries in the Learning and Teaching of Science* (provisional title), Toronto: Ontario Institute for Studies in Education.

BAKHTIN, M.M. (1986) *Speech Genres and other Late Essays*, Austin, University of Texas Press.

BEREITER, C. (1994) 'Implications of postmodernism for science, or, science as progressive discourse', *Educational Psychologist*, **29**, 1, pp. 3–12.

BRUNER, J.S. (1990) *Acts of Meaning*, Cambridge, MA, Harvard University Press.

COBB, P. (Ed.) (1994) 'Constructivism in mathematics and science education: An exchange', *Educational Researcher*, **23**, 7, pp. 4–23.

DEWEY, J. (1938) *Education and Experience*, New York, Collier Books.

DONOAHUE, Z. (1996) 'Collaboration, community and communication: Modes of discourse for teacher research', in DONOAHUE, Z., PATTERSON L. and VAN TASSELL, M.A. (Eds), *Research in the Classroom: Talk, Text and Inquiry*, Newark, DE, International Reading Association.

ENGESTRÖM, Y. (1991) '"Non scolae sed vitae discimus": Toward overcoming the encapsulation of school learning', *Learning and Instruction*, 1, pp. 243–59.

GALBRAITH, B., VAN TASSELL, M.A. and WELLS, G. (in press) 'Learning and teaching in the zone of proximal development (in Spanish translation)', in ALVAREZ, A. (Ed.), *Proceedings of the 'III Jornadas de Infancia Y Aprendizaje — CL&E' Conference*.

HALLIDAY, M.A.K. (1985) *Spoken and Written Language*, Geelong, Victoria, Deakin University Press (republished by Oxford University Press, 1989).

HALLIDAY, M.A.K. (1993) 'Towards a language-based theory of learning', *Linguistics and Education*, 5, 2, pp. 93–116.

KALANTZIS, M. and COPE, B. (1993) 'Histories of pedagogy, cultures of schooling', in COPE B. and KALANTZIS, M. (Eds), *The Powers of Literacy: A Genre Approach to Teaching Writing*, Pittsburgh, PA, University of Pittsburgh Press.

LAVE, J. and WENGER, E. (1991) *Situated Learning: Legitimate Peripheral Participation*, Cambridge: Cambridge University Press.

LOTMAN, Y.M. (1988) 'Text within a text', *Soviet Psychology*, 26, 3, pp. 32–51.

McGLYNN-STEWART, M. (1996) 'A language experience approach to elementary geometry', in DONOAHUE, Z., PATTERSON, L. and VAN TASSELL, M.A. (Eds), *Research in the Classroom: Talk, Text and Inquiry*, Newark, DE, International Reading Association.

OLSON, D.R. (1994) *The World on Paper*, Cambridge, Cambridge University Press.

ONTARIO MINISTRY OF EDUCATION AND TRAINING, (1993) *The Common Curriculum: Grades 1–9*, Toronto, The Queen's Printer for Ontario.

ROGOFF, B. (1994) 'Developing understanding of the idea of communities of learners', *Mind, Culture, and Activity*, 1, 4, pp. 209–29.

SCARDAMALIA, M. and BEREITER, C. (1994) 'Computer support for knowledge-building communities', *The Journal of the Learning Sciences*, 3, 3, pp. 265–83.

SHECHTER, M. (1994) *Learning Science: Children's Voices*, Monograph, Toronto, Ontario Institute for Studies in Education.

VYGOTSKY, L.S. (1978) *Mind in society*, Cambridge, MA, Harvard University Press.

VYGOTSKY, L.S. (1987) 'Thinking and speech', in RIEBER, R.W. and CARTON, A.S. (Eds), *The collected works of L.S. Vygotsky, Volume 1: Problems of General Psychology* (Trans. N. Minick), New York, Plenum.

WELLS, G. (1994) 'Text, talk and inquiry: Schooling as semiotic apprenticeship', in BIRD, N. *et al.* (Eds), *Language and Learning*, Hong Kong: Institute of Language in Education and University of Hong Kong Department of Curriculum Studies.

WELLS, G. (1995) 'Language and the inquiry-oriented curriculum', *Curriculum Inquiry*, 25, 3, pp. 233–69.

WELLS, G. and CHANG-WELLS, G.L. (in press) '"What have you learned?": Co-constructing the meaning of time', in FLOOD, J., HEATH, S.B. and LAPP, D. (Eds), *A Handbook for Literacy Educators: Research on Teaching the Communicative and Visual Arts*, New York, Macmillan.

14 Classroom-centered Research at Chulalongkorn University Language Institute

Anchalee Chayanuvat and Duangta Lukkunaprasit (Thailand)

It is not easy for English language teachers like us to become researchers using quantitative methods. Most of the time, we are bogged down by numbers upon numbers and to interpret a table full of unfamiliar data and terms is unimaginable. In brief, to most language teachers, research is something beyond them and therefore there is no direct effect on classroom teaching.

How We Got Interested in Classroom-centered Research (CCR)

We were first exposed to qualitative research when we attended a workshop conducted by Professor Wolcott, a renowned figure in this area, in November, 1992 at Kasetsart University, Bangkok, Thailand. He presented the various methods one might use in order to collect data, how data can be reorganized and how conclusions are derived. Through this kind of research we study phenomena that cannot be measured in terms of statistical analysis. He asked us to first start with a case study in order to get a better understanding of how the interviewing method could be carried out effectively. It was fortunate that we followed his recommendation: to pursue an experience under an experienced supervisor would be the most valuable lesson.

Due to the fact that not much time was available since it was a workshop assignment, we decided to do two case studies together: *K's Story: A Miniature Case Study* on a good student and *My Undaunted Low Achiever* on a weak student whose pseudonym is Suda. The approach and data organization of these two case studies followed the model of '*Adequate Schools and Inadequate Education: The Life History of a Sneaky Kid*' (copyright by the Council on Anthropology and Education, 1983). The topic of investigation was their learning strategies because we wanted to know what differences there were and what made one proficient in English while one was very weak. We did our studies separately but we used the same methods: (semi-)structured interviews. We tried to be good interviewers by getting our informant to speak up as much as possible. Duangta also got her informant to orally answer a questionnaire on learning strategies.

Figure 14.1: Summary of two case studies

K	Suda
enjoys extra classes	doesn't enjoy extra classes
keeps a vocabulary notebook	doesn't keep a vocabulary notebook
reads newspapers and other reading sources	doesn't read newspapers and other reading sources
develops effective learning strategies on her own	cannot develop effective learning strategies on her own
gets family support	gets family support

After the two case studies had been completed, we presented them to the workshop group with Professor Wolcott as the chairperson. He provided many useful comments. Later we presented it again to a group of teachers at CULI in a session we had organized to introduce an ethnographic approach in TEFL, and in order that other teachers could have a chance to meet and talk to Professor Wolcott in person. Most of our staff seemed to be convinced that doing research using qualitative methods could probably be another way of doing research, since most language teachers like to observe and reflect. They could probably do this more effectively than using quantitative methods. However, Prof. Wolcott emphasized that we should not rely on data from only one source, and we should countercheck the reliability of the data from various sources or another mode of data collection.

The summary of our two case studies (Lukkunaprasit and Chayanuvat, 1993) is shown in Fig. 14.1. Soon after we were invited to give a talk at another university on our studies which we combined into one study entitled *'The Making of an Ideal EFL Student'*, which received positive feedback. Our work was later published in the *Journal of Language and Linguistics*, Department of Linguistics, Faculty of Liberal Arts, Thammasart University. After that we surveyed more literature in the area. We found that the more we read, the more we were interested in the questions. You find that other people have done a great deal in the field, and it is enjoyable to read their research. For example, Carter and Leask (1994) studied how an ESL Japanese student developed her fast rate of language acquisition during an eight-week course. Through interviews and the student's journal, the student was found to be a very determined and ambitious person who employed a number of strategies outside the classroom such as reading newspapers, watching TV, keeping a vocabulary book and taking every opportunity to converse in English. Besides, the student constantly evaluated her own learning and requested for new strategies from the teacher.

Another example is Cohen's survey (1987) with 217 students who were studying in different courses which involved writing papers and receiving the teacher feedback on them. A brief, yet informative, questionnaire regarding the form and substance of teacher feedback and the ways in which learners dealt with it was used and the students' verbal reports as to what they were doing when they were responding to teachers' comments were analyzed. Part of the results indicated clearly that making a mental note of the teacher's comments is the most popular strategy of processing feedback among students. However, those self-rated poorer writers tended to rewrite their papers.

From How *Languages are Learned* (Lightbown and Spada, 1993), it seems to be an accepted fact that a good language learner has characteristics that can be attributed to five main factors: motivation, aptitude, personality, intelligence and learning style. It is interesting to learn from research findings into the role of intelligence that it plays a crucial part in the formal study of a language such as writing and vocabulary study but is not likely to influence the development of oral communication skills.

The interest in teacher research prompted Duangta to undertake another small project based on her classroom, investigating how 'dictogloss' can improve her students' confidence in writing, and how much rewriting their written work can help improve their writing ability (Lukkunaprasit, 1995). She successfully combined her classroom-based research into her teaching through which teacher and students gained. That left a tremendous impact on how we look at our classrooms. We now realize that the classroom is one inexhaustible source of information. We can obtain numerous ideas about TEFL from the classroom and if we set up some guidelines to follow strictly, using the research methods that we learnt from visiting experts in the field, and from the books we have read, our study would undoubtedly be a research project in its own right.

Our First Collaborative Effort in Classroom Research

Our first collaborative effort related to classroom study started when there was a question as to whether we should provide Foundation English II, of which the objective is to teach academic reading and writing, for a number of Thai students exempted from the first English course. Each year a group of first year Chulalonghorn University students with very high scores in English in the National Entrance Examination sit for an exemption test (English is a subject at pre-university level in Thailand). Only a small number, about 1 per cent of the 4000 first-year students, are usually exempted from Foundation English I. They then have to wait for one semester to do Foundation English II offered to the majority of students in the second semester.

As we are moving into the age of globalization where English becomes increasingly important, CULI would like to produce a new batch of graduates who are highly competent in English. If we could provide them with an FE II course immediately, we could reinforce the language skill(s) at which they are good, and address those in which they are weak as soon as possible. This would be more easily done because the class would be homogeneous in terms of their language ability, which is ideal for teaching, in our view. Thus, our classroom research was conducted primarily to investigate the profiles of this group of students to confirm our assumption that their language ability is above that expected of students enrolling in the first course, as well as to have an insight into their learning strategies. This research would then portray the ability level of the students in the four language skills. This would help determine whether it is worth arranging one section to accommodate them — and whether this will lead to any academic gains for the students.

We regard our classroom research as collaborative because the situation, in which we both had very tight schedules, required us to share the teaching of this class. In this way we planned and revised every step of this project together.

Our research tools to gather background information concerning students' study of English were two sets of questionnaires, one is meant for the students, and the other for their parents. These sets of questionnaires were given out and collected within the first two weeks. During the course, apart from the normal written assignments at the end of the units in the workbook, journal writing was required of them once every week. Students were aware that their journals would be used as our research data. Through these means we hope to judge and help to improve their writing ability, which still needs to be improved even though their other language skills are good. Through their journals, we could also gather information which is pedagogically interesting, for example, their learning strategies, their attitudes towards learning English, their comments on the workbook we use as the core material, and their opinions on the course specially arranged for them as a whole. After the mid-term exam the students were asked to do the FE I Mid-term test to confirm whether they were able to gain high scores on that paper without having to study the course.

Towards the end of the course, Wongsothorn's questionnaire (1993) which is based on the learning strategy inventory of Oxford (1990) was administered to collect more details about their learning strategies. The information we got from this questionnaire would counterbalance that gathered from the first two sets, and the students' journals. Another element of this classroom study was our observation of the class and keeping notes of what we observed in our own journals, written after every class we taught. Our deliberate observations led us to revise some of our planned steps to incorporate more oral activities in our teaching because students could read and finish each unit very quickly, and had almost no problems in finishing the reading activities. We even managed to include two oral sessions with a native English speaker for them, using the time meant for their self study in the SALC (Self-Access Learning Center). Our students had also 'projects' to do outside the class, e.g., reading an interesting story from 'Drama in Real Life' in the Reader's Digest. In the last session the class was video-recorded while the students were telling the stories they had read to the teacher and their friends, and also while they were reporting the opinions of 'the public' (i.e., their friends from various faculties) on certain topics. The recording gave an insight into the students' speaking ability. Also, watching this video recording urged us to include more interaction between the teacher and students in our teaching of another special group in the following semester.

We evaluated the students' language abilities using the Australian Second

Table 14.1: Students' language skills (based on ASLPR)

Name	Listening Level	Speaking Level	Reading level	Writing Level
Acha	5	5	5	5
Nat	5	4+	5	4+
San	3	3+	3	3
Knit	3+	3+	3	3
Auma	3	3	3	3
Pranit	2+	3	3	3
Prem	2+	2	3	2
Porn	2+	2	3	2
Nareu	2+	3	3	3
Apit	2+	3	3	2

Note: The level of language ability starts from 0 to 5.
0 — indicates the student's very low language ability and 5 indicates the student's language ability which is as high as that of an educated native speaker. Both Acha and Nat had been educated abroad for many years and were fluent in all the four language skills.

Table 14.2: Reflections of abilities through a variety of measurements

No.	Name	Grade Point Average of Pre-U Level	Entrance Exam Results (100)	Exemption Test Results* T-score	FE I Mid-Term Results (80 marks = 40%)		FE II Grade
					Raw score	%	
1	Acha	4	90	67	74	37	A
2	Nat	4	93	77	73	36.5	A
3	San	4	89	75	65	32.5	A
4	Kanit	4	83	60	70	35	A
5	Auma	4	79	51	65	32.5	A
6	Pranit	4	85	59	73	36.5	A
7	Prem	4	74	57	65	32.5	A
8	Porn	4	72	51	53	26.5	A
9	Nareu	4	78	58	68	34.2	A
10	Apit	4	83	51	54	27	B

* The exemption test results were from Paper 1 only. (Paper 1 contains 100 objective items.)

Language Proficiency Rating (ASLPR) Scale and we show the students' language profiles in Table 14.1. Table 14.2 reflects their language ability through a variety of measurements. In our report we refer to the students by their pseudonyms. On the whole, the students were fluent in the reading skills. The areas which needed to be improved were their speaking and writing skills. As for the students' learning strategies, we gathered very interesting aspects of this area, and present them in Table 14.3 and Table 14.4.

Besides these data we also obtained information from student journals, which we enjoyed reading. Below are short descriptions of the language learning strategies of some of the students.

Table 14.3: How the Students Learn English outside the Classroom (based on the questionnaires for students and parents and part of their journals)

Learning Strategies	No. of Students (10)
reading (newspapers, magazines, novels, short stories, comics, cookbooks and labels on packages)	10
watching movies or (cable) TV programmes (with soundtracks or English subtitles)	9
listening to songs	5
having pen pals	5
having extra tuition at a language institute (e.g., British Council and a private institution)	5
playing scrabble/crosswords	3
listening to recorded teaching materials	2
looking up difficult words	2
trying to translate interesting articles, songs, posters and ads, etc. (into Thai or English)	2
playing games in newspapers and magazines; answering a quiz	2
listening to news in English on radio	1
self study through 'Follow Me'	1
trying to talk and think in English	1
guessing meaning	1
trying to use certain words in everyday life	1

Table 14.4: Wongsothorn's questionnaire on language learning strategies (based on Oxford's Strategy Inventory for Language Learning)

PART 1	No. of Students (9)*				
	A	B	C	D	E
You prepare yourself for your English lessons by:					
1. skimming lessons in advance to get the main ideas, the organization and check if you have any prior knowledge about them.		1	3	5	
2. finding the meaning of words that you come across by making guesses, using dictionaries or rote memory.	5	2	1	1	
3. revising/memorizing what you have learnt by making notes in a tabular form or drawings.				4	5
4. having a diary for writing down useful or interesting information about English.		1		4	4
5. trying to grasp the main ideas when conversing with others.	2	5	1		1
6. trying to notice the native speaker's pronunciation, the use of expressions, sentence structure and gestures when you interact with native speakers.	3	3	2	1	
7. making preparations before working on language activities.	1	2	3	2	1
8. determining the objectives of your language learning in advance.	2	1	2	3	1
9. collecting language errors.		1	6	1	1
10. looking for language errors.	2	3	4		

• One student loved listening to English songs and when she found any interesting songs or articles she would try to translate them into Thai. This is another way to learn English. When alone she tried to talk and think in English.

Table 14.4: *(Cont'd)*

PART 2	No. of Students (9)				
	A	B	C	D	E
You control and manage your language learning by:					
1. practising pronunciation and speaking correctly according to the tape and correcting yourself.		1	3	4	1
2. asking for suggestions on language usage.		2	5	2	
3. trying to revise your answers when you know they are wrong.	5	3	1		
4. checking if you use the language correctly from others' facial expressions.	2	2	3	2	
5. working on a language test to evaluate your own ability.		3	3	3	
6. reading to revise and correct your own writing.	2	5	2		
7. studying the teacher's feedback on your work.	2	5	2		
8. remembering correct and appropriate language for further use.	2	7			
9. trying to eliminate grammatical errors and improve the four skills.	4	4	1		

PART 3	No. of Students (9)				
	A	B	C	D	E
You practise English by:					
1. discussing with friends or native speakers when you do not understand the activity.	1	4	2	1	1
2. exchanging viewpoints with others on language learning.	1	2	2	3	1
3. participating in language activities such as singing and acting in plays.		1	3	2	3
4. joining a ceremony for native speakers or regular users of English such as Singaporeans.		1		1	7
5. frequently asking questions while making a conversation to show interest.		1	3	5	
6. expressing interest in other people's thoughts and feelings while talking.	2	2	5		
7. showing willingness to assist when requested.	4	3	1		1
8. expressing sympathy through language and facial expressions.		3	5		1
9. contacting native speakers by having pen-pals, etc.	4	1	1	1	2
10. going to receptions where the use of English is required.	1		1	2	5

* One student was always absent from the class towards the end of the course. So the number of students who were present and answered the questionnaire was only 9.
Note: A = always, B = usually, C = sometimes, D = rarely, E = never

• Another student enjoyed playing crosswords and English games in newspapers. At home, she played scrabble with her sisters and always 'cheated' them by looking up words and gained more vocabulary.

• A third was interested in reading newspaper headlines and labels on packages of chocolate and sweets because she wanted to know the ingredients. When approaching exams, when she was in high school, she made a vocabulary list to revise the words she had learnt.

• When unsure of the meanings of some words, especially those which seemed familiar, this student preferred to guess their meanings. In some cases, though, she looked them up and memorized them, trying to use them more often.

• Sometimes, another student tried to watch 'difficult films' on politics and history. He considered this as his hobby through which he could improve his listening ability.

These students employed a variety of learning strategies, most of which are suggested or discussed by Rubin and Thompson (1982) and Oxford (1990). They not only learn English inside the classroom but also outside it. However, we also found certain strategies a few, or many of them, never or rarely use. Among them are skimming, note taking, keeping a diary for writing down interesting information about English, practising speaking with recorded materials, working on a language test to evaluate oneself, and asking questions during a conversation to show interest. For this reason we feel it is our duty to point out to the students the importance of some of these activities, such as skimming and note-taking, which are essential reading skills and need to be practised over and over.

The presentation of our classroom-centered research was well received at an International Teacher Research Conference held at University of California (Davis) in April 1995. It also had an impact on CULI's teaching programs. The findings of the case study have helped rationalize the offering of a special class for such a group of students in this academic year (1995).

In the next academic year, a special class for the exempted students will be arranged and included in our regular teaching programs. Among other things, we have recommended more emphasis on speaking and writing, inclusion of external reading materials which are more difficult and challenging, and exploitation of students' learning activities outside class in our English program e.g., an oral discussion following the watching of an assigned film. We also suggested that we should make the students aware of the learning skills that have helped them better their English, and also encourage them to develop other learning skills not many of them think very useful or necessary. Such learning skills include skimming, making notes in a tabular form, or determining the objectives of their language learning in advance.

What We Learnt From Our First CCR

Collaborative vs. Individual

There are many good points about doing collaborative research. You will never be alone for, when in doubt, you can always consult each other. When combing the library for books you want, there are at least two to do this; you save a lot of time and effort. Besides, you will be double checked all the time. Where you fail to be clear, your partner will notice it. You and your partner will complement each other with strengths in different areas, in addition, you begin to trust each other. Having done a lot of work together, you can set up a well-organized system where both are satisfied. Having achieved this, a group might then embark on a more difficult research project with confidence.

Classroom — A Source of Professional Development

In trying to collect data from our own classroom, we indirectly develop ourselves professionally because we will see and are aware of things we have never seen or known before. In other words, we seem to look at things in a new light. We are inspired to investigate what is wrong and why some activities do not work well in class. We are now more able to look at things like this with a researcher's eyes. If all teachers are engaged in classroom-based research projects, we are sure they can help improve the learning and teaching of English. Research will not be a forbidden word any longer. It is an area we as practitioners have the utmost right to enter. Actually, we should have a part in improving what and how we teach a foreign language. We totally agree that the knowledge gained through classroom research would influence teacher's decision-making. The process of research equips them with techniques for self-evaluation and with the knowledge and skills for ongoing renewal of their teaching practice (Burton and Mickan, 1992). Thus, it is something we have to do because as teachers we know our students and our class best, so why wait for others to conduct research in it.

Developing Professional Pride

In more ways than one, research provides job satisfaction. Teaching, no matter how much you like it, will start to be boring after some time and you might feel so fed up with it, that there is no incentive to continue. A teacher of English should also be an authority of a kind and he or she should have something to say with pride and confidence. From a research project, you might get plenty of information to talk about, for your presentations and your papers, and this information can be put to use in your future teaching.

Insight into our Highly Proficient EFL Students

Before doing this research project, we know what good students are like from years of teaching experience. However, we got to know our students even better and became closer to them through research. We came to know each particular one well, and why and how this student is different from that student. We remember important facts about them: what their parents and former teachers say, how they speak English, what area they are strong in and what area they are weak in. From experience, we know that they are good, but from this research, we know what probably makes them better than other students.

Conclusion: What the Future Probably Holds

Having worked on our first collaborative research project, we feel more confident in our ability to research into our own classroom. We have started to see how lucky we are to be in a classroom and how challenging it is to explore it. Nonetheless, however great this enthusiasm may be, we are aware of the need to acquire more theoretical background to support our work. For us now to study literature in this area is not only one of the initial steps to follow when conducting research. It is an access to a wealth of knowledge which we can apply to help better our work. Through a two-week workshop on classroom research recently conducted by Jill Burton, who did this kind of workshop for CULI staff for the first time, we have reinforced our theoretical background concerning the classroom study and the importance of classroom discourse of texts. Examples of texts in the reading list are

- *Educational Action Research*, an international journal published by Cambridge University Press,
- *Focus on the Language Classroom* by Dick Allwright and Kathleen Bailey (1991) and
- *The Action Research Planner* by Kemmis and Mc Taggart (1988).

Now both of us are waiting for another chance to conduct another classroom investigation and this interest might extend to some of our colleagues, who also came up with research questions during the workshop.

Since we both have a common interest in learning strategies, we should like to find an answer to the question of whether the strategies which proved successful with a proficient language learner would work with a poor language learner. It will be fruitful if we can apply our knowledge acquired from our earlier work to improve the language ability of a poor learner. If it is possible, perhaps the next effort will be collaborative on a larger scale. We may recruit our colleagues who teach the same course to be our co-researchers. Hopefully, we can combine our local experience, acquired through teaching Thai learners for years, with the universally accepted theoretical background in second language teaching in the form of collaborative research. We expect that this can be done without interrupting the process of teaching and learning, which we believe is also characteristic of classroom research. Finally, we anticipate that we will be able to grow professionally ourselves, apart from being able to improve our poor language learners.

References

ALLWRIGHT, D. and BAILEY, K. (1991) *Focus on the Language Classroom*, Cambridge: Cambridge University Press.

CARTER, S. and LEASK, B. (1994) 'A study of a successful second language learner', in BURTON, J. (Ed.), *Perspectives on the Classroom*, November 1994, pp. 105–20, Applied Linguistics, University of South Australia. Hyde Park Press.

COHEN, A.D. (1987) 'Student Processing Feedback on Their Compositions', in WENDEN, A. and RUBIN, J. (Eds), *Learner Strategies in Language Learning*, London, Prentice Hall International, pp. 59–67.

KEMMIS, S. and McTAGGART, R. (1988) *The Action Research Planner*, (3rd. ed.) Geelong, Victoria: Deakin University Press.

LIGHTBOWN, P. and SPADA, N. (1993) *How Language are Learned*, Hong Kong, Oxford University Press.

LUKKUNAPRASIT, D. (1995) 'Creating Students' Confidence in Writing', *Journal of Language and Linguistics*, **13**, 1, pp. 76–97, Bangkok, Department of Linguistics, Faculty of Liberal Arts, Thammasart University.

LUKKUNAPRASIT, D. and CHAYANUVAT, A. (1993) 'The Making of an Ideal EFL Student', *Journal of Language and Linguistics*, **11**, 2, pp. 82–105, Bangkok, Department of Linguistics, Faculty of Liberal Arts, Thammasart University.

OXFORD, R.L. (1990) *Language Learning Strategies: What Every Teacher Should Know*, New York, Newbury House/Harper & Row.

RUBIN, J. and THOMPSON, I. (1982) *How to Be a More Successful Language Learner*, Boston, MA, Heinle and Heinle Publishers.

WONGSOTHORN, A. (1993) *Guidelines for Language Test Writing.* (Unabridged) Bangkok, Chulalongkorn University Language Institute.

15 The Professional Journal, Genres and Personal Development in Higher Education

Christine O'Hanlon (United Kingdom)

The use of teachers' journals in professional development is widespread and varied. The journals can be used for reflection, or introspection and for recording events and feelings. The journals may be written solely with the author in mind, or alternatively for a wider professional audience, possibly for colleagues, a tutor, or an assessor in courses in higher education contexts. Journals are often viewed as autobiographical writing but professional journals differ in focus and in substance from personal diaries because of the different contexts in which they are being used, which in this chapter is the professional development of teachers and other associated educational professionals through higher education. Within a specific professional context i.e., action research based school development, the journal writing focuses upon an 'issue' or 'concern' under investigation in the local context of the school or local authority, or in the wider context nationally or internationally. The journal is used deliberately to foster in teachers a greater self-awareness, greater deliberation, and professional reflection. The journal when used by teachers on in-service courses which encourage change in practice, enables teachers to perceive their views of the situation in both a retrospective and prospective manner. The professionals can record their views of the concrete reality in the present, their significance in relation to past events and their implications for future planning. Then later, after their engagement in action to improve the professional situation, they can reflect on earlier writing and attempt to discover their own pre-suppositions and inherent expectations and assumptions about the situation. The journal forms a basis for self-reflection; it also allows the professionals to be self-indulgent, to express themselves freely on paper and thus create a permanent record of their professional endeavours.

The use of journals is particularly beneficial when used in association with attempts to change and improve teachers' practice through professional development based on practitioner research e.g., action research. It enables teachers to find a voice for their concerns and to unite their personal and professional values and perceptions through reflection on their activities.

Goodson (1991) expresses a similar view when he states that 'The teacher's life style both in and outside school impact on views of teaching and on practice'. He emphasizes the view that life outside the school influences in many ways the practices of teaching within the school. It is problematic to see the school life as a separate existence beyond the influences of the everyday experiences of its participants.

There are many courses in higher education which deliberately focus on the professional investigation of schools and classrooms with the aim of developing teachers' autonomy and self-awareness in their practice: A professional autonomy which is expected to lead to the amelioration of habitual or unreflective practices which hinder the creative development of the professionals in their roles. These courses are providing opportunities for intra-professional dialogue through reflexive practice-based research. They are provided in numerous colleges, polytechnics, and universities and are normally developed within an award-bearing context.

Professionals who undertake higher degree courses (these are predominantly teachers and school-linked professionals) are encouraged, but not compelled, to keep a journal for the course duration (1–4 years). The writing of a journal supports and informs the research, and planned action, through a reflective exploration of the professional issues and concerns being investigated.

The keeping of a course journal allows the deliberate dialogic process of personal/professional writing to provide the basis for self-reflection and inter-professional dialogue between course participants. It also enables intra-professional dialogue between participants with the same professional background on the course, and inter-professional dialogue between all the course participants and other professionals with whom they are in contact during their investigations. The course tutor is yet another professional who participates in this active dialogue. All participants write in a journal which encourages them to understand themselves, their actions and values in everyday routine situations, which they may share with course participants in 'collegial groups'. This is the source of the evidence and analysis of the data referred to in this chapter.

The understanding of the self in the professional context is the primary aim of writing a journal during the course. This can be best achieved through the development of reflective commentary about the professional's practice which is written regularly in a journal. This commentary becomes a dialogue with the self which may be extended to 'chosen others'. The dialogue with oneself enables professionals to become aware of their professional identity, of what their role does to influence this identity, and to understand how they view themselves in their professional lives. Nias (1989) has shown how important it is for teachers to know and understand themselves in their teaching. The writing of a journal allows the person to explore the many different perspectives of realities experienced in education. It allows teachers to record what is happening to them, what the significance of the events are to them, and how they influence their professional intentions and actions. In doing this at a specific level of awareness they can challenge hidden assumptions in their work and find a means to reinterpret their actions. By writing from their own 'lake of consciousness' they can write about their present view of the world which will change on rereading and will inform and reinform them each time to support their reconstruction.

There is a critical view in a post structural context, that a dual process occurs in the act of writing — that of the construction of the words by the writer and the deconstruction and reconstruction by the reader. The reality of the text resides in the interaction between the writer and the reader — but in journal writing the writer and the reader are the same person — it functions as part of a whole communication event that occurs when the created narrative text is opened up to a wider audience, then to be understood by different individuals. The writer is continually reading what has been written previously in order to develop the ideas further. Journal writing becomes a kind of silent dialogue which can be made available to a wider audience when appropriate.

Teachers are recording their own processes of thinking and development for themselves. In the future this can serve as an archival resource of their own professional development. It encourages reflection which may become reflexive and also opens the possibility for new ways of thinking and theorizing. The theme of knowing oneself through a dialogue with a text is supported by Gadamer (1976): 'To understand a text is to understand oneself in a kind of dialogue' (p. 76).

The professional carries out an inner dialogue or conversation with themselves. They are not merely logging factual events in their journals but learning how to benefit from understanding their professional activities. Each professional understands events in their lives in a manner that speaks and finds answers in the words of their own personal language. They learn to understand their own lives by discovering their interaction with, and making sense of, the lives of others. They are involved in an ongoing, questioning dialectic in search of meaning. For Berthoff (1981) writing a personal journal enables the writers to become aware of themselves as meaning makers by following the 'dialogic-action,' 'inner dialogue' or 'dialectical thinking' inherent in critical consciousness and meaning making i.e., reformulating questions and answers, reconsideration and reflection.

The process of journal writing allows for the emergence and development of sustained critical thought. It helps the professional to modify, develop or criticize their own activities through the recognition of inherent values. In writing they can discover their own ideas, express them, rehearse them and evaluate them. The process of keeping a professional journal is a process of self-evaluation. It is also a reflective practice which has been advocated by Dewey (1963) and later by Schon (1983).

The actual journals take many forms in practice, this is because, in the higher degree courses, they are the teacher's personal reflexive record of the current investigation, and are normally supplementary to the completion of a case study, which is their primary research concern. The written case study forms the dissertation or thesis which is the subject of assessment, therefore the journal often merely forms an appendix for reference to the main study. However, it may become the foundation of the thesis itself, if it is sufficiently developed at a reflexive and integrated level.

As well as writing the journal for themselves, teachers are encouraged to share selections from the journal with course participants/colleagues when they meet at regular university seminars. Each professional may use his/her 'time' in the seminar to share his/her thinking on their educational issues and concerns with the group.

The group consists of colleagues and fellow professionals following the same or a similar research focus. They may wish to share aspects of the journal in the sessions to elicit responses from colleagues for feedback or critique. If the journal is not literally read out to others during the session for further discussion, it may be used as background evidence about a situation in the school, or a critical incident that needs unpacking, with help, during the seminar. Colleagues can ask questions and give feedback to help each other to uncover hidden assumptions. Collegial feedback is essential when, or if, the teacher is considering taking action — this often needs some consideration, challenge and debate.

The whole journal, or selections, may be submitted as substantiating evidence for any change in practice referred to in the main case study. There is complete freedom for the professional to write what and how they wish. This leads to a variety of professional practices which I will attempt to identify. The actual process of writing itself is not a problem if the professionals are clear about what they are doing and what they want to say. Where to start is often the first problem that is faced. This can be resolved by the proposition that there is some issue in the professional's practice which needs further investigation or improvement. The broad idea of the identification of an 'issue' becomes clearer and more focused when the professionals start to observe, or collect evidence from, their real practices. The teachers/professionals then develop their awareness surrounding their concerns and issues, and devise a plan for improving the situation within the classroom, school or wider professional context. In the process of investigation through action research, the professional collects data, reviews and analyzes the data and either resolves to, or actually takes, certain action to throw a clearer light on the situation. This action is reviewed and further analyzed through a process of action steps planned to improve the professional's practice (Elliott, 1991).

My experience working with teachers keeping journals is that every professional in his/her own spontaneous manner starts to write a journal in their preferred intuitive personal/idiosyncratic style. Some may adopt an open and free personal style, whereas others may write in a more formal and informative manner, passing on the essential information to the reader in a detached and definitive manner. It is more than just a question of audience, there is either an intuitive feel for the writing process and 'opening up' to yourself on paper which involves trusting yourself, your ideas, thoughts and feelings, or it is a minimalist response to a request from the course tutor/supervisor which becomes an exercise in the simple recording of events without unnecessary embellishment. If it becomes the latter there is little chance of the writing becoming reflexive.

Sara begins her journal writing in an informing narrative style, more in the style of writing a log, in which she refers to herself in a detached manner. She begins with an initial description of the context for her 'issue' which she wishes to investigate. She writes in a formal, descriptive manner. She appears to be writing for another reader other than herself;

> My class parents are being interviewed this week with regard to their children's performance so far on verbal reasoning tests. Parents are normally

interviewed between tests, and teachers would also discuss results and the child's performance on practice tests in school with the parents. I passed on a number of children to another class.

Professionals begin to use the journal as a background for the more detailed investigation of their practice. They use it as a log or to describe significant events and generally record their school lives according to their own priorities. They are given no specific instructions about keeping the journal, therefore there is a variety of genre which characterizes each writer's personal mode of expression. The narrative-descriptive genre is predominant. However, the genre does not have to be formal; it may be casual, conversational, poetic, or one liners. It may vary from week to week. A natural personalized writing style seems to emerge individually during the journaling process over a period of time, which is important to reflect a more personal involvement in the total professional development experienced through the research. I would describe the very early attempts undertaken by professionals as predominantly detached from themselves and as descriptive i.e., setting the scene. The teachers begin by describing their situation for the reader and simply log facts and events. However, the professionals who successfully initiate change in their practice, who influence their situations in a confident and competent manner, are the persons who write the more introspective, open and reflexive journals.

The professionals who experience contradictions in their practice, who analyze the conflicting evidence which is exposed, who confront the issues which emerge and attempt to resolve them in a sensitive and positive way, inevitably involve themselves personally in the process. Taking risks in the professional world involves dilemma resolution and a search for a deeper understanding of the surface and immediate evidence. Critical self-examination is a necessity in the process of professional autonomy and professional realization, which implies a personal engagement in the professional process. Strengths and weaknesses, which appear within the situation, may on closer examination, prove to reside within the person him/herself, as the journey of self discovery may reveal.

It is a process of professional development from unconscious actions to self-awareness and critical self-examination which is supported and accelerated through the reflective writing in a journal. Yet how does the professional make progress to self-evaluation from the mere logging of facts or the description of events in the school and classroom?

Is there a developmental process involved in the evolution of reflexive writing or are there professionals who are naturally reflective and self-aware, who can write about themselves in the educational reality in an honest and authentic manner without direction?

I have analysed a large number of professional journals and have found that there are four spontaneous modes or initial genre of journal practice as follows:

1 Report writing — is the logging of events in a factual manner. It is the recording of observational data, or the narrative description of facts and events in the professional situation.

2   Interpretive writing — includes reporting and also involves the writer in the explanation of events. Interpretive writing interprets the events in the context of the person's intentions and purposes of action. There is explication of significant factors for meaning. This may involve feelings and responses to events encountered during the day. The writer explains his/her understanding of the incidents and events referred to in the text.

3   Deliberative writing — includes reporting and interpretation. It involves conjecture and deduction as well as description and explanation. It is reflective and interactional. It involves the writer in deliberation and self-evaluation, and refers to retrospective and prospective ideas and their consequences or (un)expected outcomes. There is evidence of reflexivity. The writer attempts to explain his/her own responses to the situation involving emotions, judgments and intentions. The writer shows self-awareness and willingness to criticize his/herself, and aspects of the situation under investigation.

4   Integrated writing — includes all of the three above i.e., reporting, interpreting, and deliberating, yet moves beyond them into writing which fully integrates the personal and the professional aspects of situational understanding. Professional action and events are interpreted and analyzed in a holistic manner without distinction between the private and the personal domain. The writer does not deliberately hold back or censor his/her thoughts and ideas. There is integrity in the purpose of the writing i.e., to explore aspects of the situation in an authentic manner. All the different views and perspectives are recorded or defined in an attempt to fully understand the situation in an honest and integrated way. The person becomes fully reflexive in his/her writing and attempts to understand the situation from a critical, self-analytic viewpoint. S/he integrates personal values and assumptions with professional action.

The four writing genres refer implicitly to modes of thinking and reflection which range in depth from a mere description of educational events to a more profound self-aware and evaluative mode. The four genres are not necessarily exclusive of each other, but indicate a degree or level of professional identification with a reflexive process within journalizing. I will now develop this model of the four genres of journal writing with reference to actual journal material written by the teachers.

Report Writing

After singing, children helped me to get the new water trough filled (it's called a water playcentre). Mrs D. is at coffee. Got aprons on and everyone had a great time playing with the water. I was just supervising mainly keeping an eye on E, who was standing at one end of the trough. Mrs D returned. She joined in watching and talking to the children as they played. Children fascinated by water-wheel and plastic dams and using water pump.

The teacher writes in a reporting manner, she describes the classroom situation in a concise and factual manner. The description is both objective and subjective. It involves herself too, but not her responses, feelings or judgment about the events. It is written for herself as a bald record/log, or for another person as basic information of what has occurred in the situation. She is reporting.

Interpretive Writing

I stayed with the first group and gave them some assistance to get started and then moved on to the boys' group. There I found that the boys could not really get started, they had to list the stages of building the house, and their discussion was pretty pathetic. I had to encourage them to think about each stage and then go on to the next one. Perhaps the next time they will find it more relaxing, and not be so reticent . . .

Next time I will try giving each group the same topic to discuss. Then we can have a general discussion on the points raised by each group. Then all the children should learn from the discussion time.

This teacher describes her work with the classroom groups. She uses evaluative terms about the pupils' attempts at discussion i.e., pathetic. She describes her own efforts and her intentions for future action. She surmises about the pupils' possible responses to her plans. She interprets pupils' responses in relation to her actions. She is using reporting, explanation and interpretation. She is making decisions for future action based on the evidence of the situation. She is writing with situational interpretation and personal understanding. She is interpreting.

Deliberative Writing

My organization was very poor. I'm wondering whether I should keep particular groups for one week or change them around. I have to choose their activity otherwise all the children go to the sand or the house. I think I need to ask a colleague to observe me in action and tell me what I am achieving in the groups. Is it more play or more learning through play? I need to focus my teaching on one group at a time and concentrate on language, maths or science during that time. At present I am too worried about being in control of everything all of the time. I can't allow the pupils free exploration. It is too disruptive to my view of quiet learning. I never realized before how little I thought about these things in my teaching. I am now really trying to find something that works for the children and for my teaching too. I need to challenge myself daily on this course, and that's not easy!

I just feel I want to get a few thoughts down on paper. I feel that I am pulled between doing this course and doing my best for the children in school. My dilemma is related to the fact that we are having a general inspection soon and I am doing my best to change my teaching methods — to improve the situation for the children. This term I am really trying to extend their play time, organize group teaching and do more conversation and drama. Will I ever feel totally satisfied with my school work?

This primary school teacher is describing activities in the classroom e.g., her organization of the play groups. She is reporting and interpreting the situation in her own way, i.e., she sees a contradiction between her teaching for improvement of pupil learning and what she feels is expected for a general inspection. Comments are not factually based on present events, she has moved beyond reporting and interpretation to make deductions about her own activities. She uses conjecture about the consequences of her actions. She deliberates about her school work. She writes in a personal idiom with reference to her feelings. She is aware of her own personal change in the process of professional development. There is evidence of self-evaluation, deliberation and reflexive thinking. Her audience is primarily herself but she shows reflexivity in the questioning of herself. She is deliberating.

Integrated Writing

Looking back through my work on the school discipline policy I realized that I presumed a lot. Knowing the pupils in the group I assumed that all the teachers were having discipline problems with them but I never presented evidence of this. Did I mention in any part of my journal earlier that any of this group was on report or on detention? Did I see any form of discipline being used on the group? No! Surely I was operating on my own, independently of the school policy. Did the children realize that I wasn't using the system and did I, and my teaching suffer as a result?

I believe that my action research will only be of genuine aid and assistance to me in my teaching, if it is carried out on the basis of the full extent of my own honesty (even if it does hurt and often shows me in a very bad light), when describing my situation, in investigating and analyzing. Consequently, I constantly remind myself to be open in my thinking, by deciding before I make any journal entry that I must above all else try to be honest. This does not mean that I deliberately lie, but I am human and unless I challenge my motives continually I know it would be tempting to leave skeletons safely in the cupboard.

This secondary teacher is reflecting about her past writing, and her attempts to understand the school discipline policy. She identifies her own omissions in thinking and questions herself about them. She understands her own self-development through her action research, and can evaluate her own position now as being a stronger more informed professional than previously. This teacher is reflexive in relation to her own problem of being totally honest and authentic in her investigation and analysis, which must, she believes, involve her personally in a reappraisal of her motives in writing a journal. She is committed to her professional role, she feels she must be totally present in her work and this involves an honest appraisal of all her motives, both personal and professional. She resolves to undertake her investigation and reflection through action research in a tough manner, even though it may be painful for her, and reveal her in a less attractive manner to colleagues. She genuinely wants to uncover the 'truth' for herself in the professional situation.

She integrates her personal and professional attitudes in this intention. She is fully reflexive in a self-critical manner. She is self-analytical, honest and uncensored. She is holistically examining the professional situation in retrospect with an awareness of her own learning which will influence her future actions. She is living her professional contradictions and dilemmas through the definition of her own personal values and beliefs. She is integrating the previous three genres together in a reflexive manner.

The main reason for promoting journal writing in teachers' professional development is to enable teachers to effectively use their practical knowledge. The journal is a form of autobiographical writing which emancipates and frees the teacher from unreflective and constraining professional practices. I see each individual journal, its underpinning of the case study, and its sharing with colleagues, as the professional's personal endeavour for professional improvement. Dewey, too, (1963) saw personal experience as the primary source of education. As educators we can gain much from attempting to understand how teachers continue to learn and develop their own individual knowledge and professional competence through the analysis and review of their efforts to become reflexive in journal writing.

The professional, in order to develop a real self knowledge must enter into a dialogue with him/herself in the writing of the journal. This dialogue performs the function of linking the inner and the outer self, or the 'I' and the 'other' (Bakhtin, 1986). For Bakhtin too, all language is inherently dialogic, and the particular discourse is dependent upon the context in which the text must function.

Journal writing, though obviously monologic, is also dialogic in its communicative form. Each point at which the writer chooses one particular expressive genre, one example rather than another, one term rather than another, certain comparisons rather than others, is influenced by what the writer has to say and also by the needs of the reader or readers to understand. This is demonstrated in the four genres outlined above.

The journal may be written by the author for his/her readership only, or it may be written for a wider professional audience. Whichever audience is in mind, however, the person him/her self will, through the journal reading, or re-reading be presented with material that is previously completed. The thoughts and ideas have already occurred. The writing and the ideas may be deliberated upon again by the writer or by another reader. It is archival material in any context. The professional is developing and evolving a sense of identity and of self knowledge through him/her reflexive writing, particularly when it takes place within a social process as developed in higher education courses in group discourse. The person's self-awareness becomes explicit in his/her writing which can be repeatedly re-examined and reconstructed. A deeper and truer self-understanding becomes possible, especially when the writing is opened up in discussion to a wider audience. The work of G.H. Mead (1934) explores similar issues in his writing about the social nature of the constitution of the self.

Teachers attempt their professional development through journal writing in different ways, some are more authentic and self-challenging than others, using a range of genres from report writing to integrated writing. They can be brought to understand the nature and purposes of their writing through reading extracts to others in the collegial group. They can be shown the value of integrated writing through identifying different modes of writing and their functions in the process of professional development. Teachers who develop the deepest understanding and professional knowledge are those who use their journals as a form of genuine dialogue with the self, writing in a deliberative or integrated genre within a professional dimension. The dialogue forms the foundation of dialectical knowledge, where the professional develops an argument with him/herself about the truth of their beliefs and values inherent in their educational practice.

During this process, the practical actions which the teacher engages in, and their self-critical stance in the analysis of the evidence are essential to the development of real dialectic. This development can be painful and difficult at times, but it leads to clearer thinking and to intentional and deliberate change in practices. However, the journal writing and the management of its wider audience are aspects of course work that require sensitive and careful handling. Discussing the hidden assumptions and values underpinning events offers an outsider perspective to professionals and breaks the 'inner' centredness of the problems and dilemmas experienced.

In the wider journal sharing, the professional engaging in dialectic is acting as both an insider and an outsider in the deliberation of his/her intentions and actions in the professional world of education. The act of writing removes the unconscious, the unknowable or inside purpose, to the conscious, to the outside awareness of actions and events. It allows the writer the opportunity to examine his/her motivation in action and the influences, both internal and external, on professional practices. They are learning to act in the role of observers and monitors of their own practice. They are learning to evaluate their own professional roles. Holly (1989) supports this view when she writes that as teachers become consistent journal writers, they begin to observe experience as it happens, almost as outside observers.

There is evidence that teachers and other professionals are developing a risky questioning stance to their practice, which is leading to many real practical improvements in the education of children and young people in the schools concerned. The teachers who are developing their reflexive writing and keeping professional journals are becoming more confident and competent through their improved professional and self-understanding. They are involved in dialogue with themselves — the inner dialogue. They are also engaging in a social dialogue with professionals and colleagues in their search for meaning and truth — the social dialogue. And finally, they are developing new ideas through the restructuring of their past action in the rereading and reconstruction of their own texts. The discourse is emerging dialectically from the basis of personal writing in higher educational contexts.

References

BAKHTIN, M. (1986) in NYSTRAND, M. *The Structure of Written Communication*, New York, Academic Press Inc.

BERTHOFF, A. (1981) *The Making of Meaning: Metaphors, Models and Maxims for Writing Teachers*, New York, Boynton/Cook.

DEWEY, J. (1963) *Experience and Education*, New York, Macmillan.

ELLIOTT, J. (1991) *Action Research for Educational Change*, Milton Keynes, Open University Press.

GADAMER, H.G. (1976) *Philosophical Hermeneutics*, translated from the German and edited by Davis Berkeley, London, University of California Press.

GOODSON, I. (1991) 'Sponsoring the Teachers Voice: Teachers' Lives and Teacher Development', *Cambridge Journal of Education*, **21**, 1, pp. 35–45.

HOLLY, M.L. (1989) 'Reflective writing and the Spirit of Inquiry', *Cambridge Journal of Education*, **19**, 1.

MEAD, G.H. (1934) *Mind, Self and Society, from the Standpoint of a Social Behaviourist*, Chicago/London, Chicago University Press.

NIAS, J. (1989) *Primary Teachers Talking*, New York, Routledge.

SCHON, D. (1983) *The Reflective Practitioner: How Professionals Think in Action*, New York, Basic Books.

16   Gender Equity in an Elementary Classroom: The Power of Praxis in Action Research

Robyn S. Lock and Leslie Turner Minarik
(United States)

For the past nine years Leslie Minarik has participated in monthly conversations with a small group of colleagues and peers who support each other in teacher research and related school projects. This peer group has spent these years together as teacher researchers, learning to teach and to conduct research on their own teaching. Their initial work (the first six years) resulted in the publication of the book, *Teacher Research and Urban Literacy Education. Lessons and Conversations in Feminist Key* (Hollingsworth, 1994).

Leslie joined teaching and the group after leaving a career in business. The years of interaction with the peer group were helpful to Leslie in that she had gained the confidence and ability to develop and research her own teaching. She also recognized that learning to teach was an on-going process. It was through this process of inquiry that she became more knowledgeable about the process of teaching and gained a stronger sense of self worth. She learned what she needed to know to transform her practice and claim the power to teach for social change. However, for more than a year after the publication of the book, she continued to question her own practice. But it was these initial revelations through the teacher research project that led Leslie to questions relating to the relationships of playground behavior, sports and gender.

The Teaching Situation

The elementary school in which Leslie teaches is located in an urban, residential community in the North Bay Area of San Francisco. With 553 students in kindergarten through sixth grade and twenty-three credentialed teachers, the school is committed to providing the collaborative education of teachers that will support and enrich the basic program. There is a clear commitment to language arts.

The students who attend the elementary school reflect six ethnic groups: 47 per cent are Black, 10 per cent are Caucasians, 25 per cent are Hispanic, 12 per cent are Asian, less than 1 per cent are Pacific Islander, Filipino, and Native American. Thirty-eight per cent of the families within the school community are on Aid for

Dependent Children. Eighty per cent of the students qualify for free or reduced lunches. Class size averages thirty students. In addition, students at all grade levels score below other schools in the district on the Iowa Tests of Basic Skills (WCCUSD Schools Report, 1994–95).

Defining the Action Research Problem

In conversations with the group as related in the book Leslie consistently demonstrated a concern for equitable teaching practice. She stated, 'It appears that once I finally realized that the class environment was not equitable . . . I began to look at new ways to make the situation more equitable and successful for kids . . .' (Hollingsworth, 1994; p. 119). Grounded in this commitment to equity and a deep sense of the ethics of caring (see Noddings, 1984) she identified the problem of gender inequality specifically in a sport situation. She describes the situation, 'Every year I've heard it. "Well, the girls can't have the ball. They're girls"' (Hollingsworth, 1994). This discovery and her commitment to researching her own teaching helped Leslie to frame the questions which directed this action research project.

Leslie considered her reasons for the study on gender inequality within the context of sports at the American Educational Research Association annual conference in 1995:

> Over the last five years I have looked at the issue of empowerment relative to classroom power structure and the impact this has on self esteem. I have set up programs to make the discipline system more equitable and empowering. I have struggled with sharing power with regard to managing the classroom and on the question of choosing curriculum. At the back of it has been the nagging issue of gender equity. Has empowering the students as a whole improved the situation for girls in particular? My question is what does gender equity/inequity look like in my classroom, and what role do I have in promoting it? (Minarik, 1995)

In addition, she was becoming more aware of some of the issues female students faced in terms of feeling inadequate in school on academic and social levels (The AAUW Report, 1992), but also particularly in terms of sports participation.

In defining the action research problem Leslie was forced to reconsider the meaning of 'elementary classroom'.

> I believe that my definition of 'the classroom', relative to this study, was preconditioned by the past gender research I was aware of. Yet, as I got further into my research, I began listening more carefully to the students for the origin of their ideas. I should have known that the 'classroom' is where the students and teacher are. The research, among other things, showed me that children learn in a variety of ways and places, the interior of a building with a 'teacher' standing in front of them being only one. To

look only within the four walls of a school for a solution to gender equity would seem too narrow. (personal communication, January 26, 1996)

So as Leslie conceptualized the research project she expanded the definition of 'classroom' to include the school playground, where much dynamic learning and teaching takes place with or without a 'teacher'.

The Action Research Project

Since Leslie was not a stranger to action research methods, she followed the approach she had used previously: 1) observe the situation, 2) define the question, 3) seek solutions from those she trusted, 4) conduct her own classroom investigation, 5) come to conclusions, 6) modify her methods, and 7) continue the process with other problems and situations (Hollingsworth, 1994; Minarik, 1995).

Thirty students (ten girls, twenty boys) comprised her combination second and third grade class. Only three of the students were designated at second grade level. Reading ability included beginning levels to the third grade. This class was designated as 'full inclusion', a program in which children designated as special education students are fully included in a regular class all day when appropriate, as well as 'sheltered English', a program in which teachers trained in English language development make modifications in curriculum and presentation to include students who do not speak English as their primary language, with half of the students classified as limited English speaking. Two-thirds of the third grade students had been in Leslie's second grade class the previous year.

Initial interviews with the children revealed very stereotypical views of gender roles even though further probing indicated that their views were not supported by the reality in their homes where many boys did jobs considered to be 'women's jobs' and many of the girls did jobs that were classified as 'men's jobs'. Gender separation that stressed gender difference was the norm. Specifically, the boys thought they had more natural ability and were 'better' than the girls in sports. Consider these responses by three boys in Leslie's class when they were asked directly about the discrimination that was occurring in a kickball game: Boy A, 'Girls can't be better'; Boy B, 'Men practice harder'; and Boy C, 'Girls get hurt.' (Minarik, 1995).

Leslie's initial attempts to reconstruct class interactions described above through indirect teaching were straight forward and traditional. Leslie tried to become more aware of the interaction between boys and girls by recording conversations and taking field notes. Also, she made a concerted effort to deal with the 'boy/girl' issue more often by making sure a girl acted as a team captain during recess, that girls were given equipment management responsibilities, and that the girls were called on more frequently and praised for their scholastic efforts. She monitored her calling patterns to be certain they were equitable, increased wait time for the girls' responses and monitored their class chores to make sure that traditional gender roles were not being reinforced. At this point Leslie continued to think that the solution to discrimination lay in modifications within the four classroom walls despite increasing information from the interviews that sports were a dominant area of interest and interaction for boys and a key arena for discrimination against girls. She wrote about these efforts,

> I initially thought that the gender discrimination that I found within my classroom could be solved within the classroom. The discrimination studies I was aware of encouraged teachers to correct this by doing the following: 1) watching calling patterns, 2) watching roles assigned to boy vs. girl students, and 3) giving girls more opportunity to answer (questions). I believed that I tried this initially, however, it had little effect on changing the classroom, or perhaps I was impatient. In any case, several ideas came to mind during this period of impatience: 1) I kept remembering comments boys made about how much better they were at sports — proof of their superiority, 2) I focused on my goal of empowering girls and related that to girls' soccer teams and how I had seen them become stronger over my two year observation, and 3) I encountered articles on team building in 'Teaching Tolerance' and *voilà* a light bulb went on — get out of the class and go teach where the power problem is — on the playground. (Minarek, 1995)

Further investigation into the interaction between the boys and the girls revealed that the girls were indeed having sporting experiences at home, yet at school the girls were not getting involved, partly because of the negative reaction of the boys, but also because of their own inhibitions. Unfortunately, Leslie noticed little change in the girls' behavior as a result of the indirect traditional teaching practices but did notice the more obvious problem, i.e., the boys' attitudes and behaviors. Faced with this realization, Leslie decided to try a different teaching strategy, one that would take her out of the classroom and to the playground.

After considering different possibilities, Leslie decided on the 'direct teaching' method as advocated by Lisa Delpit (1988). Coupled with insight from an inspirational piece on the damage of silence in the face of blatant discrimination that Leslie had just finished reading and the urgency of speaking out about injustice as well as some readings in sport motivation, Leslie devised a direct method to confront the discrimination the girls in her class faced.

At the beginning of October Leslie had a direct discussion with the members of the class on the meaning of discrimination and how it was occurring in the classroom, specifically on the playground and in sport situations. The transcript of the session revealed that five of the six girls described sporting experiences at home. As the conversation progressed more of the boys tried to be supportive as the issues were laid bare. Leslie stated in her notes, 'Notice how some of the boys try to be supportive. One of the boys even changes his opinion' (Minarik, 1995). By mid-October the boys demonstrated increasing supportive attitudes as well as open verbal support of the girls. Boys were beginning to openly acknowledge girls as friends and demonstrated an awareness of the need to include girls in team sport activities.

By the end of October the change in the boys was very noticeable. Leslie wrote, 'I was hearing supportive comments about girls from a growing number of boys which I had never heard in seven years' (Minarik, 1995). Pleased by what she was seeing and feeling, Leslie asked one of the boys, who had been in her second grade class the previous as well as the current year, 'Why is it working so well . . . better than last year?' The boy responded, 'Because you didn't tell us about this last year' (Minarik, 1995).

Leslie then moved to explore the hypothesis that sports was a key to creating more supportive and equitable relationships between the girls and boys. The boys had most often used their accomplishments in sports as examples of their seeming natural superiority. Most notable was the fact that the most overt discrimination against the girls occurred within the context of sports. Leslie's plan to improve the interaction between the girls and boys was to 1) provide instruction in the sport skills in which the girls were lacking, 2) modify the rules of the games to make the situations less competitive, and 3) downplay the emphasis on winning while encouraging a spirit of fun in its place.

To this end Leslie, with the aid of a volunteer, divided the class into smaller groups for instruction. Smaller teams and teams of players of similar skill proved to be more comfortable formats for the girls and some other less competitive boys. Skills practiced within the small groups were specific to each team sport commonly played during recess and physical education. The boys who expressed competence were allowed to continue their team sport play on their own. Interestingly, after a period of time, several boys asked permission to practice with the girls. At the same time, two girls transferred themselves to the ongoing soccer game. Those students who had been practicing skills began their own game when they were ready.

In her field notes Leslie described the progress the students seemed to be making, 'I am not only noticing a change in their [boys'] attitudes, a genuine effort to be kinder to the girls, but they also seem to like the interaction and have begun to appreciate the athletic skills of many of the girls. Several comments also indicated that the class perceived that they were doing the right thing, so to speak or that they were better people for what they were doing. They felt proud of themselves' (Minarik, 1995).

The change in behavior and attitudes in these students continued. Leslie noted in her field notes that increasingly the girls and boys were playing together during recess. Girls were speaking up whenever they perceived that the sports equipment was being distributed inequitably. In a class discussion in February the students described and analyzed their own behavior:

Boy: Now it's getting more fun to play with the girls.
Girl: The boys changed. About thinking more better.
Girl: I think it's better when they play with girls because they used to fight games and they'd get in trouble — but when they play with girls — like tag games — it's fun but safer.
Boy: I thought girls' things were no fun — but I — and I didn't even try playing with girls because I never even tried it. But now I tried it.

Girl:	Boys don't like to play with girls cause they play house stuff. Now we are chasing boys and girls.
Mrs. M:	So if girls play too much house stuff it's boring for the boys?
Girl:	You know when girls play dolls they're trying to figure out why moms and dads have to do things. Girls keep on trying to figure it out. It's really not boring.
Mrs. M:	What are boys doing when they play?
Boy:	Just having fun.
Boy:	When boys play it teaches you how to fight.
Mrs. M:	Is learning to fight important?

(*Note from Leslie*: All boys — in some cases after a thoughtful pause — said no.)

Boy:	I think this is one of the best things I am going to say. Girls are feeling more comfortable with the boys.
Boy:	After school we were playing, me, D., B. and T. (all girls)
Boy:	I like — I'm fit to like girls' stuff.
Boy:	I think girls is more fun because the boys fight and the girls don't. I kick one boy with a ball and said sorry but he was mad.
Girl:	At recess it was pretty fun. When we played chase with the girls it was kind of boring like the same thing over and over. When the boys started to play it changed and we learned different ways to run.
Boy:	I wanted to play with girls but my mind said no.

In some cases the societal/cultural lessons seemed so ingrained in these 7-year-olds that they cut themselves off from new experiences. Some non-aggressive males still felt fear when they did not fit other boys' expectations of playground behavior. Still, making the classroom more empowering for girls meant making changes that fostered a supportive environment enabling them to express who they were. In this situation the boys' opinions had to change. Creating a space for change resulted in a liberating experience for the boys. The option of having more comfortable and equitable relationships with girls gave the boys a safer space. Leslie concluded in her field notes,

> Obtaining gender equity in my classroom relative to participation may mean creating a better balance in the types of formats I give students to share their ideas. Whole class discussions tend to benefit boys who can be more vocal. Smaller group discussions may provide a less competitive arena where girls can find their voice. Contrary to my notion that the girls should be integrated the majority of the time into learning groups, perhaps time for girls to work with girls can be less stressful.
>
> If boys tend to define themselves by their physical abilities at this age and use this to reinforce stereotypical ideas of gender roles and superiority, then it is critical to find ways for the girls to participate fully in sports and to do so equitably, meaning they must be given the skill training necessary

to compete fully. This means rethinking our own views of girls and sports, reshaping how we teach sports and physical education classes, how we set the tone for the games, i.e., less competitive and more team building.

While there is no question that we must help the girls expand their view of possibilities and work diligently to improve self esteem, we might also need to look very carefully at how we can alter boys' notions of sports.

The Context of Sport

Leslie's exploration of the intersection of gender and sports through action research is critical for a number of reasons. First, her willingness to explore possible social change in her classroom through action research using gender and sport as the elements to be invested is a statement about her belief in the power of action research as praxis. Second, the possibility for social change within the context of sport can be seen. She did not shy away from a difficult investigation of the powerful nature of play and sport as socializing agents in children's lives.

Through numerous experiences at home, in school, and on the playground these children learned the lessons of power and domination which all too often undergird the team sport context. The references the boys and girls used in regards to the meaning of sport are reflections of current attitudes in mainstream society. The hegemonic practice voiced and exhibited by these children has been accepted as natural and right by both girls and boys.

Leslie's observations concerning the interaction between the girls and boys are consistent with previous research. On the playground where adults exert little influence on behavior, there is extensive division of space by gender. Space, activities and equipment are gender-typed. Boys typically spread out playing games requiring more space (as much as ten times the space of the girls), usually team sports, and exercise control over this area. The space the girls occupy is typically much smaller and closer to the school building. Boys see the activities in which girls are engaged as trivial, interruptable and treat their (girls') presence as contaminating. Boys treat any object associated with being a girl with the same disdain and social distance, although the reverse does not occur. Allocation of equipment can also fall along gender lines. Girls rarely request footballs or basketballs. In the same spirit, boys rarely ask for jump ropes. In fact, boys disdain anything associated with being like or associated with girls. Power and social superiority are central to the social relations of gender. As Thorne (1993, p. 84) stated, '. . . in several notable ways, girls act from a one-down position.' And, teachers continue to reinforce this one-down position (1) by their silence and failure to give girls the skills they need to succeed in sports, (2) when they do not modify the boys' attitudes and make them more sensitive, and (3) when they do not modify the rules of games to make the games less competitive and more cooperative.

The control of space on the playground by boys is also an issue of entitlement. While the boys control more space, they also violate the girls' activities and treat girls as contaminating, thus reinforcing the socially constructed notion of the naturalness of male dominance. Nancy Henley (1977) noted that adult men to take up more space personally and publicly than do adult women. The importance of body sense and space is crucial to the development of male gender identity (Whitson, 1990). Through sport boys are empowered since they are encouraged to experience their bodies in space-occupying, forceful and dominant ways. In contrast, women are culturally encouraged to take up as little space as possible (Bordo, 1993).

Contrast the different cultural experiences between girls and boys using their participation in and value placed on team sports. Team sport involvement for boys may be related to boys' tendency to organize in larger groups and help explain their preoccupation with competition. Boys engage in more physical aggression and intimidation of each other than do girls, and boys' social relations tend to be very hierarchical and competitive. Team sports typically require a large number of participants and have rather extensive rules to govern play. Boys make, break and argue more about the rules of a game than do girls. Girls' games, on the other hand, tend to be structured with fewer and more simple rules and focus on turn taking (Thorne, 1993). For the most part, girls are less likely to play team sports than are boys. Both girls and boys learn that the vehicle to acceptance and social prominence is through team sports.

In addition, play itself can have a variety of meanings for children. It can be drama filled with ritual, or it can be 'gender play' where the play is serious and laden with gender related messages about worth and social position (Thorne, 1993). This last point is particularly true for team sports where the message is that girls are not able nor are they valued. Dewar (1991) argued that sporting practices are historically produced, socially constructed, and culturally defined to serve the interests of the powerful groups in society. Sport can be viewed as a cultural representation of social practices and relations. The unintended consequences of never challenging or intervening are many. But play and sport can also be a space for action in that girls and boys can come together and learn new ways of relating to one another. Sport can be a site for social change as evidenced by Leslie's research.

Since gender is socially constructed, children are socialized into gender roles and appropriate gender behavior. But as Thorne has stated, we 'do gender', that is, gender is not something that one passively 'is'. Gender behavior changes according to the situation, even though from birth the way children are treated is a function of their gender. Gender is a dichotomous variable at the individual/personal level. In the social world 'doing gender' varies according to the context.

As born out by Leslie's initial investigation into classroom interactions, gender separation was most likely to occur: 1) in groups that are more near aged rather than mixed age, sex separation emerges in peer groups; 2) in crowded settings such as school where there are sufficient numbers of students who can self-segregate into groups that reflect sameness; 3) through forced choice, as in choosing teams; and 4) in games that require more technical skill and experience, that is, the more gender separated the activity becomes, it earns the label as a girls' or boys' activity. Leslie's decision to consider/investigate methods of more positive interaction was an admirable one. Finding ways for girls and boys to interact with one another in positive, mutually reinforcing ways was a difficult challenge in the face of the reality of playground interaction.

There is a taken for granted view within schools that gender differences between boys and girls are 'natural' and expected. The assumption of natural difference is legitimized by school practice. Gender provides a convenient line of difference and division that is ongoing in schools. Although at times gender itself may be highlighted or played down depending on the situation, the fact is that students separate by gender first (Thorne, 1993). This practice is reinforced via the language as forms of address used by teachers and administrators as in 'boys and girls', via seating arrangements within classrooms, or when arranging students for entry into or exiting from a building or classroom by lines. These practices merely reinforce children's experience of gender difference as natural.

Action Research in Physical Education and Sport

Even though action research has a broad base of support within education, in the field of physical education action research has had a limited impact. As Richard Tinning (1992) has said, as a research phenomena, action research seems to have completely bypassed the field of physical education. The reasons for this are many and varied and this chapter is not intended to review those. Suffice to say, the historical dominance of the empirical paradigm has limited action research's acceptance as a legitimate form of research. The empirical paradigm was thought to enhance the credibility of physical education and the study of sport. Secondly, play itself has been viewed as trivial and not a serious focus for analysis. Yet, play can be deadly serious, a place where powerful emotions are acted out. 'Child's play' can be a forceful lesson in power and gender relations (Thorne, 1993). In addition, in my review of the research in physical education and sport, I found that the empirical paradigm has historically ignored the issue of power and gender relationships in the context of the gymnasium or playground (Lock, 1993). Unequal power relations exist within the gymnasium and playgrounds. Social reality and expectation do not check themselves at the school doors.

Leslie's project was openly ideological in that her interests and concerns were explicitly defined. The aim was quite simply to challenge the children's behavior and promote a new social order within her classroom. Leslie's initial idea was to use a more traditional approach to support and build girls' self esteem. This approach had little noticeable effect on the discrimination that existed in the classroom. By listening to student stories and by studying power sources and relations she was able to construct new approaches to change. Emancipatory research calls for a form of engagement different from that of the traditional empirical approach. Participatory forms of engagement are required to provide insights that serve for action and change (Bain, 1990).

To improve interactions and promote cooperative relations between the girls and boys Leslie

1   used criteria other than gender for grouping her students,
2   reinforced and affirmed the values of cooperation,

3   organized the children into small, heterogeneous and cooperative groups,
4   facilitated the girls' access to all activities by providing the skill practice in the games that enhance self esteem and social acceptance, and
5   actively intervened to challenge the dynamics of stereotyping and of power.

Without guidance and positive intervention, boys adopt behaviors that reproduce male dominance and girls remain marginal to the power structure altogether.

Leslie's deep sense of caring about her students brought her to examine the naturalness of difference within gender relations. In doing so she created an alternative lens for the children to view their being in the world. And as Sandra Hollingsworth (1994, p. 182) said, 'Leslie's story reminds us that learning to work in communities for change may be a matter of knowing how, and having a commitment to that work, with persistence and support, leads to action.' And as the narrator of Leslie's story, I was acutely aware of the importance and the power of Leslie's action research project and the project's potential contribution to the examination of gender equity in physical education and sport.

References

BAIN, L. (1990) 'Interpretive and critical research in sport and physical education', *Research Quarterly for Exercise Science and Sport*, **60**, 1, pp. 21–4.

BORDO, S. (1993) *Unbearable Weight*, Berkeley, CA, University of California Press.

DELPIT, L. (1988) 'The silenced dialogue: Power and pedagogy in educating other people's children', *Harvard Educational Review*, **58**, pp. 280–98.

DEWAR, A. (1991) 'Incorporation or resistance?: Towards an analysis of women's responses to sexual oppression in sport', *International Review for the Sociology of Sport*, **26**, 1, pp. 15–23.

HENLEY, N. (1977) *Body Politics: Power, Sex, and Nonverbal Communication*, Englewood, NJ, Prentice-Hall.

HOLLINGSWORTH, S.H. (1994) *Teacher Research and Urban Literacy. Education Lessons and Communications in A Feminist Key*, New York, Teachers College Press.

LOCK, R.S. (1993) 'Women in sport and physical education: A review of the literature in selected journals', *Women in Sport and Physical Activity Journal*, **2**, 2, pp. 21–49.

MINARIK, L. (1995, April) *Gender Equity in an Elementary Classroom. A Teacher/Researcher Project*, paper presented at the meeting of the American Educational Research Association.

NODDINGS, N. (1984) *Caring: A Feminine Approach to Ethics and Moral Education*, Berkeley, University of California Press.

Teaching Tolerance (1993) *California News Letter*, Spring Edition.

THE AAUW REPORT (1992) *How Schools Shortchange Girls*, Washington, DC, AAUW Educational Foundation.

THORNE, B. (1993) *Gender Play: Girls and Boys in School*, New Brunswick, NJ, Rutgers University Press.

TINNING, R. (1992) 'Action research as epistemology and practice: Towards transformative educational practice in physical education', in SPARKES, A. (Ed.), *Research in Physical Education and Sport*, London, Falmer Press, pp. 188–209.

WCCUSD Schools Report (1995) *The West Contra Costa Unified School District Accountability Report 1994–95.*

Whitson, D. (1990) 'Sport in the social construction of masculinity', in Messner, M. and Sabo, D. (Eds), *Sport, Men, and the Gender Order*, Champaign, IL, Human Kinetics Books, pp. 19–29.

17 Working with the Different Selves of Teachers: Beyond Comfortable Collaboration

Christopher Day (United Kingdom)

In a recent review of research on teachers' beliefs and practices it was suggested that an accurate portrayal of the relationship between teachers' situational beliefs, knowledge, teaching behaviours and contextual factors (i.e., cultural environment, life histories and narratives) will contribute to a more complete picture of teachers' cognitive activity and, ultimately, improve teaching effectiveness (Fang, 1996; p. 51). This chapter attempts to do this by presenting the case of one (high) school teacher of English in some detail. Only one example is provided because work of this kind, in which an external collaborator works with teachers over time, in order to assist in raising to an explicit level the thinking that underpins practice, observe that practice, gather views of practice from other sources, and continue to work with teachers in processes of change, is rarely documented.

The process was designed collaboratively and involved extensive interviewing — with the teacher about the effect of his life histories upon his thinking and espoused practices of teaching, with students about their perspectives on the teacher and their teaching — and observation of teaching, using video recording and stimulated recall as an aid to reflection on practice. The teacher chose the lessons to be observed; and he amended and authenticated the interpretations of data. My designated role was to film the lessons, interview teacher and students, manage the data collection processes but not control them, analyze the data but not have exclusive rights to their interpreted meaning. Systematic feedback was built into a negotiated fieldwork process. In short, I was acting as 'critical friend' (Day, 1991). The work, which took place over a one-year period, was characterized by principles of voluntarism (the teacher himself invited me to work with him), ownership (information provided by myself and the teacher was regarded as jointly owned), equity (no one had more rights than the other) and ethical contracting (the making of agreements through which both participants gained from the process). Because the teacher wanted to examine possible contradictions between his ideas, ideals and practices and to act upon the information generated from this, the action research cycles were divided into five phases of reflection **on** and **about** the action within personal, professional, institutional and socio-political contexts:

Collaborative Action Research Phases

Phase 1:   Pre-teaching (1) Here the teacher reflected upon his life histories, ideologies (e.g., views of students, teaching, knowledge, schooling) and decided upon his focus of interest (the lessons which he wished to investigate) and the process for investigation.

Phase 2:   Teaching (1) Here the teacher taught and reflected on the teaching through the iterative process enabled by the stimulated recall process, autobiographical interviews and student feedback.

Phase 3:   Pre-teaching (2) Here the teacher reflected upon the first teaching sequence, with the additional feedback provided by the students (through researcher interviews) and made decisions about the purposes and design of a second sequence of lessons with the same students.

Phase 4:   Teaching (2) As in Teaching (1), but with the focus of the stimulated recall process being upon the success or otherwise of the changed teaching ideology and/or strategies.

Phase 5:   Post action: Here interpretation of the data analyzed by the researcher were fed back, and discussed with the teacher, thus enabling further reflection on and about the action.

Michael

Michael had been a mature entrant into teaching. He had left school at 16, lived abroad, been a member of the armed services, and qualified for entrance into teacher training as a result of part-time study. Whilst at college he had been president of the students' union. He had been president of the local branch of a teachers' union, and was an active member of a political party. He was, therefore, well aware and had particular views of the socio-political context of schools and students and of his purposes as an English teacher. He described the major influences as being his mother who, as a widow, 'brought me up to be self-sufficient and self-contained'; his History teacher, 'who encouraged me to raise my opinions and be true to my ideals; a school which, 'taught me the discipline of hard, organized work . . . to be responsible for things in my charge . . . and to do a job even in the face of deplorable conditions'; and the armed services which where, 'influential in teaching me something about group cooperation . . . (and) . . . how easy it is to stifle youthful inquisitiveness and individuality of expression and thought. This merely reinforced my awareness of class inequality, which has been the major influence on my life.'

These influences had caused him to believe that:

a child must not be educated to fill an economic position but to be shown how to explore for himself, but with guidance, his/her own potential and to develop his/her own values rather than to receive them. In this way, dissatisfaction with a society that will attempt to control and suppress his/

her maturing awareness will lead to rebellion against that suppression. . . . I suppose my own erratic development — academic failure at school but later development, has shown me never to underestimate a student and never to put them in a position where they lose faith in themselves. If you treat people with respect then eventually they may respect you — with mutual respect between a teacher and student, then I think the sky is the limit . . .

These indicators formed the basis of Michael's ideological and planning frameworks for teaching.

Sequence 1: The Three 'Selves' of Michael

By his own admission, Michael's teaching focused, 'somewhere around the middle, giving bias to the kids who are less competent'. He had never been able, 'to produce a programme tailored to the individual needs of each student'. There was a tension between his 'educative' self in which he wanted to encourage 'creative processes' whilst 'giving students the basic tools or skills of written expression', his 'ideological' or 'emancipatory' self in which he believed that students should acquire through him a knowledge of content selected for its social relevance; and his 'personal' self which was itself complicated by his need for control. In the lessons observed, his espoused values of self-sufficiency, individuality, self-searching, were constrained by his personal need to maintain a dominating teaching role.

The first sequence of six forty-minute lessons which Michael asked me to observe was on the theme of 'Cinema and Television'. His intentions were to begin through whole class discussion in which, as central coordinator, he would encourage a free flow of ideas, 'creating an environment for free exploration'. 'Whatever the kids pick up as being important during that time I intend to develop that area rather than try to develop an area that I think is important . . .'

However: '. . . if the free flow doesn't come, I'm going to have to keep on stimulating it, and I'm going to have to throw out questions to provide the answers. . . . I know that basically I'm quite a forceful person in the classroom, and I do tend to sit on top of discussions'.

The twenty-two 14-year-old students sat in six free-choice friendship groups. The first two lessons (a double period) consisted of an hour long class discussion in which the final ten minutes were spent by students in reading teacher constructed handouts on cinema and TV. He constantly related the discussion to the students' experiences, but maintained control over selection of topics, the flow of information and direction of discussion. The discussion itself was characterized by the teacher's acceptance, and thus legitimization, of opinions offered by the students. Although he felt that he had allowed the discussion to go on for too long, characteristics of Michael's style of teaching and organization of lessons which were to appear throughout the sequence had emerged. His style was 'charismatic', relying on his own dynamism, use of humour and friendly 'banter'. He 'walked and talked', stopping at particular groups of students, by his proximity persuading them to participate, or naming students he wished to contribute. He often sought class consensus — 'testing the market' — all designed to gain student verbal participation while at the same time ensuring that this was relayed through him. On reflection, he thought that it might have been more productive for students to discuss in small groups.

The third lesson also took the form of class discussion, despite his stated intentions to devote it to small group discussion. He was concerned to ensure that students had read the handout (for homework) and assimilated the information in it, so that they were well prepared for an essay he was to set. The essay was an important one to cover, and he didn't want to take too long getting to it. The discussion was closed guided discovery with the teacher seeking 'correct' answers from students. He himself, in the post lesson discussion, characterized it as instructional, an 'oral comprehension test'. This had been his intention, he said. However, on reviewing the lesson he was concerned at the effect of this on the expectations of students:

Michael: . . . I signal what answers I want, and signal what answers I'm rejecting without actually saying I reject them. I'm consciously saying to myself . . . 'No, you mustn't quash somebody by saying "No" . . .'. But by the very fact that I say 'Yes', and move on to the next person, it's clearly obvious to the person who's just answered that I'm rejecting it . . .

In the final two lessons (a double period), the students continued writing their essays for the first half hour, when Michael introduced the final topic for class discussion — 'Sex and Violence in the Cinema'. The students' responses were minimal, until one mentioned a topical film. There was an immediate buzz of conversation with students discussing with each other directly and initiating conversations. Michael, sensing the high level of interest, encouraged the discussion on this topic to develop by challenging the view of the students that it was a good film. Later, he asked them to continue the discussion in small groups, and for the final ten minutes of the lesson focused the class discussion on 'Violence and Television':

Michael: It's very much a change from lessons 1 and 2. . . . The class is choosing the areas. The class is very much guiding me in the content. I'm focusing the discussion process. I took my clues from the kids this time. For the first time they're responding to each other instead of just going through me. . . . At times I became superfluous . . . they were developing thoughts and ideas from themselves. . . . It happened because we'd caught on to something where they had opinions of their own which they could discuss out of their own interest. . . . It was more real for them. . .

Students' Views

All the students enjoyed the freedom they had been given to talk in class. Some preferred small group discussions. It was 'better than sitting down working all the time' and less inhibiting than class discussion, 'cos when you're in a large group, and you're sitting there, you feel alone when you're saying something, you feel as though everyone's looking at you, you feel small . . .' However, all but two of the rest of the class (who enjoyed both discussion settings) positively preferred the class discussions which had formed a large part of the lessons.

The comment of one student aptly illustrates the feeling expressed by the majority of students:

> **Andrew**: I prefer class discussion. You seem to get more out of it. In a group you only tend to talk about what you're meant to be talking about when the teacher's there. And you don't seem to learn very much. Certain facts never come out when you're talking in a group.

For the most part, then, Michael's intentions for the lessons had been fulfilled. However, because of his emphasis on teacher-directed class discussion in which students were dependent on him, he had not encouraged 'self-searching' in a way with which he was satisfied.

Sequence 2: The Personal and Ideological Selves Prevail

In the first sequence, Michael had perceived a conflict in action — between his responsibility to 'teach' (his 'ideological' and 'personal' selves), and his desire to encourage students to think about problems in new ways so that they could make their own meanings (his 'educative' self). His second teaching sequence was on the theme of 'Race', which he regarded as 'a vehicle, not only for English teaching, but to try and break down prejudices . . .'. He described his intentions for the sequence:

> **Michael**:   . . . as a result of looking at myself last time, what I want to try and get away from is . . . me as the focal point of the group . . . from the group looking towards me for guidance and leadership . . . I don't want my attitudes to come through. . . . What I'm trying to do specifically — and I think this is probably different from . . . before . . . is that I want them to come to conclusions, hopefully the right ones . . . about their own racial attitudes . . . because there's not going to be any kind of internalization taking place if I tell them what they should be thinking . . . there's got to be a lot of factual input. . . .

He wanted, in effect, to attempt to take a role of 'procedural neutrality'. (Elliott, 1975) He stated that his organizational emphasis would be on small group discussion work, and also that he found it 'difficult to participate, while leaving them to generate'. He recognized the difficulties — 'I tend to feel that I have got answers . . . and that I make sure that they explore and are exposed to what I hold to be of value . . .'. Clearly, within his wish to increase participation, he intended to ensure the transmission of certain items of knowledge which he regarded as crucial to the understanding of any given topic. Nevertheless, he wished to attempt a resolution of the conflict.

However, a new factor intervened from his life outside the classroom which affected his plans and which serves as a reminder of the complex interplay of person and professional in every teacher's life. The most significant unplanned feature of the lessons in this sequence was the constraining effect of events outside the classroom (department politics) on the teacher's teaching. These pressures were expressed in uncharacteristic short-temperedness by the teacher during the lessons, which marred both his intended strategies for the lessons and his interpersonal relationships with his students.

In the second lesson Michael intended to attempt the role of neutral chairperson:

Michael: Well, tomorrow, we're really going to open up this racial question. I'm going to give them enough rope to really hang themselves on their own prejudices. I certainly don't intend to take very much part in tomorrow's lesson. Really what I want to do is get to the core, try and get them to be as honest as possible about their own racial attitudes, and what they particularly dislike about particular races. I'm going to try and leave it to the whole class to examine their own and each other's prejudices . . . So it'll basically be a class discussion. Hopefully, it'll develop into the group controlling the group, rather than me having any real part in it, other than perhaps spreading questions about from one individual to another. But I certainly want to get away from channelling it through me, because I don't want my attitudes to come through. . . .

The class discussion was designed to elicit students' opinions about immigrants, and he achieved his intention of orchestrating the process of the discussion rather than its content. The openness of the discussion was illustrated by the number of student-initiated conversations. Michael was: 'pleased by the response . . . I was having no struggle at all to keep them talking . . . people in the class were very forthcoming, very ready to come out with what they thought. I think just about everybody participated . . .' He was, however, getting 'a little bit concerned about . . . how I'm going to actually get somewhere. Because I'm conscious of the constraints and requirements of the course, I'm wondering how . . . I'm going to utilize what we've got so far into something that is assessable . . . I would have liked to develop some sort of project, but it's very difficult . . .'.

Michael organized the next two lessons (a double period) into six stages:

1 general criticism of students' level of commitment followed by individuals writing about their attitudes to immigrants (10 mins);
2 individuals making lists of attitudes 'for' and 'against' (15 mins);
3 individuals reading their lists to the class (30 mins);
4 teacher selected groups discussing attitudes privately (10 mins);
5 group spokespersons reporting back to class (5 mins);
6 teacher-led class discussion (10 mins).

Michael was again pleased and felt that he had achieved his intention of giving more opportunity to individual students to clarify and express their opinions. In lesson five, he distributed a printed factsheet on the topic, and the lesson was spent in individual silent reading. He was 'very impressed' by the concentration of students.

The grey skies outside the classroom reflected the sombre mood of the teacher in lesson six. As with other lessons in this sequence, he arrived in class late (10 minutes). Again he began by 'telling off' a student, and once more his plan to 'let things go as they come' through small group discussion, was altered. He reverted first to whole-class discussion with himself as director, relayer of opinion and information.

> **Michael**: . . . I realized the night before when I was writing it out that I had far too much to try and do in that lesson . . . I had to try and get something out of it, not because I really felt that there was any necessity . . . as such, but again it comes down to the constraints of what's required . . .

In the small group discussions which followed he found himself under constant attack from students for the bias of the 'factsheet'. Michael was unhappy with the lesson.

He pinpointed the causes:

> **Michael**: . . . It's a combination of causes, really. I was dog-tired . . . because I'd been doing . . . that (work) . . . until about half-past two in the morning . . . I was feeling up-tight still about . . . the departmental business. I was feeling very annoyed . . . I just couldn't cope with it all.

Student Views

Michael's intentions for the second sequence of lessons had been to place more emphasis on small group work as a means of encouraging more exploratory learning by the students, to make himself a less dominating figure in the classroom by taking the procedural role of 'neutral chairman', and to encourage more talking by the students and less by himself. His overall aim was to change the attitudes of students whom he perceived to be racially prejudiced. In responding to the question, 'Do you think Michael is a teacher who tends to ask you things or tell you things? Or does he do both?' Nine felt that he mainly asked questions (of the closed guided discovery kind) and ten students stated categorically that he told them things:

He does both
Oliver . . . He dominates the lessons. You can put your points, but what you say, he changes a bit, and then he gives it back to you, and then you're stuck with that.
Lynne . . . He doesn't do much talking. When he wants to make a point, he leads round to it so that

Ian. . . . He does a mixture, really. First of all he'll ask you a question, and then, if nobody answers, he'll start shouting at you and get in a bad mood, saying that no-one's trying. And then he'll tell you, really.

The practice of attempting to involve all the students at the same time in the same activity effectively placed him in the public position of controller of behaviour, pace and content. Michael had partly modified his emphasis on teacher-centred content, and through his wider variety of organizational structures increased the students' access to participation in knowledge making. However, class discussion as an organizational strategy still predominated, thus ensuring the teacher's overt authoritative, director role.

It would seem, then, that the teacher had become more strict in the class-room, more moody, and less inclined to deal with individuals in a sympathetic way. The reasons for this lay in part in his continued reliance on class discussion as a teaching technique, and, perhaps more important, the conditions under which the second sequence of lessons observed were taught. Despite his original intention to modify his teaching strategies the constraints proved too strong; and he reverted to the style of teaching in which his personal self felt most confident.

Discussion

Despite a widespread recognition of the benefits and potential benefits of action research which essentially asserts teachers as active participants in their own learning, there are a number of issues concerning its different forms, intentions and purposes which this work serves to highlight.

Revisiting Personal Solutions

The purpose of the action research had been described by Michael as 'to devise a means by which I can evaluate the extent to which I achieve my stated aims and objectives . . .' It became evident that the identification of his aims and objectives in relation to his observable teaching acts in the classroom had the effect of clarifying these, and revealing for Michael certain inconsistencies.

It is important that teacher educators concerned with promoting or supporting this process of change should recognize that most teachers will, like Michael, already have found their own personal solution to perceived problems. They will have constructed a balance between the major opposing interests, i.e., 1) teacher personality factors; 2) ideological factors; 3) presentation and nature of material; 4) external requirements (e.g., ordered classroom, examination results) and 5) the characteristics of the class i.e., social and academic characteristics of students (Lacey, 1977). It is only where teachers perceive that their personal solutions are themselves inadequate that they will be moved to search for means by which they can change.

In terms of teacher change, however, what must be investigated is the value and permanence of the 'personal solution'. When I met Michael, he had, in one sense, achieved a 'personal solution' which enabled him to 'cope' with teaching. However, he 'coped' with varying degrees of satisfaction, because he felt he was not realizing the potential which his espoused theories led him to expect. He had not been given the opportunity to engage in any systematic reflection (on the different selves of his teaching). Thus he had not been able to assess critically any of what Lacey termed 'opposing interests', and he was bound within 'taken for granted' norms and assumptions.

Teachers do not normally have the time nor the energy to engage in a constant re-examination of their teaching. But under the special circumstances where collaboration with a trusted other is made available, it would appear to be possible for them to invest more time and energy than 'normal'; and this condensed but thorough period of self-examination may have long-term if not life-long effects. Ideally external agents would not be a necessary part of this process. However, most situations are not ideal, and teachers are not afforded the opportunity for reflection on their teaching. This is not to say that teachers do not reflect in the normal course. Conditions in most schools for most teachers continue to prohibit any detailed consideration of the complex factors which contribute — often in conflicting ways — to their classroom practices. Teachers, then, are likely to operate on a model of restricted professionality. Once they have developed a personal solution to any problems of teaching which they perceive — and this is usually achieved without any systematic assistance by others — it is unlikely that this solution (or theory of action) will again be significantly questioned. The opportunity for Michael to confront himself which collaborative action research of the kind described in this chapter enabled, had the effect of altering his perceptions, not only of himself as teacher, but also of the different selves and voices that played their parts in his life and work as a teacher. There was no assumption in this work that Michael would continue with the process of fundamental re-examination, but it has been taken for granted that his increased confidence would maintain a mood of being willing to try out new ideas and an increased sensitivity to student responses to his teaching.

Taking Account of the Different Selves

The research process had raised 'a number of important factors' for Michael:

> **Michael**: . . . the main one being the need for the teacher to examine carefully his understanding of his role in the classroom. My inclination is to accept student directed learning and questioning rather than stating is necessary if the student is to be encouraged to question the world in which he lives and those values he and his society holds, and I feel that both sequence 1 and 2 indicate a willingness on my part to enable this to take place. However, the teacher has an experience of the world that is necessary for him to impart to the student, and it is important that this takes place. There is a body of knowledge that needs to be taught, and the ability

to assimilate it is, in itself, an important skill. Questioning may not be an appropriate way to impart this. At what time does it became necessary to give hard facts? I see this as a dilemma created in the main by the relegation of education to being a service agency for industry and a transmitter of a culture and values so often in conflict with those of a large number of students. . . I think the meeting by the teacher of his objectives whatever his methodology is more important than how the students perceives them. A teacher must be concerned with the students' opinions of him, only insofar as it affects the establishment of a rapport conducive to learning, but there are widely differing methods of teaching that will establish this rapport.

The strength of Michael's personal self is illustrated by his assertion of his beliefs in his right to determine his own course of action in the light of his theories of action, and his questioning of the extent to which a teacher '**can** change his overall classroom style'.

Michael: . . . How much is this 'style' and subsequently 'method' determined by his personality? A teacher 'teaches' in the way in which he feels secure (is in control of the situation) and by the way he understands his role . . . while he can change his role from i.e., an importer of unchallengeable truth, to that of neutral chairman, can he change the basic make-up of his personality i.e., the reticent teacher becoming a skilled leader of class discussion? I think this is questionable.

Michael had stated that he found it difficult to modify his 'charismatic' teaching style where he was at the centre of the teaching-learning process, dominating its content pacing and procedures for ideological reasons. Sustaining attempts at change was made more difficult both by stress felt by the teacher as a result of events which were occurring outside the classroom and his difficulties in managing conflicts within the 'educative' and 'ideological' selves of his espoused theory. As a person, he was beset with intra-departmental conflict relating to his own role in the future, and to the way in which he perceived he was being treated by his Head of Department and the school in general, and his workload: 'I have felt, as the year has gone on, that . . . I haven't been able to give it the preparation time, the thought time in terms of development, that I'd like to have done.'

It is important that the different selves and contexts of the teacher are recognized. As a professional ideologue Michael believed in the importance of the teacher transmitting a 'relevant' body of knowledge to students which was value laden. As an educator he believed in the importance of encouraging students to be 'self-searching'. While the two values are not intrinsically inconsistent and indeed may be complementary, it would appear upon reflection that whilst both were considered when planning the second sequence of lessons, they were irreconcilable in action. So what was revealed to Michael during and as a result of the research process was his commitment to a teaching approach in which students and content must fit in with the teacher, and to his need for dominance in the classroom which appeared to conflict with his wish to 'emancipate' students. The dominance of the personal and ideological selves was a constraining factor on teacher change. It was the process of collaborative action research which clarified this; and though his teaching did not change significantly, his understanding of his different selves did.

Beyond Comfortable Collaboration

There have been many criticisms of the different purposes, processes and outcomes of action research. For example: 1) processes of reflection, central to learning, may not in themselves lead to confrontation of thinking and practices nor take account of broad institutional and social contexts, necessary as precursors to decisions about change when carried out by the teacher alone (Day, 1993); 2) some of those engaged in studying teachers' thinking and action (an inevitable part of action research though not confined to it) attach importance to the narrative of teachers' stories without always locating them in broader social and political contexts; 3) action research, now 'colonized' by many who support educational reform, is being used to serve the 'academic knowledge' interests of teacher educators rather than teachers; and 4) policymakers and managers of organizations have adopted the term as a means of ensuring that teachers investigate their practice with a view to improving it without close or explicit investigation of the contexts in which the practice occurs.

Put briefly, the potential for genuine teacher development through 'reflection' has been undermined by:

1 a focus on helping teachers better reproduce practices suggested by university-sponsored research, and neglect of the theories and expertise embedded in teachers' own practices;
2 a means-end thinking which limits the substance of teachers' reflections to technical questions of teaching techniques and internal classroom organization and a neglect of questions of curriculum and education purposes;
3 neglect of the social and institutional context in which teaching takes place;
4 a focus on helping teachers reflect individually, referring to their own research. (Gore and Zeichner, 1995, p. 204)

All of these practices, it is claimed, help create a situation 'where there is merely the illusion of teacher development'.

Further criticisms may be levelled at the myriad of published collaborative action research reports which seem to imply that the researchers (usually drawn from higher education) and the teacher-researchers (usually drawn from schools) must share the same (usually humanistic, radical or progressive-liberal, educational ideologies, (Burbules, 1985); and where the reported direction of change in thinking and practice is almost always towards the 'social justice' end of the political continuum (characterized by emancipatory social action research espoused by, for example Carr and Kemmis, 1986; Zeichner, 1993). There are dangers, therefore, in assuming that the teachers' voice, once liberated, will provide an authentic account. Andy Hargreaves (Hargreaves, 1996) supports the promotion of teachers' voices through research, but questions those advocates who 'selectively appropriate' those voices which are consonant with the value positions and educational ideologies of the researcher which they themselves hold so that the effect is to present them as 'the voices' which are representative of teachers as a whole.

Authentic portrayals of teaching should contain other voices in addition to those of teachers so that they may be interpreted 'with reference to the contexts of teachers' lives and work that help give them meaning' (p. 16). The information from students reported in this chapter added significantly to understanding Michael's teaching. His response to the collaborative learning process and new perspectives gained illustrates the 'thin red line' which has to be walked by the collaborative action researcher if teachers are not to ascribe to him the role of indoctrinator, and in doing so, resist the very process of self-evaluation which they are attempting to encourage.

Teachers change or do not change according to whether they perceive a need, diagnose a problem, and conceive of a response to the problem that is both within their intellectual and emotional capacity, and appropriate to their personal, educative and ideological perspectives and the context in which they work. The possibilities for emotional turmoil, which work of this kind generates, are beginning to be documented. Research into one's own practice can entail destabilization risks to both personal and professional self-image and self-esteem (Argyris and Schon, 1976; Nias, 1989; Holly, 1991; Winter, 1989). Adverse external circumstances can complicate efforts to change. Those engaged in action research collaboration must recognize and work with the different 'images' or 'selves' (Day and Hayfield, 1996) and the emotional factors central to processes of investigation and change which are personally as well as ideologically and educatively significant. These non-rational processes can cause ripples of change throughout all facets of life (Dadds, 1993) which are not always positive.

In assisting individuals who are attempting to build upon their own theory of practice, those engaged in collaborative action research are engaged in 'a synthesis of research technique with human correspondence'. The former has often been overemphasized at the expense of the latter. Teachers' personal and professional selves are inextricably bound up in their teaching and thus research into their teaching. Although there is much lip service to this, there is still limited evidence of account being taken in collaborative action research which combines both the story, the action and the change. For those collaborators who are ideologically committed to particular purposes and practices of teaching, collaboration may not always be comfortable.

References

ARGYRIS, C. and SCHON, D.A. (1976) *Theory in Practice: Increasing Professional Effectiveness*, New York, Jossey-Bass.

BOLAM, R. (1990) 'Recent Developments in England and Wales', in JOYCE, B. (Ed.), *Changing Culture through Staff Development*, Alexandria, VA, Association for Supervision and Curriculum Development.

BURBULES, N.C. (1985) 'Education Under Siege', *Educational Theory*, 36, pp. 301–13.

CALDERHEAD, J. (1989) 'Reflective Teaching and Teacher Education', *Teaching and Teaching Education*, **5**, 1, pp. 43–51.

CARR, W. and KEMMIS, S. (1986) *Becoming Critical: Education, Knowledge and Action Research*, London, Falmer Press.

CARR, W. (Ed.) (1989) *Quality in Teaching*, London, The Falmer Press.

CONNELLY, F.M. and CLANDININ, D.J. (1990) 'Stories of Experience and Narrative Inquiry', *Educational Researcher*, **19**, 5, pp. 2–14.

DADDS, M. (1993) 'The Feeling of Thinking in Professional Self-Study', *Educational Action Research*, **1**, 2, 1993, pp. 287–303.

DAY, C. (1991) 'Roles and Relationships in Qualitative Research', *Teaching and Teacher Education*, **7**, 5/6, pp. 537–47.

DAY, C. (1993) 'Reflection: A Necessary but not Sufficient Condition for Professional Development', *British Educational Research Journal*, **19**, 1, pp. 83–93.

DAY, C. and HAYFIELD, M. (1996) 'Metaphors for Movement: Accounts of Professional Development', in KOMPF, M., BOAK, R.T., BOND, W.R, and DWURET, D.H. (Eds), *Changing Research and Practice: Teachers' Professionalism, Identities and Knowledge*, London, The Falmer Press.

DAY, C. and BAKIOGLU, A. (1996) 'Development and Disenchantment in the Professional Lives of Headteachers', in GOODSON I.F and HARGREAVES, A. (Eds), *Teachers' Professional Lives*, London, Falmer Press.

DREYFUS, H.L. and DREYFUS, S.E. (1986) *Mind over Machine: The Power of Human Intuition and Expertise in the Era of the Computer*, New York, The Free Press.

ELLIOTT, J. (1975) 'The Values of the Neutral Teacher', in BRIDGES, D. and SCRIMSHAW, P. (Eds), *Values and Authority in Schools*, London, Hodder and Stoughton.

FANG, Z. (1996) 'A review of research on teacher beliefs and practices', *Educational Research*, **38**, 1, Spring, 1996, pp. 47–65.

FEIMAN-NEMSER, S. (1990) 'Teacher Preparation: Structural and Conceptual Alternatives', in HOUSTON, W.T. (Ed.), *Handbook of Research on Teacher Education*, New York: McMillan.

FESSLER, R. (1995) 'Dynamics of Career Stages', in *Guskey*, T.R. and HUBERMAN (Eds), *Professional Development in Education: New Paradigms and Practices*, New York, Teachers College Press.

FULLAN, M. and HARGREAVES, A. (1992) 'Teacher Development and Education Change', in FULLAN, M. and HARGREAVES, A. (Eds), *Teacher Development and Educational Change*, London, Falmer Press.

GOODSON, I.F. (1992) 'Sponsoring the teachers' voice', in HARGREAVES, A. and FULLAN, M. (Eds), *Understanding Teacher Development*, London, Cassell.

GOODSON, I.F. (1995) 'Studying the Teacher's Life and Work', in SMYTH, J. (Ed.), *Critical Discourses on Teacher Development*, London, Cassell.

GORE, J.M. and ZEICHNER, K.M. (1995) 'Connecting Action Research to Genuine Teacher Development', in SMYTH, J. (Ed.), *Critical Discourses on Teacher Development*, London, Cassell.

HARGREAVES, A. (1996) 'Revisiting Voice', *Educational Researcher*, **25**, 1, Jan/Feb, 1996, pp. 12–19.

HATTON, N. and SMITH, D. (1995) 'Facilitating Reflection: Issues and Research', *Forum of Education*, **50**, 1, April 1995, pp. 49–65.

HOLLY, M.L. (1991) *Personal and Professional Learning: on Teaching and Self-Knowledge*, paper presented to the CARN Conference, University of Nottingham, April.

HUBERMAN, M. (1995) *The Lives of Teachers*, London, Cassell.

LACEY, C. (1977) *The Socialisation of Teachers*, London, Methnen.

LEITHWOOD, K. (1990) 'The Principal's Role in Teacher Development', in JOYCE, B. (Ed.), *Changing School through Staff Development*, Alexandria, VA, Association for Supervision and Curriculum Development.

LISTON, D. and ZEICHNER, K. (1991) *Teacher Education and the Social Conditions of Schooling*, New York, Routledge and Chapman Hill.

NIAS, J. (1989) *Primary Teachers Talking*, London, Routledge & Kegan Paul.

NODDINGS, N. (1992) *The Challenge to Care in Schools*, New York, Teachers' College Press.

PETERSON, K.D. (1990) 'Assistance and Assessment for Beginning Teachers', in MILLMAN, I. and DARLING HAMMOND, L. (Eds), *The New Handbook of Teacher Evaluation*, New York, Sage Publications.

SCHON, D.A. (1983) *The Reflective Practitioner: How Professionals Think in Action*, New York, Basic Books.

SCHON, D.A. (1987) *Educating the Reflective Practitioner: Toward a New Design for Teaching and Learning in the Professions*, San Francisco, Jossey Bass.

SIKES, P., MEASOR, L. and WOODS, P. (1985) *Teacher Careers: Crises and Continuities*, London, Falmer Press.

SMITH, D. and LOVAT, T. (1991) *Curriculum: Action on Reflection*, Wentworth Falls, Social Science Press (2nd edition).

SMYTH, J. (Ed.) (1995) *Critical Discourses on Teacher Development*, London, Cassell.

TOM, A. (1985) 'Inquiring into Inquiry-Oriented Teacher Education', *Journal of Teacher Education*, **36**, 5, pp. 35–44.

WINTER, R. (1989) *Learning from Experience: Principles and Practice in Action Research*, Lewes, Falmer Press.

ZEICHNER, K. and LISTON, D. (1990) *Traditions of Reform and Reflective Teaching in US Teacher Education*, Lansing, Michigan, National Centre for Research in Teacher Education, Michigan State University.

ZEICHNER, K. (1993) 'Action Research: Personal Renewal and Social Reconstruction', *Education Action Research*, **1**, 2, pp. 199–220.

18   Action Research and
'The Reflexive Project of Selves'

Ivor F. Goodson (Canada)

> Here we have a poem which is holding Eliot together as much as he is
> holding the poem together.
> **Peter Ackroyd on T.S. Eliot's 'The Wasteland'**

A common way of proceeding in exploring a project's impact and dissemination
has often been through textual analysis. Following this mode, it is assumed that a
project is disseminated through the textual production of the key players. Here it is
tacitly asserted that new recruits to action research would be persuaded by reading
the texts and hearing the interpretations of the main advocates of the movements.
Hence, by intertextual exchange and intersubjective negotiation, new recruits join
the movement and the movement develops and expands.

A countervailing view to this rational/textual view would be that here we are
more, or at least as much, concerned with issues of personal knowledge and construction; we might argue that new recruits are less concerned with textual justification than with issues of lifestyle and identity. Hence, counterpoised against textual
conversion would be a possibility that new recruits to social movements such as
action research are actually involved in identity or lifestyle shopping. What they
would be more concerned with by this view would be the kind of lifestyles or identities which are carried in suspension within new social movements. Hence, rather
than a view of action research as dissemination, as proceeding through rational
adoption after textual conversion, here we would be looking for a more personal
set of transitions. These would be closely meshed with issues of identity and lifestyle and hence, the best mode for enquiring into this countervailing view would
be the collection of a number of life histories.

The Teachers as Researchers project at the University of East Anglia has
allowed us to test this view of social action as identity politics. In the fieldwork
stage of the project a range of life history interviews have been conducted with
teachers who employed action research modalities and/or were members of action
research projects and groups. The group included a number of the 'key players' in
action research.

This move towards the analysis of identity politics, whilst partially no doubt
a response to postmodern discourses, is related to changes in the economy and
superstructure. As Wolf has argued, it is probable that it will not only be the welfare

state which is dismantled in the new epoch 'following the end of history' but also aspects of the superstructure (Wolf, 1989). In particular, he argues, some of the median associations such as universities and schools may well be diminished and decoupled in significant ways. This means that institutional sites, institutional missions, institutional objectives and institutional movements may not any longer be the most significant sites of struggle and analysis. It further means that methodological genres which focus on institutional analysis and institutional theorizing may be similarly diminished and hence, the need to develop new genres becomes pressing.

One of the new arenas for struggle and definition will undoubtedly be personal life and identity. It is here that perhaps one of the most interesting projects, what Giddens (1991) calls 'the reflexive project of the self' will be contested in the new epoch. Life politics, the politics of identity construction and ongoing identity maintenance will become a major growing site of ideological and intellectual construction and contestation.

Of course, the link between identity politics, the reflexive project of the self and broader social and institutional movements and missions has always been there. In analyzing that interrelationship, we need to develop broader patterns of data and data analysis which focus on the reflexive project of the self. Indeed, we need to broaden and deepen the conception of self away from a singular, unitary, linear notion of narrative of self towards a multiple and more fluid notion of self. Hence, the focus in this work is on the reflexive project of selves which is meant to refer to the multi-faceted aspect of the self project. It is argued that whilst singularly embodied and embedded the self has multiple facets and prospects.

Before dealing with some of the themes and topics which emerge in interviews and in subsequent data analysis, let me by way of exemplification provide an extended quote from a leading action research proponent which shows the close relationship between the reflexive project of the self and the development of action research. We have tried in this report to carry as much of the 'voice' of the interviewees as is possible, whilst noting that their voice is in fact a 'third voice' — the voice constructed by the interviewee and interviewer in interactive negotiations. There has certainly been no attempt for the interviewer to play 'neutral chairman' in these interviews. Emerging themes and ideas are paraded, tested and often times rejected. There has been little attempt to keep 'theories' hidden until the interviews are completed. In this model which has not been employed, theorist can emerge from the undergrowth of the interview and provide the pristine theory that has been hatching unbeknown to the interviewee. So we see a third voice being negotiated, contested and constructed in these interviews.

Interviewee:	Well I don't know I grew up with a lot of aggression that I turned towards myself and then gradually learned how to externalize that aggression. And I've always had this tension between being in many ways an extreme extrovert, I mean the life and the soul of the party, very articulate, verbal and er do you know what I mean?
Ivor:	That's just performance though.

Int:	That's just performance, that's act. And then there's been this rather sort of neurotic introverted character as well. Most people don't see that now ...
Ivor:	Mm. You just mentioned there —
Int:	Er that macho thing and then this sort of rather shy sensitive retiring recluse.
Ivor:	Mm. Which is the real you, the latter?
Int:	No I think they're both me, hence action research and the theory practice problem. I think they're both me and I try to keep them together in some way interactive with one another. Um so why would *Sailing* be my favourite song? Rod Stewart right? — a) because it's a —
Ivor:	It's transcendent It's a bloody transcendent song.
Int:	Yes, because you see the sea. The sea and sailing, I mean the navy was another vision I had of a vocation which didn't come to fruition. Um but I've always seen myself as a man of action and as an intellectual.
Ivor:	Why do you think that? I mean just go back to this thing about, early on you said something about this aggression that you were able to internalize, where did the aggression come from? What was that about?
Int:	Well I always thought it was aggression against my strict father.
Ivor:	I bet it was the other way.
Int:	What?
Ivor:	It was more your mother wasn't it?
Int:	Yeah, I think it was now, aggression towards my mother, and so I've had a tremendous problem that I live with to this day aggression towards women.
Ivor:	And was it aggression that she wasn't, although she was there she wasn't really interested? I mean what —
Int:	No, no not at all. My mother doted on her sons, I was a spoilt mother's boy in some ways.
Ivor:	Smothered?
Int:	I've had a great fear of getting tied down by women, which is a fear most men have to some extent.
Ivor:	Mm, so it was the smothering that lead to the aggression?
Int:	It took me until I was about 45 to be able to relate to an emotional woman. All the women I was attracted to before then were the kind of cool, ice-cool Grace Kelly types, who I saw as a profound challenge breaking down the barrier, of course I never did, and never wanting to get into the emotional stuff because I always associated emotionality with manipulation.

Ivor:	So that action research is a way of taking back that sense of autonomy is it?
Int:	Yeah, yeah.
Ivor:	Taking back power.
Int:	Oh yeah, that's why I'm talking about power. Autonomy, control over your life. And developing a distinction between taking control and being in control, I mean I do have a concept that you can't in fact control your circumstances, the behaviour of everyone in the world, what you can do is you can always be in control over your own self, the construction of your own self in relationship to the situation.

The elements covered in this interview provide a useful backcloth for the thematic analysis of the range of interviews conducted with action research proponents. A number of the themes touched upon in this interview can be discerned more generally in the interview material. Three themes seem particularly salient. Firstly, the issue of the teacher as intellectual, the teacher as scientist, the teacher as researcher. These positional statements run in similar form across all of the interviews conducted. It is as if the interviewees are at pains to point out that they renounce a narrow definition of the teacher as technician, as deliverer, as implementer of other people's objectives. There is a strong stress on the autonomy of teacher's work and this seems clearly related to a definition of self as intellectual or scientist or researcher. A number of the interviewees speak eloquently of the sense of self and autonomy that is expressed through the spaces and locations associated with intellectual visions and work.

This issue which deals with the autonomous space to undertake the 'reflective project of the self' relates to two other themes. These may be seen as different routes of movement or escape. So as a second theme, there is what may be described as the 'escape from the self'. The attempt to transcend initial social definitions and locations through movement to another locational place and psyche. Thirdly, there is the movement beyond the classroom towards a more purist notion of intellectual location. The themes of escape from the classroom and escape from the original self seem common within the interviews conducted. But before we examine notion of escape, we need to define starting points.

Origins and Destinations

Before exploring the main themes discerned in the interviews, it is important to provide some contextual background of the origins and destinations of the main interviewees. Some of the interviewees spoke frankly of some of the trials and traumas of their early years. These experiences may go some way to explaining the appeal of a social movement like action research in terms of its general missionary posture but also in terms of its potential for 'playing out' more broader psychic struggles. This relates specifically to its core belief — its psychic promise if you will — that action can be 'researched', intellectualized, rationalized as a guide to behaviour and as a means of asserting control in a precarious and sometimes hostile psychic and, later, workaday world.

One of the interviewees spoke of her mother before analyzing some of her early experiences. The interview makes clear some of the links between early experiences and the appeal of the 'action research movement' in which she has now become a key player.

Int: She was a very independent spirit. She learnt to drive in India. She insisted upon driving as much as my father drove. She insisted on having her own bank account, which she saw as a matter of pride that they didn't have a joint account. So when she was left money by an old aunt, she had control over that. It cost her very hard that she couldn't work. But her father was so ashamed that his wife, (my grandmother), had been a nurse. She was the vicar's daughter and they had to work because they weren't really very wealthy, but when she married a doctor nobody knew any more that she'd been a nurse, they didn't discover that she'd been a nurse until after she died and they found documents in her possession which showed that she had this qualification and she had worked as a nurse before her marriage. My grandfather saw it as a matter of real pride that he supported his family, even though he never had any money, they were always incredibly hard up. So this was a very, this was no doubt a very, very powerful influence in me, it still is. I find the hardest thing to understand about one of my children is that she has absolutely no desire to have a career, she lives in a bus, she's a, a new age traveller or whatever. And that's fine, I understand it intellectually but it was so important to me to do, what I saw at the time as doing something with my life. To me just spending my life on bringing up the next generation of children wasn't making any mark, you know, I felt that life would be purposeless, that my own statement would have been lost if I simply become the person who produced the next generation. And I felt that really strongly.

Ivor: Tell me what it was.

Int: Because I felt so trapped.

The feeling of being 'trapped' or 'smothered' or encased in a very circumscribed class or regional environment was a common theme. This often led to a desire for forms of 'escape' or 'transcendence'.

The scholarship route to grammar school as 'an area of self transcendence' was commented on by most of the interviewees. Clear gender differences emerge in the telling of these tales of scholarship success.

I was the first person to go to university in my family — you know, the usual story. I was an only child — there was my mother and me, my father had died when I was very small. There was no-one in the family to offer any kind of advice about higher education. Going to university was really quite a big step and we were also very poor so it was also quite a strain. I was growing up in south-east London — I'd always lived in London.

My mother was a Harris and there was a rich end of the family who owned Harris' Bread and Cakes. I don't think the firm exists any longer. The family was committed to educating the boys. They paid for the boys to go to grammar schools but the girls left school early — presumably with the expectation that they would marry. So my mother left school at 14 and went into a variety of jobs, but she also spent a long time then going to evening sessions at Morley College. It offered a range of music. She didn't win any qualifications because she was always in and out of things. There was a lot of music in the family. The men drank a bit and gambled a bit and I was brought up in a female setting — with none of the females having any qualifications. The pattern was that the women saved and the men spent — and I had to learn to break out of the female habit!

But they knew it was important to go to university. I remember going for interviews in Nottingham and various places but chose to go to London because my mother was ill and wanted me to see her at weekends. I went to Westfield College in Hampstead.

My father had trained as a chemist but he died when I was very small. I don't know much about my father's side of the family.

The 'scholarship boys' and 'scholarship girls' who went to grammar schools in the fifties and sixties experienced considerable uncertainty at their cultural marginality. This has been closely documented by Hoggart (1958), Steedman (1986) and perhaps most influentially in Jackson and Marsden (1962).

The salience of scholarship boy and girl stories in the accounts collected is of considerable significance and in all probability provides a natural seedbed for transition to stories of 'the teacher as intellectual'. It would seem that the arena of schooling provided the location for the acts of transcendence and rationalizing engagement recounted by the interviewees. In this sense, it is probable that schools have a mythic place in the stories and dreams for these people. It is almost as if, therefore, they were socialized into modernism because of the close link with the reflexive project of the self. Not surprisingly then, later in life, their work turned to using action research to seek to improve (sometimes in transcendent ways) public schooling. In this sense, the relationship between the individual reflexive projects of selves and their collective outcome in the social movement of action research is an important locus for our social analysis.

Teachers as Intellectuals

The possibility of a conception of 'teachers as intellectuals' or 'teachers as researchers' depends very much on the social and political conditions of particular historical periods. It is significant that much of the exploration and operationalization of the 'teacher as researcher' and 'teacher as intellectual' conception were undertaken in the 1960s. In the United Kingdom, this was a time when the Labour government was sponsoring the search for a number of solutions through schooling as part of the broad implementation of comprehensive schooling. This is the period Eric Hobsbawm (1994) has characterized as the 'golden age' — an age of social democratic capitalism where patterns of profit and accumulation allowed degrees of looseness in social reproduction and construction which would be entirely unthinkable in current times. Hence, the encouragement of teachers as researchers and intellectuals as part of a broader, albeit partial, social and political project was specific to the late 1950s and 1960s.

> *Ivor*: But would it be fair to say just going back through the biography there and sifting through, what you're really saying in terms of why the teacher as researcher thing began for you in a school that you were trying in teaching to carve out the biographical space that you'd always wanted.
>
> *Int*: Yes.
>
> *Ivor*: You'd wanted to be a researcher?
>
> *Int*: Yes, absolutely right.
>
> *Ivor*: You'd wanted to be a scientific researcher but this was a way of parleying that in to where you ended up which was teaching?
>
> *Int*: Yes, but don't forget my research was always action research in one sense. I mean as a nuclear physicist I wanted to —
>
> *Ivor*: Yeah, sure.
>
> *Int*: Split the atom and get bombs going off, laughs.
>
> *Ivor*: Yeah, that's pretty active.

For this reason, it is of considerable interest that many of the interviewees express opinions that are similar to Henry Giroux's notion of 'teachers as intellectuals' a conception that derives a considerable amount, possibly unknowingly, from the earlier conceptions of the teacher as researcher — that were pioneered in Europe. Giroux writes:

> As intellectuals, they will combine reflection and action in the interest of empowering students with the skills and knowledge needed to address injustices and to be critical actors committed to developing a world free of oppression and exploitation. (Giroux, 1988, p. xxxiv)

He goes on to define the transformative and transcendent aspects of this conceptualization of self and work.

The material conditions under which teachers work constitute the basis for either delimiting or empowering their practices as intellectuals. Therefore teachers and intellectuals will need to reconsider and, possibly, transform the fundamental nature of the conditions under which they work. That is teachers must be able to shake the way in which time, space, activity, and knowledge organize everyday life in schools. More specifically, in order to function as intellectuals, teachers must create the ideology and structural conditions necessary for them to write, research, and work with each other in producing curricula and sharing power. In the final analysis, teachers need to develop a discourse and set of assumptions that allow them to function more specifically as transformative intellectuals. (Giroux, 1988, p. xxiv)

One of the interviewees talked about the salience of this conception of being 'an intellectual' and the way that it dawned upon her in the months she spent in Ireland recovering from a divorce. Planning the conception of self as intellectual plays a crucial role in the reflexive project of self-building that has been undertaken, and what is described in the interview.

Ivor: You've just used the phrase there 'taking control with all the ideas put together', interestingly I have noted just before rational/intellectual taking control, is that notion of being an academic, being an intellectual linked with this idea of how one takes control of one's life and one's biography from what has been a fairly rootless and fragmented childhood, do you think that issue of how one takes control through books and the imagination is very much part of the motif for you?

Int: Yes, I do. Yes, I think that's quite perceptive. Yes.

Ivor: So when you talk about becoming academic, becoming intellectual it must have a kind of biographical meaning about how one takes control of a life?

Int: Yes. I'm sure it does. I'm sure it's easy to see the roots in my childhood, but I think also if you are a lonely child and you turn to books very strongly, one of the few things I remember telling the psychoanalyst in Dublin for the short time I lay on the couch was that I had really lived in books for part of my childhood, and then suddenly found that people were interesting. I suppose this was when I made some very good friends in the last two or three years I was at that school in Dublin. I've always thought it was a very odd idea actually, this does relate to the way I feel about action research, the idea that you can't learn from books is very peculiar to me actually. I do see what the problems are, but I think one of the major problems about a lot of action research work is that it hasn't been sufficiently rooted in knowledge of other people's ideas. I'm impatient of people who ridicule something called propositional knowledge. I think one wants to have every kind of experience and reading is a hell of an interesting experience. And I include vicarious experience, I mean a lot of my childhood was locked up in pretty boring places but you could get tremendous vicarious experience through reading. So a big image for me was lying in that boarding school in Malvern which was in the old railway hotel and hearing the trains go past by night. It was so bloody wonderful to hear these trains whistling and to think of them going out there through the night, and free. I think I had practically no freedom during my entire childhood so when I finally got myself to Trinity, I was booked into one of the women's halls of residence, but I basically never ate a single meal there the whole term because it was something like a four mile bicycle ride out there, and it just wasn't worth going home because it would have meant that I couldn't do anything in the evening. So I just took off, I mean my memory of being a student was just riding around Dublin on a bicycle, luxuriously, thinking I can go anywhere I bloody like and do anything I bloody want. I'm completely free.

Patterns of Transcendence

Later on, in discussing a period of secondment following years of teaching, the interviewee in the foregoing section referred to the 'absolutely transformative event in my entire career' certainly an absolutely crucial transition in the continuing project of self-building, of which the trajectory was emerging with increasing clarity: It happened while she was at the Cambridge Institute on a full time secondment from her teaching job.

> *Int*: So over coffee somebody said to me that the big thing was curriculum studies and that he was going to do curriculum studies with this person called John Elliott, and I said, 'Well, I'll come along'. So I went to John's first session although I wasn't enrolled as his student and said to him, 'Would it be allright if I sat in because I was interested'. At the end of the session I went straight out thinking that this was the most mind-blowing thing, you know, because suddenly instead of it being just a great relief year there was a chance of something that would be absolutely riveting, i.e., going to schools to carry out research on behalf of teachers. This is what he told us in the first session, this is what he had lined up for us, he'd got these schools where teachers were coming up with problems, they wanted his students to go in, work with them on something and carry out research on their behalf and help them to improve their practice. And I thought —
>
> *Ivor*: And why did that appeal to you so much?

Int: I just thought it sounded the most exciting and interesting possibility of — why, [laughs]. Oh I think, I don't know, Ivor, really. I think, I suppose the word 'research' meant a lot, you know I still, you see I never thought I was doing something called, I did call it action research but I didn't differentiate it from research. I felt it was just as valuable as, I didn't really have any hang-ups that what I was doing wasn't proper research. I felt affronted when I found out that other people didn't necessarily feel it was, you know.

One of the recurrent themes in the interviews of people's backgrounds and lifestories is the notice of what one interviewee actually calls 'transcendence', the move from one vision of self to a wider range of alternatives or multiple selves. One of the interviewees spoke specifically of how notions of multiple selves began to emerge in her work as an action researcher.

So I wrote a thing about my multiple selves and constructing my self for personnel managers, and the self-positioning, and the way in which what you are as a self has to act politically. Therefore you can't have this notion of the one true self because you have to be a political actor otherwise you're powerless. So you have to be conscious of the different selves you can employ.

The development of these reflexive project of selves often could be retrospectively, yet partially and selectively, reconstructed in the interviews. One episode, for instance, spoke of a 'breathtaking moment' where the person realized that there were a range of alternative futures which would make possible a different conceptualization of self. The episode took place when the teacher who, as we have seen earlier, aspired to a vision of himself as a scientific and ornithological researcher, was involved in catching birds.

Int: I mean I remember one night, just while we're talking about Kenneth Allsopp and stuff, catching these wag-tails, which we did in huge numbers, and a little falcon twigged on to what was happening and it just hovered around for a while for this big pile of wag-tails to come in and just took the weakest one out and I mean it was just a breath-taking moment so there were those sort of moments but that's aside. Yeah, it gave me, it gave a connection with that, that world, that it was tangential to it and not part of it and, and at the same time there were beginning to be pressures like, oughtn't I, you know I was a Scale 4 head of science, oughtn't I to be getting on to be deputy-head? which I could never visualise myself as. So what that gave, and I don't think I knew it at the time, but what it gave was an alternative vision of a future and that's a Stenhousian phrase as you probably recognize, you know —

Ivor: Mm, yes.

> *Int*:   Sort of dreams of, of possible futures and, not having read Stenhouse at that point, that's how I would characterize it.

The visions of alternative futures and alternative selves often arose from a recognition that the original social location and pattern of socialization was unacceptable. As one interviewee put it, she came to, 'understand that certain aspects of the way I was brought up stank'. Because of this background, she continued

> it was difficult for me to be the kind of person I wanted to be. To have the kind of democratic values I wanted to aspire to wasn't something that I could automatically do, you know, every time I opened my mouth, I made some other Englishman despise me. It was not only the way I sounded but the sort of phrases I used, my discourse. It was terribly difficult to unpick an entire discourse system you've been brought up in, even if rationally you've come to understand you don't want to be part of it.

This seems as articulate and concise a statement of the desire to escape from the original social location and socially constructed self as it is possible to imagine.

Leaving Teaching

Alongside the desire to escape from the original social location and pattern of socialization, was a subsequent desire to escape from the classroom, a similarly embedded site of self definition and socialization as systematic and penetrative as anything experienced in family life.

> *Ivor*:   so you didn't really think hard about leaving teaching, it was an easy decision?
> *Int*:   Mm, I didn't want to go back. I knew it was risky but I felt confident and just went ahead with it.
> *Ivor*:   When you say you didn't want to go back had you at that stage had enough of teaching and if so why?
> *Int*:   Yes, I think I had. Well, because I felt like somebody who had gradually peeled off more and more protective layers as a result of trying to get away from the routines, the protective techniques that teachers had wrapped around themselves. You know that sense originally when I started that my personality was under attack, which I used to feel because I had to discipline people and force people to do things they didn't want to do. It was very good for me because I was actually very lacking in confidence in many ways when I first became a teacher. It was a curious mixture but there was a part of me which was very lacking in confidence and it toughened me up no end that I had to take this role all the time. But then when I started doing action research the investigation into the

interaction between myself and students and the examination of my own motives and tacit assumptions and all that stuff, and also looking carefully at what learning tasks I was setting meant that I was setting more and more challenging work really, so I was losing out on some of the, you know, reciprocal negotiation that people would get on comfortably because I wasn't challenging them too much. So the job was quite demanding and the more that you peel off these protective layers and try to engage with every individual student and then people just say, 'Bugger off' because they're teenagers and they don't want to be there. It's crushing. I began losing my temper sometimes because my big dilemma was always, how do you engage in one-to-one conversation with people sufficiently to actually take them forward intellectually? You know, how do you listen to what they've said, come back with a response which will enable them to take their thinking forward. In other words, how do you have some kind of Socratic dialogue when you've got twenty-nine other people in the room? Well, the only way you do is by changing the whole responsibility for learning and creating a new ambience where they take responsibility for their own learning — And I tried to achieve that and I achieved a lot of in my classes but I didn't achieve it with, you know, groups who were in a sense —

Ivor: I mean how were the other staff of the school responding to your Socratic interventions?

Int: I don't think they knew much about it, I think that I had to keep quiet about what I was doing. Although interestingly my dissertation for my MA, in fact all of my research for my MA, made me a lot more popular in the school in the end, because I interviewed people and I interviewed them having divested myself from my role as Head of English. And I listened to them and wrote down what they said and they liked that enormously.

Ivor: But in terms of what you're saying, I mean here you are, you're going through this very reflective practitioner mode, but somehow it's led you to the conclusion that you'd be best to move onto something else rather than going on in teaching, hasn't it?

Int: Well, yes, I know, but that is the rub and that is the guilt. That's why, you know, when you first get your first job outside teaching you don't feel good about being in a town during a school day. You actually feel bad about going down to buy a pair of shoes or — you know for a long time after you give up teaching, you know precisely what people are doing at this moment if you were still in school. So you go past the school gate, to drive from Thatchar to Redmona and instead of thinking, 'shit, how awful I've got an hour and a quarter to drive before I get to work', you think this is a wonderful trade-off for marking all those exercise books which I used to have to do all day on Sunday. And gone is the feeling of dread on Sundays about Monday morning. And I don't know why that's an integral part of teaching, but I've never yet, you'll probably, you'll probably tell me you're the exception, but I've never yet met a teacher who didn't own up to feeling a sense of dread on Sunday afternoon.

The problems of the escape from the classroom are made very clear in the experience of one of the interviewees. After a sustained period on action research projects based in university, she spoke of the problems of re-entering teaching.

Int: So I had to fall backwards on the authority and they said, 'OK, you can go onto supply here.' And I went to a school in Cambridgeshire on supply and all of the cues that I thought I knew how to handle about kids just came totally unstuck. So I mean in a school that I had taught at for nine years I could cough and the whole school would come quiet, you know that? You know that they knew me, I knew them, they knew when I was serious and stuff, and yet in this other school I did that and a small kid came from the front and gave me a cough sweet, you know. Er, cheeky little sod. And all, all my practical skills had gone, and it was a nightmare actually, the whole summer term there, trying to stay with your head above water in a situation that formerly you could have wellied with your arm behind your back, you know, it was just a nightmare.

Ivor: It's very paradoxical, isn't it? As I mean after a long immersion in practitioner based action research what you ended up being was deskilled.

Int: Totally so, totally so.

Ivor: And that is the paradox isn't it?

Int: Yes.

Ivor: How do you explain it?

Int: I think, I mean there's numerous ways that you could explain it, I think it's a bit like this thing that people say horses can smell fear. It wasn't fear the kids could smell but they knew my lack of motivation, that I was being where I didn't want to be, in a world I didn't want to be in.

Ivor: Had your view of yourself changed then really during the years?

Int: Oh yes.

Ivor: From what to what? From practitioner —

Int: To researcher, I think would be the, the [pause] — and in the end I'd got masters in the process and so I'd begun to see myself in that metier. And that's where I wanted to be and to be elsewhere was if you like a failure in that project. Um —

Ivor: What do you mean?

Int: Well in the project to be within the research world. To have to dump yourself back in school. I mean I was doing the kids no service, not where I wanted to be and they knew it. I knew it.

What is so clear about this interview is the way that a new sense of self had emerged whilst on action research project in universities. And it was, as it were, impossible to take that sense of self back into the classroom. As he says 'I'd begun to see myself in that metier'. And it was difficult, therefore, to re-enter the world of classrooms.

Conclusion

The range of themes which emerge in the interviews are compelling but also in their nature, selective. We chose to interview a number of the 'key players' from the action research movement and as a result we have a cohort of people who moved into elite positions inside the university sector. What is made clear, however, is that taking the notion of the teacher as intellectual and the teacher as researcher seriously, often led to the logical conclusion of moving from being a teacher to being, in a pure sense, a researcher or intellectual. This logic was built into the paradigm from the beginning and it is perhaps not surprising that some of the key players in the movement followed this metier to its conclusion.

The selective nature of the sample provokes other questions. Most notably, what about the large army of teachers who do not leave the classroom but continue to practice notions of the teacher as researcher or teacher as intellectual within their classrooms? Associated with this is perhaps the most critical question of all. Which is: is action research institutionalized in university courses in ways that foster notions of escape and transcendence? Does action research as realized and institutionalized in universities take a particular form which encourages patterns of abstraction and intellectualization which are convenient for the university milieu and the careers pursued therein, but inappropriate and decontextualized for those wishing to take action research back into the classroom?

This links to questions of the relationship between private lives (and self projects) and professional trajectories (and careers). The patterns of status and resources which structure professional careers influence the patterns of knowledge which are embraced and institutionalized. These patterns influence even countervailing traditions such as action research in ways that penetrate both private and public projects. They warn us that as C. Wright Mills argued: 'No social study that does not come back to the problems of biography, of history and of their intersections within a society has completed its intellectual journey.' (Mills, 1959, p. 6)

References

APPLE, M. (1979) *Ideology and Curriculum*, London, Routledge.
GIDDENS, A. (1991) *Modernity and Self-identity: Self and Society in the Late Modern Age*, Cambridge, Polity Press (in association with Basil Blackwell).

Ivor F. Goodson

GIROUX, H.A. (1988) *Teachers and Intellectuals: Towards a Critical Pedagogy of Learning?*, MA, Bergen & Garvey.

HOBSBAWM, E. (1994) *Age of Extremes: The Short Twentieth Century, 1914–1991*, London, Michael Joseph.

HOGGART, R. (1958) *The Uses of Literacy*, Harmondworth, Middlesex, Penguin Books, in association with Chatto and Windus.

JACKSON, B. and MARSDEN, D. (1962) *Education and the Working Class*, London, Routledge and Kegan Paul.

MILLS, C. WRIGHT (1959) *The Sociological Imagination*, London, Oxford University Press.

STEEDMAN, C. (1986) *Landscape for a Good Woman*, London, Virago Press.

STENHOUSE, L. (1975) *An Introduction to Curriculum Research and Development*, London, Heinemann.

WOLF, A. (1989) *Whose Keeper? Social Science and Moral Obligation*, Berkeley, CA, University of California Press.

19 Using Participatory Action Research for the Reconceptualization of Educational Practice

Lesvia Olivia Rosas C. (Mexico)

The Reconceptualization of Educational Practice as a Necessary Element for Improvement of Educational Quality

Research and studies made during the past few years about basic education in Mexico have paid close attention to teaching as the primary determinant in the improvement of educational quality. Of course, there is nothing new about that; if one only recalls educational reforms made during the past thirty years, one will see that teachers have always been at the top of the list, and that attention to their preparation is one of the most important aspects of any educational reform. Given that situation, what has educational research contributed to our current understanding and development of teaching?

By centering attention on teaching, educational research during the last decade has helped uncover teaching from very different angles: some have concentrated on how working conditions hinder professional fulfilment. This type of study eliminates the romanticism of teaching and presents it as simply the job of workers who require but often lack, particular working conditions and salary levels to perform their tasks well (Lavín, 1992; Fierro, 1991). Other researchers have analyzed teacher preparation programs and critiqued them both for their exhausting pace and lack of 'realistic' content (Alvarez, 1975; Calvo, 1980; Ulloa, 1989). Still others have investigated the way in which teachers conceive and execute their duties, the roles they play within the educational process, the capacity they display for making decisions (Vera, 1985). All this has been done in the spirit of helping the teacher play a more decisive role in educational reform and societal development.

The actions proposed to solve the designated problems of teaching, until a few years ago, were made from outside the classroom. They took the form of new curricular designs, new textbooks, didactic materials, training courses, etc. It was not until the beginning of the 1980s that a discourse emerged about the necessity of restoring teachers' position as central subjects in the educational process. Educators began to talk about teachers' 'reconceptualization of educational practice' as a fundamental to improving education.

As is well known, the teacher of basic education has little or no say in material features that determine their practices: curricular design, creation of textbooks and the formation of programs, etc. Teachers' roles are generally passive, since they are required to translate orders that are given to them. Only in exceptional cases does one find teachers who make of their classrooms a space in which 'knowledge is reconceptualized' (going back to Paulo Freire).

Another problem is the solitude in which teachers work; regardless of how much knowledge their experiences in schools have given them, seldom, if ever, do they have the chance of sharing this with their colleagues. If we add to that the fact that many teachers, particularly those who work in poorer areas, are not provided with the means for further study, they run the risk of becoming routinized and outdated. Without such support, teachers must resolve problems of practice by finding the quickest and least complex solution. Faced with these realities, how can teachers manage to reconceptualize their practices by creating a space for reflection, for creating knowledge, for communicating with their colleagues and their students?

Methodological Strategies for the Reconceptualization and Analysis of Teaching Practice: The Scheme of the Six Dimensions

The main objective of teaching is the education of human beings; it is a social practice and a praxis. As a social practice, it is normed by the relationships between scholar and social agents. As a praxis, it is concerned with a dialectical relationship between theory and practice, between reflection and action.

The teaching task may be seen as a complex of relationships, established among the different agents that make it happen, and a group of objective as well as subjective elements, that determine how it comes into play. Among the former are politics, administration, standards and facilities, and among the latter are the sense, the perceptions and the actions of the persons involved. The objective of reconceptualizing practice is not only that of analyzing it, but to do it critically: recognizing incongruities, successes, shortcomings and possibilities, and above all, placing oneself personally inside of teaching as a practice.

For teachers, re-creating their practices implies managing to distance themselves from it, but at the same time getting closer to it with a different perspective. To achieve that, teachers must rely on an 'instrument' of some sort. In the search for this instrument, a group of researchers from the Educational Research Center[1] elaborated a scheme which we have called 'The Six Dimensions of Educational Practice' (Fierro, Rosas and Fortoul, 1995). The scheme shows the complexity of the teaching practice, conceptualized as a gathering of relationships that are established as much inside as outside the classroom.

The six dimensions that comprise the scheme are the following:

1 The Personal Dimension: This concerns teachers as human beings with personal histories, explicit experiences, skills and limitations. This dimension permits teachers to recover, within the trajectory of their lives, biographical factors that made them become teachers and the story of their lives within the profession. The most important thing about this dimension

is that it helps teachers become conscious of their role as subjects of their work in teaching.

2   The Institutional Dimension: Here teachers embrace all the working relationships that their jobs imply. The analysis of this dimension permits teachers to reconceptualize their practices by reflecting upon the institutional aspects that determine their work.

3   The Interpersonal Dimension: This concerns teachers in relation to the other members of the school, their students and students' families. In analyzing those relationships, they discover the importance of communication and dialogue.

4   The Social Dimension: When reflecting upon this dimension, teachers reconceptualize their practices in education as social spaces, realizing that they are heavily influenced by the social majority, and that they can also transcend that influence.

5   The Didactic Dimension: In analyzing this dimension, teachers can understand why they teach as they do, and discover their particular learning needs. In this dimension, too, teachers have a chance to reconsider the sort of relationships that they have made with their students, the standards that regulate classroom work, and the ways that they evaluate this work.

6   The Value Dimension: Finally, this dimension helps teachers reconceptualize themselves as persons who have inside themselves beliefs, ideals and values which orient all of their activities, and therefore, their work. This dimension enables teachers to reconceptualize their practices as a place in which they mold their values, but also where those values can be questioned and re-evaluated.

As they move through the six dimensions, teachers formulate questions, postulate hypotheses and find explanations which lead them to a different relationship with accumulated knowledge. They no longer seek 'formulas' for their teaching practices, but rather new ideas with which they can interact until they transform the ideas into their own words. Another result is that, by standing back from their practices, teachers may be able to reconsider all those situations that seemed to hinder their work. This doesn't mean that the teachers will be able to resolve them all, but they will realize that there is much more they can do than they imagined before. Thus, the scheme of the six dimensions becomes the first step in a process of engaging in participatory action research, leading to a reconceptualization and even transformation of teaching practice.

Participatory Action Research as a Process for the Reconceptualization of Educational Practice

Participatory action research, (Kemmis and McTaggart, 1988: 9) seeks the transformation of social practices through a process in which social actors understand the rationality of their own practices and the social conditions that determine them. Applied to education, participatory research seeks the transformation of educational practices through the participation of educational agents in reflective action groups.

In an effort to offer teachers a systematic way to understand the rationality of their own practices and transform them, we continue from the scheme of the six dimensions to an 'Analysis of Our Educational Practice'. In this analysis, teachers collectively identify classroom problems to be solved and the required knowledge to solve them. The second step — 'Seeking New Answers' — requires the group to select appropriate solutions, try them in action, gather evidence about students' responses to the attempted solutions, and analyze the results. The final step is 'Transforming Our Educational Practices' — or asking the group to note the ways in which practices have been transformed through participatory research. Once the project has been finished and evaluated, the process can begin again, as many times as the group wishes.

There are two important points to stress in the process: (1) teachers must learn to distance themselves from practice and reflect upon the action, so that reflection and action mutually nourish each other; and (2) teachers must learn to communicate and work in a group.

A Case Example of the Participatory Action Research Process in the Reconceptualization of Educational Practice

The case presented here refers to a project carried out by the Centro de Estudios Educativos — Educational Research Center — with teachers from a group of private schools. The project was foundation funded. All the schools were located in marginal rural or urban areas. Some of the former were located in regions with both indigenous and 'mestizo' populations. The project objective was to offer teachers in the schools a permanent educational process for facing and solving daily problems of practice — and ultimately prepare them to give their students a higher quality education. The teacher population was characterized by the lack of opportunity for ongoing professional development and constant mobility due to their working conditions. Nevertheless, the degree of enthusiasm and commitment of the teachers increased as the process advanced.

The first stage of the work was the analysis teachers made of their own teaching practices based on the six dimensions scheme described earlier. The analysis was done by means of group exercises especially designed for that purpose. In this stage, teachers defined the universe of problems they faced — but not easily. Teachers were not used to this level of abstraction.

The second stage involved analyses of the problems, specifying their causes and consequences, and the degree of knowledge required for their solutions. This was also a new process for the teachers and difficult to achieve. The analysis of problems led teachers and principals from each school to develop small action research projects. The projects were characterized by forming processes to solve the problems over the long term, and not on discovering immediate answers. A common focus of the processes was to facilitate communication between principals, teachers, students and their families. The projects were initially constructed around four study areas: academic improvement, community and school relations, teachers' and parents' relations and the development of values. The most long lasting projects involved community and school relations.

In one of the rural schools with indigenous students, the project revolved around a study of the culture and the language of the region in order to improve the communication with students and their parents. In an urban school, the project was directed at achieving better communication with parents based on dialogue, rather than on impersonally-distributed information. We at the Educational Research Center visited the teachers in their schools and supported them as they developed these projects.

There were two major difficulties which required our support: (1) The reactions of the participating teachers' colleagues, students and their parents to the new and different approaches to practice. (2) The process of changing from an isolated form of work to a participatory structure in which teachers were encouraged to make decisions. To achieve this support, we arranged special workshops in each region. One of the objectives of these workshops was to identify the common foci within the participating schools. In the rural school, the main focus was understanding the local culture and preserving its language. In the urban school, the main foci were authority, liberty and responsibility in school.

The workshops allowed us to conclude that the systematic reconceptualizing of teachers' experiences and skills through participatory action research is important to the improvement of educational practice. We were able to see that some teachers were reluctant to change their practices because they lacked information which would help them know what to do to resolve instructional problems. Thus, the next step in this process will be to provide teachers with the knowledge that will help them extend their teaching methods.

Some of our main learnings from this case example have been:

1　The importance of having teachers reconceptualize their vocation and their specific functions in educational process. It is important to provide experiences where teachers can see themselves as subjects of teaching, so that they can participate in educational reforms and improve educational practices.

2　The importance of teachers seeing the difficulties they face as problems that are capable of solution.

3　The importance of communication between teachers, not only to share anecdotes about their teaching experiences, but to learn together how to be better teachers.

Note

1　The Educational Research Center I am referring to was the first Research Center specializing in education founded in Mexico. It started working in 1963 and today is one of the most important research centers of this type in Latin America. It is not government sponsored, but a type of institution known in Mexico as a Civil Association.

References

ALVAREZ, I. (1975) 'La difusión de las ideas y el cambio en la formación de maestros de primaria en México'. *Revista Latinoamericana de Estudios Educativos*, **V**, 3, pp. 13–62, México.

CALVO, B. (1980) 'El estudiante normalista: su origen de clase y su relación con el Estado', *Simposio sobre magisterio Nacional*, **2**, CIS-INAH, Cuadernos de la Casa Chata No. 30, México.

FIERRO, C. (1991) 'Ser maestro rural: ¿una labor imposible?', CEE-SEP, México.

FIERRO, C. ROSAS, L. and FORTOUL, B. (1995) 'Más allá del Salón de Clases', 2a. Ed. México, CEE.

KEMMIS, S. and McTAGGART, R. (Ed.) (1988) 'Como planificar la Investigación Acción', Lartes, Barcelona España,.

LAVÍN, S. (1992) 'Informe Técnico Final del Proyecto: Educación Rural Comunitaria', CEE, México.

STREET, S. (1994) 'Magisterio Chiapaneco: la Democracia como un modo de vida', *La Jornada Laboral*, 27 enero.

ULLOA, M. (Coordinador) (1989) 'Propuesta de Reforma de la Educación', (mimeo), CEE, México.

VERA, R. (1985) 'Capacitación de Profesores de Educación Básica para jóvenes y adultos: Elementos para formular estrategias de capacitación fundadas en una revisión crítica de las prácticas educativas', Seminario Internacional de Educación Básica para Jóvenes y Adultos, IICA. PREDE/OEA Río de Janeiro, (mimeo).

Section IV

Cross-professional Perspectives on Action Research

Section Editor: Richard Winter

Section IV explores issues in action research and professional development not only in the fields of education, but in social work, nursing and management. A key theme of this section concerns the relationship between the values and processes of action research and those of the various professional and cultural contexts.

The chapter by Hugh Sockett and Michael Zellermayer speaks to cultural differences in applying action research to teacher education in institutions of higher education. Two other chapters — one by Bridget Somekh and Micheala Thaler, and a second by Bruno Losito and Graziella Pozzo, address how an organization outside of and across IHE's influence conduct collaborative action research. Angie Titchen argues that action research is concerned with the creation of 'learning cultures' and she describes in detail how an action research process was used to develop a learning culture on a hospital ward among a group of nurses.

Peter Posch and Mag Gottfried Mair, like Angie Titchen, report a process in which a practitioner working in a specific professional context works alongside an 'outside' action research 'consultant' — showing the wider cultural and political implications of the action research process. Finally, the chapter by Richard Winter and his colleagues argues that the action research process requires a general emphasis on 'empowering' relationships and that this emphasis is (ideally at least) equally central to the professional values of education, social work and management.

20　The Ambiguities of Educational Reform: Action Research and Competence Specification in Social Work Education

Richard Winter, John Brown Lee, Leo Bishop, Maire Maisch, Christine McMillan and Paula Sobieschowska (United Kingdom)

Introduction

'Reform' is an ambiguous conception in any educational context — whether we are talking about schools, universities, vocational training or professional development. On the one hand it has in-built positive connotations: a reform implies a specific change which is supposed to be an 'improvement' on a prior state of affairs. On the other hand, any actual reform is a practical compromise between the problems of the status quo and ideals which in their pure form could not be directly implemented because they are too 'radical' to be generally acceptable. This means that most reforms, whatever their apparent political purpose, open up a 'space' which can be interpreted and occupied in different ways (i.e., more or less conservative, more or less radical).

The background to the work reported in this chapter is an educational reform which seemed to contain unpromising elements of managerial control and prescription, namely the 'competence-based' format for vocational education initiated in the UK by the National Council for Vocational Qualifications (NCVQ)[1]. The approach to vocational education promoted by NCVQ consists of detailed specifications of the competences 'required in employment', to be demonstrated in portfolios of evidence derived from workplace practice. This can be presented as a (positive, progressive) reform in that it represents an attempt to:

1　derive curriculum aims from practitioners' experiences (rather than merely from academics' theories) through a process of 'functional analysis' of work roles[2];

2　expand educational opportunity by ensuring that access to qualifications is not limited by practitioners' inability to afford or attend expensive or distant 'courses' — because educational requirements are entirely embodied in 'outcome' statements describing professional practice;

3 give learners greater control over their education by making explicit in advance the criteria by which their work will be assessed;

4 ensure that vocational curricula and qualifications are directly 'relevant' to the work roles to which they refer. (Jessup, 1991)

However, these claims are frequently met by counterclaims, criticizing competence-based curricula as fragmented and reductionist, as a denial of the creativity and autonomy of professional work and the subjection of professional education to crude managerial control (Ashworth and Saxton, 1990; Field, 1991). In particular, such criticisms have been advanced by writers with a commitment to an action research oriented version of professional development (Elliott, 1991; Norris, 1991) and we have much sympathy with their point of view (see Winter, 1992).

This chapter, then, is an attempt to intervene in this debate: it reports a number of ways in which, within an innovative programme designed to incorporate competence specifications into a post qualifying professional curriculum for social work, a model of professional learning based on action research was used to make the emphasis of the 'competence-based' curriculum format *less* reductionist or prescriptive and more holistic and developmental.

Over the past few years Anglia Polytechnic University has developed a format for professional post qualifying education, the 'ASSET' Model[3] which attempts to combine the NCVQ competence-based curriculum model with some of the values and processes characteristic of action research. The details of the ASSET model are fully described and analyzed in Winter and Maisch (1996); the features of the approach which are significant for the argument of this paper are as follows:

1 Competence statements are derived through a process of 'functional analysis' in which groups of practitioners create a detailed description of their tasks;

2 Portfolios of evidence are presented not only in terms of detailed 'task' competences but also in terms of a set of 'Core' assessment criteria which portray in holistic terms the responsibilities and values of the professional role — including: commitment to professional values (respect for individual differences, equal opportunities, 'anti-oppressive' interactions and interpretations), commitment to learning from practice, affective awareness, interpretive application of bodies of knowledge, etc.;

3 Specific emphasis is given to the process of interpreting competence statements in individual candidates' varying practice contexts;

4 'Competence' is presented not simply in terms of practice evidence but also through analytical commentaries upon practice;

5 Support for the development of portfolios of practice-derived material is provided not simply by relations within the workplace and between candidates and tutors but by a series of group meetings of candidates (the

'Peer Group process') which are specifically devoted to sharing ideas as to how the competence statements and Core assessment criteria may be variously interpreted.

One colleague from another university, using the ASSET model as the starting point for the development of a curriculum for further education teaching staff, described our approach in the following way:

The ASSET Model
Action research, reflective practice, experiential learning are linked in a subtle way.
This means:
- all knowledge is viewed as situated knowledge related to particular forms of practice;
- critical reflection becomes a central feature of work-based learning;
- all work-based learning is viewed as 'context-driven' and context-dependent.
(Guile, 1994, p. 9)

Although we would not claim that the ASSET model actually constitutes a synthesis of action research and competence-based education, it is certainly true that our commitment to action research values and processes inspired us to attempt to 'push' the NCVQ competence-based format in a particular direction, and it is one of the contentions of this paper that the ambiguities of educational 'reforms' create opportunities and scope for such redefinitions. In the remainder of the chapter we give three examples of such 'redefinitions' in more detail. The first example shows how the specification of competences can be an activity of *individualized* clarification of professional purposes; in the second example a senior social work manager describes how he used the method for devising competence statements to enable a group of practitioners to develop their own specification of a new role, rather than imposing a definition 'from above'; and in the third example, a social worker talks about the overall similarities and differences he experienced when undertaking a) competence-based and b) action research-based forms of professional education. The text of the chapter has been co-ordinated and edited by Richard Winter, writing as one of the Directors of the ASSET Programme; the first two examples are 'editorial' descriptions of work carried out by the named co-authors, and most of the third example consists of John Brown Lee's own description of his work, taken from a taped interview.

Example 1: The Development of 'Personal' Competence Statements

(Maire Maisch, Christine McMillan, Paula Sobieschowska)

Although the process of describing practice in terms of competence statements is intended, within the ASSET model, to give practitioners a voice in the definition of a vocational curriculum, it does not avoid facing individuals with the task of identifying their own work in relation to a collectively formalized statement, and thus (initially at least) presents them with an external prescription. Furthermore, no matter how comprehensive the range of optional units dealing with different aspects of the role, different specialisms, etc., there will always be some aspects of practice or some professional experiences which do not fall within the areas defined by existing competence statements.

For these reasons, the ASSET Programme has begun to develop the use of 'personal' competence statements. This means that tutors work with a candidate to help her/him to formulate in competence terms an aspect of their work not covered by the existing documentation. In this way, the competence format is used as an exercise in self-clarification, a way of understanding and analyzing one's practice and a way of planning the future development of one's practice. The following example was developed by Christine McMillan (a social worker specializing in working with clients with mental health problems and a graduate of the ASSET Programme), Maire Maisch (formerly ASSET Programme Director) and Paula Sobieschowska (ASSET Programme Tutor and current Programme Director).

Example of a 'Personal' Module: 'Counselling with Clients as a Method of Social Work Practice'

1 Evaluate the effectiveness of an intervention in a counselling relationship,
2 Demonstrate the use of particular models of intervention in the counselling process,
3 Give a detailed account of the progress of sessional-sequential work with a client,
4 Evaluate the effects on personal learning in the counselling relationship,
5 Consider the relevance of the agency context in relation to the counselling process,
6 Demonstrate a sensitive response to ethical concerns in counselling,
7 Work with the client to establish and maintain a framework and boundaries for on-going work,
8 Analyze the significance of the counselling process within the social work profession, and
9 Demonstrate the effects of a counselling intervention in direct work with a client.

This personal 'plan' for documenting, analyzing, evaluating, and developing practice was used in conjunction with the core assessment criteria (see above), concerning general professional and educational values. Christine herself defines the experience of working with Maire and Paula to formulate these 'objectives' for her professional role in terms of Kolb's 'adult experiential learning cycle' and was very conscious of the tutors' efforts to 'dismantle' their own authority (as potential definers of what students 'should do') in order to 'empower' her (Christine) as the author of her own curriculum. She notes that this approach seemed to represent both the educational value-base of the ASSET Programme and also the value-base of the social worker's stance towards clients. Paula, one of the tutors involved, comments that within the ASSET Programme the tutorial relationship is always a two-way process of nego-tiation, involving a Freirean form of 'liberation': in order for the 'student' to exer-cise self-determination the tutor must 'lose' preconceptions and assumptions. Hence, the 'personal module' represents merely an *extension* of the attempt by the ASSET Programme to take a particular aspect of an institutionalized educational reform (i.e., the formulation of competence statements) and reinterpret it in a way which avoids what we (and others) see as negative features of prescription and managerial imposition.

Example 2: Functional Analysis: Management as Action Research

(Leo Bishop)

Leo Bishop is currently (December 1995) Director of Mid-Essex Social Services Department. His previous role was Director of Inspection and Training for Essex as a whole, and this included managing groups of staff carrying out inspections of residential accommodation and day-care provision for children. In that capacity he carried out an action research inquiry (Bishop, 1995) with the purpose of helping inspection staff to clarify what they meant by 'good practice', when all they had by way of guidance was a series of rather abstract declarations of principles from cent-ral government. Leo saw his management task in this context as problematic: how could he encourage his staff to define a set of desirable practice procedures which they would feel as genuinely 'their own', rather than as yet another proclamation from on high? How could he, as a senior manager in a hierarchical organization, play a part in facilitating his staff's discussions of their aims, values and experi-ences without being cast by them in the role of 'prescriber'?

Leo decided, independently of any external suggestion, that he might be able to resolve this problem by using the 'functional analysis' method for eliciting practitioners' accounts of their work (see Note 2) which he had noted during the period when he had been a member of the steering committee of the ASSET Pro-gramme. His action research project, therefore, centred around the use of functional analysis as a minimally intrusive method for facilitating discussion and description of staff roles, which he then used as a basis for formulating practice guidelines and circulated to participating staff in draft form for amendment. Staff evaluation of this process suggested that they had felt they were indeed genuinely contributing to the production of an agreed document, and half of them also described the process as 'empowering'. Clearly, non-hierarchical organizational relationships are not built in a day, but there is an important and encouraging lesson to be learned from the fact that Leo was able to achieve even a modest success in this respect through the establishment of an action research process. There is also a nice irony in the fact that Leo's action research definition of his managerial process involved the application of a technique otherwise often associated with the establishment of rigidly prescriptive procedures (see earlier references to criticisms of the work of NCVQ). Again, we have a good illustration of how ambiguities in educational reforms can create opportunities for action research redefinitions.

Example 3: **A Convergent Experience**

(John Brown Lee)

John Brown Lee is a senior social worker with Essex Social Services; his current responsibility is to manage the establishment of contracts with providers of domiciliary care services for social services clients (i.e., support for clients in their own homes), and to oversee arrangements which guarantee the 'quality' of these services. He undertook two competence-based modules within the ASSET Programme, one on 'Anti-oppressive Practice' and the other on 'Sustaining Professional Morale', each of which entailed working with the core assessment criteria referred to above and a set of 'competence statements' similar in format to the 'personal' module quoted in Example 1, above. He then undertook an Action Research module, in which he explored the concept of 'quality' in the provision of domiciliary care by interviewing a number of managers of agencies which provided such services. Concern had been expressed in a number of quarters about the quality of the services being provided, and John felt that the current guidance on quality provided by the Social Services department was not clear or effective. His project, therefore, was to create a fresh set of guidelines based on a concept of quality which would be both effective (in terms of clients' needs) and practical (acceptable in detail to care providers rather than merely a set of pious generalizations). One key problem, consequently, was how to 'interview' service providers (with whom, as the representative of Social Services, he was in a power-oriented relationship) in such a way that they would feel able to provide him with sufficiently rich and honest data and ideas, from their perspective, which would help him improve his understanding of the issues, and thus help him formulate new guidelines (which could then be evaluated).

It was after undertaking the project outlined above, that John initiated the suggestion that working with the ASSET competence statements and core assessment criteria and working with the values and processes of action research had not been two highly contrasted experiences, but instead, surprisingly, rather similar. In the following edited extracts from a discussion of his experiences, John explains. Interviews, of course, tend to have a rather freely associative flow of ideas, so in order to make the argument clearer, the interview material has been ordered into separate, but obviously linked, 'themes', each of which indicates how the competence-based format and the action research format 'converge' to provide a certain type of educational experience which is, at the same time, closely linked to the professional values of social work practice.

Theme One: Learning for Oneself, as Opposed to 'Being Taught'

My original experience of education was always about 'being taught', sitting there as a passive receiver of information. Doing the ASSET competence-based modules has been very different for me, because no one is sitting there telling me what to think and how to think about something. You are actually going out, looking at what you are doing, thinking about what you have been doing and why you are doing it and finally coming to conclusions. So it's very much teaching yourself, with the aid of other people there for you to bounce your ideas off, to help you to formulate your ideas: why you are doing something and how you can improve it.

In the same way, the action research fitted in nicely with the social work that I had been doing. The project was to look at quality, and my job is all about looking at quality. What the action research project allowed me to do was to look at what I was doing in a much more formalized way: to stand back and ask people for help and to advice about the job I am supposed to be doing, to read what other people have done in this field, looking at myself and saying, 'Why am I doing this? What am I intending to find out? Am I going to find out what I think I should be looking at by doing it this way?'

I would have found the action research a lot harder if I hadn't done the ASSET competence-based modules beforehand, because I had never ever experienced that form of education before. For me, that talk about the difference between action research and the ASSET modules, that's not the way I actually thought about it: when I said that there were such strong links between them, I was thinking of the way I had experienced education. I know I have learned things, and my confidence in various skills has developed through education, but I don't think I understood how it developed, because I was just sitting there absorbing information, and people were saying, 'Yes you have done it right' or 'You have done it wrong' and giving you a mark. But in both ASSET and Action Research you are being asked to assess your own competence and to be specific about it.

Theme Two: Individualized Learning

> *Richard Winter: Could you take the influence back the other way? You have shown how there was a sense in which you could use what you learnt in the competence modules in the work you did for the action research. Could you also reverse the argument? Did the competence statements nevertheless remain sufficiently open for you to engage with them in a way which you later realized wasn't very different from the action research? I mean: did the competence statements leave you free to explore? Because a lot of people would say they are very directed.*

Well, they are directed, in the sense that you have to demonstrate certain specified competences but there are many different ways you can demonstrate them. We were all working to the same competence statements within the peer group but we all produced very, very different work and we demonstrated our competences in very, very different ways, because we are individuals and competence is about individuality, because if we were all demonstrating the same competence in exactly the same way, then we would all be doing social work in exactly the same way. No, we all started from a different stage of learning and all finished up with different level of learning as well, so it was very open. The competences weren't constricted, they gave us a focus but it wasn't prescriptive as such. The same with the action research: you gave us general guidelines throughout what we did, so that we were all working in very similar ways but our projects were all very different.

Maire Maisch: Yes, I notice this as a tutor. The competence statements do sound prescriptive, as though they tell you what to do, but people somehow take them and, because, I suppose, of their own individual personalities, the context in which they work, the peer group support process, the influence of managers, or because of their personal lives, they mould the competence statements into their own particular thing, their own interests or whatever. For example, they may have started to apply it, then changed it to fit the situation, and then reinterpreted it because the circumstances or their ideas about what they are trying to do have changed.

Theme Three: Valuing Learning, Valuing Practice

I think that the one thing this type of learning has done for me that school work had never done for me, was to make me more confident. I still feel very insecure about academic work and I don't think that will ever go, but once I had completed the first competence-based module I felt I knew more about me and the way that I work. I didn't go away thinking I've learnt about this or about these writers or this theory or that model, I went away thinking I know more about what I'm doing, why I'm doing it and being more confident about doing it.

And in the action research work, thinking about how you discover things (about how you are actually going out to do the research) gives more value to your work. You realize that you don't have to have someone from outside come in to look at it, that you can actually do a valuable piece of work yourself. There are a few people in the department doing this all the time, but I think most of us don't value the work that we are doing; you feel that you can't influence anyone, and that if you need some research done you're going to need someone else to do it for you. But it doesn't have to be that way.

Theme Four: Collaborative Process

At first, in the peer group for the ASSET competence-based modules, we all had our own agendas. We started off with, 'This what I've got to do', but then each of us had various problems where we needed the help of the others, and at that stage we suddenly realized how much we were getting from each other in terms of support, help, and advice about how to achieve the competences. So then we were actually understanding the needs of the other person and we were no longer just focusing within ourselves. And that was the benefit of both the ASSET modules and the action research module. The three of us in the action research group didn't meet very often, but when we got into the work we were very much focused on, 'How can we help this person to move forward?' and 'What can I gain from other people to move me forward?' With the ASSET modules it was the same thing: once we started truly supporting one another in the peer support group we were seeing the value of working in different ways and helping each other to assess ourselves.

In my action research project, a number of people assisted me, but they saw themselves as helping me to complete my piece of work; they didn't see it as their work; and at one point I actually said, 'I want to *own* this because it is important to me. But then, after that, I realized that it wasn't just *mine*; it was as much *their* piece of work, because they were supplying the information: they were as anxious to get the information across as I was to have it, and they were as anxious for the report to reflect that as I was. So, it was very much a collaborative piece of work amongst all these people: we were discovering things about ourselves. We were working closely together and producing a piece of work which reflected our shared knowledge. In the ASSET modules we worked as individuals, but we all had a vested interest in seeing each other through, so it was working as part of a team. In that way they are very much alike, in that you're not on your own. But in conventional education you *are* on your own.

Theme Five: Empowering Others

Throughout the ASSET Programme competence-based modules there is a continual emphasis on looking at yourself and saying, 'Am I working in an anti-discriminatory way? In an anti-oppressive way? Am I *enabling* the people I work with?' When I was doing the action research project there was a lot of talk about the questionnaire that I used, about not using 'leading questions' but framing questions that would allow people to give the information they had to give more freely. In the same way, if I'm working with clients that's what I want from them: I don't want to tell them what they should be telling me. So, some of the things I had done for the ASSET modules helped me to think how I actually phrased things to other people, and this helped me when I moved onto the action research. One of the problems that I found with my questionnaire was that I wasn't asking open questions: I thought I knew the answers already and therefore I was asking questions to draw those answers out of people, but having worked through some of those issues on the ASSET modules helped me with the action research questionnaire, to think along the lines of: I didn't want to impose my views, I wanted to truly find out what other people thought.

Theme Six: Continuing Development

I think that from both the ASSET modules and the action research project you come away not feeling that you have finished something but you've just begun something. That's very clear in the action research because once you have done a piece of work that isn't the end: it's a cycle that goes on.

RW: So how is it clear in the competence modules?

Well, you should be continuing to look at what you are doing and why you are doing it and re-examining it. After you have done an ASSET module and passed it, that's not the end to it; you can't just stop there, because things change; policies change; everything is changing all the time, so you have to look at it again and re-examine why you're doing things. The competences that you have demonstrated — are you still keeping them up to date? Are you still continuing to learn?

RW: But isn't that equally true when you read a book which introduces you to a powerful way of thinking about something, so that when you have finished your essay that way of thinking still stays with you and is equally relevant to the next one?

It may very well be, but I think that the ASSET modules and action research leave you with a much stronger feeling that you've got to keep on looking at why you are doing things, that you've got to keep re-examining, a sense that you can't be satisfied with the fact that you did it well *there* because the question is: are you still doing it well *here*? Whereas with reading a book, it may give you a certain theory and certain ideas but then you read another book and it contradicts it and you think, 'Oh well!' I agree that books can *change* your ideas. But with the competence statements, once you have achieved a level of competence and looked at it and recognized it, what you read just increases your awareness of it and your desire to keep moving. So it doesn't work the same way, because it's *growth*, not a change.

I think also that it then makes you feel more confident in reading something and being critical about it, not just accepting it because you are more confident in what you have done and what you feel. A lot of it was about feelings and about examining feelings, and the same with the action research: it's about examining relationships, not just paper relationships but relationships between people, between organizations and what can be done to move them on. I think that once the process has started it's something that you've gained so much from it, that it just continues. It changes you as a person, I think.

Conclusion: 'Reform', 'Authority' and 'Self-determination'

So far we have interpreted the ambiguities of educational reform as constituting opportunities. We have argued that what can easily be seen as a rather prescriptive reform — the UK competence-based format for vocational qualifications — nevertheless contains elements which can be taken in directions which facilitate an empowerment of the learner (examples 1 and 3) and an empowerment of relationships within the processes of professional practice (examples 2 and 3). But our argument, of course, cuts both ways. What we have also experienced is that hierarchical relationships remain within curricula and professional relationships which intend empowerment. In example 1, Christine's work has to remain within the format set by a predetermined format for the expression of competence statements. In example 2, Leo's use of functional analysis was not experienced as empowering by half of his staff. And John Brown Lee noted a further similarity between undertaking competence-based modules and undertaking an action research project, namely that in spite of the increased degree of self-determination which they permit, they are also similar in that the exercise of authority remains: there is a limit to the variety of individual interpretations of competence statements, and there is a set of criteria indicating desirable qualities for action research projects, and both are embodied in documentation validated by what John calls, 'the academic establishment'.

There is a crucial theme here, for action research and for education, and one which is rendered even more problematic within a 'pluralist' society: the relationship between cultural authority and self-determination. In opening up definitions of 'education' or of 'research' one nevertheless remains subject to (and indeed committed to) the values implicit in the concept of an educational or an action research process. But values always imply judgments of what ought to be, and, consequently, questions as to the basis for such judgments, who should make them, and how. Similarly, if professional work is defined as having a particular value-base, then it also entails the same issues: the autonomy of professional staff collides both with the inescapable responsibilities of organizations and with the civic rights of clients, leading to dilemmas as to how judgments are to be arrived at.

Educational 'reforms' are doubly ambiguous, then; not only because they can be 'implemented' in different ways, but also because any changes in forms of self-determination which they may introduce also require a rethinking of the forms of cultural authority (i.e., the criteria for judgment) within which self determination is exercised. Clearly, this will never be a simple matter, since it involves a broad context of relationships which can only change substantially over a lengthy period of time. From this point of view, it is important to note that action research is at the same time both an expression of general professional values (providing ideas and aims for reform) and at the same time a means for effecting reform. All this suggests that, on the one hand, the development of action research is likely to create a particularly complex set of controversies, but, on the other hand, as we have tried to show in this chapter, that the values and processes of action research can be induced to blossom in apparently unpromising soil.

Notes

1   In New Zealand a similar approach is promoted by the New Zealand Qualifications Authority.
2   'Functional Analysis' is a procedure for eliciting and organizing accounts of practice. It consists of asking a simple series of questions:
   a   What is the key purpose of your work?
   b   What do you have to do in order to achieve this purpose (*leading to a series of subpurposes'*)
   c   What do you have to do to achieve these [sub-]purposes?
   The question is repeated several times, leading to progressively more detailed descriptions of the practices required, up to the point where the activities of individual workers are being described (See Fennell, 1989; NCVQ, 1995, p. 17).
3   'ASSET', i.e., Accreditation and Support for Specified Expertise and Training.

References

ASHWORTH, P. and SAXTON, J. (1990) 'On "competence"', *Journal of Further and Higher Education*, **16**, 3, pp. 8–17.

BISHOP, L. (1995) '*An approach to managing changing professional roles through exploring "What is inspection?"*', Chelmsford, Anglia Polytechnic University, unpublished MSc Dissertation.

ELLIOTT, J. (1991) 'Competence-based training and the education of the professions: Is a happy marriage possible?', *Action Research For Educational Change*, Buckingham.

FENNELL, E. (1989) 'Training agency guidance note number 2: Developing standards by reference to functions', *Competence and Assessment*, **8**, pp. 2–6.

FIELD, J. (1991) 'Competency and the pedagogy of labour', *Studies in the Education of Adults*, **23**, 1, pp. 41–52.

GUILE, D. (1994) *Accreditation of Work-based Learning Project, Development Paper 2*, London, University of London Institute of Education, Post 16 Education Centre.

JESSUP, G. (1991) *Outcomes*, London, Falmer Press.

NCVQ (1995) *National Vocational Qualifications: Criteria and Guidance*, London, National Council For Vocational Qualifications.

NORRIS, N. (1991) 'The trouble with competence', *Cambridge Journal of Education*, **21**, 3, pp. 331–41.

WINTER, R. (1992) '"Quality management" or "The educative workplace: Alternative versions of competence-based education"', *Journal of Further and Higher Education*, **16**, 3, pp. 100–115.

WINTER, R. and MAISCH, M. (1996) *Professional Competence and Higher Education: The ASSET Programme*, London, Falmer Press.

21   The Environments of Action Research in Malaysia

Kim Phaik-Lah (Malaysia)

Introduction

Over the past ten years, action research projects of various sizes and scope have been carried out throughout Malaysia. Although the main aim of action research is to conduct collaborative inquiry for the improvement of educational practices, the nature of interventions for change and the action research approaches used, differed from project to project. The establishment of the Malaysian Action Research Network (MARNET) is an attempt to create a research culture and learning organization which links information exchanges, professional support and system facilitation to the teachers in schools. This chapter attempts to examine a number of action research projects in Malaysia and the learning environments which promote collaborative inquiry, educational improvement and teachers' professional development.

Small Scale Action Research Projects

In the past few years, there were several small scale action research projects initiated by the academic staff of higher educational institutions such as teachers' colleges and universities. For example, the Science University of Malaysia organized action research programmes to develop remedial teaching processes in selected Malaysian schools (Zainal, *et al.*, 1990). More recently, programmes on literacy development in schools were organized using collaborative action research approaches (Kim, 1994, 1995; Syed, 1996). The main aims of the programmes were to promote curricular innovation, teacher empowerment and shared ownership of problems. Informal contacts and meetings were used to encourage teachers to voice their concerns, their reflections-on-actions and their self-evaluation of practices in schools. The lack of formal structures in the collaborative action research environment enabled the teacher researchers and field researchers from the university to construct deeper understandings of teaching; and to develop their sense of self-esteem and satisfaction in conducting school-based research. Although formal written reports by individual participants were encouraged; verbal, visual representations and the use of metaphoric reflections were often used to relate the experiences of teacher change and pupils' learning.

Other small scale action research projects include projects carried out by individual teacher education colleges as school-based inquiry with cooperating schools. Various action research approaches were used by teacher educators, student teachers and school teachers as a means to construct and understand the life experiences of teaching, and to provide opportunities to develop school-based research programmes. Local as well as overseas consultants and lecturers were invited to lead the workshops and discussion sessions. An example of such collaborative inquiry is the project carried out in the Keningau Teachers College in Sabah where a group of teacher educators and teachers under the leadership of college lecturer, Tham Soo Koon, collaboratively investigated the implementation of a model of teaching mathematics. In early January, 1995, the college organized workshops, led by Professor Sandra Hollingsworth from the United States of America, to promote active participation in action research.

Another higher education institution which has been actively promoting action research programmes is RECSAM (the Regional Educational Centre for Science and Mathematics), a Southeast Asian teacher education institution in Penang. In the late eighties, there were various small scale school-based research projects on the teaching and learning of science and mathematics organized under the sponsorship of an Australian funded programme, ADEP (Asian Development Education Project). The projects were organized to facilitate teachers' professional development and school-based action research (Sim and Tan, 1991; Leong and Ferrer, 1991). Regular formal meetings and interactive sessions were conducted by the teachers and RECSAM staff and consultants from Australia. Discussions on improvement of teaching and learning were based around reflections on a number of events such as lessons taught and activities carried out by teachers; issues and problems encountered. Minutes of formal meetings and other documents were also used as a basis for reflections on teaching. The stimuli and encouragement of the RECSAM staff who acted as consultants, provided valuable inputs for presenting different viewpoints and perspectives to school teachers and their administrators.

A review of the state-of-practice of research environments of small scale action research projects in Malaysia reveals that there are glimpses of complexity and simplicity as well as diversity and unity in the attempts to conduct school-based action research. Stories of critical incidents, meaningful dialogues and voices regarding conflicts, contradictions, dilemmas and struggles to understand and implement teaching are some of the important elements which create cultures for school improvements and teachers' professional development. The review also recognizes that there are inherent problems of small scale action research projects. The main problem is that almost all of the projects have a very short life span (i.e., projects did not go beyond two or three years). Very often, the processes of the projects were not systematically recorded, adequately documented or frequently reported to the team members. Thus, there is very little opportunity for deep understanding and exchanges among members. As a result, the collaborative inquiries were not disseminated widely; and the breadth of challenges in action research were not known to larger audiences, both nationally in Malaysia and globally, to the international communities of action researchers.

Large Scale System-Wide Adoption of Action Research Programmes

Action research is currently taking place in Malaysia on an unprecedented scale which has involved all levels of the educational system; namely the schools, the district, state and national educational agencies (Ellerton, *et al.*, 1996). More than 900 action research projects were approved by the Malaysian Ministry of Education under a World Bank funded programme (1993–1996) called PIER (Programme for Innovation, Excellence and Research). In 1995–1996, the project is being jointly managed by the Educational Planning and Policy Research Division (EPPRD) of the Malaysian Ministry of Education and the IDP Educational Australia. The main objectives of the action research projects are:

- to establish action research as a viable and alternative approach to addressing problems in education;

- to develop school-based research in order to improve teaching and learning processes;

- to nurture a research culture in schools; and

- to use action research as a tool towards achieving educational excellence.

These action research projects were funded and facilitated through a number of ways. Proposals and applications for funding were submitted by the school action research teams to be processed through the district and state offices; and the final approval of funding came from the EPPRD, Malaysian Ministry of Education. Regular meetings, seminars and talks were organized by the school action research teams in conjunction with the district and state educational offices to facilitate the organization and management of the school-based research. Reading materials such as action research guidelines, reports and modules were provided as support to project members. Workshops were organized both locally and overseas (in Australia and United Kingdom) to upgrade the knowledge and skills of teachers, principals, educational administrators at district, state and national levels in conducting action research projects. Scheduled site visits by educational personnel and consultants to action research projects in schools and district offices were carried out to assist in specific areas of concerns and clarify questions regarding action research concepts and methodologies.

There is evidence that this large scale nation-wide action research programme has created an impact on the collaborative research environments in Malaysia. Some of evidence includes increased teachers' participation in research and better cooperation and collaboration at all levels of the education system to promote school improvements. It is apparent that action research has just begun to gather momentum, and it has great potential as an alternative approach used by educators to understand the problems of teaching and learning. It is difficult at this stage to judge the outcomes of improvements on learning and teaching in schools; however, the spirit of cooperation and collaboration among educational personnel at three levels (school, district and state); and the willingness to conduct systematic school-based studies are basic values which build the foundation of a good educational practice.

Although many action research teams face problems regarding how to use appropriate research techniques and methodologies for systematic inquiries in the classrooms and into their own practices; and lack of skills and knowledge often hinder project teams' abilities to conduct their inquiries successfully, there are attempts to gain support through getting expertise from outside the research teams and having regular workshop sessions. Many of the project members also recognized that conducting action research projects are over and above their normal duties in schools. Thus, they felt that they have very little time to share and discuss their projects with the team members after beginning their own inquiries. However, the ideas of self-management, self-monitoring and teacher empowerment were often practised by many action research teams without much difficulty. In many instances, leadership in process management is crucial in determining the success of the action research partnerships.

With regard to sustaining the motivation of action research, some team members felt that beside the personal satisfaction of experiencing professional development, incentives and rewards can be used to motivate and support team members. It is apparent that action research has motivated those who act with commitment to realize the vision of a better world, and those who find the enterprise of action research as a stepping stone for the reward system in the teaching profession.

Networking Communities of Action Researchers

Several plans are currently operating to establish MARNET (Malaysian Action Research Networks) as a national networking system to collect and disseminate information on action research both locally and internationally. Each of the Malaysian states has its own key personnel to provide the vital links in promoting and sustaining action research activities. Newsletters, bulletins and an electronic mail system will be widely used to inform and exchange experiences in action research activities at school, district, state and national levels. The communication system is designed to provide the constant contact needed in networking communities. The learning environments and cultures for action research will be greatly enhanced if more information flow is available through the networking system. The organizational culture of working as an action research team in an individual school and in isolation may be a thing of the past if the networking system of action researchers is fully developed.

Managing Environments in Action Research

Most of the teachers, teacher educators and educational researchers in Malaysia received a strong foundation in the philosophies and methods of quantitative educational research during their professional training and education. The educational research environment in Malaysia is very much influenced by the experimental research designs and methodologies (Zainal, *et al.*, 1988; Kim, 1993). Thus, knowledge, skills and dispositions to conduct and facilitate action research which are based on collaborative inquiry and teachers' reflective thinking need to be further developed. The environment for cultivating reflective teaching in Malaysia has been critically examined and suggestions for future directions in teachers' continuing professional development include teachers' self-directions in learning and conducting collaborative research (Kim, in press). Both the western and non-western cultural traditions of thinking and reflective skills can be used as powerful tools to motivate educators to create their own frameworks for educational improvements. The focus of inculcating a religious and ethical value system in all Malaysian school curricula and systems of education can further enhance the attempts to promote action research.

In developing collaborative inquiry, the leadership in steering, organizing and managing of collaborative action research can come from various institutions. If the main vehicle for school improvements across all education systems in Malaysia is to practise action research, the success of the vehicle will have to rely on programmes which support teacher researchers and practitioner research. Partnerships such as building innovative links between schools and other agencies to promote teacher professional development and encouraging teachers' professional judgments and decisions are essential elements in this support system.

Conclusion

Groundwater-Smith (1996) points out that:

> In an educational world where the activists in education are more likely to be governments than educators it is essential that the professional voice is strengthened.

The increasing interest of action research activities in Malaysia can be an indicator to denote that more and more professional voices can be heard. However, the sustainability of the interest needs to be strengthened through constant support and understanding in developing partnerships, collaboration and cooperation in all systems of education.

Acknowledgments

I wish to acknowledge the constant encouragement of my tutor, Professor John Elliott, University of East Anglia, England and the participation of Professor Nerida F. Ellerton of the Edith Cowan University, Australia, Ms Madzniyah Md. Jaafar of the Malaysian Ministry of Education, and my colleagues at all levels of the education system in sharing the vision of developing action research as a global movement.

References

ELLERTON, N.F., KIM, P.L., MADZNIYAH, M.J. and NORJIAH, S. (1996) *System-wide Adoption of Action research: A Case Study*, a paper presented at the Annual Conference of Mathematics Education in Australia, June, 1996.

GROUNDWATER-SMITH, S. (1996) *Putting Teacher Professional Judgment to Work*, a paper presented at the Practitioner Research and Academic Practices Conference at Cambridge Institute of Education, England, July, 1996.

KIM, P.L. (1993) 'The Environment for Action Research', in TOH, K.A. (Ed.), The Proceedings of the Seventh Annual Conference of the Educational Research Association, Singapore. Singapore, Institute of Education.

KIM, P.L. (1994) 'Developing Literacy in Schools', in MOIRA, A. and WHITE, J., *The Proceedings of World Congress on Action Learning, Action Research and Process Management*, Bath, University of Bath, England.

KIM, P.L. (in press) 'Reflective Teaching and Teacher Education', in KIM, P.L. and LEE, N.N., *Teacher Education: the Challenges of the 21st Century*, Kuala Lumpur, Dewan Bahasa dan Pustaka.

KIM, P.L., SIM, P.K., CHIN, J. and LAW, C.G. (1995) 'Helping Children to Write: An Action Research Project Children's Literacy Development', in LOO, S.P. and MAZNAH, I. (Eds), *The Proceedings of International Conference on Innovation in Education*, Penang, USM.

LEONG, Y.P. and FERRER, L.M. (1991) *Working Towards Teacher Change*, Penang, SEAMEO, RECSAM.

SIM, J.T. and TAN, S.H. (1991) *Teacher Change Through Action Research*, paper presented at the Regional Seminar on Teacher Education: Challenges of the Twenty-first Century, Penang, November, 1991.

SYED, I.S.A. (1996) 'Literacy Development in Malaysian Schools with reference to Creative Writing through the Method of Action Research,' paper presented at the World Conference on Literacy, Philadelphia, Pennsylvania, USA, March, 1996.

ZAINAL, G., *et al.* (1988) 'The Educational Research Environment in Malaysia' in GOPINATHAN, S. and NIELSEN, S. (Eds), *Educational research environment in Southeast Asia*, Singapore, Chopman Publication.

ZAINAL G., *et al.* (1990) 'A Study of Remedial Teaching Process in Selected Malaysian Schools through Action Research', *Singapore Journal of Education*, Singapore, Institute of Education.

22 Creating a Learning Culture: A Story of Change in Hospital Nursing

Angie Titchen (United Kingdom)

This chapter tells a story of a cultural change in a British National Health Service hospital ward. It is one of the many stories arising from a major action research project conducted by Alison Binnie, a practising nurse and clinical leader, and myself, an educationist, researcher and development worker in health care. The project was set up to help nurses in the Medical Unit at the John Radcliffe Hospital, Oxford, to transform their traditional nursing practice to a patient-centred service. In addition, the aims of the study were to generate and test theory about effective change strategies and to theorize the experience of change for those involved in, or affected, by it. Our objective was to provide a 'map' of the journey for other nurses in the UK, to help them to manage and evaluate change effectively, to alert them to possible problems and solutions and to speed up changes that take several years to achieve.

Traditionally in the West, nursing was task-focused to ensure maximum efficiency and a safe, universal standard of care. Tasks were carried out in rounds and routines, strictly adhering to procedures defined by the ward sister, in accordance to instructions laid down by the senior nursing hierarchy. Thus patients received the same care regardless of personal preferences or individual needs. Bedside nurses were responsible for carrying out these routines on a large number of patients. Patients were, therefore, looked after by many nurses on any one shift and by different nurses from day to day. In addition, as the bedside nurses were not responsible for making decisions about a particular patient's care, they were not able to involve patients in decision-making.

Short encounters with different nurses tended to encourage superficial and distant relationships which, Menzies (1960) suggests, protected the nurse against anxiety and stress. She argues that the heart of anxiety for nurses lay within their relationships with patients; the closer the relationship, the more the nurse would experience anxiety arising from daily confrontation with the threat and reality of suffering and death. The social structure of the nursing service therefore developed, often unconsciously, as a system of socially constructed defence mechanisms against this anxiety. Discontinuous care, centralized decision-making and distant nurse-patient relationships are examples of such mechanisms.

In line with society's values at that time, this routinized, depersonalized style of care was accepted by nurses. Patients expected it and were grateful for it. However, as values in society changed towards an emphasis on respecting the rights of the individual and the consumer, nurses' and patients' values and expectations also changed. Nurses began to recognize that traditional nursing did not meet individual needs and that it denied both the patient and nurse the benefits of a close, therapeutic relationship. Patients began to express a preference for a personalized and individualized nursing service (e.g., Moores and Thompson, 1986; Audit Commission, 1991).

In response to changing values, patient-centred nursing emerged as a style of nursing based on close nurse-patient relationships that are claimed to be therapeutic in themselves. Nursing practices have also been developed to promote healing and a movement towards health and wellness. However, this style of nursing cannot be practised within a traditional system because continuity of care is necessary to allow close relationships to develop. In addition, to practise therapeutically and to meet individual needs, nurses need to be able to make decisions about care with their patients. New structures and ways of working are, therefore, essential. Innovative nurses began to experiment with various decentralized work organization systems which provided the conditions necessary for patient-centred nursing to grow and flourish.

In the early eighties, as a senior ward sister, Alison introduced one such organizational system in an acute ward which had been previously used a task-focused approach. She found that the nurses required enormous support to develop the necessary knowledge and skills to practise in a therapeutic, patient-centred way. In 1989, she accepted the challenge of leading a similar change in the Medical Unit of the John Radcliffe Hospital and initiated this action research project. The study was set up collaboratively by the Oxford Health Authority and the National Institute for Nursing, Oxford, and I was appointed by the Institute, in 1989, to work with Alison as her action research partner.

Early in the work, we found that the development of a ward learning culture was an essential prerequisite to enable the nurses to learn effectively from Alison, as a patient-centred nurse, and from their own practice and change experience. A ward learning culture can be defined as the norms, shared meanings, values, beliefs and attitudes held by nurses that support professional learning at work. This chapter tells the story of how a learning culture was created in Alison's ward. It is offered, primarily, to disseminate a professional development strategy for promoting a learning culture that is not described in the literature, and, to demonstrate the possibilities of action research as a strategy for effectively achieving cultural change in hospital nursing. The secondary purpose is to show the similarities and parallels between the values and processes of professional development and of action research and to demonstrate how action research itself facilitates the creation of a learning culture.

Background, Values and Processes

Research exploring the traditional culture in which qualified nurses learn appears to be non-existent. However, there are studies which identify two cultural norms which, one could argue, do not support the existence of a learning culture within traditional nursing. The first norm, 'getting through the work', is the constant activity of nurses and their compulsion to rush about completing task routines by set times of the shift (Bendall, 1975; Clarke, 1978; Melia, 1987; Johns, 1989). Working by the clock appears to have been expected by the sister to meet the organizational goal of efficiency. These findings could be interpreted, especially in the light of later studies, as nurses rarely seeing traditional nursing work as legitimizing, or providing opportunities for, learning. Later studies have shown that practising nurses have little time for reflection upon their practice experience (e.g., MacLeod, 1990; Mander, 1992) and that there is a perceived need to create ward learning cultures for nursing students (e.g., Fretwell, 1980, 1983a, 1983b; Orton, 1981).

The second cultural norm is nurses seeing senior nurses as supervisors checking up on them to ensure that the work has been carried out satisfactorily. They expected senior nurses to distrust them, to be looking for mistakes and to be ceaselessly disciplining them (Menzies, 1960, MacGuire, 1961; Revans, 1964). Such evidence does not support a view of senior nurses as facilitators of learning. This interpretation becomes more robust when we consider the research which established a need to develop the ward sister as a facilitator of work-based learning (e.g., Runciman, 1983; Fretwell, 1983a; 1983b; Marson, 1982; Ogier, 1989). These studies and recent reports and documents (e.g., NHSME, 1993; UKCC, 1992) provide evidence that the importance of promoting learning at work is now recognized in nursing for practising nurses, as well as for students. However, there is no research that looks specifically at how to create a learning culture for practising nurses. This research helps to fill that gap.

We developed an action research strategy drawing on two theoretical perspectives: a critical social science perspective using the work of Habermas (1970), Carr and Kemmis (1986) and Kemmis and McTaggart (1988), and a phenomenological perspective using the ideas of Schutz (1967; 1970), Heidegger (1962) and Gadamer (1975). The critical perspective underpinned our action research scheme which built on Lewin's (1946) action research spiral. We adopted the refinements suggested by Kemmis and McTaggart (1988) and Elliott (1991) and made some of our own (Titchen and Binnie, 1994). The phenomenological perspective informed a simultaneous, parallel observational study in which a phenomenological understanding of the 'lived experience' of change was sought.

The data gathering strategy consisted of observing, questioning and listening, and reflective dialogue. Data were collected over two and a half years, primarily on Alison's wards, using participant observation of ward life and nursing practice, indepth interviews with nurses, patients, relatives and health care professionals, reflective conversations and writing, story-telling and review of documentation. Knowledge about effective change strategies was generated and tested in the critical perspective, using debate of the findings in groups of participants and engaging in critical reflective conversations with individuals. Knowledge about the 'lived experience' of the change was generated through our indepth analysis and interpretation of phenomenological data at the end of the fieldwork, using ideas developed by Titchen and McIntyre (1993). Data and interpretations were fed back to participants for critique, debate and validation (Titchen, 1995).

Within our action research partnership, there was a sharing of responsibilities which made our large scale project manageable for Alison, as practising nurse and clinical leader. By each of us contributing to both the action and the research, these two elements of the work remained integrated and focused in a complementary way. Alison's role was mainly that of 'actor', as the key facilitator of change. She was familiar with the setting, she had a legitimate and influential involvement with everyday practice and she had authority to initiate and manage change. Complementing Alison's role, I worked mainly as 'researcher'. I was responsible for developing the theoretical perspectives of the study and for developing data collection, analysis and interpretation strategies. Initially, then, responsibility for the action and for the research was taken by Alison and myself, but as the nurses grew in confidence and were supported by us, they took on responsibilities in varying degrees, in different areas. All the staff nurses took responsibility for ward developments, for their own professional learning and for providing data for the research. Most nurses were involved with interpreting and validating data. Some took on responsibilities for facilitating colleagues' learning, for example, running workshops, developing resource materials or being clinical supervisors. Two nurses accepted full responsibility with us for all the research decisions and conduct of research activities within one of the action research spirals. More detail about our action research strategy and how we collaborated with the nurses is reported elsewhere (Titchen, 1993; Titchen, 1994; Titchen and Binnie, 1993a; 1993b; 1994).

Embedded in the above account are our values relating to action research within our context. More explicitly, these values are:

- Researching one's own practice is part of a professional role.
- The action research should help nurses to think, to feel and to behave as professionals and to empower themselves.
- Our conduct should demonstrate that we respect the nurses as professional people.
- We should display sensitivity and attunement to the nurses' feelings and pressure of work.
- Collaborative relationships between us and participants should be based on a genuine care and concern for each other, on honesty, openess, trust, and on giving constructive criticism sensitively and receiving it non-defensively.
- We should share responsibility for the action research with the nurses.
- Time has to be built into the working day for participating in the action research.

The processes by which we realized our values in practice are embodied in the action research strategy. In other words, the nurses' actual experience of the action research strategy facilitated their learning. The process of collaboration in the action and in designing, directing and being involved in research activities gave the nurses the experience of sharing responsibility for a piece of work and of working together.

The articulation of, and reflection upon, practice knowledge, facilitated by the data gathering strategy, raised to consciousness the tacit knowledge hitherto embedded in practice. Making this knowledge accessible, reflecting upon it and sharing it enabled nurses to deepen their own knowledge and to learn from others. Feeding back data sensitively and constructively enabled the nurses to confront their own behaviour and the effect that it had on others. This experience often motivated them to change themselves or their practice in some way. Self and peer evaluation helped the nurses to evaluate the effects of their actions and to revise, refine or elaborate their action plans. A process of high challenge with high support enabled nurses to learn from challenge and to cope with it at the same time. Theorization as a means for generalizing the findings to other settings (see Titchen and Binnie, 1994) was achieved through critical reflection upon, and debate about, the data and through drawing, where relevant, on social science theory. As individuals and groups engaged in these theorization processes, they learned about their own practice. Identification and solution of problems was facilitated by reflection upon practice and by theorization. Understanding gained in these ways was motivating and helped them to look for achievable solutions, to devise plans and to carry them out.

In the story, the reader will be able to see how these processes were carried over into our professional development strategy for creating a learning culture. The processes are clarified further within the theorized account. But first, the story needs to be put into the context of the rest of the change experience.

The story begins some seven months after Alison took up her post as sister on Oriel Ward. Many of the nurses on the ward had been attracted to work in the hospital because of its reputation for supporting professional learning. The nurses had welcomed the proposed change to patient-centred nursing and the new work system had been in place for several months. As a ward culture is embedded in the way that people think and behave, the story describes the nurses' and our own thinking and behaviour in the context of professional learning. The names of the ward, the teams and the staff nurses have been changed to protect anonymity.

Learning at Work

From previous empirical work (Clarke, 1978; Pearson, 1985; Binnie, 1988; Johns, 1989; Titchen and Binnie, 1993c; 1993d), we expected that the nurses would still be influenced to some degree by traditional nursing culture. We were not surprised, therefore, to find traditional norms still shaping nurses' thinking and behaviour in Oriel Ward. We called the norms we found operating at that time, 'needing to get away' and 'seeing criticism as reprimand'.

Needing to Get Away

We were seeing the nurses working extremely hard, using all their energy and often staying late to finish work, which, at times, they resented. Work drained them and they sought recreation, stimulation and relief from stress outside their work.

Janice, 17/8/89:   I'm not prepared to stay behind after my working hours on the ward. I have to go. I need to go home to have a break. . . . When Alison asks if nurses would like to go to the library, surely she must know that people are not likely to go, that they are more likely to go home. You need to get away from the stress to have a break.

Janice explained that working within shift hours was necessary to cope with the heavy, sometimes boring work. Other nurses reserved their breaks for social discussion only, as a coping mechanism to recover from 'what was going on out there', in a similar way to the nurses in Clarke's (1978) study. Although the nurses expressed a desire to participate in professional development, finding the motivation and energy to sustain it was difficult, 'I need a kick up the backside' or 'I'm too tired to sit in the library and study'.

The nurses required extrinsic motivation for professional development and looked to Alison for this motivation. It seemed to us that the culture and the tiring nature of the work were stifling their spirit of inquiry. We believed that a wealth of learning opportunities were being missed. Other evidence (Fretwell, 1980; Pearson, 1985; 1992) and our personal experience led us to conclude that the situation would not be unusual in other hospital settings.

Seeing Criticism as Reprimand

In the early days, there was evidence that the nurses recognized the value of learning from practice. They negotiated with Alison for her to give them feedback and the agreement was that Alison should work collaboratively, as a team member, and ask questions and challenge the nurses' thinking. This approach was new for the staff nurses, as qualified professionals, and their initial reactions showed that although they wanted constructive criticism, they had not shaken off the old expectation of a senior nurse to be looking for mistakes and to giving feedback in the form of a reprimand. The most common reactions were nurses feeling anxious, inadequate, defensive or threatened because they felt that Alison would be making a judgment about their performance, despite her assurances that she would be there to help them to learn.

Fieldnote, 16/10/90:   Mark described how he and Rachel were getting into a panic because a patient didn't have a care plan and Alison was coming onto the team on the late shift. In retrospect, he realized that this was 'ridiculous' and 'not at all in line with what Alison was hoping to be able to offer the team'.

When Alison gave feedback, the nurses tended to construe it as criticism.

Rachel, 20/9/91:   When she said, 'Have you tried this? Have you done that?', I immediately got my defences up because I had tried really hard with this patient. It has been a real slog lately and . . . I am not very good at taking criticism, but also maybe because nobody has ever questioned what I do and they still don't. None of us criticize each other and, therefore, when Alison does and is trying to be construct-ive, it is a bit of a shock . . . and you think it is Alison criticizing you.

Alison sensed Rachel's defensiveness.

AB, 15/5/91:   When I first went onto the Ash Team, I made a suggestion to Rachel. I had acknowledged, I thought, the good work and then I said, 'Have you thought of this?' Rachel said to Mark that she was really upset that that was all I could find to say. It's my perception that when I try to use my experience to take them fur-ther . . . they often react negatively. Maybe it's the way I'm doing it — I say 'I'd like to make some time with you to talk about your care plan'.

Johns (1990) also found that nurses have difficulty in receiving constructive feed-back and tend to respond defensively. This evidence shows how pervasive cultural norms are and how difficult it is to change feelings and behaviour, despite a rational decision to do so.

The Strategy: Promoting Challenge, Openess and Debate

We wanted the nurses to see their work as a source of energy and excitement and as offering opportunities for personal and professional growth; in other words, giv-ing as much as it took. We also wanted to help them to receive constructive criti-cism non-defensively. To create this kind of learning culture, we adopted a strategy of challenge, openness and debate.

We built learning opportunities into the working day, informally by asking questions, taking an interest in the nurses as professionals and being sensitive to their readiness to learn. The aim of asking questions about their work, their feelings and reasoning, opportunistically at handovers and during breaks, was to help them to think about their work and the issues beyond the tasks to be completed. To help the nurses to experience constructive criticism positively, we brought their negat-ive feelings into the open, formally, by feeding back the data. We then pointed out where and how they were being influenced by old ways of thinking and behaving that they had explicitly rejected, encouraged discussion about the problem and about what could be done and agreed a way forward. We also recognized that we must be sensitive to the nurses' readiness to learn before offering help. Being attuned to the way the nurses were feeling (at work and in their personal lives) and knowing the pressure that they were working under enabled us to be sensitive here.

By articulating our own thoughts, tacit knowledge and interpretations, we hoped to encourage the nurses to do the same and to think through their own practice. We also encouraged professional reading specific to the nurses' patients or the nurses' own identified learning needs and facilitated peer group teaching and learning in the staff room:

Fieldnote, 5/8/91: In the staff room, Henrietta is struggling to write a care plan. Four staff nurses try to help her to identify her patient's problems and aims of care. They help her to see what she, as a nurse, can do . . . Later, Alison told me that she had deliberately allowed silences and had been consciously not leaping in and taking over to enable the peer teaching and learning.

Formal, traditional 'time-out' opportunities were provided by encouraging nurses to attend local courses and by setting up staff development interviews and professional development sessions. Although offering people a few hours in the library was not successful, as we saw earlier, we found that offering a week or several days for study was more successful. Using a 'top-down' approach (Ottaway, 1976), the sisters in the Medical Unit set up unit seminars, a journal club and support groups, but these intiatives never became firmly established, despite the sisters' support. They were often cancelled due to lack of interest and were finally abandoned with the conclusion that staff nurses would establish their own groups when they were ready for them. We concluded that our time would be better spent supporting a 'shared responsibility' (Beer, 1980) approach.

Professional development sessions in the ward were more successful. The sessions were not prepared talks, they merely offered nurses the time and space to ask questions about patient-centred nursing. There were always plenty of questions which arose directly from their experiences of the new system and ways of working. Even though these sessions were helpful to the nurses because of their relevance, the logistics of getting people together in busy wards made the sessions a less important strand in our strategy than opportunistic, individual work.

Less traditional 'time-out' was encouraged in the form of peer group review and evaluation by suggesting that team meetings should be used to look honestly, openly and critically at each others' patient care, as well as giving and receiving constructive criticism. But despite agreeing to be more honest and open with each other, the nurses found it very difficult because of the desire to avoid conflict and because they wanted people to like them.

Janice, 25/7/91: I'm finding the treading on other peoples' toes a problem at the moment . . . and I think that something could be done slightly differently or slightly better. I wonder whether we ought to discuss people's care. I know we are supposed to do that, but I don't know if we really do . . . Sometimes, I mention it and then think, 'I hope they didn't think I was being snotty, trying to take over their role, bossy. . . . I wonder how I would feel if I'd worked hard over a care plan and someone said. "What do you think about such and such?" and no-one's ever said that to me'.

Although seeing it as legitimate behaviour, nurses still had difficulty challenging colleagues. This reflects Johns' (1992) findings in a study of a similar change in a community hospital in which he describes the 'harmonious team' brushing conflict under the carpet.

Our next action was to encourage 'time-out' in the form of critical friendships between peers. Some decided to give each other feedback on care plans, but they found that they were being 'too nice' to each other. We then suggested an honesty and trust session at the formal ward 'time-out' — the 1991 Away Day. The idea was that, in their teams and in a safe environment away from the pressures of the ward, nurses would raise concerns, issues, and 'undercurents' which they had been reticent about sharing. The suggestion was taken up and the nurses found it very helpful, for example, one team negotiated ground rules for giving constructive criticism to each other.

Overall, we found that we had to make all our suggestions repeatedly, because people found it hard to accept that they could challenge and debate ideas and actions and still maintain good working relationships with colleagues.

The Lively Critical Community

Becoming a lively critical community was a difficult, slow and, in some ways, painful cultural change to make. Gradually, as the nurses came to see learning at work as possible and potentially exciting, challenging and worthwhile, they began to respond to our encouragement and suggestions, but they found it difficult to sustain their efforts without support, and few initiatives came from them. Learning at work became part of the culture to a point where they relied much less on Alison. There was more evidence of working together and learning from peers.

In the early days, professional discussion was observed at the shift handovers, but at breaks and during slack time, discussion tended to be social, rather than professional in nature. Later, we observed:

AT, 30/7/91:   It's really quite different coming on to the ward now . . . There is no reticence about using coffee breaks to discuss patients, interesting issues, articles or books.

AB: And this business of sharing care plans, showing each other their work, that wasn't happening six months ago.

Several months later, the depth of the discussion had increased.

AB, 15/1/92:   Yesterday we were having coffee and Rachel bounced into the staff room and sat down and said, 'I've got an ethical problem I want to discuss with you all' . . . They really discussed this problem properly and discovered that there are no easy answers. They were using each other and me and taking it seriously.

Individual project work in the library failed to sustain enthusiasm and motivation, but collaborative projects were successful. At the 1990 Away Days, teams identified a number of areas they wanted to work on. Each team negotiated 'time-out' with the rest of the ward team, to plan their programme of work. These meetings were fun, engendered enthusiasm and stimulated the nurses to start working on the various projects in their own time. We came to see the nurses' need for variety, and the difference between these kinds of 'time-out' experiences and sitting studying alone in the library. The former was more energizing for the nurses, particularly when they were feeling bogged down by busy periods on the ward.

Nurses were looking for their own professional development opportunities and were organizing rotas to have time with a critical friend or to do project work. Nurses commented that they had never worked anywhere where so many people were involved in projects to develop the ward or patient care. When I asked Rosemary what she had learned from working on a care plan project, she replied:

Rosemary, 28/1/92:   Time-out to focus on one issue, to do it in a partnership with Rachel has definitely been brilliant . . . and to have been able to spark off some of the care plan discussion. It has given me confidence in myself when speaking in groups . . . It has improved my interpersonal skills in dealing with people who, as an ordinary staff nurse, I couldn't even dream to speak to — like (Director of Nursing Services). I've learned to think on my feet a lot more through facilitating the workshops . . . It helped to develop my patient-centredness, having the opportunity to observe Alison closely with patients and ask her all those things.

The projects often arose from the staff nurses identifying a problem and then doing something about it to improve the situation. Their taking on of responsibility surprised a visiting sister who was more used to observing nurses generally sitting back and letting problems continue.

Another indication that our strategy had been successful was the new openness. Firstly, nurses were confronting tensions in relationships, they were engaging in frank discussion on painful interpersonal issues, challenging each others' decisions and giving each other constructive criticism. Secondly, nurses were responding nondefensively to supervision by Alison and their team leaders:

Sophie, 16/8/90:   Alison opens our eyes to new ideas, new ways of looking at things . . . She helps us to be more organized in our thoughts and to think ahead . . . I used to only think one or two hours ahead. She also helps me to think about a much wider area than I have been used to thinking.

Fieldnote, Team Leaders Meeting 25/11/91:   Alison reported that she had observed Sharon (team leader) and Kate in a supervision session. There had been a past history of tension between the two and Kate had been defensive when Sharon had tried to give her feedback before. In this session, Kate looked slightly defensive, but then when she suddenly got some sense of why she was stuck and what the problem was that Sharon was trying to get across to her, her body language changed (arms unfolded and body leaned forwards) and she started to accept the criticisms.

In summary, the nurses' experiences of the transition to a learning culture were often difficult, uncomfortable and painful. They sometimes felt angry, threatened or defensive. Although they had understood and accepted the new norms and meanings when standing back from practice, it was much more difficult for them to change their actual behaviour, feeling and thinking. But to counter these negative aspects, they enjoyed collaborative working and the time and space to think, to learn and to contribute to the development. They experienced the energizing 'buzz' and excitement of learning. They felt empowered through understanding their problems and coming to see them as solvable and challenging, rather than as overwhelming. They also enjoyed critical debate and learned to handle giving and receiving constructive criticism.

Our experience was that the cultural change was slow (it took three years) and painstaking and required tolerance and the patient repetition of suggestions and interpretations. We knew from our previous experience that it would take time for nurses to match their understanding with actual thinking, feeling and behaving. Knowing this made us tolerant of any inconsistencies. This journey was very challenging for us and we were well rewarded when we and other colleagues could see evidence of cultural change.

A Theorized Account

I have theorized this story by drawing on cultural theory (e.g., Bredemeier and Stephenson, 1962; Merton, 1968; Eldridge and Crombie, 1974; Smircich, 1983) and by showing how how the action research processes were carried over into the professional development. Providing a theorized account that is grounded in the data offers readers an opportunity to judge whether the findings and interpretations are transferable to their own settings.

The ward culture is a unique configuration of cultural norms, shared meanings, values, attitudes and beliefs. Shared meanings shape, and are shaped by, cultural norms. This configuration influences the ways in which nurses interact as a group or as individuals, as they go about their everyday work. Their behaviour is also shaped by organizational goals that are culturally-defined and legitimized by the organization. Ways of achieving the goals are defined and controlled by the organization through norms and rules of conduct. In other words, cultural goals are coupled with regulations for ways of moving towards them. Such rules are carried in people's heads, rather than being explicit in policy and procedure documents. For cultural change to occur there has to be consistent change in organizational goals and in the configuration of cultural norms, shared meanings, values, attitudes and beliefs.

At the beginning of the project, the nurses welcomed the new organizational goal of professional learning at work; a goal legitimized by senior nursing management. Whilst the nurses' values, beliefs and attitudes appeared to be consistent at first with the goal, we soon discovered inconsistencies in the configuration. The old norms of 'needing to get away' and 'criticism as reprimand' were not congruent with learning at work and there was evidence that they were preventing the creation of a learning culture. Although the nurses' values were consistent with the values of the new goal, for example, they valued learning from their patients, and although they realized those values in practice by negotiating constructive feedback on their work, there was an inconsistency in their negative response to it. This suggests a dissonance between 'espoused theory' and 'theory-in-use' (Argyris and Schon, 1974). It would appear that this dissonance, observed also in the nurses' wanting to learn, but not wanting to use the library in less busy times, was occurring because the nurses had not yet overcome the influence of the old norms, despite have identified and negotiated new ones. Thus the nurses' experiences of the early changes alerted us to the focus of our professional development strategy. It was necessary not only to help nurses to create new norms and meanings, but also to overcome the pervasive influence of the old ones. We, therefore, had to help them to understand what was happening and to legitimize the new norms through our actions. In other words, we had to demonstrate a congruence between our own 'espoused theories' and 'theories-in-use'.

Small collaborative projects often arose from identifying problems and by being motivated to do something about them. These projects were developed on the ward by groups or pairs of nurses. They promoted professional learning and nurses felt empowered by solving practice problems. Nurses were helped to articulate their practice knowledge by using the same processes as those in our research strategy, namely, observing, questioning and listening, story-telling and reflective writing. This helped the nurses to describe their feelings, thinking and knowledge, thereby making them available for critique by expert nurses and peers. Using these processes also encouraged them to reflect deeply on their practice and on themselves, as people and as nurses, to see things in new ways and to theorize their own practice. They also learned from experienced nurses by observing and questioning them and listening to their stories (as shown in Titchen and Binnie, 1995).

By feeding back data sensitively and constructively, Alison and I acted as role models for the nurses to help them to develop the skills for confronting difficult interpersonal issues and for giving each other constructive criticism. Feedback was constructive in nature because as well as challenging the nurse, it also offered new possibilities and ways forward. Support was also given by helping nurses to work through problems themselves and to deal with uncomfortable or painful feelings. Critical debate of the data and interpretations also facilitated our own and the nurses' ability to theorize and to learn from practice, as demonstrated in their diaries (Miller, 1992; Hedges, 1993), a research report (Hedges and Firmin, 1992) and reflective conversations.

Three principles for action emerged as important for us, as the key facilitators of change, in creating a learning culture in a ward:

1   The facilitator's action reflects a commitment to the values of a professional learning culture.

2   The concepts of values, beliefs, attitudes, cultural norms and meanings that make up a culture are used explicitly, for example, in the following ways:

   • making current values, shared meanings, cultural norms and so on explicit by naming and exploring them;

- making them more visible by pointing them out when their influence can be discerned in action, feelings or behaviours;
- exploring new values, meanings, norms and so on by articulating new possibilities;
- demonstrating new ways of thinking and behaving in practice and pointing them out;
- negotiating new norms and ground rules;
- legitimizing new norms by role-modelling them;
- pointing out when there is an inconsistency between the agreed organizational goal and the values, norms, meanings and so on actually influencing behaviour and thinking;
- making the dissonance between 'espoused theory' and 'theory-in-use' explicit; and
- being tolerant and understanding.

3 Building 'time-out' opportunities into work-time is essential, in addition to using opportunities afforded by shift handovers and breaks. Once nurses experience the excitement and challenge of learning at work and negotiating 'time-out' to do so, it is likely that they will be prepared to use their own time as well.

There was evidence that the strategy and the principles derived from it were effective because cultural norms and shared meanings were consistent with the organizational goal of professional learning at work. The norms, 'seeing criticism as helpful' and 'lively critical community' were established and sustained. New shared meanings about studying in the library, feed-back from senior nurses and giving constructive criticism to peers evolved as the nurses worked with us in the identification and negotiation of new norms and ground rules.

Conclusion

An effective strategy for creating a learning culture that is not described in the nursing literature has been identified in this work. Fretwell's (1980; 1983a; 1983b) action research shows that the sister is a key figure in creating a ward learning culture for nursing students. Our work shows that this finding also holds for the professional development of practising nurses. But Fretwell does not provide practical detail about the nature of learning opportunities or about how the learning environment is created. Our findings make a contribution in both these areas. Other action researchers give practical details of formal staff development programmes for practising nurses (e.g., Pearson, 1992) and formal supervision (e.g., Johns, 1994), but collaborative 'time-out', opportunistic individual work and critical friendships have not been described before. In addition, the principles for creating a learning culture are new. I conclude that although the professional development milieux will vary according to setting and resources, the principles and processes of the theorized account are likely to be transferable to other settings and other cultural changes.

It has been demonstrated that action research can be an effective strategy for achieving cultural change in hospital nursing. In summary, other facilitators of cultural change may find it helpful to:

1　find out how the configuration of cultural norms, shared meanings, values, beliefs, and attitudes is influencing thinking and behaviour of participants at the outset of a development;

2　identify any inconsistencies between this configuration and the new organizational goal and between 'espoused theories' and 'theories-in-use';

3　develop facilitative roles and relationships with participants;

4　provide new conditions, milieux, opportunities and time for participants to grow and change;

5　use the principles and processes described in this work;

6　re-examine the configuration and its relationship to the goal and 'espoused theories' and their relationship to 'theories-in-use' to assess whether the desired change has occurred.

Finally, how action research itself facilitates the creation of a learning culture has been shown and a cultural change has been described in which there was an attempt to ensure congruence between the values and processes of the action and the research strategies. As the desired change was effectively achieved, it may be that this congruence contributed to our success.

Acknowledgment

I should like to acknowledge that the story, 'Learning at work', was developed with Alison during the life of the project.

References

ARGYRIS, C. and SCHON, D. (1974) *Theory in Practice: Increasing Professional Effectiveness*, London, Jossey-Bass.

AUDIT COMMISSION (1991) *The Virtue of Patients: Making Best Use of Ward Nursing Resources*, London, HMSO.

BEER, M. (1980) *Organization Change and Development: A Systems View*, Santa Monica, CA, Goodyear.

BENDALL, E. (1975) *So You Passed, Nurse*, London, Royal College of Nursing.

BINNIE, A. (1988) *The Working Lives of Staff Nurses: A Sociological Perspective*, Warwick University, MA dissertation in Sociological Research in Health Care.

BREDEMEIER, H.C. and STEPHENSON, R.M. (1962) *The Analysis of Social Systems*, London, Holt, Rinehart & Winston.

BRUNER, J.S. (1967) *Toward a Theory of Instruction*, Cambridge, MA, Harvard University Press.

CARR, W. and KEMMIS, S. (1986) *Becoming Critical: Education, Knowledge and Action Research*, London, Falmer Press.

CLARKE, M. (1978) 'Getting through the work', in DINGWALL, R. and McINTOSH, J. (Eds), *Readings in the Sociology of Nursing*, London, Churchill Livingstone, pp. 67–86.

ELDRIDGE, J.E.T. and CROMBIE, A.D. (1974) *A Sociology of Organisations*, London, Allen & Unwin.

ELLIOTT, J. (1991) *Action Research for Educational Change*, Buckingham, Open University Press.

FRETWELL, J.E. (1980) 'An inquiry into the ward learning environment', *Nursing Times*, **76**, 16, pp. 69–75.

FRETWELL, J.E. (1983a) 'Creating a ward learning environment: the sister's role — 1', *Nursing Times*, **79**, 21, pp. 37–9.

FRETWELL, J.E. (1983b) 'Creating a ward learning environment: the sister's role — 2'. *Nursing Times*, **79**, 22, pp. 42–4.

GADAMER, H-G. (1975) *Truth and Method*, New York, Seabury Press.

HABERMAS, J. (1970) 'Knowledge and Interest', in EMMET, D. and MacINTYRE, A. (Eds), *Sociological Theory and Philosophical Analysis*, London, Macmillan, pp. 36–54.

HEDGES, J. (1993) 'Into new life: a reflective account', *Journal of Clinical Nursing*, **2**, 4, pp. 194–95.

HEDGES, J. and FIRMIN, H. (1992) *Care Plan Project Paper*, unpublished paper, Oxford, National Institute for Nursing.

HEIDEGGER, M. (1962) *Being and Time*, New York, Harper & Row.

JOHNS, C. (1989) *The Impact of Introducing Primary Nursing on the Culture of a Community Hospital*, Master of Nursing dissertation, Cardiff, University of Wales.

JOHNS, C. (1990) 'Autonomy of primary nurses: the need to both facilitate and limit autonomy in practice', *Journal of Advanced Nursing*, **15**, pp. 886–94.

JOHNS, C. (1992) 'Ownership and the harmonious team: barriers to developing the therapeutic nursing team in primary nursing', *Journal of Clinical Nursing*, **1**, pp. 89–94.

JOHNS, C. (1994) 'Guided reflection', in PALMER, A., BURNS, S. and BULMAN, C. (Eds), *Reflective Practice in Nursing: The Growth of the Professional Practitioner*, Oxford, Blackwell Scientific Publications, pp. 110–30.

KEMMIS, S., McTAGGART, R. (1988) *The Action Research Planner*, 3rd ed., Victoria, Deakin University Press.

LEWIN, K. (1946) 'Action research and minority problems', *Journal of Social Issues*, **2**, pp. 34–46.

MACGUIRE, J. (1961) *From Student to Nurse. Part 1: the Induction Period*, Oxford, Oxford Area Nurse Training Committee.

MACLEOD, M. (1990) *Experience in Everyday Nursing Practice: A Study of 'Experienced' Ward Sisters*, Doctoral Thesis, Edinburgh, University of Edinburgh.

MANDER, R. (1992) 'See how they learn: experience as the basis of practice', *Nurse Education Today*, **12**, pp. 11–18.

MARSON, S.N. (1982) 'Ward sister — teacher or facilitator? An investigation into the behavioural characteristics of effective ward teachers', *Journal of Advanced Nursing*, **7**, pp. 347–57.

MELIA, K.M. (1987) *Learning and Working: The Occupational Socialization of Nurses*, London, Tavistock Publications.

MENZIES, I.E.P. (1960) 'Nurses under stress', *International Nursing Review*, December, pp. 9–16.

MERTON, R.K. (1968) *Social Theory and Social Structure*, 3rd ed., New York, Free Press.

MILLER, A. (1992) 'From theory to practice', *Journal of Clinical Nursing*, **1**, 6, pp. 295–96.

MOORES, B. and THOMPSON, A.G.H. (1986) 'What 1357 hospital inpatients think about aspects of their stay in British acute hospitals', *Journal of Advanced Nursing*, **11**, pp. 87–102.

NHSME (1993) *A Vision for the Future: The Nursing, Midwifery and Health Visiting Contribution to Health and Health Care*, London, Department of Health; National Health Service Management Executive.

OGIER, M. (1989) *Working and Learning: The Learning Environment in Clinical Nursing*, London, Scutari Press.

ORTON, H.D. (1981) *Ward Learning Climate: A Study of the Role of the Ward Sister in Relation to Student Nurse Learning on the Ward*, London, The Royal College of Nursing of the United Kingdom.

OTTAWAY, R.N. (1976) 'A change strategy to implement new norms, new styles and new environment in the work organisation', *Personnel Review*, **5**, 1, pp. 13–18.

PEARSON, A. (1985) *The Effects of Introducing New Norms in a Nursing Unit and an Analysis of the Process of Change*, Doctoral Thesis, London, Goldsmith's College, Department of Social Science and Administration, University of London.

PEARSON, A. (1992) *Nursing at Burford: A Story of Change*, Harrow, Scutari Press.

REVANS, R. (1964) *Standards for Morale, Cause and Effect in Hospitals*, Nuffield Provincial Hospitals Trust, Oxford, Oxford University Press.

RUNCIMAN, P.J. (1983) *Ward Sister at Work*, London, Churchill Livingstone.

SCHUTZ, A. (1967) *The Phenomenology of the Social World*, Evanston, IL, Northwestern University Press.

SCHUTZ, A. (1970) *On Phenomenology and Social Relations*, London, The University of Chicago Press.

SMIRCICH, L. (1983) 'Studying organizations as cultures', in MORGAN, G. (Ed.), *Beyond Method*, London, Sage, pp. 160–72.

TITCHEN, A. (1993) 'Action research as a research strategy: finding our way through a philosophical and methodological maze', in TITCHEN, A. (Ed.), *Changing Nursing Practice through Action Research*, Oxford, National Institute for Nursing, pp. 49–58.

TITCHEN, A. (1994) 'Roles and relationships in collaborative research', *Surgical Nurse*, **7**, 5, pp. 15–19.

TITCHEN, A. (1995) 'Issues of validity in action research', *Nurse Researcher*, **2**, 3, pp. 38–48.

TITCHEN, A. and BINNIE, A. (1993a) 'A unified action research strategy in nursing', *Educational Action Research*, **1**, 1, pp. 25–33.

TITCHEN, A. and BINNIE, A. (1993b) 'Research partnerships: collaborative action research in nursing', *Journal of Advanced Nursing*, **18**, pp. 858–65.

TITCHEN, A. and BINNIE, A. (1993c) 'What am I meant to be doing? Putting practice into theory and back again', *Journal of Advanced Nursing*, **18**, pp. 1054–65.

TITCHEN, A. and BINNIE, A. (1993d) 'Changing power relationships between nurses: a case study of early changes towards patient-centred nursing', *Journal of Clinical Nursing*, **2**, 4, pp. 219–29.

TITCHEN, A. and BINNIE, A. (1994) 'Action research: A strategy for theory generation and testing', *International Journal of Nursing Studies*, **31**, 1, pp. 1–12.

TITCHEN, A. and BINNIE, A. (1995) 'The art of clinical supervision', *Journal of Clinical Nursing*, 4, pp. 327–34.

TITCHEN, A. and MCINTYRE, D. (1993) 'A phenomenological approach to qualitative data analysis in nursing research', in TITCHEN, A. (Ed.), *Changing Nursing Practice through Action Research*, Report No. 6, Oxford, National Institute for Nursing, pp. 29–48.

UKCC (1992) *The Scope of Professional Practice*, London, United Kingdom Central Council for Nursing, Midwifery and Health Visiting.

23 Dynamic Networking and Community Collaboration: The Cultural Scope of Educational Action Research

Peter Posch and Mag Gottfried Mair (Austria)

In this chapter challenges are described which are facing schools today (section 1) and which ask for a redefinition of the professional services demanded from teachers (section 2). One of the emerging answers to social change is the development of 'dynamic networks' breaking the barriers between school and community and creating strong demands for a reflective and communicative approach to teaching and learning through action research. Such a network is illustrated in a case study based on the remarkable initiative of a biology teacher (section 3). In section 4 the characteristics of dynamic networks are described and illustrated in some detail. The final section deals with some implications of these networks for the professional development of teachers.

Challenges Facing Schools

Profound and irreversible changes in industrialized societies create new and challenging demands on schools. Some of these challenges are sketched in this section (Posch, 1994a).

The Quest for a Future

An increasing number of students find it difficult to connect their school experience with a positive vision of the future for themselves and therefore lose motivation to succeed at school. Academic success, defined in terms of mastery over the contents of traditional school subjects is no longer a guarantee of success in the labor market (Elliott, 1995). Increasing numbers of people will be unemployed at least for part of their lives. Mass unemployment appears to be an intrinsic feature of the societies of the twenty-first century.

If young people are to live satisfactory and fullfilling lives, they will need to construct personal identities which are less dependent on job-satisfaction, and learn to participate in society as active citizens capable of influencing the social conditions which shape their lives.

The traditional legitimation of content to be learned is losing credibility and weakens the position of teachers who have to rely on external justification of teaching and learning tasks; they are confronted with the challenge to enabling students to actively create meaning and construct their own futures.

Redefinition of Teachers' Professional Services

The Quest for Negotiation of Tasks

The learner has always been a contributor to the educational process. The aims of education are not achievable in a direct way but only indirectly by stimulating and directing the activities of the learner. This is not new. What is new, however, is that the importance of the student in learning is increasing at an enormous pace. More and more students limit their contribution to learning those activities which can plausibly be legitimated, which appear meaningful to them and which they can influence. This phenomenon has to do with the weakening of established social networks and of social control, with value diversity, with the increase of options outside school, with their early confrontation with contradictory demands.

Probably one of the most important reasons behind this new social order is the dramatically changing authority relationship in families. The interaction between parents and children is becoming more like a partnership in which arguments are replacing orders and commands. What is allowed and not allowed is becoming a matter of negotiation between parents and children and the age in which this process starts is still decreasing. This is the experience with which more and more children come to school. There, however, they meet a context in which they have hardly any influence on procedures. Many problems in the interaction between teachers and pupils can be explained by this clash of a 'negotiation culture' with a 'command culture', because the teachers' traditional position as authority figures no longer corresponds to the authority relations between parents and children.

Teachers are not in a position to mandate learning activities and to control the educational process through their formal authority as in the past, and this means that they have to be able to legitimate learning activities (because external legitimations have insufficient credibility for many students) and to negotiate them with their students.

The Quest for Accountability

In many countries, teachers and schools have traditionally been the last ring in a chain of local, regional or central administrative regulations. At present we see a tendency in these countries to increase the autonomy of schools, that means that the influence of authorities on the educational process through input factors (such as prescribed curricula, regulations concerning instructional organization and time structure, prescribed materials and modes of assessment) is reduced. As decision-making power is devolved to the school and to the individual teacher, the public interest grows to hold teachers accountable for the educational process and its outcomes. Teachers are required to provide public evidence for the quality of their work.

The challenges described above produce considerably higher demands on teachers than their traditional task to transmit predefined sets of information. Teachers lose to some extent the safety-net provided by clear, predefined and undisputed standards of quality and have to negotiate them with their students. They need the dynamic qualities which they are requested to foster in their students. Moves towards a more dynamic culture of learning imply that the question of what should be taught can only partially be answered by regulations and national curricula. To a considerable degree, teachers have to involve themselves in reflection on educational aims and practices, that is in action research on the school level and on the classroom level. It also implies a move from 'first order change' to 'second order change' (Cuban, 1988) or in Argyris and Schön's (1974) terms from 'single loop learning' to 'double loop learning'. Second order change or double loop learning imply that teachers are not only expected to become more effective and efficient in carrying out their tasks, but also to reflect on aims and, if necessary, to modify them. And they will have to reflectively tap an increasing variety of sources of knowledge and experience in the schools environment. These challenges ask for a reconceptualization of the professional tasks of the teacher.

Changes in the Concept of Professional Services

The emergence of networks that extend traditional relationships in school is the subject of the following sections. They will heavily draw on the research in an international project which is in the front-rank of attempts to provide constructive anwers to the changing contexts of schooling. The 'Environment and School Initiatives (ENSI) Project' was designed as a piece of cross-national curriculum development in which schools developed environmental education curricula that were consistent with two basic aims:

- to help students develop an understanding of the complex relationships between human beings and their environment by interdisciplinary learning and generation of knowledge about their environment;

- to foster a learning process which requires students to develop 'dynamic' qualities, e.g., 'exercising initiative', 'accepting responsibility' and 'taking action' to resolve real environmental problems within their locality (e.g., OECD, 1991 and 1995; Elliott, 1994; Posch, 1994a).

All of the following examples selected to illustrate the dimensions of networking and of their implications for professional development are taken from this international project.

A Case Study in Networking

In a secondary school in the Tyrol, Austria, a biology teacher (Mag Gottfried Mair) started an 'energy network' with a group of 14-year-old students (Mair, Mallaun and Montibeller, 1992; Mallaun, 1994; and personal communication). In a pilot phase they began to study the energy situation in their school building and in their own homes. A year later they tackled a major task: to analyze the use of energy in four small villages (the home communities of most of the pupils). The first step was the elaboration of a questionnaire with fifty questions and — supported by an energy expert — an intensive learning phase to understand the issues and to master the theoretical and social demands of collecting the necessary data. Through role plays possible reactions of inhabitants were anticipated and discussed, then groups of two to three students went from house to house with their questionnaire, informed people about their intentions and offered assistance in filling it in. Nearly 70 per cent of the households completed the questionnaire.

The students processed the data at school and produced a comparative analysis of the use of energy for each house and for each village, and of possibilities to use renewable energies (such as biogas, wood and solar energy). The teachers involved, and their students, kept 'research diaries' to facilitate reflection on the progress of work. The results were presented by the students at a public event, where they enacted sketches to illustrate experiences and conflicts during data collection. The main part was the presentation and discussion of findings and proposals.

Two months after the event, a few pupils with their parents started to build sun collectors for their own house. This stimulated the foundation of an association for renewable energy and within two years 700 installations for solar water-heating were built in the whole region. A number of other investments followed. In one village, for example, the school building was insulated to reduce energy consumption.

In this project a number of relationships were established:

- contacts with an energy expert to receive professional assistance in the design of the questionnaire;

- cooperation with a teacher of computer science in order to get classroom time and assistance in processing the data for comparative analysis and presentation;

- contacts with the mayors of the communities to get the support of the community councils and financial assistance.

This project showed students and teachers that with relatively little effort a considerable amount of energy could be saved and public approval could be gained. The next step appeared to be a logical consequence; to link up with other schools and to find solutions for a number of new questions: how to inform schools, how to identify persons and institutions who would provide financial, political, and other kinds of support, etc. The first issue of a network-newspaper was published in which the project was described and support was offered (advice by teachers and students, computer software, the questionnaire etc.). The project was presented at several fairs and exhibitions, and a number of schools reacted and invited the teachers and students for short introductory courses to become familiar with the ideas, the logistics and the computer software, which was being improved continuously.

In a school in a larger community, for example, the two teachers and a group of students were invited to act as expert advisers in launching a major energy project involving several teachers and several forms. In joint meetings they developed the design and sequence of events: an information phase (to get things going and to inform the public), a project week (to prepare the students), data gathering, data analysis and synthesis, public presentation of results. An important strategic manoeuvre was to involve political figures, and to inform the public from the very beginning of the project. As a result, the new school organized public evenings to inform the community, initiated discussions in the community council, held press conferences to involve the regional media, etc. In most of these activities students were involved: for example, they held the first press conference and produced articles for the local paper.

More and more schools as well as local authorities in communities became interested and were given the opportunity to learn about the concept on site and/ or be visited. In subsequent years the logistics were continually improved, and local enterprises were also involved (such as chimney sweepers and plumbers). From 1991 to 1994 almost thirty schools had taken over the idea to contribute to the development of an energy policy in their communities. This created an enormous demand for advice and external support and communication across schools, most of which was accomplished through informal contacts, presentations at school conferences and by the regular network newspaper.

The teacher who had initiated the energy network originally gained a high reputation, won with his students a number of national and international awards, and was offered financial and infrastructural support through the authorities. The regional government provided the funds for the production of the newsletter and the central government provided resources for part-time secondment and operational money for the energy network.

In 1994 an interesting shift in emphasis occurred. The teacher was convinced that in order to stabilize the energy network it had to have many 'fathers and mothers'. In other words: the understanding had to 'grow' in the local population that the saving of energy was both a valuable and a feasible endeavour. The question was how such a feeling of collective ownership could develop. His strategy was: All persons and institutions who have influence or vested interests or know-how on energy matters should be involved in the design and realization of initiatives. Thereby he moved beyond school initiatives to community initiatives. The network newspaper (originally school-based) became a newspaper of community environmental projects. The teacher's main interest became the creation of local groups with broad participation and strong emphasis on the training of local coordinators. Schools (teachers and pupils) were still (and in some cases heavily) involved but the community projects were no longer fully dependent on their participation.

For example, he selected a small community, which had a rather bad reputation with respect to energy consumption as most of the families heated their houses with coal of low quality (Gstrein and Krabacher, 1995 and personal communication). He started with studying documentary data on the village and with interviewing people to find out about their perceptions of the situation, about the social structure, who were the opinion leaders in the village, etc. His intention was to build up trust and to look for a person who would be interested in organizing an energy project in this village. Finally a small team of persons was gathered (from local trade and business, from administration, from a bank, etc.) who agreed to support the project, to give advice and/or financial assistance.

Then a questionnaire was developed and sent to each household. The questionnaire gave instructions on the calculation of an energy index (the consumption of energy per square meter), some information on simple means to save energy, and offered advice through the local coordinator. Everybody who agreed to take concrete measures was invited to participate in a competition for prizes. This initiative created a remarkable collective interest in improving the local conditions of life in the village and more than 50 per cent of the households participated and within the first year 100 square meters of sun collectors were built and 20 per cent of the households invested in insulation.

Initially, the elementary school of the village did not participate but moved in after some pressure from children and parents. After this the children became highly involved in symbolic and creative activities, such as painting posters on the idea of a 'sun village'.

At the moment the network is further expanding and although schools are still playing an important role, the main thrust is in establishing local groups which provide continuity and in linking the local coordinators into a regional network in order to facilitate training and the exchange of experience. Last but not least, is the further development of the underlying philosophy: It emphasizes communication and joint reflection on shared values, on the situation, and on feasible improvements. Energy saving is not merely regarded as a matter of technical solutions and expert services but primarily as a matter of reflection on one's conditions of life and on personal communication and negotiation. It seems that the tangible effects of these activities are not results of personality changes of the participating persons; they are much rather results of the values embedded in the social structures which these people have participated in creating and feel part of. This is an essential characteristic of 'dynamic networks', in which teachers, students and other parties actively create relationships with each other.

The Emergence of Dynamic Networks in Education

Networks of communication and 'joint ventures' are international phenomena and, in part, results of increasing complexity in industrialized societies. To be able to cope with complexity and uncertainty, institutions and individuals are stimulated to actively create relationships with each other. These 'dynamic' networks complement and to some extent even replace the traditional 'hierarchical' relationships that have characterized the infrastructure of social life (Posch, 1994b).

The essential feature of dynamic networks is the autonomous and flexible establishment of relationships to assist responsible action in the face of complexity and uncertainty. They are a social correlate of action research and answers to specific situational characteristics:

- unstructured situations, in which often even the problems are in need of being defined, with a call for specific knowledge to cope with them; 'general knowledge' is not sufficient.

- this specific knowledge can only be generated within the situations and by those persons who through their action (or non-action) are elements of it. It cannot be produced in another context but is derived from a 'situational understanding' (Elliott and Rice, 1990); and

- the knowledge thus generated is not applied instrumentally to solve the problems but expresses itself holistically in actions comprising cognitions, value orientations, and feelings.

Dynamic networks contradict one of the traditional assumptions of schooling: the assumption of a separation of school and society. If dynamic networks develop it is difficult to say where the educational organization ends and where society and its abundance of personal and institutional relationships begin. It is interesting that quite similar developments have been identified in the economic system (cf. Ochsenbauer, 1989, pp. 264ff). Dynamic networks are in a sense an extension of the idea of specialization by providing access to a variety of external resources (and know-how) to teachers as well as students, they are generally initiated and sustained by the teachers and students of one or more schools. The following examples illustrate the variety of such networks.

A School Network for a Joint Purpose

A typical example is the Water Analysis Project (Mantova) originally comprising teachers and students of five vocational secondary schools and a number of local and regional institutions. The schools co-operated for several years to study the quality and the degree of pollution of ground and surface waters in the communities of Mantova (Italy). The activities were coordinated by a group of students and teachers and were financed by the communities on the basis of contracts. The responsibilities of the pupils ranged from the selection and drawing of water samples and on the spot analysis, via a detailed chemical, bacteriological and micro-plancton analysis in their school laboratories, to reporting and discussing the results with the authorities (Sutti, 1991 and personal communication). In 1991 the project was extended to comprise thirteen junior schools. The older students of the original five schools now acted as tutors to the younger ones, trained them, invited them to their schools for laboratory work, and visited them. It seemed that the mere fact of close co-operation with younger students and of joint reflection on action also widened the perspective of the project from a rather narrow technical orientation to a broader more holistic one, including artistic and social aspects (Project Mincio, 1992).

The Children's Parliament

A different kind of dynamic network is the 'children's parliament' (an idea originally coming from France) organized by an ENSI school teacher (Elke Ammann) in Western Austria (Thonhauser, *et al.*, 1993, pp. 47ff.). It links a number of elementary and lower secondary schools of a community and gives children of these schools the opportunity to develop and submit proposals for improvements in their environment to their mayor and the aldermen, and subsequently discuss them in public.

In workshops, these children develop ideas, organize them in projects and present the results of these activities through elected representatives ('parliamentarians') in a democratic forum. There children experience the need to produce evidence for their situational analyses and convincing arguments for their demands. Those bearing political responsibility (the participating mayor and councillors of the community) are expected to take the proposals seriously and give adequate answers to questions that are asked. A number of proposals have been realized already (e.g., by diverting traffic away from a school). The network is heavily supported by the local community which, for example, provides secretarial assistance as well as resources for the teachers who run the workshops. The emergence of dynamic networks in environmental education exemplifies such a horizontal division of labor. 'The network idea (. . .) sought to replace rigid control from the centre by a process of negotiation partnership and consensus' (Department of Education for Northern Ireland, 1994, p. 16).

The main strengths of dynamic networks are their functional integration into the activities of an environmental project. They are results of initiatives taken by teachers and students of the schools concerned and of the knowledge and situational understanding which they gained through action research. The usefulness of investments into the network can be discerned relatively easily by all participants. A weakness of these networks is their relatively low institutional stability because they are anchored in specific school initiatives. They are limited to those persons, groups or institutions which are expected to contribute to the schools' project activities. The conclusion of the project therefore, in general, is also the end of the network. Another limiting factor of dynamic networks is size. If they grow larger, the demands on time and management capacity increase rapidly. There are, however, attempts to stabilize such projects by integrating them into the mainstream curriculum. This was accomplished by the Water Analysis Project (Sutti, 1991).

Dynamic Networks and Professional Development

Dynamic networks appear to be an increasingly important framework for professional development. They permit the effective utilization of know-how, abilities and energies that emerge in the teaching profession. The following features of dynamic networks should give an idea of the potential and the prerequisites.

Co-operation Resulting from the Nature of the Tasks

Dynamic networks develop if co-operation is needed in order to accomplish what teachers and students wish to achieve. Co-operation among teachers students and 'third parties' is not just a matter of 'good will' but depends on the character of the tasks encountered. Typical tasks which demand co-operation are attempts to generate local knowledge on environmental issues or to change environmental conditions. If projects are aimed 'at solving real problems, in a real situation, a partnership with decision-makers, local authorities or non-govermental organizations is essential' (Clary, 1993, p. 16).

The following example (Axelsson, 1993, p. 42) gives a vivid illustration of the need to create links if the school wants to move from knowledge transmission to knowledge utilization: All teachers and students of Pårydskolan in Sweden have taken up challenges in their own vicinity and reserved two hours per week for environmental projects. They started from their own interests and from requests from outside. A parent, for example, had ponds that were now overgrown with trees and plants — could the school help them with these? The school now has fish breeding in the ponds. Similar initiatives resulted in a shop in which the school sells environmentally friendly detergents, in a green house, and in the restoration of a water mill. Some of these initiatives involved hard work, and if it turned out too hard for students to do themselves, parents came to the school on Saturdays to help.

The school has managed to become the centre of the small village. When there is an open house, not only individual parents come but the whole family, including grandparents and aunts; even people who have no children at school may come along. People also come to the school asking for help about ponds, about acid water in their wells, and about different environmental issues: The school is a place where knowledge is to be found.

Bustin (1993, pp. 14, 20) reveals some characteristics of the emerging relationships between children involved in an environmental initiative and other parties: The third year pupils of a school in the French-speaking community of Belgium acted on a request by the Solvay Industrial Group to recover plastic (PVC) bottles by setting up a sorting and storage centre open to the people of the commune: 'They canvassed not only the other pupils and teachers of the school but also the local population, the commune authorities and the press.' One of the major practical problems they had to cope with was to persuade the commune authorities to run the storage centre during the summer holidays. In September 1993, the commune authorities, at the children's suggestion, proposed organizing a container park and the responsibility for action moved over to politicians.

The initiative of the school was well timed. First, the inspectorate for elementary education was encouraging teachers to take steps in favour of environmental education. Second, it was started just a few weeks before the Rio summit. There the Minister of the Environment used the initiative as an positive example which in turn had consequences for the school: The children were invited to visit schools in Brazil. After their trip the pupils invented another side of the project, the idea to establish an exchange with Brazilian schools facing social and environmental problems. 'Beginning with a local initiative, the pupils quite naturally moved on to a more world-encompassing project that enters into the framework of necessary North-South solidarity.' This example illustrates salient features of networking:

- Dynamic networks are not super-structures searching for a *raison-d'être*, rather they emerge from an environmental initiative and are, in a sense, the 'logical' result of its design. The cooperation of the community was in a sense 'needed' in order to sustain the initiative. This need provided the basis for the co-operation.

- Dynamic networks are time-bound. In the example, the contacts between the school and the other partners had fulfilled their purpose when the commune had taken over responsibility. They had come to an end but it is likely that the potential for their activation in the future was higher than at the beginning of the initiative.

- Interaction of interests is an important condition for networking, dynamic networks are based on mutual interests. Some of the motives of the commune politicians to assist the pupils in establishing the sorting and storage centre (e.g., their interest in re-election) may have been quite different from those of the students. Nonetheless, the centre was the result of a linkage between these interests. Dynamic networks, in this sense, have a micropolitical dimension.

Accessible Competence and Ownership

Dynamic networks among teachers develop if innovative activities and knowledge produced through action research are accessible to other teachers, e.g., by opportunities to visit teachers whose work appears to be stimulating or to invite them into one's own school.

Two of the ENSI Schools in Scotland (Peel Primary and Inveralmond High) shared some visiting teachers 'so there was an opportunity for both schools to benefit from one another; a mutual understanding had developed of what Peel Primary School's environmental ethos was, and the contribution which the secondary school's subject expertise could make to its environmental work' (McAndrew and Pascoe, 1993, p. 51).

Observing how other teachers and students develop their initiatives and discussing with them how they cope with difficulties and how they utilize strengths can be a strong stimulus to innovation (cf. Ekholm, 1988). Although experiences gained in one complex situation cannot be technically applied to other situations, a direct or mediated understanding of an innovation in another teacher can generate a set of illuminating hypotheses which allow a fresh perspective of one's own situation.

One can grasp an idea that materialized in one context and can use its power to construct one's own concretization, adapted to one's own situational context and personal strengths and weaknesses. The result then is not a copy nor an application of a general principle but is a new solution for which ownership can be claimed. In this sense, dynamic networks provide cross-situational links which allow a 'reflective transformation of ideas' (Schön, 1983) and thereby a spread of innovative activities without 'disseminating' anything, in a technical sense. 'From the evaluations we received from teachers it is apparent that the opportunity to learn from others and reflect on their own work has given fresh impetus to their commitment to developing environmental education in their schools' (*ibid.*, p. 46).

An Atmosphere of Mutual Trust

Any innovation — especially school initiatives that depart from the transmission mode of teaching — can be (and often are) interpreted as a threat to prevailing interpretations of the tasks of teachers and to the persons who practice them: 'Active teaching exerts pressure on others . . . One does not like to destabilize one's colleagues or let them know indirectly that they could do more' (Kyburz-Graber, *et al.*, 1993, p. 29f.).

Personal, informal contacts are breeding grounds for dynamic networks. 'Ideas move along the social network of personal acquaintance' (House, 1974, p. 10). Dynamic networks develop if personal relationships are created and if mutual trust is built up. In a group involved in a project 'there must already be an atmosphere of mutual trust, a network of affective relations able to integrate each person's experience' (Losito and Mayer, 1993, p. 58). 'Building a relationship of trust and mutual understanding, establishing realistic goals and maintaining good communication were . . . paramount' (McAndrew and Pascoe, 1993, p. 50).

The building of the ENSI teams in the different countries shows the important role of a 'group spirit'. The development of mutual acceptance and trust needed losely structured and self-organized opportunities to get to know each other. A 'fundamental element for developing a group spirit in teachers and in students that work on an environmental education project together is the collective use of "free time" (. . .). Chatting, walks, songs, games, all generally self-managed (. . .) were a cohesive element for the group' (Losito and Mayer, 1993, p. 15). Also the continuity of relationships seems to play an important role: 'The periodic meetings of the groups were considered important and if only one teacher per school could participate this was considered a problem' (Kurtakko, *et al.*, 1993, p. 48).

Generation of Professional Knowledge

Dynamic networks develop if teachers produce professional knowledge about their work. Teachers who leave the 'stable state' or systematic knowledge transmission have to cope with open-ended, uncertain, unpredictable, sometimes contradictory situations, entailing risks. The professional knowledge that is necessary to cope with such situations can only partially be transmitted in advance; most of it has to be produced by the practitioners themselves reflecting on what they do, clarifying their own values and developing their practices through action research (Elliott, 1989; Altrichter, *et al.*, 1993). The practicalities of mutual assistance in gathering and interpreting data are a basis from which professional communication and sharing of knowledge may emerge. Losito and Mayer (1993, p. 15) give a vivid illustration:

> From October 1991, the research group worked in subgroups — always including a mix of different school levels and competence (...). The three chosen themes of action research, dynamic quality and complexity, although interlinked, provided the guiding thread. The projects carried out by the schools were the raw materials on which to reflect and discuss. Each meeting required teachers' contributions: reflections on the development of dynamic qualities within one's own project or reflections on complexity; an example of data gathering; the outline of the school report, etc. (...). We added some element for reflection and stimulation in every meeting: articles, questionnaires, role-play and simulations.

In Finland (Kurtakko, *et al.*, 1993, p. 37) schools were asked to invite at least two other persons (teachers, students, parents, representatives of the local school authority or local media, etc.) not directly involved in their environmental initiatives to evaluate the project. Starting points were questions and data produced by the project teachers. By being asked to evaluate these teachers' activities they were challenged to seriously reflect available data and had the chance to 'leave traces' by being given a voice. Both opportunities are likely to induce some of these persons to involve themselves in similar initiatives.

Conclusion

The growth of dynamic networks — and at the same time a smooth transition to a more dynamic learning culture asks for a redefinition of the role of educational support. The most difficult reorientation will be to complement technical rationality or the doctrine of 'transferability' (House, 1974) by a reflective rationality and a logic of 'supporting growth'. The doctrine of transferability implies that innovations can be developed and tested outside schools and be transferred to them. The logic of supporting growth is based on the understanding that local initiatives exist already and that their growth process can be supported symbolically and instrumentally through action research. House (1974, p. 243) provides another metaphor to indicate the direction of this shift: 'Government activity should be stimulating and regulating like withdrawing or inserting a lead rod in an atomic stock pile. . . Directions and energies must be mobilized within the system itself.' The metaphor acknowledges that innovative potential need not be imported and imposed but is already there. Moreover, if specific innovations are forced upon schools this tends to reduce their coping power and problem-solving capacity and increases their dependence. This understanding implies a fundamental change in perspective on the side of educational support.

Main challenges for any infrastructural support system are:

- to counteract the quasi-natural tendency to define and to solve problems for the teachers and to tell them what they should do, assuming that their problem definitions and solutions are by nature better than those which the teachers and students develop in situ. This may well be the case sometimes. But it is likely to reduce enormously the energy invested and the educational value of the initiatives. So, in balance, it may have more negative effects than positive ones;

- to invest their knowhow and potential for the seemingly less respected, but in fact more demanding tasks, to increase the visibility and accessibility of high quality school initiatives and to create opportunities and stimuli for the reflective generation of local knowledge through action research and for communication between teachers and other social groups affected by school initiatives.

References

ALTRICHTER, H., POSCH, P. and SOMEKH, B. (1993) *Teachers Investigate their Work — An Introduction to the Methods of Action Research*, London, Routledge.

ARGYRIS, C. and SCHÖN, D. (1974) *Organisational Learning*, Reading, MA, Addison-Wesley.

AXELSSON, H. (1993) *Environment and School Initiatives (ENSI) — The Swedish Report*, Göteborg, Dept. of Education and Educational Research of the University of Göteborg.

BUSTIN, C. (1993) *Environment and School Initiatives (ENSI) — Report from the French Community of Belgium*, Bruxelles.

CUBAN, L. (1988) 'A fundamental puzzle of school reforms', *Phi Delta Kappan*, 70, pp. 341–52.

DEPARTMENT OF EDUCATION FOR NORTHERN IRELAND (1994) *Environment and School Initiatives in Northern Ireland — Report*, Belfast, Department of Education for Northern Ireland.

EKHOLM, M. (1988) *Inservice Education of Teachers and School Development*, Stockholm, Swedish National Board of Education.

ELLIOTT, J. (1989) 'Educational theory and the professional learning of teachers: An overview', *Cambridge Journal of Education*, **19**, 1, pp. 81–101.

ELLIOTT, J. (1994) 'Developing community-focused environmental education through action research', in OECD/CERI (Ed.), *Evaluation and Innovation in Environmental Education*. Paris, OECD. pp. 31–60.

ELLIOTT, J. (1995) *Social Change: The Challenge for Schooling in the 21st Century*, Norwich, University of East Anglia (CARE). Ms.

ELLIOTT, J. and RICE, J. (1990) 'The relationship between disciplinary knowledge and situational understanding in the development of environmental awareness', in PIETERS,

M. (Ed.), *Teaching for sustainable development — Report on a workshop at Veldhoven-Netherlands, 23rd–25th April 1990*, Enschede, Institute for Curriculum Development, pp. 66–72.

FISCHER-KOWALSKI, M. (1991) 'Das pyramidale und das unbegrenzte Netz', in PELLERT, A. (Ed.), *Vernetzung und Widerspruch — Zur Neuorganisation in Wissenschaft*, München, Profil-Verlag, pp. 165–94.

GSTREIN, J. and KRABACHER, O. (1995) 'In Karrösten gehen die Uhren vor', *Gemeinde-Netzwerkzeitung*, Oktober 1995, pp. 10–11.

HOUSE, E. (1974) *The Politics of Educational Innovation*, Berkeley, McCutchan.

KURTAKKO, K., LAUKKANEN, R. and IZADI, P. (1993) *Report on the Implementation of the Environment and School Initiatives Project in Finland*, Helsinki, Ministry of Education.

KYBURZ-GRABER, R., GINGINS, F. and KUHN, U. (1993) *Environment and School Initiatives in Switzerland — Final Report*, Zürich, École polytechnique fédérale.

LOSITO, B. and MAYER, M. (1993) *Environmental Education and Educational Innovation — Italian Report on ENSI research 'Environment and School Initiatives'*, Frascati, Centro Europeo dell'Educazione (CEDE).

MAIR, G., MALLAUN, K. and MONTIBELLER, R. (1992) *Projekthandbuch Energie*, Imst, Bundesrealgymnasium.

MALLAUN, K. (1994) *Zur Teamarbeit bei Umweltprojekten*, Wien, ARGE Umwelterziehung. USI-Reihe, Nr. 25.

MCANDREW, C. and PASCOE, I. (1993) *Environment and School Initiatives (ENSI). The Scottish National Report*, Dundee, Scottish Consultative Council on the Curriculum.

OCHSENBAUER, C. (1989) *Organisatorische Alternativen zur Hierachie*, München, GBI-Verlag.

OECD (1991) *Environment, Schools and Active Learning*, Paris, OECD.

OECD (1995) *Environmental Learning for the 21st Century*, Paris, OECD/CERI.

POSCH, P. (1994a) 'Changes in the culture of teaching and learning and implications for action research', *Educational Action Research*, **2**, 2, pp. 153–60.

POSCH, P. (1994b) 'Networking in environmental education', in PETTIGREW, M. and SOMEKH, B. (Eds), *Evaluation and Innovation in Environmental Education*, Paris, OECD/CERI. pp. 61–87.

POSCH, P. and ALTRICHTER, H. (1992) *Bildung in Österreich — Analysen und Entwicklungsperspektiven*, Innsbruck, Österreichischer Studienverlag.

PROJECT MINCIO (1992) *Research Report*, Frascati, Centro Europeo dell'Educazione (CEDE).

SCHÖN, D. (1983) *The Reflective Practitioner*, London, Temple Smith.

SUTTI, A. (1991) 'The Water Analysis Project — An Alternative Model for Environmental Study', in OECD/CERI (Ed.), *Environment, Schools and Active Learning*, Paris, OECD, pp. 59–65.

THONHAUSER, J., MOOSBRUGGER, B. and RAUCH, F. (1993) *The Achievements of the Austrian Team in the Framework of the OECD/CERI Project 'Environment and School Initiatives' — A Review*, Klagenfurt, Institute for Interdisciplinary Research and Continuing Education (IFF).

24 Contradictions of Management Theory, Organizational Cultures and the Self[1]

Bridget Somekh (Scotland) and Michaela Thaler (Austria)[2]

Towards Learning Organizations

This article is based on the Project 'Management of Human and Organizational Development' (MOHD). The main research focus of this project is on understanding learning at the level of the whole organization and identifying strategies for organizational development which give high priority to human resource management and quality assurance[3]. MOHD is a cooperative project funded by the European Union (1994–96) and involves six research centres in five European countries. These institutions are working within a network carrying out a series of interlinked small scale research projects in a range of organizations (mainly in the educational and health services). Specifically, MOHD is exploring the effectiveness of participatory action research as a strategy for creating 'learning organizations' (Peters and Waterman, 1982). The project assumes that power infiltrates all aspects of organizational structure and culture, through inter-personal, micro-political and formal-hierarchical relationships; that it acts negatively rather than positively when it becomes bi-polarized into patterns of coercion and resistance; and that these patterns are often the result of individuals lacking understanding of their own potential power and constructing for themselves (or acquiescing in) the role of the oppressed. Thus the central question for MOHD is whether involvement in participatory action research can enable individuals, regardless of their formal position in the hierarchy, to understand their own power and make a conscious contribution to organizational development.

In our understanding, the 'learning organization' is not brought about simply by training individuals; it can only happen as a result of learning at the level of the whole organization. It is also not brought about simply by interventions introduced by management; importantly, change processes need to be implemented by individuals in their own organizational context. In a genuine learning organization, every individual member should not only take part in change processes, but contribute positively — even initiate — these processes. Much has been written about what the learning organization is or is not, and there have been attempts to present piecemeal approaches for bringing it into being. However, despite its origins in Peters and Waterman's analysis of practice in actual companies, few attempts appear to have been made to develop a coherent strategy for creating a learning organization.

Normally the words are used to create a powerful aspiration intended as the focal point for change — but because there is no strategy to put the dream into place, very little actual change occurs. Participatory action research which tries to involve members at all levels of formal organizational hierarchies seems to be a useful strategy for this demanding purpose. What is often not understood is that taking part in the conscious development of organizations is a powerful means of professional learning. Thus participatory action research is a strategy which integrates organizational development with professional learning.

In this paper we present theoretical understandings which we have developed in collaboration with five organizations involved in the MOHD project in Scotland[4]. Our ideas are grounded in understandings of their experience of change as well as intensive debates with our international partners. We will argue that in order to develop strategies to make the aspiration of the learning organization into a reality, it is essential to rethink common management theories and the concept of the single, unique self.

'I Am'

Written in Northampton County Asylum:

> I am—yet what I am, who cares or knows;
>> My friends forsake me like a memory lost:—
> I am the self-consumer of my woes;—
>> They rise and vanish in oblivion's host,
> Like shadows in love's frenzied stifled throes:—
> And yet I am, and live—like vapours tost
>
> Into the nothingness of scorn and noise,—
>> Into the living sea of waking dreams,
> Where there is neither sense of life or joys,
>> But the vast shipwreck of my lifes esteems;
> Even the dearest, that I love the best
> Are strange—nay, they are stranger than the rest.
>> John Clare, 1793–1864[5]

This poem was read aloud in a recent radio programme about the nineteenth century Northamptonshire poet, John Clare (1939). He was much praised in his day for his nature poetry but is now valued most for the poetry he wrote while living against his will in Northampton mental asylum as a result of increasingly bizarre behaviour.

The self is fragile as a concept. Listening to the poem, it was immediately clear to us that John Clare's 'madness' was as much created by his imprisonment in a mental asylum as it was its cause. Bereft of his friends and family, deprived of the lionization as 'peasant poet' that he had experienced during his brief sojourn in London, John Clare lost a part of his self in his incarceration. The self who wrote this extraordinary poem was a different self, constructed through and within the context of the asylum, as Clare's self-critical faculty responded to the constructions placed upon his words and actions by doctors, fellow-sufferers and male nurses. Our interpretation of the poem is informed by George Herbert Mead's theory of the self. Mead sees 'mind' or 'consciousness' as three-fold: the 'I' who is the actor and problem-solver within the environment; the 'me' who is the object of self-scrutiny, continuously linked to the 'I' by a process which Schön calls reflection-in-action; and the 'generalized other' which can perhaps be summarized as the culture and norms of the group, represented by individuals with whom we interact. Only through 'engagement' of the 'I' and the 'me' with the 'generalized other', according to Mead, does the individual 'develop a complete self':

> It is in the form of the generalized other that the social process influences the behaviour of the individuals involved in it and carrying it on, i.e., that the community exercises control over the conduct of its individual members; for it is in this form that the social process or community enters as a determining factor in the individual's thinking. (Mead, 1934, p. 155)

Individuals are able to interpret changing stimuli or interactions even within an interaction. This means that the identities of individuals are not only multiple and overlapping, they are also continuously reconstructed. Identities are therefore not rigid, they are continuously transforming in response to changing demands in the individual's social environment. Krappmann (1969, quoted in Hanft, 1991, pp. 169ff.) called this process the 'balancing identity.' To explain this he uses the concepts of 'social identity' and 'personal identity.' The 'social identity' consists of the various norms and expectations of others, which the individual has to face in the interactive process. The 'personal identity' characterizes the individual: it consists of a unique combination of capabilities, attitudes, values, etc. In order to meet the demands of different 'others' and the demands of our own personalities we have to subordinate ourselves to circumstances while at the same time wanting to present ourselves as unique persons, and this entails a process of balancing identity between social and personal identities. The balancing identity allows us to accept demands (arising from one social identity) but also to reject them at the same time according to other demands (arising from other social identities or from personal identity). Hence, as individuals we have the capability to represent ourselves not only within a single interaction, but also in relation to former interactions or over-lapping interactions. According to this theory the balancing identity represents the 'I' within the different social identities and the personal identity.

The self is, therefore, inter-dependent with others rather than being an isolated and wholly independent identity. Understanding this is crucial to understanding the processes of social change — in all contexts, including the family and the workplace. Bettelheim (1961) and Goffman (1961) help us to understand John Clare's descent into madness. The peasant poet was perhaps torn between the intensive, compulsive isolation of the writer and the fierce passions of the lover and father. His 'madness' was a convenient label others could give to his inability to position himself successfully between these two extremes.

The concept of the 'self' consisting of many balancing identities is reinforced when we consider Foucault's insight that societies and sub-cultures of societies construct realities and values through categorization and naming (Foucault, 1972, p. 131), and enforce behaviours through unrecognized but deeply-embedded traditions such as the ritual of confession that 'unfolds within a power relationship' (Foucault, 1978, p. 61). Foucault works to resist the oppression of these regimes of truth expressed through social structures and signified through discourse. He does not willingly submit to being constructed and named as a single identity. In the metaphor of the labyrinth he describes his attempt to express his self in a language cleansed of the constructs, and hence of the power, of any discourse. And he reserves the right to remain essentially free and fluid in identity.

> What, do you imagine that I would take so much trouble and so much pleasure in writing, do you think that I would keep so persistently to my task, if I were not preparing — with a rather shaky hand — a labyrinth into which I can venture, in which I can move my discourse, opening up underground passages, forcing it to go far from itself, finding overhangs that reduce and deform its itinerary, in which I can lose myself and appear at last to eyes that I will never have to meet again. I am no doubt not the only one who writes in order to have no face. Do not ask who I am and do not ask me to remain the same: leave it to our bureaucrats and our police to see that our papers are in order. At least spare us their morality when we write. (Foucault, 1974, p. 17)

For us, this passage from Foucault reveals a basic human dilemma. On the one hand, it seems that our constructed selves are caught in overlapping group identities whose constraining power is embodied in discourse; but on the other hand, if we could break free it would only be at the price of our known world and our security. We would be free spirits but stateless, so to speak. Our selves are not separate and single; without others we have no 'voice'. Few of us would knowingly choose to go down Foucault's labyrinthine path beyond social constraints, even supposing it were possible, but paradoxically our reliance upon societal structures, social groupings and sub-cultures leaves us ultimately vulnerable to disintegration of identity through the kind of rejection meted out to John Clare. The concept of the learning organization has a new imperative when we understand that, through inter-personal and intra-personal positionings, the organizations in which we work play an important role in shaping our sense of identity and self-worth.

Management Theories and the 'Self'

If we accept this concept of multiple 'selves', what are the implications for developmental processes in organizations? In our current state of knowledge about management of organizations, which concepts of the 'self' are prevalent and how do these relate to the theory of multiple selves? Management theories of both organizations and leadership define the relationships between people in organizations, including authority relationships, control systems and informal structures. By defining relationships these theories deal explicitly or implicitly with change processes in organization, insofar as they try to explain which approaches interact most positively with internal or external conditions like tradition, growth, economic constraints, new technologies etc. Arising from different values embedded in these theories the ways of conceptualizing human behaviour are very different. But most of them fail to take account of the implications of the self consisting of 'multiple, overlapping and balancing identities'.

Traditional approaches which can be summarized as rational-functional theories assume that both individuals and organizations have clear-cut needs and that progress will result from setting clear goals and monitoring performance. On the one hand, individuals have more or less firm and inflexible needs, motives, values and attitudes which determine their actions within the organization. On the other hand, the organizational environment sets clear tasks and expectations through knowledge of which variables affect individual performance and satisfaction. The organization also has the power to coerce individuals by rewards or sanctions to meet its demands. Hence, the leadership's task is to create a system, and individual action is seen as the product of individual pre-assumptions, stimuli and organizational demands. The assumption is that the 'right use' of the 'right means' will determine individual action as required by the organizational goals. Role conflicts, disagreement and differences of interpretation are seen as resulting from insufficient management. However, this assumption seem to be ill-founded as repeated examples demonstrates that these 'failures' cannot be avoided (Hanft, 1991, pp. 152ff.).

The work of the MOHD project shows that, although different organizations experience very similar external pressures for change within the same societal environment (i.e., in the context of common political, ideological and economic factors), their particular organizational cultures, the degree of involvement of individuals and their own understanding of their contribution to organizational development make every change process unique. This diversity in itself is nothing new. But our understanding of the underlying reasons for diversity in the process of change has been greatly enriched by interpreting events and relationships in the light of the concept of multiple selves.

Individuals at different levels in organizational hierarchies who want to contribute to organizational development, mostly do more than traditional roles would request, and therefore position themselves politically within the organization. Explicitly or implicitly they are enacting multiple selves. This very often causes them (and others) to experience role conflicts and uncertainty. If the individual who is promoting change processes is a manager, this often leads to continuing conflicts between the demand to act professionally and personally. When this is understood, not as a simple conflict between private and public goals, but in terms of Krappmann's concept of the 'balancing identity' the complexity of the situation becomes clear: in working towards *both* professional and personal goals the manager engages in the intrapersonal process of balancing personal identity and social identity — and those who interpret the manager's decisions and actions are themselves engaged in the same process. For example, this explains why attempts to address the problems experienced by staff who are subordinates can be interpreted by them either as manipulation or as a personal effort on their behalf: whatever the manager's espoused intentions, the concept of multiple selves suggests that both motives almost certainly played a part in the manager's decision and subsequent actions. This in turn makes the manager vulnerable to criticisms which will result in different 'self-positionings' in subsequent decisions. What we commonly refer to as strength of personality is clearly essential if the manager is to function effectively, given this complexity.

Some of the newer management theories deny the capability of organizations to develop. In this ecological-darwinistic view (Aldrich, 1992, p. 17) organizations experience new beginnings and self-destructive downward spirals which can be explained through a life cycle metaphor of birth and death. They are shaped for an epoque and a context and become non-functional as a result of changing conditions — radical rebirth or closure then becoming the only possibilities. These models thus tend to neglect individuals in organizations and 'down-play the role of individual actors and their interpretation' (Aldrich, 1992, p. 20).

Other so-called institutional approaches see organizational processes as mainly political rather than functional[6]. Organizations are not only focused upon the tasks of their core business, but are also driven by the demands and expectations stemming from the organizational environment itself and its cultural norms. According to these theories, organizations are created and developed through politically-generated decisions rather than through decisions taken upon rational grounds (see, for example, Powell and DiMaggio, 1991). These new approaches still ignore the interaction process as a basic element of organizational behaviour: change in organizations is seen to occur as a reaction to external demands in order to obtain continuing external approval, legitimacy and support from institutions within the organizational environment. Again the individual's part in the change process is passive: organizations and their members either have the capability to act appropriately in response to external demands or they do not.

Other management theories see political interactive processes as an essential part of organizational behaviour. For example, in a micro-political analysis of organizations it is argued that people use interaction to enhance or protect the personal interests of individuals or groups. As Pfeffer writes, the degree of influence depends on the sources of power and on personal qualities, but is also a result of interaction and interpretation:

> Power is at once a consequence of the constraints and resource contingencies facing the organization, the ability of those in the organization to advocate their skills and capacities for handling those problems as well as shaping the definition of the situation, and the knowledge and advocacy skills that help in the exercise of structurally-derived power. Definitions of the situation are part and parcel of power strategies and must compete

with other definitions which are advocated by other interests.' (Pfeffer, 1981, p. 135)

This micropolitical approach is useful, because it shows very clearly that individuals and groups are not just objects in organizational processes. Each individual and each group has many possibilities of influencing these processes. On the other hand, micropolitical analyses sometimes have a negative flavour, in that by recognizing the use of power as a means of achieving individually preferred outcomes, they appear to legitimatize all possible strategies like intrigues, betrayal, control of information flow, etc. The purpose of these strategies is mainly to enhance personal interests, and this leads to continuing conflicts over limited material and immaterial resources within organizations. Although the micropolitical approach seems to integrate the concept of multiple selves, it sometimes seem to overemphasize 'the dark side of organizational life' (Altrichter and Salzgeber, 1995, p. 20), and from our point of view it does not give sufficient recognition to individual efforts to contribute to organizational development. The strength of this approach lies in recognizing and stressing the frequent use of power in organizations to enhance personal interests (and group-interests of strategic coalitions); but its weakness lies in taking insufficient account of those initiatives within organizations which promote both individual and organizational development. The work of the MOHD project suggests that people contribute to organizational development, not only because it is a way of gaining power over resources, but because making a commitment and contribution to the development of the organization in which they spend most of their time supports their own professional development.

To summarize: traditional management theories assume that individuals respond to social demands, while micropolitical approaches assume that individual action is determined by enhancing individual power. We think that both views are insufficient, partly, at least, as a result of assuming over-simplistic models of the self. Our approach is in line with research such as (Nias, 1989) and Dadds (1995), who provide detailed analysis of teachers' experiences of working within organizations.

On the contrary, reflection on the change processes within the organizations participating in the MOHD project has shown that individuals with strong personal beliefs about the 'mission' of the organization are motivated to suggest and promote organizational development. At the same time they are conscious of organizational structures, cultural pecularities, constraints and links. In interpreting and using the given situation (e.g., by establishing informal networks, using opportunities such as any kind of available resources) the individual has to accept compromises and ongoing role-conflicts. These conflicts are experienced as 'disturbing the smooth running' of organizations, but they are also positive. In MOHD we have found that experiences of conflicts of any kind seem to be important occasions for searching shared understandings of situations and possibilities for development. These shared understandings are based on the positioning of interests and interpretations in discussion with others. In organizations where individuals do not engage in the (often abrasive) process of coming to shared understandings, development hardly occurs.

The Role of Action Research Within Change Processes

We are interested in ways of developing the power that already exists within individuals in organizations. We believe that action research provides the means of developing the kind of intuitive knowledge necessary for this. Specifically, we refer to Aristotle's definition of intuitive knowledge (nous) — the state of mind that 'apprehends first principles', an unreasoned state of knowing. Aristotle distinguishes knowledge from 'judgment and opinion' which he says are 'liable to be quite mistaken' (Aristotle, 1955). We have become intrigued with pondering on this distinction. As a first step we have found it helpful to think of 'judgment and opinion' in terms of what is often today called 'common sense'. Both terms have the initial appearance of being a kind of knowledge, but upon investigation turn out to be 'often quite mistaken'. This mistaken substitute for knowledge is, we believe, commonly used as the basis for decision-making and action in organizations.

In the MOHD project our central strategy has been to explore participatory action research as a means of enabling individuals to develop *nous* as an essential base for action. This *intuitive knowledge* enables them to handle the complexity of adopting an active stance and make a conscious contribution to organizational development. It is fundamentally different from intuitive common sense.

Understanding of action research, however, commences with individual research and development, as Altrichter, *et al.* writes:

- action research is about people reflecting upon and improving their own practice;

- by tightly interlinking their reflection and action;

- and making their experiences public to other people concerned by and interested in the respective practice (Altrichter, *et al.*, 1991, p. 7).

In this sense action research provides possibilities to improve 'judgment and opinion' at the individual level. Many examples show that action research carried out by individuals supports the process of reflecting on roles and relationships, and improves the social situations in which the action research takes place. Of course, these action research processes also have some impact on organizations, but the influence is not direct and very often not intended. In order to enhance learning at the whole organizational level, we need to conceptualize and carry out action research in slightly different ways.

Strategies and Principles of Participatory Action Research

John Elliott (1991) defines action research as: 'the study of a social situation with a view to improving the quality of action within it' (p. 69). This does not imply that the research process should only be concentrated on the individual's point of view of a social situation. In the MOHD project we have found that *involving as many people as possible who are likely to be affected by the action research*, in the action research process, at an early stage, can be a way of greatly enlarging the potential power of action research to support change. Involvement here means more than simply becoming informants. In participatory action research the roles of researchers and participants are intentionally blurred: a small group within an organization, often including an external research partner, is promoting the research, but they conceive of their action research as a collaborative endeavour with the other participants in the organization, including those who are not close colleagues. In a school this would include students and possibly parents or other members of the local community, e.g., corporations which promote projects or sponsor the school and its students in various ways. The aim of this little core group, who are knowingly engaged in action research, is to encourage as much participation as possible in the action research, typically — at least at first — without naming the activities involved as 'research'. For example, a wide range of individuals can become involved in the analysis and interpretation of data if 'data summaries' are prepared by the core team and tabled for discussion, say at the end of a regular meeting. This kind of participation is itself a strategy of bringing about improvement and development: if people are involved in discussing, analyzing and interpreting data they can share in developing any necessary action strategies. This develops quite a different kind of ownership of the ideas from anything that normally results from action research conducted by one or two individuals without this explicit aim of engendering participation. Whyte (1991), in an excellent book on participatory action research, stresses that the level of participation can never be predicted in advance. Depending upon the organization and the individuals within it, and upon the skills of the core group, wide variation is to be expected in the levels of participation achieved. But the underlying rationale remains the same — any participation in the action research process from individuals beyond the core group strengthens its power as a lever for change.

Reinforcement for these ideas can be found, of course, in Fullan's (1982; 1991) theory of innovation. Those who are responsible for implementing change need to 'make sense' of what the change is about and the reasoning behind its introduction. This 'personal meaning' is essential because of the strong link between the commitment to change of individuals and their personal and professional values. Fullan also stresses the importance of 'integrating general knowledge of change with detailed knowledge of the politics, personalities and history peculiar to the setting in question' (1982, p. x). Here we can find the link to the notion of 'multiple, balancing selves'. The successful implementation of change processes depends on the significance which it has for the individual within the 'local' setting of various organizational and personal conditions. It seems that the idea of 'ownership' is mainly based on participation and involvement of people as well as mutual understanding and open discussion of different points of view.

To involve people in participatory action research on the basis of their own particular (organizational) background, fits well with our understanding of the interactive and interpretative nature of identity and identification. The process of analyzing and reflecting upon formal and informal roles arising from different demands supports the individual's capability for 'role-taking'. This means, that it enables individuals to determine their role within the interaction by anticipating the demands of others and understanding the roles of others in terms of their own personal needs. Although the organizational situation causes conflict, action research provides the possiblity of a deeper understanding of these conflicts. Understanding and enduring these conflicts is necessary for individuals, in order to sustain their 'balancing identity'.

By encouraging the increasing participation of colleagues and other interested parties in action research across the whole organization, the core 'initiating group' begins to lose control over the focus and developmental direction of the action research. As more people become more involved and move from being participants and informants towards being researchers, they make an increasing input into the analysis and interpretation of data and the planning and implementation of development strategies. There is a resulting shift of control over change processes from senior managers (and possibly external consultants) who helped to initiate the research to other participants; but the opportunities for change are much more powerful than they are in 'traditional' approaches to the management of change. It has to be said that there may be certain features of organizational policy which senior managers see as being of such central importance that they cannot be changed. If this is the case, it is important for managers to be clear about this possibility from the start, and honest about identifying these features when they become clear. This ensures that these assumptions become part of the data, and can at least be discussed and considered within the decision-making process.

Possible Risks and Problems of Participatory Action Research

Participatory action research is open to the charge that it can be used as a means for manipulating people to act and react in a certain way. In this it is no different from many other forms of management. When the motivation or impetus comes from an individual or a small group (e.g., the core initiating group in participatory action research) there is always a danger of manipulation, especially if participants have different formal power within the organization, which is an important feature of participatory action research. The multiple self, engaged in a process of 'balancing' personal identity and social identity, is continuously positioning and repositioning *vis a vis* others who will have differential awareness of the significance of these complex intra-personal and inter-personal interactions. Inescapably, greater understanding of this process means greater power. Essentially, this is a moral question. It is one that does not arise in many approaches to management which assume that a manager's job is to gain compliance from others by whatever means is most effective and efficient. In participatory action research it is an important issue which must be addressed. In the MOHD project we have placed emphasis upon negotiating clear (written) guidelines which determine the access to and use of information in advance of the research process. As participatory action research is an 'evolving' approach, changing conditions or unexpected results may cause a change of the guidelines: the participants for instance could see the necessity of reporting the research findings to another group than originally expected. But, fundamentally, participatory action research needs to be based on moral and ethical groundrules. This means that participatory action research only can be applied in a climate of openness and honesty as well as mutual trust between the participants. Without this basis participatory action research cannot be successful in promoting change. Of course, not all members of the organization need to participate in the action research — there will always be those who have become tired, or disillusioned, or whose motivation for one reason or another has little connection with organizational goals, and they are best seen as constituting part of the organizational context for change. There is no need to aim for total participation (which is normally unattainable). Effective whole organizational change can occur with the involvement of a sufficient number to create what is commonly called a 'critical mass'. If the basis of openness, honesty and trust exists within this group, participatory action research is a powerful strategy to enhance understanding and communication between individuals and their roles at different levels in the organizational hierarchy.

The second 'risk' to be mentioned is the application of participatory action research as a means of crisis management. Whereas it seems to be most likely that organizations start to learn when external or internal conditions enforce them to do so, the ideal of a learning organization goes beyond managing an organization in critical situations. The ideal seems to be to create an acting rather than a reacting organization. To quote Argyris and Schön (1991, p. 94) this means engaging in 'double loop learning' instead of 'single loop learning'. Single loop learning means that actions which produce errors are identified and changed, whereas 'double loop learning' involves a more sophisticated understanding of the underlying causes or the actions. For instance: in one of our MOHD projects the new headteacher of a school changed the existing structure of communication by abolishing a senior teachers' meeting and replacing it with other meetings because it appeared to be inefficient. Double loop learning would ask not only: 'Was this meeting an efficient way of taking decisions in the school?' but would also ask: 'Why did this meeting exist for such a long time, when it was so inefficient?'; 'What function had it for the participating teachers?'; 'Does the new meeting meet the demands of these teachers?' If not, 'what (possibly unintended) impact will the abolition of the meeting have on the teachers and on the organisation?'. This example also shows that change processes in crisis situations very often affect organizational structures in a way which would not happen in more normal circumstances. Change processes in crisis situations have the power to break taboos and 'undiscussibles', which usually sustain the existing organizational structures. Argyris and Schön (1991) call these 'undiscussibles':

> defensive routines, which may be defined as any policy or practice that prevents organizations (and their agents) from experiencing embarrassment or threat and at the same time prevents them from identifying and reducing the causes of embarrassment or threat. . . . Defensive routines, at any level, are anti-learning (p. 94).

The success of participatory action research as a strategy for creating a learning organization depends on its capability to surface such defensives routines in an active way. If action research is not able to enhance change processes, by identifying anti-learning routines without the threat of a crisis in the organization, it degenerates to little more than a 'pretty' instrument, of little more use than other management techniques. To succeed in this difficult endeavour of breaking down established routines of interaction and what, in effect, are taboos established by the culture and traditions of the group, we maintain that it is essential to have an understanding of the multiple nature of the many 'selves' involved. Rational planning and decision-making are doomed to failure in the face of the remarkable complexity of human motivation, encompassing interlocking disappointments, hurts, confessions, affections and aspirations.

Notes

1 Part of this paper is a re-working of ideas included in: 'Reflections on First Encounters with Human Resource Manager', by Bridget Somekh in Congress Papers of World Congress 3 on Action Learning, Action Research and Process Management, University of Bath, July 1994, pp. 216 ff.
2 Michaela Thaler worked with the MOHD project at the Scottish Council for Research in Education from January to June 1996.
3 The other main aim is to train and to support young researchers, who are working for six months in one of the other centres abroad.
4 The Mary Erskine and Stewart's Melville Junior School, Edinburgh; Craigmillar Primary School, Edinburgh; the University of Glasgow TILT (Teaching with Independent Learning Technologies) project; Strathclyde University Faculty of Education at Jordanhill; and Stranraer Academy.
5 The poem ends with four further lines which provide a Christian resolution, but it is likely that these lines were an afterthought (possibly suggested to Clare by his carers).
6 Some authors refer to these approaches as new paradigms (Donaldson 1995, p. 16).

References

ALDRICH, H.E. (1992) 'Incommensurable Paradigms? Vital Signs from Three Perspectives', in: REED, M. and HUGHES, M. (Eds), *Rethinking Organization. New Directions in Organization Theory and Analysis*, London, Sage, pp. 17–45.
ALTRICHTER, H. and SALZGEBER, S. (1995) 'Mikropolitik der Schule', in ROLFF, H.G. (Ed.), *Zukunftsfelder von Schulforschung*, Weinheim, Deutscher Studienverlag, pp. 9–40.
ALTRICHTER, H., KEMMIS, S., McTAGGART, R. and ZUBER-SKERRITT, O. (1991) 'Defining, Confining or Refining Action Research?', in ZUBER-SKERRITT, O. (Ed.) *Action Research for Change and Development*, Aldershot/Brookfield: Avebury, pp. 3–9.
ARGYRIS, C. and SCHÖN, D.A. (1991) 'Participatory Action Research and Action Science Compared: A commentary', in WHYTE, W.F. (Ed.), *Participatory Action Research*, Newbury Park, Sage, pp. 85–96.
ARISTOTLE (1955) *Ethics*, translated by THOMSON, J.A.K., London, Pengium Classics.

BETTELHEIM, B. (1961) *The Informed Heart: The Human Condition in Mass Society*, London, Paladin.

BLUMER, H. (1946) 'Collective Behavior', in LEE, A.M. (Ed.), *New Outlines of the Principles of Sociology*, New York, Barnes and Noble, pp. 163–222.

CLARE, J. (1939) 'Written in Northhampton County Asylum', reprinted and edited by QUILLER-COUCH, A. *The Oxford Book of English Verse*.

DADDS, M. (1995) *Passionate Enquiry and School Development: A Story About Teacher Action Research*, London, Falmer Press.

DONALDSON, L. (1995) *American Anti-management Theories of Organization: A Critque of Paradigm Proliferation*, Cambridge, Cambridge Studies in Management. Cambridge University press.

EBBUTT, D. and ELLIOTT, J. (Eds) (1984), *Issues in Teaching for Understanding*, London, Longman for the SCDC.

ELLIOTT, J. (1989) 'Educational theory and the professional learning of teachers: An overview', *Cambridge Journal of Education*, **19**, pp. 81–101.

ELLIOTT, J. (1991) *Action Research for Educational Change*, Buckingham, UK, and Bristol PA, Open University Press.

ELLIOTT, J. (1993 Ed.) *Reconstructing Teacher Education*, London, Falmer Press.

FOUCAULT, M. (1972) *Power/Knowledge: Selected Interviews and Other Writings: 1972–77*, edited by GORDON, C., Bury St Edmunds, Harvester Press.

FOUCAULT, M. (1974) *The Archeology of Knowledge*, London, Tavistock Publication.

FOUCAULT, M. (1978) *The History of Sexuality*, Vol. 1, English translation by Robert Hurley. London, Penguin Books.

FREUD, S. (1986) *The Essentials of Psycho-Analysis*, London, Penguin Books.

FULLAN, M.G. (1982) *The Meaning of Educational Change*, New York, Teachers College Press.

FULLAN, M.G. (WITH STIEGELBAUER, S.) (1991) *The New Meaning of Educational Change*, London, Cassell.

GARFINKEL, H. (1967) *Studies in Ethnomethodology*, in particular: Chapter 2, pp. 35–75, 'Studies of the routine grounds of everyday activities', 1984 edition, Polity Press: Cambridge and Oxford.

GOFFMAN, E. (1959) *The Presentation of Self in Everyday Life*, London, Penguin.

GOFFMAN, E. (1961) *Asylums*, London, Penguin.

HANFT, A. (1991) *Identifikation als Einstellung zur Organisation. Eine kritische Analyse aus interaktionistischer Perspektive*, Muenchen und Mering, Rainer Hampp Verla.

MEAD, G.H. (1934) *The works of George Herbert Mead, Vol. 1. Mind, Self and Society*, Chicago, IL, University of Chicago Press.

NIAS, J. (1989) *Primary Teachers Talking: A Study of Reading as Work*, London and New York, Routledge.

PEDLER, M., BURGOYNE, J. and BOYDELL, T. (1991) *The Learning Company: A Strategy for Sustainable Development*, London, McGraw Hill.

PETERS, T.J. and WATERMAN, R.H. (1982) *In Search of Excellence: Lessons from America's Best-run Companies*, New York, Harper-Row.

PFEFFER, J. (1981) *Power in Organizations*, Pitman Publishing Inc., London, Marshfield.

POWELL, W.W. and DiMAGGIO, P.J. (1991, edition) *The New Institutionalism in Organizational Analysis*, London, Chicago, The University of Chicago Press.

SENGE, P.M. (1990) *The Fifth Discipline: The Art and Practice of the Learning Organization*, London, Century Business.

WHYTE, W.F. (1991) *Participatory Action Research*, Newbury Park, CA, and London, Sage.

25   The Double Track: The Dichotomy of Roles in Action Research

Bruno Losito and Graziella Pozzo (Italy)

This chapter is the result of a collaborative discussion within a project, that of MOHD.[1] The experiences of action research that we both brought to the project are different, partly because we work and have worked in very different institutions: one is a regional centre for innovation and in-service teacher training and the other, a national centre for educational research. Both these institutions are dependent upon the Ministry of Education.[2] In these contexts we have taken part in action research projects as facilitators and as outside researchers, developing a second order reflection on our own roles and professional practice (Elliott, 1991).

In recent years, we have tried to develop a collaborative debate with other researchers on the role and the functions of the outside researcher/facilitator in action research. The reflections in this chapter were, therefore, made possible within the context of the MOHD project but are also a result of our past experiences. They are offered as they emerged from our common reflection. The epistolary format of the excerpts in the chapter reflects the modality we adopted for distant communication.

Roles, Functions, Contexts

Action research can be considered simultaneously on many levels. It is a professional development strategy which focuses on practitioners' own reflection upon and within their professional practice. It is a research methodology through which investigative processes can be pursued and knowledge produced. It is a strategy for change both at an individual level and within the internal professional context. But it is also a very flexible strategy and it is this flexibility which allows for the processes of action research to be pursued in different contexts, with the emphasis moving from one to another of these dimensions. The role of the outside researcher along with his/her position within the research process and his/her relationships with the researcher teachers (and more generally, with practitioners) varies depending on the context within which action research is being carried out. Outside researcher, facilitator, expert, consultant, evaluator, these are some of the possible roles he/she may be called upon to play.

At times there can be tension between these different roles (Messner and Rauch, 1995). At other times, the outside researcher has to take on different roles at different phases of an action research project (Losito and Mayer, 1995). In any case, the reflection of the outside researcher/facilitator cannot be developed only *a posteriori*. The facilitator should rather develop her/his research identifying questions and problems, collecting data and analyzing them. Her/his reflection should develop in parallel with the reflection of the practitioners, interwoven with theirs and following analogous and congruent research modalities (Elliott, 1993; Jansen and Dijkstra, 1992).

The Context: The MOHD Project

The MOHD project is a collaborative one which involves six European centres.[3] The objectives of the project are two-fold:

- generation of knowledge and explanatory theories relating to the processes of whole organizational development;
- improvement of the effectiveness and efficiency of the participating organizations in fulfilment of their organizational mission, and of the educational processes which enable that improvement through the creation of 'learning organisations'.[4]

From a methodological point of view, the project has adopted the action research methodology with the aim of developing a 'reflective transformation of practice'. It is therefore an action research project in which moments of knowledge production, of professional development and of organisational change are fused together. Its more general guidelines have been identified and elaborated by researchers from different Centres and Institutes participating at a European level. The Italian project is made up of two sub projects with different aims, one of which prioritises the development of a reflection on the role and function of heads of school through the setting up of of two action research groups, one in Turin and one in Rome, which each have a facilitator.

In Italy, there is no specific training for heads of school before being appointed. In recent years several initiatives for their in-service training have been developed both at national and regional level, but they have been very different both in terms of aims and quality. Furthermore, it is not possible to speak of a 'national system' for in-service training. Institutional people are still paying homage to a top-down culture where inquiry and the effort to understand better is seen as threatening to the institution itself. Critical dialogue has no institutionalized space but just happens to be there. There have been extensive top-down innovations which have left almost unchanged the dominant culture of heads of school as well as that of teachers. Professionals in Italy are still largely attuned to the obeyance of fixed rules set by others: teachers' actions have to conform to the heads' expectations; heads have to conform to and respond to inspectors, *provveditorati* (local education authorities) and to the Ministry of Education. This does not mean that that is how things actually are but that is how everyone expects things to be. Another feature is the 'isolation' in which both teachers and heads work. Also expectations seem to be geared to highly structured situations rather than to flexible and experimental attitudes.

Separate Roles or the Coexistence of Several? Two Metaphors

When we first started work we thought it would be useful to start our common reflection by trying to express through metaphors how each one of us perceived our own role in the project. We often use this technique when carrying out our (and practitioners') reflection because metaphors allow to make explicit the implicit images people have of their professional roles. They allow a freer exploration and the starting of a process of clarification without freezing the concepts in a definition. So they allow the development of reflection through free and accumulative associations.

These are two major metaphors that we developed at the beginning of the project, when we started to reflect on our role in the group. Bruno writes to Graziella:

A good metaphor for me I think, could be that of an 'experienced' sailor travelling with other sailors on a boat without a captain.

A breakdown of the metaphor.

1 There is no 'captain'. I don't feel like a captain who charts the course, who makes decisions and gives orders. At the same time, I don't reject the responsibility I know I have. I am aware that, compared to the others, I am

2 not just a 'sailor' but an 'experienced' one. I should like to navigate with others, putting my experience and the skills I have learnt from that experience at their disposal. I am prepared to tell them in what direction I think we should be heading and to take on practical tasks which this entails. I'm also committed to 'transferring' my 'expertise' to others (in action research, in methodology, and in particular areas — for example my experience in environmental education as I did in the ENSI project[5])

3 I, too, am a traveller (in research), just like the others and obviously, like everyone else involved, I bring my values and meanings to the voyage, which may be different to those of the other 'sailors'. I am 'on the boat' with them and yet my position is not the same as theirs. It is this difference which allows for the comparing and sharing of choices or at least for them to be make known and made explicit to all those who are on the boat

4 The 'voyage' doesn't have a preconceived destination, or rather in part it does, but so many things can happen during the journey, adventure/the unexpected are hidden round each corner waiting to pounce! The land to be reached may be known, the course to be taken perhaps less so, depending upon the chart, on sea conditions, on the ability of the sailors — especially since for many of

them it is (or may be) their first journey — and on the provisions made along the way. What we do know is that the voyage has to have a destination, that it can't be an end in itself and that it can't go on forever. Once a destination is reached, another can be set. Hopefully, the experience will not have diminished the desire to travel in any way. Indeed, hopefully, having become experts, the sailors will develop a real taste for sailing.

5   The boat symbolizes all the contextual elements — the project, the group, the abilities of each of its members. The vessel may be more or less well-equipped, more or less in one piece but this need not be an obstacle to the voyage itself. What is important is to be conscious of its condition so that the destination chosen is not impossible to reach and that the course chosen will be appropriate (currents, distance . . .).

I like this metaphor especially because it captures the non-separate nature of my role, acknowledging at the same time my responsibilities but above all because it puts me in the context of an adventure, which excites me a lot.

What do you think? I was thinking about your metaphors and how different they are from mine in a very substantial way, obviously because of our different experiences: you always make references to 'concrete' facilitation activities within internal group processes whereas my metaphors tend to be more about 'roles' and particularly about my fear of 'using' other people's work. In other words, a problem of 'power'. Maybe this is what is at the root of my metaphor.

Graziella answers:

I read with interest the metaphor you have developed for the way you feel in the group: if you had to retranslate the metaphor into a role figure, would you still say you were a facilitator? or an expert? The task of a facilitator is to facilitate processes, the role of the expert is to offer knowledge (declarative or procedural) along the way. You define yourself as an 'experienced sailor' with other sailors. In the case of the heads of school they can also be experienced sailors, but their expertise is in other areas. In this sense, I don't think I agree with the fact that your role is not separate from the others. Precisely because you are an expert and that the others aren't, means that they will turn to you as the expert and that you will have more of a voice.

While I was thinking about your metaphor I was trying to develop one which now and again crosses my mind but which I've never written down: that of the weaver (Penelope without Ulysses!). The metaphor centres around the role I have in the group of heads of schools: I have no meaning without those participants and without them providing the raw materials (the threads — their ideas, values, beliefs); we are all involved in the creation of something (a tapestry) which will exist as a product (the knowledge which will be constructed together), even if the task is not completed. And probably by the end, Penelope isn't bothered about keeping the tapestry: it is a collective artefact made so that others too can see it (communicating to the outside). The raw materials may have knots (obstacles) and in any case it is the role of the weaver to work in those knots while keeping the threads together (written feedback of the threads the participants bring) and to create a pattern warp and weft). And this is where the skills of the weaver can be crucial (bringing together the threads and the connections) and in bringing out certain colours (the cognitive styles, nature of the contributions).

You are going on a voyage with others. I am participating in the production of an artefact, the tapestry. You are living an adventure, I am participating in the production of a collective work but have a different function to the other participants, that of facilitating and structuring (which doesn't give me more rights over the tapestry). It's true that I am more in a 'doing' mode whereas you are in a 'going' one. . . .

Facilitation

Reflection through the use of metaphors brought out another difference in roles. This is what Bruno sees as the major task he set himself.

In the first phase of the project's development, I, as the outside researcher, took on a variety of tasks.

As *outside researcher responsible for the project* I took on a lot of tasks that I would define as ones of *organizational and institutional support*.

First of all, *the research group had to be put together*: I had to identify which heads of school were to be asked to participate in the project, then present the aims, bring the two groups together and set out a draft plan. What I did was in some way to take on the responsibility for 'selecting' the participants. I decided that openness to the general aims of the project and an interest in becoming involved in action research would be the main criteria.

I realize that in this way, I 'got around' what for me is one of the open questions in action research, that of what 'prerequisites' are necessary for action research to really be an efficient strategy for professional development and research. Is action research a strategy that 'suits everyone'? Or can it be useful only if professionals come with prior motivation, an already developed interest or at the very least a 'willingness to change'?[6]

The groups I worked with until now were always made up of particularly motivated teachers who in some sense were already 'in research'. For the MOHD project I re-used the same model for constituting the group construction and chose to work with just a handful of school heads.

As outside researcher I took on another role. As the heads of school were participating on a voluntary basis, it was important that their reflection and the research they were to be engaged in within the project were recognised as in-service training by the school authorities. This was a task that I, as outside researcher, took on, by making the necessary steps to get the recognition I felt was appropriate from the Ministry of Education and the local school authorities.

This is where the outside researcher can use his/her institutional position (in research or training centres) in order to create conditions conducive to reflection and the carrying out of research by practitioners.

Graziella is no longer working within the institution. While her new position makes her role certainly 'weaker' in terms of power and releases her from organizational tasks, it makes her facilitatory function in a way 'cleaner'. So she writes:

> Unlike you, as a freelance or outsider I can no longer be a mediator between practitioners and the institution. A lot of the tasks you are taking on are the responsibility of one of the heads of school in our group (e.g., identifying group members, contacting the local authorities, etc., explaining the aims of the research.). This makes my role as facilitator somewhat easier in the sense that it is not 'contaminated' by other kinds of roles. I don't know whether it needs to be said, but that's how it is, and as someone working outside the institution I no longer have any power. I am certainly not as strong a link as you. So I feel quite distant from the question of what the advantages are for me in being involved in research except in terms of professional development (which is very important to me) and the opportunity to forge links/make contact with a wider public than that of Torino, which includes you and eventually, colleagues in other countries.

Negotiation

In this phase the different approaches seem to mirror the degree of complexity in the relationships due to the different background and amount of power the two researchers supposedly have. A person working within the institution on set tasks cannot avoid addressing such questions as expectations, motivations, tasks and possible rewards from the very beginning. Graziella writes:

> In the first session a kind of contract was drawn up, liable to re-negotiations and changes at any moment, which would make both 'cold' (objective) and 'warm' (subjective) data available. Each session would be recorded and then

a transcription made of it. This would give a concrete idea of the importance of data.

At the beginning of each session I also found it essential to remind
the group what the purpose of our being together is: to see that heads of
school can become agents of change and how they can have a role in the
creation of a culture that values learning more than teaching. In short,
what role they can have in the creation of a learning environment (where
every member, head included, has something to learn). Later, I noticed that
the general feeling of elation of the first meetings was giving way to more
restrained reactions and participation. Does less enthusiasm in fact indicate deeper reflection on the way? Or an awareness that the issues at stake
are no easy ones and that the involvement requested is of a rigorous type?

A complex situation demands not so much solutions but rather the skill to see the
controversial issues that inhabit it. Controversial issues have to be identified and
named in order to be seen. The better if the identification is carried out by a community of people who share them. From this follows the need to find spaces and
opportunities to make them visible and to share them. The context in which we live
provides few opportunities for the description of what one does and of how one
does it. We even lack the language to say things. In this respect:

a) MOHD is providing a space where heads of school can meet and pour out
problems, puzzles and perplexities within the frame of AR. The existence of a space where controversial issues may be aired is in itself something new in a culture of topdown initiatives where the old saying 'One
problem aired, one problem shared' has never found a fertile ground. The
hypothesis is that the modality chosen for the meetings, one of reflective
dialogue, will produce a space favourable to:

— identifying and articulating tensions
— exchanging ideas, sharing experiences and socializing problems
— providing opportunities for feedback of what one does
— providing opportunities for the restructuring of one's own culture
in the direction of a culture of learning (just as AR in my experience helps teachers to restructure the culture of teaching and
learning).

b) MOHD provides the space and the opportunity to create a language for
the discovery of things related to the profession being investigated and to
then articulate them in terms of professional development, the transition
being carried through by the professionals themselves, working with their
peers and using their peers as resources for moving forward.

c) In the process, the meetings generate what I would call a 'pool of reflection'. Let me explore the metaphor further.
In order for the pool to form, people have to start pouring out impressions,

ideas and perplexities, give vent to their own problems and dilemmas. The element of the pool is just as fluid as the unstructured conversations and reflections of the group. A pool has borders: the time and space of the meetings. The pool can act as a mirror for the self; it also allows others to see themselves mirrored in it. The contents of the pool are renovated at each meeting. New ideas fall onto the deposits at the bottom (elements from previous reflections), which provides the *humus* for further reflections.

For those members of the group who cannot take part in a particular session, what falls into the pool (the result of unstructured critical conversations) is made physically visible through the transcription of the recorded data, as well as exportable to the parallel group in Rome by means of faxes. In short, the creation of a pool seems to respond to one of the problems identified by participants: the utter isolation of the head of school.

For once, heads of school can have a better grasp of their problems by looking at them from without, as it were: once a problem is taken out of the self, it is made visible and can be looked at from a distance and even contemplated. At the same time, if dilemmas are found to be the same as one's colleagues, this very fact can work as an anxiety reliever which makes one say: 'I have problems just like my colleagues', 'it is not me that creates the problem, the problem is inherent in my job'.

Methodological Support

What kind of methodological skills or competences do practitioners need to acquire in order to be able to carry out action research? How can the dilemma of 'relevance *versus* rigour' which so often comes out of the common reflection, be dealt with? Graziella writes:

The methodology of action research is rigorous. It demands that the data be collected from different sources and be interpreted in a shared context. In my previous experience with teachers I had found that they tended to value the relevance of the action being taken more than the rigour of the investigation. Was it because of the way I had started? I still have to explore this aspect at a deeper level, but now, with heads of schools I should also try and consider what different shades it takes in the new context.

For certain I can say that, because of the context in which they work, teachers tend to be generalists and globalists: when they start an action, they want to see if an alternative route 'works in my classroom'. They like to talk about the beneficial effects the action has had on the classroom rather than see the effects on the individual pupils. Also they find it difficult to be analytical about the procedure they set about.

Now that I was starting to work with heads of school, I found myself caught once again in the same dilemma about what I should do: shall I ask them to 'suspend disbelief', that is to accept as an act of faith that the collection of data is crucial? Or shall we wait for the moment when the need for data becomes imperative? I thought I was not going to see the dilemma in terms of 'either/or', but that I would rather try to create a situation which would ask for the use of data from the very beginning. Parallel to the first-level research, I stimulated an interest towards the method followed by the group in the various sessions. With this second focus, the use of data would become of paramount importance from the very beginning. All the meetings would be recorded and transcribed. The keeping of a personal diary would guarantee a space for more informal impressions and comments.

Usually, the term 'second-order reflection' is used with reference to the outside researcher/facilitator. Practitioners are rarely encouraged to develop reflection of a methodological or an epistemological order. Is it possible to ask the practitioner to engage in this kind of reflection and if so, to what extent?

Bruno writes:

As an 'expert' I was asked to provide 'methodological support' in terms of applying the procedures and techniques of action research.

Except for two of the heads of school, none of the practitioners have had previous experience in action research. Indeed, none of them have conducted any kind of individual research in education. In some cases, they have 'collaborated' in research projects developed by academics but without being individually involved as actual researchers. So I have to take on not only the responsibility of presenting and discussing with them the characteristics and potentials of action research but also to give a general introduction to the more widely used techniques for data collection and analysis. In practice, what I will have to give the practioners as a group is a sort of 'research training', gradually helping them to build up the necessary procedural and methodological competences required for research in general and action research in particular. This leads to another knotty issue. What is actually expected of practitioners is that they take on all the responsibilities of the researcher, from identifying the problem to formulating the hypothesis, to the development and implementation of the research, to the collection and analysis of the data and their interpretations. They are usually excluded from the second level of the reflection, a methodological and epistomological one. Is it possible that it is this exclusion, along with the particular positions within the institution which seem to reproduce a power relationship, which still favours the outside researcher? This is where the outside researcher continues to 'claim his/her territory' but in so doing is he/she not maintaining a position of power based on the possession of specific competences that the practitioner lacks?

Faced with this dilemma, I have tried in previous experiences of action research with teachers to develop the second level of reflection with them, opening up the opportunity for researcher teachers with more experience, to progressively take on the role of facilitating other teachers.

I believe that we have to work towards practitioner *autonomy* in two senses: autonomy in their professional practice but also in the sense of no longer depending on the outside researcher. At the same time, the very real constraints that exist within their organisational and institutional contexts that do not encourage research need to be acknowledged.

In this sense, the experience of research which the heads of school are having could have indirect consequences: through them, their schools may become places where conditions become more favourable for teachers to engage in their own action research. Becoming aware of their own need to claim autonomy and the space and time for reflection could lead these heads of school to offer the same opportunities and conditions to their teachers.

Conclusion

Our research has left unanswered a number of questions related to the methodology of action research. These are the issues that we have in mind and that we hope to address in the future when the project will have allowed for more self-observation and data.

1 *The negotiation issue.* Should negotiation be carried out at the beginning, once and for all, or rather be the result of continuous shifting in the process?
2 *Collecting data through writing.* This is related to the negotiation issue. How far can the necessity to collect data through writing, and the time to collect them, be liable to negotiation? Writing can provide a lot of data to be used later on to feed reflection. And yet the attitude to writing is one where strong differences can be detected among individuals. Some even say that writing is a modality they will never feel confident with. Thus, should writing be a clause of the contract from the very beginning? at least when time constraints (and the time schedule of MOHD is particularly tight) seem to impose a time limit to the space for personal growth? or may be even when time constraints are not so tight, in order to give a sense that actions have borders and are not unlimited? Can time constraints be used productively to force, as it were, reflection? How far can the distinction between cold, documentary writing and personal, reflective writing be useful in tackling the dilemma?
3 *The facilitator's strategies.* This is connected with the 'how' of facilitation. How far should meetings be structured and in what direction? Are there strategies that seem to be more effective in terms of facilitating learning and professional development and of clarifying the issues at stake?
4 *The distinction between 'first and second order' research.* We often used in

this chapter the terms 'first order' and 'second order' research referring to the research carried out by the practitioners and by the outside researchers/ facilitators. Is this distinction really useful? Does it give the idea of the actual difference — in terms of both role and position — between practitioners and facilitators? In fact, we found ourselves not only playing different roles, but also carrying out reflection and research at different levels and on different issues, both of 'first' and 'second' order: our roles and our strategies for facilitating practitioners' research, the roles of the heads of school in school development, the organizational development. At the same time we tried (and we are still trying) to involve the heads of school in a reflection upon the process of professional development they are engaged in, upon action research as a strategy for their professional development and about methods and data collection techniques.

Could it be useful to look at the difference between practitioners and facilitators in terms of difference of 'position', of 'perspective' in an action research process rather than distinguish different 'orders' of research? In other terms, can we say that one of the aims of action research could be to 'go beyond' the distinction between 'first and second order' research? If so, what are the theoretical, methodological and practical implications we have to explore further?

Acknowledgments

Anna Magyar (CARE, University of East Anglia) for revising the English version of this text.

Notes

1 The MOHD Project (Management for Organizational and Human Development) is partially funded by the Commission of the European Communities — DG XII.
2 Bruno Losito is a researcher at CEDE (European Centre for Education), Frascati (Rome), an educational research centre which depends on the Ministry of Education. Graziella Pozzo, now retired, worked with IRRSAF, Piemonte, based in Torino, a regional institute for educational research and in-service training for teachers.
3 Scottish Council for Research in Education (Edinburgh); Centro Europeo dell'Educazione (CEDE) Frascati; University of Malaga — Departamento de Didactica y Organizacion Escolar — Facultad de Ciencias de la Education; University of Innsbruck — Department of Business Education and Personnel Management; University of Klagenfurt-Institut fuer Schulpaedagogik und Socialpaedagogik; University of Northumbria at Newcastle — Department of Education; University of East Anglia — Centre for Applied Research in Education: School of Education. The international coordinator is Dr. Bridget Somekh from SCRE.
4 See *Management for Organisational and Human Development*, proposal presented to the Commission of the European Communities DG XII.

5 The Environment and School Initiatives (ENSI) Project was carried out by the OECD
   Centre for Educational Research and Innovation. The teachers participating in the project
   constructed environmental initiatives and developed action research within those initiatives. The project was carried out in 1990–1993 and schools from over 20 countries were
   involved.
6 House, 1995; Elliott, 1995.

References

ELLIOTT, J. (1991) *Action Research for Educational Change*, Milton Keynes, Open Univer-
   sity Press.
ELLIOTT, J. (1993) 'Academics and Action Research: The Training Workshop as an Exercise
   in Ideological Deconstruction', in ELLIOTT, J. (Ed.), *Reconstructing Teacher Education*,
   London, The Falmer Press, pp. 176–92.
ELLIOTT, J. (1995) 'Recherche-action et initiatives des établissements scolaires dans l'éducation
   à l'environnement' in OCDE-CERI *L'éducation à l'environnement pour le XXI siècle*,
   Paris, pp. 71–85.
HOUSE, E. (1995) 'Politiques d'éducation à l'environnement: études approfondies de cinq
   pays' in OCDE-CERI *L'éducation à l'environnement pour le XXI siècle*, Paris, pp. 87–
   106.
JANSEN, B.J. and DIJKSTRA, M.J. (1992) 'Congruency in Attitudes and Behaviour of Parti-
   cipants in Action Research', paper presented at CARN International Conference 'Cultures
   for Change', Worcester, September.
LOSITO, B. and MAYER, M. (1995) *Environmental Education and Educational Innovation*,
   Italian National Report on ENSI Research 'Environment and School Initiatives', Frascati,
   CEDE.
MESSNER, E. and RAUCH, F. (1995) 'Dilemmas of Facilitating Action Research', *Educational
   Action Research*, **3**, 1, pp. 41–53.
SOMEKH, B. (1993) 'Teachers generating knowledge: Constructing practical and theoretical
   understanding from multi-site case studies', in DAY, C., CALDERHEAD, J. and DENICOLO,
   P. (Eds), *Research on Teacher Understanding Professional Development*, London, The
   Falmer Press, pp. 124–46.
WOODWORD, T. (1991) *Models on Metaphors in Language Teacher Training: Loop Input and
   other Strategies*, Cambridge, Cambridge University Press.

26   An Exploration in Cross-cultural Pedagogical Innovation

Hugh Sockett (United States) and
Michal Zellermayer (Israel)

Introduction

Since 1992, the Institute for Educational Transformation (IET) at George Mason University, Fairfax, Virginia has been teaching an innovative Masters Degree program for serving teachers, which represents a root and branch change from the traditional American experience. In 1994, Michal Zellermayer, from Levinsky College of Education, Israel attended the summer session of the American program. As a result, the problems of cultural roots and transferability were manifest as links between the institutions were explored.

This chapter is in two parts. In the first, Hugh Sockett portrays the innovation. In the second, Michal Zellermayer reflects on the program from the point of view of a scholar exploring the Jewish Humanistic Tradition in the context of modern Israel, and a teacher considering the development of a program with similar commitments and directions. Both authors align themselves with those who see the legacy of positivism as profoundly destructive to the moral and intellectual life of schools and teachers, severely diminishing our ability to live, talk and work at educational tasks in a morally sophisticated way. They are committed to recovering a moral conversation about teaching from intellectual ancestors and between colleagues in different cultures.

Hugh Sockett: The Program and its Development

Beliefs, Principles and Practices

The conviction underlying this School-Based Masters Degree is that teacher professionalism is both a moral and an intellectual business (Sockett, 1993). In 1994, the teaching faculty wrote a document which describes the innovation, initially to clarify their own understanding. This has been retitled 'Beliefs and Principles in IET Practice'. The reflective character of the document is stressed by the interrogative:

> The degree is dedicated to the examination of four central questions: How do we understand ourselves as people and as teachers? How do we create knowledge of our world through the forms and genres of language? How do we seek knowledge and understanding of our world, of students,

classrooms, and schools? How do we build learning communities and reflective practice?

The document also acts as a touchstone for internal governance as well as for teaching, emphasizing the ideological core of IET as a learning community:

> Since, matters of governance are not separable from practice, the document becomes an explicit and comprehensive statement of beliefs and principles, a *modus operandi*, and a set of standards against which improvement can be measured, and individual and team conduct judged.

Yet it is also a position statement inviting critique, and a continuing attempt to articulate beliefs and principles. Finally, it is a curriculum design:

> Our principles of procedure are not goals. They describe, rather like guidelines, the ways in which we intend to work, both in teaching and management of the whole program, as well as in our own thinking and planning. (IET, p. 3)

The program itself is characterized by seven seminal features: Curriculum and pedagogy as primary intellectual and practical interests; work in teams; reflective practice; school-based inquiry; intensive scheduling; integrated technology, and continuous improvement. Each is spelled out in the document against the beliefs, principles and experiences relevant to that feature.

For example, the 'reflective practice' feature is presently described as follows:

Figure 26.1: On Reflective Practice

i   *Beliefs*
- Effective and moral teaching requires deliberate, ongoing reflection and the careful articulation of the moral and epistemological assumptions made by individuals.
- Reflective practitioners strive to uncover and critique their own values, assumptions and biases, examining constantly their day-to-day strategies, intentions and decisions.
- Reflective practice demands individual contemplation and collegial dialogue.

ii *Principles of Procedure*
- Articulate and critique practical knowledge, emergent theories, deeply held beliefs and values.
- Inquire into the interactions among practice, theory, belief and cultural influences.
- Move beyond consideration of 'what works' to imagine, invent and enact 'what is possible'.
- Create an agenda moving constantly beyond cultural constraints to reclaim personal professional perspectives.
- Build the capacity to view schooling from multiple perspectives.

iii *Varieties of Experience*
- Write journals and autobiographical narratives about experiences in learning and teaching.
- Articulate, analyze, and debate practical knowledge, emergent theories, deeply held beliefs and values in conversational, seminar, and forum settings.
- Experience uncertainty and indeterminacy as valuable concomitants in reflection along with discovery.
- Think and act as a member of a learning community with questions: What has this society made of me that I no longer want to be? What has this society made of teaching and learning that I no longer want them to be?

A similar description of each of the seven features provides an extensive document for all associated with program: i.e., for the articulation of the epistemology on which our practice is built, the articulation of moral relationships we search for in our teaching, and as a model for use in classrooms.

Organizational Characteristics

We attempt to install modes of work which fit the pattern of teachers' personal and working lives. We recruit only in teams from individual schools. This provides a strong supportive arrangement for teachers wanting to change their school culture. Everyone starts the program at the same time and finishes at the same time, an unusual characteristic at this level in the American academy. A typical class (100) is divided not only into the teams which constitute it, but into four cohorts. This promotes conversation across all grade levels and across school districts, undermining still further the sense of isolation so many American teachers feel. The creation of a professional community and identity is further enhanced by technological communications, specifically in electronic conferences. Class meetings are entirely in summer two-week sessions, day release from schools or Saturdays, although weekly team meetings, attended regularly by IET faculty, become an essential ingredient of the study. Half the credits are for research projects conducted in the workplace which promotes an intensive relationship of dialogue between practice and theory. Individual and team-based projects are publicly presented to the community. All teachers keep a journal.

Continuous Improvement, Evaluation and Redesign

Yet the program continues to evolve. We are committed to continuous improvement of the program, but also of fostering in teachers this stance towards their own work and away from the triviality of grading. Teachers read each other's work and critique it. But the major part of the program's evolution arises from IET's own reflective practice, manifest, for example, in a very recent funding proposal which describes differently the underpinning ideology of Beliefs and Principles in IET Practice.

The program confronts fundamental moral and epistemological issues, we now say, by taking seriously the lived experiences of teachers, by eliciting from them autobiographical narratives and written reflections on experiences, and by helping teachers develop multiple lenses for interpreting them. Hence, readings are required in sociology, psychology, philosophy of mind, history, moral theory, epistemology, ethnography, and imaginative literature, and teachers are asked to hold these readings in dialogue with their experiences as learners and teachers. Teachers work collectively within and across school teams to discuss and critique their emerging ideas and insights, to articulate the issues and challenges most salient to their present practices which defines their workplace research, and to present these in individual assignments and in a major team project which concludes the program. Ambitiously, we indicate that we seek the transformation of public education and the improvement of student learning through a radical redesign of degree-based in-service teacher education. We now believe that 'restructuring the schools' is bound to be unsuccessful without reinvented teacher education: and that requires lengthy, teacher-friendly rigorous work and study, and a whole-hearted openness to innovation.

What evidence do we have that our program is effective? The claims we make rest in evidence from multiple sources; a detailed one year evaluation study of the program (1993), teachers' journals, daily evaluation reports, individual and team-based research projects, reports by principals and superintendents, and records, evaluations and journals by faculty. Indeed as we now see it, the core of the program is the enhancement of the critical inferences and judgments professionals make about their work. Four major items are indicative of its effectiveness, each of which connect to improved student learning:

1. Critical reflection Critical reflective methods used in teaching teachers has had three impacts: 1) emancipated open examination of school administrative practice, 2) improved intellectual quality of teacher-student discourse, instantiating the interrogative and intellectual questioning as the classroom mode, and 3) profound growth in the maturity of teachers' self-perceptions and understandings of their personhood and role, evidenced throughout teacher journals.

2. Critical reading of educational theory and imaginative literature is influential in 3 ways: 1) It challenges teachers to examine the ideological underpinnings of structures of schooling; 2) it enhances teachers' focus on the practical difficulty of structural reform in schools, and 3) it cracks the carapace of professional socialization.

3. Dialogue within a community of interpretation and critique establishes a different set of parameters of inquiry: 1) it has facilitated teacher interchange and the end of isolation; 2) it has changed the way teachers view theory in relation to practice, enabling them to hold the theory in dialogue with their practice, thereby facilitating understanding the critical inferences they make about student learning, and 3) it has encouraged some teachers to create within their own schools similar communities.

4. On-going documentation, observation and analysis of practice and experience. This central feature of teachers' work provides them with primary data. From it, they report that 1) student learning has improved; 2) the intensity of studying their own practice in teams facilitates breaking through taken-for-granted assumptions about teaching and learning, and 3) the research process has an emancipatory effect as evidenced by widespread and consistent self-reports that they become autonomous in their thinking and judgment, develop more flexible ways of reasoning and interpreting, and understand better the multiple — and sometimes contradictory — social demands placed on schooling.

We are thus in a position to be constantly redesigning the program as we expand it. We are moved, shocked, delighted, embarrassed and sometimes downcast by the closeness of the relationship we build with teachers. 'My family say I am now a much more interesting person', said a teacher, a remark that embodies so much about teachers, their professional status, and the alienation from themselves which the job seems to promote. 'I have never done such heavy thinking', wrote another, revealing how inadequately professional teachers have been educated, but also how undeveloped is our understanding of individual intellectual growth. 'What have you done to me? A real Southern gal trying to think seriously about prejudice!' wrote another.

Interest in the program has spread locally across school districts and nationally. Close at hand, the enthusiastic attitude of superintendents has been a great bonus. Further afield, more than a dozen universities in the US have asked for the details and mechanics of the design. Internationally, we are talking with universities and colleges in Brazil and the West Indies, and we have had long conversations with Levinsky College of Education in Tel-Aviv.

Michal Zellermayer: Seeing the Program through the Jewish Humanist Tradition

Since its establishment in 1913, Levinsky College of Education, has cherished the idea that the personhood of the teacher was central to teacher education; yet, though discussed from time to time, it seemed to be too big a project of teacher education in a country that is always in some kind of a crisis. Now that we are painfully heading for peace, there is a general feeling that this is a time for reflection, and that reflection is no longer an abstract noun. While thinking about it, we can envision particular spaces — such as action research — where teachers conceive of themselves as intellectuals, who engage with colleagues and students in inquiry that produces knowledge rather than consumes it. Furthermore, we can now devise detailed plans for helping teachers to understand themselves as people and as teachers through collaboration and reflection. On the basis of the IET program, Levinsky College has constructed its own plan for graduate studies in teaching.

The two-year development process was complex: What did we want from the IET program and how should we conceive our own differences? Each program has different points of departure: IET faculty conceive their work with teachers as innovative and revolutionary. The program's status as a 'revolt against positivism' is apparent in that it has developed some of its principles negatively (Figure 26.1).

Think and act as a member of a learning community with questions: What has this society made of me that I no longer want to be? What has this society made of teaching and learning that I no longer want them to be?

These are crucial queries for teachers in IET who 'see themselves unfree without a rich understanding of their traditions, and trapped in a political and bureaucratic system'. The Levinsky prospective program, however, addresses a different question:

'What has society made me give up for the sake of winning wars and building a country, that I can now hope to realize?' Hope 'is the acknowledgement of more openness in a situation than the situation easily reveals; openness above all to possibilities for human attachments, expressions, and assertions' (Simon, 1992, p. 3).

Considering the detail of IET's program, we remembered Simon's thought that any pedagogical innovation must stay in tune with teachers' viable choices constituted by the real and present conditions in their lives as well as by certain conditions still to come. Simon calls not only for 'the enhancement of an individual's potential for the acquisition of skills and knowledge but the development of resources as well, within which people can begin to challenge and transform those relations which structure the available opportunities from which to choose' (p. 19). In this view, Levinsky sees the IET program as a framework for the enhancement of teachers' potential for the acquisition of skills and knowledge, but Levinsky needs to create opportunities for students to develop cultural resources that they can choose from in order to challenge and transform their work.

Teachers in Israel gave up the Jewish Humanist Tradition, but they are now beginning to reconsider it from new contemporary perspectives. This source will help our students see their work from within the most crucial intersections of their lives at the present: 1) What it means to be an Israeli today; and 2) the pervasive experience of living every day in a society that is founded on a long history of contradiction between difference and solidarity.

Our Humanist Heritage

The paradox of being an individual in society, the yearning to experience ourselves as well connected and well differentiated is a major problem in Israeli society in general and for teachers in particular. The growing feeling of teachers and students that there is no room for the individual to make a moral choice has led Levinsky faculty in recent decades to turn to our humanist tradition for support, and motivated me to look for a model of a learning environment for teachers where some of the important ideas of this tradition can be implemented.

Indeed, many of the ideas that underline the IET program were expressed by Jewish educators of the humanistic tradition who worked in Germany between the two World Wars and moved to Palestine before the establishment of the state of Israel. In the early 1920s, Franz Rosenzweig claimed that teaching and research are complementary and that teacher research improves practice since it develops the practitioner's capacity for discrimination and judgment in complex situations. He also argued for the importance of illuminating through research teachable moments, where there is revelation, where the teacher as a professional and a human being is revealed to him or herself. In 1939 Martin Buber, better known, perhaps, than Rosenzweig in European and American circles, addressed the National Conference of Palestinian Teachers at Tel Aviv. He spoke of the responsibility of the teacher to initiate a genuine dialogue with his pupils, and the gains for the educator who engages in such dialogue.

The first gain, according to Buber (1939, p. 106), is humility,

> the feeling of being only one element amidst the fullness of life, only one single existence in the midst of all the tremendous inrush of reality on the pupil; secondly, self-awareness . . . the feeling of responsibility for the selection of reality which he represents for the pupil. And a third thing emerges from all this, the recognition that in this realm of education of character, of wholeness, there is only one access to the pupil: his confidence. For the adolescent who is frightened and disappointed by an unreliable world, confidence means the liberating insight that there is human truth, the truth of human existence. When the pupil's confidence has been won, his resistance against being educated gives way to a singular happening: he accepts the educator as a person. He feels he may trust this man, that this man is not making a business out of him, but is taking part in his life, accepting him before desiring to influence him. And so he learns to ask.

Following Buber, we therefore emphasize the education of character for the teacher, the importance of seeing the teacher as a whole. We talk about the teacher's confidence and about a trusting relationship between the teacher and the teacher educator that leads to such confidence. What is inherently Jewish within that tradition is the basic assumption that the liberating insight of human truth is connected to one's being able to participate in a communal and individual recollection of Being taking place by virtue of the retrieval of our pre-ontological experience with Being.

This tradition emphasizes the particular ways that our culture offers possibilities for such an insight through a two-way communication between the knower and the known, and a sense of immediacy of contact between the speaker and the audience, the reader and the writer, the teacher and the pupil that is built upon their mutual historical experience. The idea is that we use these cultural sensitivities for discovering continuity in history, for constructing a common memory and for transferring the contents of this memory from generation to generation through a process of recontextualization. Such interpretive 'connection-making skills' become a source of support for the individual and for the community at a time of deep moral crisis.

> In order to illustrate the way that in times of crisis we 're-establish a sphere of values common to mankind', Buber cites a discussion between teacher and pupil, taking place at the time of the Arab terror in Palestine, when there were single Jewish acts of reprisal. He shows how the pupil gains the insight that one's group is much larger than one thinks and that, inevitably, it includes all the past generations:
> At this point the teacher felt the moment had come to leave the narrow compass of the present and to invoke historical destiny. ....he said.......
> 'Yes; all past generations. But what was it that made those past generations of the Exile live? What made them out-live and overcome all their trials? Wasn't it that the cry "Thou shalt not" never faded from their hearts and ears?' (1939, p. 109)

The past in the present. Life in Israel provides many opportunities for such insights to take place. For example, following the 1995 death of Prime Minister Yitzhak Rabin, our link with our own humanity was recurrently associated through language, through music and through various visual media with the ancient theme of sacrifice, as though something of us has to be torn away or immolated if we are to be more fully human. This association was supported by the fact that his death occurred during the week of the reading of the story of Abraham's sacrifice of his son, Yitzhak. For many in Israel this was not a simple coincidence. It was perceived as yet another affirmation of the understanding that man is positioned by God in the center of the universe, so that he could be tested for his abilities to take risks and to become God's social agent. Furthermore, it confirmed man's power to put God in a test as well as man's ability to participate in an authentic dialogue with God.

As we thought of our history of persecution, of our families lost in the holocaust and our children endangering their lives during military service, we wondered whether Rabin's death, like the sacrifice of Yitzhak, was what contemporary therapists call 'a necessary loss'. We felt positioned between loss and renewal, accepting that psychologically something has to die before a new self can be born. Indeed, many spoke about the death of our first adulthood, of how our first adulthood as a modernist nation ruled by ideologies, doctrines, and other objectivist interpretations of reality has come to an end. As we cried for the loss of an objectively knowable world, we realized that we were still able to evoke moral sources from outside our time and place through language that resonate within us. It was then that we grasped the existence of an order, which is not only communal but is inseparably indexed to one's personal vision. We felt more fully human.

The moral significance of gathering the past into the present has been extensively discussed by Walter Benjamin and Theodore Adorno, whose work illustrates how the bringing back and the granting give to the present a very significant and fulfilling understanding: The retrieval, 'transforms this experience into an authentically ontological understanding; the implicit is made explicit; the potential is realized a rudimentary understanding is developed; and the primordial claim of Being is redeemed by a thoughtful life' (Levin, 1989, p. 206).

Levin cites Heidegger and Gadamer in order to stress that such granting is inherently tied to our listening abilities:

> In the recollection of Being, we ourselves, as listening beings, are gathered into the in-gathering of Being. By lending our ears to this appropriation, we open ourselves to being attuned by Being. It is possible — and this is my hope — that, from out of this attunement, we shall learn some new ways to respond to the nihilism of our time. (p. 208)

Levin, like Buber and Rosenzweig, reminds us that the potential for such listening is an inherent feature of Jewish culture.

Buber, however, warns us that pursuing communal recollection means taking a very narrow road that runs between the mindful and the sensual: between the adoption of preset values and principles and the evocation of voices from the past.

On the one hand there is a danger of not being original and innovative, and on the other, of parodizing. And while explaining to others the way it works, one inevitably risks turning this phenomenon into a banality. While watching the thousands of youngsters mourn for Rabin, one could not ignore their plea for help. Standing quietly outside Rabin's home and in the place of his assassination, they asked for self transformation without mutilation and without banality. What stronger incentives do Israeli teacher educators need for beginning to consider more seriously the possibilities of

> a curriculum and a pedagogy that will not require the obliteration of the past and its replacement with a new 'truth', but rather a fundamental reconfiguration and rereading of our tradition in a way that reveals the present as a revolutionary moment? (Simon, 1992, p. 139)

Similarities and Differences

Beliefs and Principles in IET Practice welcomes the various ways the curriculum demonstrates hospitality to the students' life history. Teacher learning is based very much on their work in schools and the scheduling of academic activities attempts to fit their lives. Serious efforts are made to show the participating teachers that they are not required to leave their old loyalties to their school and to their families at the door of the Institute.

But there are four main points of cultural difference: First, the IET document emphasizes innovation, urging teachers to 'continuously develop new forms and styles of teaching as part of a need for more interesting pedagogies'. It encourages variation in models of pedagogy and curriculum. It seeks to represent pedagogy and curriculum as a way of looking sensitively and self-consciously at the conditions of the present, to show that curriculum is a means for appropriating new ways of knowing unencumbered by traditional assumptions or conventions. An Israeli program, however, would attempt to provide students with a sense of identity through the gathering of history. As we engage in a search for continuity, we intend to try to provide the moral support for looking backwards in order to go forwards; to make connections to big ideas of the past, that may help our students find coherence, identify patterns of experience, and satisfy the need for individual transformation through communal recollection.

Second, such communal recollection is quite a different collaborative experience than is apparent in IET, where the focus is on the benefits that can be gained from working in teams, and on the importance of practicing certain skills of group dynamics for conflict resolution. Levinsky will seek to provide a collaborative context in which all interested parties can create a vision or a purpose they can collectively uphold, while engaging in the individual reflexive embodiment of knowledge and knowing.

Third, reflective practice is not simply a direct outcome of collegial collaborative learning. It depends on genuine listening that is often aroused through conflict:

'A way has to be found through conflict into life, into a life, I must add, where confidence continues unshaken — more, is even mysteriously strengthened' (Buber, 1939; p. 110). We must, therefore, cultivate our hearing and try to make it more responsive and more compassionate. Through conversation and through action research we can extend the reach and range of our listening, making this extension a practice.

IET emphasizes the importance of teacher research as an instrument for the development of teacher authority and autonomy, but we should also make our students and teacher educators aware of the possibilities offered by action research to hear things we had never heard before and to communicate with people we had never listened to before. The literature on action research is filled with stories of teacher educators and teachers who find themselves affected by the people to whom they listen to the extent that their lives correspondingly change. We should encourage phenomenological accounts that are dialectical and self-referential.

Fourth, with that background, the integration of technology that the IET espouses is not merely an instrument for educational reform and for venturing into the future. The impact of integrating television in our process of moral transformation during the recent political events in Israel has shown that technology can provide an important context for cultivating our hearing, for deepening our involvement with each other and with the situation, and for exposing layers of possible connections between the knower and the known, self and other. While incorporating technology in our teacher education program, we must stay on the narrow path, described by Buber. It is a harrowing walk. As we try to listen for the ways that technology echoes and resonates our Being, we should take care not to slip into the abyss of the banal.

Conclusion

Our conversations and writing together have revealed for us much more than attention to program development would suggest. First, it seems possible to create a large 'public sphere' in Habermas' terms in Israel rather than in the US, a space in which public discourse about education is seen as having deep common roots which cross the secular, the spiritual and the religious. In both countries, we have to learn how to explore the domain of the spiritual and the religious in the public sphere (including teacher education) if we are to be authentic, irrespective of our own religious commitments. Second, this strong sense of 'the past in the present' may add up to an abandonment of the belief in progress, and a turning back, not a reaction, to our past selves for understanding. Third, the notion of community might lead us into a sense of ourselves and a more developed sense of others as selves, as centers of consciousness, not simply in terms of professional groups, but searching for community within two countries that are differently 'nations of immigrants'. Yet contemporary Israelis do not see themselves as a homogeneous society, and differences among them cannot be easily reduced to a common denominator. They don't even agree about what it means to be Jewish or on who is a Jew. Hence, dialogue in the humanistic sense is problematic here, as it is elsewhere, and the correlation of the dialogue between man and God and that between man and man is not a sufficient model for teacher education.

In conclusion, maybe teacher education programs should be sites for teachers and teacher educators to: a) grow more self-consciously aware of the complexity of their situation; b) see that the teachers who want to work against the grain within the system must aim for small scale changes that are sometimes confined to the context of the their classrooms; c) realize the one goal that encompasses human difference is that of responsibility for the other, encountered face-to-face (Gibbs, 1992), for freedom and autonomy depend on the other, and d) to understand the way each human being uses language. Words can become lethal weapons. We need to listen to our own languages, to be able to understand the way language positions the speaker vis-a-vis significant others, and to examine the multiple perspectives embedded in language and culture. Programs that fail to do at least these things fail teachers, American or Israeli.

Acknowledgments

We wish to thank our colleagues at our respective institutions for their contributions to the evolution of the ideas which we express, as it were on their behalf, in this paper: In Fairfax, Virginia, Wendy Atwell-Vasey, Mark Jacobs, Diane Wood, Gail Matthews-DeNatale, Sharon Jeffrey and Ann Sevcik. In Tel-Aviv, Rina Barkol, Dan Gibton, Abraham Rochelli Raphael Shiniak, and Arie Shirion.

Comments on this chapter or requests for information can be addressed to hsockett@gmu.edu or michalz@mofet.macam.ac.il. The IET Home Page is http://www.gmu.edu/~amoore2/iet.html.

References

BUBER, M. (1939) *Between Man and Man*, Boston, MA, Beacon Press.

GIBBS, R. (1992) *Correlations in Rosenzweig and Levinas*, Princeton, NJ, Princeton University Press.

GLATZER, N. (1953) *Frank Rosenzweig — His Life and Thought*, New York, Schocken Books.

INSTITUTE FOR EDUCATIONAL TRANSFORMATION (unpublished) *Beliefs and Principles in IET Practice*, George Mason University.

LEVIN, D.M. (1989) *The Listening Self: Personal Growth, Social Change and the Closure of Metaphysics*, London and New York, Routledge.

SIMON, R. (1992) *Teaching Against the Grain*, New York, Bergin & Garvey.

SOCKETT, H.T. (1993) *The Moral Base for Teacher Professionalism*, New York, Teachers College Press.

Section V

Looking Across Political, Personal and Professional Perspectives

Section Editor: Sandra Hollingsworth

The last chapter in the book asks the question: so what? While we have attempted to collect the best case examples of action research around the world, this volume is worth little unless it serves to give us insight into the use of action research for educational reform. The section editors have identified six themes which speak to the relevance of action research for the education of teachers, nurses, social workers, children around the world:

1 Action Research, Education and the Creation of a Just and Caring Society;
2 Building Coalitions of Shared Knowledge across Domains, Institutions and Cultures;
3 Encouraging Practitioners to take Responsibility for the Development of the Professional;
4 Action Research on Action Research Courses;
5 Action Research and Personal Development; and
6 Questioning the Meaning of 'Research' as it Relates to Professional 'Knowledge' and 'Improvement.'

27 Epilogue: What Have We Learned From These Cases on Action Research and Educational Reform?

Sandra Hollingsworth (United States), Susan E. Noffke (United States), Melanie Walker (Scotland) and Richard Winter (United Kingdom)

Each of us, if asked this question individually, would undoubtedly answer it from different cultural and positional perspectives. If there is one single pattern that emerges from these chapters, it is that the forms, purposes, methods and results of action research around the world differ widely. As Susan Noffke wrote in preparation for this chapter:

> That, more than anything, to me, is a point well worth underlining: Action research has 'multiple' meanings and uses. Its 'potential' cannot be judged apart from the 'ideological' bases which drive its practices, as well as the material contexts. The history and culture surrounding action research projects (and here I mean ideology as well as material and social practices) are great influences. What we need to look for is NOT whose version of action research is THE correct one, but rather, what it is that needs to be done, and how action research can further those aims.

What do these chapters tell us about the relevance of action research for the education of teachers, nurses, social workers, children around the world?

Action Research, Education and the Creation of a Just and Caring Society

Action research projects such as Robyn S. Lock and Leslie T. Minarik's attempt to degenderize relations through play (Chapter 16) is an excellent example of beginning with young children in school to achieve that goal. Andrew Gitlin and Johanna Hadden (Chapter 7) presented a case report of the use of educative research to foster a type of teacher-initiated change that acts on overly narrow and authoritarian types of power relations in the classroom. Their central point was that the political/

humanist approaches can lead to emergent political theories which can foster resistance to structural constraints and more democratic classrooms. Eileen Adams, Rosaleen McGonagle, Pauline Watts and Gaby Weiner (Chapter 8) continued that theme through action research for school improvement. Their chapter used action research at both a political level — to show government that inner city schools and teacher colleges are addressing low standards — and at a professional level — to help improve professional practice. Both occur in the context of striving for increased social justice in a country where the gap between the rich and poor is increasing by the minute.

David Hursh (Chapter 11) contended that action research is a necessary critical, collaborative activity for educational reform, because education is a political and ethical activity embedded within conflicting views of social and individual goals. Sue Davidoff (Chapter 9) picked up that theme as she presents a case of whole school teacher action research in South Africa to investigate whether innovations in the way in which schools operate can impact on social transformation. Susan E. Noffke and Marie Brennan (Chapter 6) extended that notion by arguing that all forms of action research are political. They called for a broad definition for action research in order to achieve social justice. 'While social justice issues seem, at times, far afield from issues of the techniques of classroom practice, forms of privilege and domination (including those of academics) must be considered as part of the work of educational action research. Only by considering both can the politics of action research be reconstructed'.

The authors in this text also collectively illustrate both the difficulty and importance of conducting action research for social justice. Their spirit reminds us of a nineteenth century US educator, Susan B. Anthony spoke to the personal challenges in working for social justice:

> Cautious, careful people, always casting about to preserve their reputation and social standing, never can bring about a reform. Those who are really in earnest must be willing to be anything or nothing in the world's estimate, and publicly and privately in season and out, avow their sympathies with despised and persecuted ideas and their advocates, and bear the consequences.

Building Coalitions of Shared Knowledge Across Domains, Institutions and Cultures

Action research is the vehicle for cross-role investigations. Gen Ling Chang-Wells and Gordon Wells (Chapter 13) clearly addressed the need in educational action research to be aware of, and make connections between, the three levels of community involved: classroom, school staff, university teacher education. Inquiry is the means of discovering how best to encourage a relationship of interdependence among them. Bruno Losito and Graziella Pozzo (Chapter 25) went into those relations by illustrating the different roles that the outside researcher/facilitator actually plays in action research projects, highlighting the power relationships between outside researchers and practitioners and illustrating strategies that enable an open negotiation among them.

Collaboration is not an easy task. Chris Day made explicit in his chapter (17), Yet persistence in collaborative action research often yields significant results. Stephen Kemmis and Shirley Grundy (Chapter 4) explained how the Innovative Links Network in Australia is helping to bridge the tensions between 'systems and lifeworlds'. Kim Phaik-Lah (Chapter 21) described the Malaysian Action Research Network (MARNET) as an attempt to create a research culture and learning organization which links information exchanges, professional support and system facilitation to the teachers in schools. Peter Posch and Mag Gottfried Mair (Chapter 23) argued that there is a direct relationship between educational network development and the emergence of an action research movement in Austria. Herbert Altrichter (Chapter 3) also analyzed the development of action research within the Austrian national setting.

The case of Austria is interesting because this country has seen an amazing growth of interest in (and practice of) action research within the last ten years, set against a background of a long-standing tradition of centralist governance of education. Bridget Somekh and Michela Thaler (Chapter 24) wrote about Project 'Management of Human and Organizational Development' (MOHD) as a cooperative project funded by the European Union (1994–96) and involving six research centres in five European countries. 'These institutions are working within a network carrying out a series of interlinked small scale research projects in a range of organizations (mainly in the educational and health services). Specifically, MOHD is exploring the effectiveness of participatory action research [not as a means for identifying indelible answers, but] as a strategy for creating "learning organisations".'

Encouraging Practitioners to Take Responsibility for the Development of the Profession

Angie Titchen's chapter (22) showed how action research created cultural change among professionals in a British National Health Service hospital ward. Richard Winter, John Brown Lee, Leo Bishop, Maire Maish, Christine McMillan, and Paula Sobieschowska (Chapter 20) agree with the power of action research to transform professional cultures. They argued that action research in itself is a conception of professionalism. Engaging in it empowers professional practitioners as formulators of their practices and (consequently) as those who are in a position to empower the 'recipients' of their practice as 'co-constructors' of the meaning of professional interaction. Leo Bishop currently struggles with such conceptions as a Social Services Department Manager:

> Management in England has traditionally been hierarchical, the King tells — his subjects enact. As Head of Inspection for residential and day care services, I struggled with my staff to create a different approach to management. Action research enables managers to know what they need

to know about the professional processes they are managing and thus enables them to provide appropriate leadership. With the current emphasis on the management of professionals, there is a significant risk of there being two agendas within one organization, one which is based on the professional role and the other on the efficiency and effectiveness of the organization. They do not have to be different; however, without a cross-over of understanding between roles, there is a probability that they will.

Action research as a management tool enables and facilitates learning. True understanding starts and develops from reflection on one's own experience. Theory therefore develops from practice and, as a result, is owned by all who are involved in delivering this service. The manager is no longer the King. By managers encouraging workers to reflect on their experience, reflection becomes a legitimate use of time, encouraging challenge, opening up lines of argument and discussion, bouncing back and forth between what happened and what that means for the emerging service. Managers are enabling, facilitative and authoritative in speaking the mind of the organization; however, as the leader, the manager values his staff, recognizes the unique contributions individuals make to the organization, thus allowing for creativity. The fact that the manager can be both enabling and authoritative challenges the traditional notion of management control.

Authoritative statements of today are not final, they are part of a process of inevitable change allowing for continuous improvement, necessary in my view, for an organization to survive. The enabling managers engage all staff in the process of continuously contributing to change. Theory and practice co-exist — one driving the other, rather than hierarchical reactive approaches to pending problems.

Action Research on Action Research Courses

Do our theories and our methods work? Do they move 'knowledge of the profession' outside the award bearing context into the work, to help practitioners create a more just society through education? Anchalee Chayanuvat and Duangta Lukkunaprasit (Chapter 14) took a step toward this goal in realizing that engaging in action research has made 'a tremendous impact on how we look at our classrooms'. Hugh Sockett and Michal Zellermayer (Chapter 26) held up for examination the extent to which universities have to re-examine their role and relationships with teachers and the content of their programs if the potential of action research for teachers is to be unlocked.

Action Research and Personal Development

Authors in this volume spoke to the personal rewards in collaborative action research. Lesvia Olivia Rosas C. (Chapter 19) argued that participation in reflective action research makes teachers better able to solve their own problems of practice. Ivor Goodson (Chapter 18) suggested that, rather than a view of action research as dissemination of text, new recruits to the movement are interested in 'issues of lifestyle and identity'. Moving away from the focus of institutional analysis and practices, action research can be employed in a range of strategies which focus on the politics of identity. Christine O'Hanlon (Chapter 15) addressed the role of action research as a catalyst for deeper self-awareness and understanding — to enable teachers to find voices for their concerns and 'to unite their personal and professional values and perceptions through reflection on their activities'. Sandra Hollingsworth, Marion Dadds and Janet Miller (Chapter 5) spoke not only of personal transformation as a salient result of action research — but in the connections and relationships that develop through this work which allow groups to sustain these efforts over time.

Questioning the Meaning of 'Research' as it Relates to Professional 'Knowledge' and 'Improvement'

The traditional separation of theory from practice separates the academic researcher from the teacher and social worker. These chapters demonstrated boldly that theory/practice/knowledge/and action are dialectically related. Melanie Walker (Chapter 12) raised the central question about what counts as legitimate knowledge about education and who makes this decision? She asked: 'Why was it that within universities academic discourse seemed to be privileged as the authoritative version/s of educational life? Why was it accepted that specialized discourses restricted access to ideas? Did communities outside the academy not also have cultural resources of value in addressing social inequities'? Michaela Mayer (Chapter 10) responded to these issues by showing how teachers have used action research 'to produce knowledge that is not only relevant to their practice but that constitutes a contribution to a more theoretical and general process of construction of knowledge'. John Brown Lee (Chapter 20) partially answers this question from the perspective of social workers, by reflecting on the worth of action research:

> Social workers, care managers and home carers are becoming increasingly involved in monitoring services for their quality and reliability. Indeed they are gathering and collating more and more information which is vital to the process of developing and planning new services. To me it is clear that practitioner action research as a means of acquiring knowledge in the area of social care is, undoubtedly, a powerful tool. As practitioners, we have both the intimate knowledge of the consumer and the detachment that permits the evidence to be gathered and viewed objectively but without losing sight of the individual. Other forms of research may have the objectivity, but invariably fail to apportion value to the personal aspect appropriate to the caring professions. With action research we are not looking for 'ultimate truths', we seek to enhance our knowledge of and improve local services.

The results may or may not be transferable to other services or locations, but the process by which this change is achieved is accessible to all individuals and teams who are interested in developing and improving services. The fact that the process of research, evaluation and service development is carried out by those who will need to implement and act upon any changes results in a strong commitment to that change. Where the commitment is high, then the outcome is more likely to be successful. As more practitioners and managers become aware of practitioner action research and its value, we will increasingly see it being used to inform policy decisions and affect change at all levels within the Personal Social Services.

Action research stands in the face of research that is valued only for itself and furthers Lewin's idea that 'research that produces nothing but books' will not do. Action research must be evaluated not only in terms of its 'research' — or knowledge producing — value, but also for its ability to improve the human condition. The results of action research thereby must be evaluated along with judgments about what counts as 'improvement,' and by whom (Winter, 1987).

In the face of so much public despair over the general state of the educational and welfare services, the people working together across these chapters show the hope and potential of collective action research. As long as there are persistent, intense and crippling social problems such as the disaffection from schools described by John Elliott (see Chapter 2), and as long as institutionalised, academic research presents such distant and abstract 'solutions' to such problems, the alternative resolutions made available by means of collaborative action research (as described in this volume) will continue to grow in importance.

Reference

WINTER, R. (1987) *Action Research and the Nature of Social Inquiry: Professional Innovation and Educational Work*, Aldershot, Avebury.

Notes on Contributors

Eileen Adams is a Research Fellow at South Bank University. She has wide experience in education, having worked as a teacher, teacher educator, in curriculum development and educational research. Her work creates links between art, design and environmental education. Particular interests are interprofessional collaboration in education and children's participation in the design process. Current research interests include the role of public art and art in the environment. She writes and lectures in the UK and abroad.

Herbert Altrichter is currently Professor for Education and Educational Psychology at the Department of Education and Psychology, Johannes-Kepler-University Linz, Austria. His main research interests are in action research, school development, teacher education, evaluation and research methodology. Publications include *Teachers Investigate their Work* (Routledge: London 1993, co-authored with Peter Posch and Bridget Somekh), *Windows: Research and Evaluation on a Distance Education Course* (Deakin University: Geelong 1991, co-authored with Terry Evans and Alistair Morgan) and several other books and papers in German, Italian and English.

Leo Bishop has worked within Social Services Departments since 1975, initially as a practitioner within the child care arena, progressing through middle management covering all client groups; older people, mental health, physical disability, learning disability — including child care. With Anglia Polytechnic University, he developed the Diploma in Social Work and Post Qualifying Awards including the introduction of a first degree in social work through the accreditation of Social Services experience and training programmes. In February 1996, he was appointed to head up Learning Disability Services for the County of Essex. Within this post he is currently undertaking a major review of services.

Marie Brennan is Associate Professor and Associate Dean (Postgraduate Education) and coordinates the Master of School Management for the Faculty of Education at Central Queensland University, Australia. She has been involved as researcher and facilitator for action research projects with educators and students in a variety of settings for almost twenty years.

Gen Ling Chang-Wells has, during her career, taught at the elementary, secondary and university levels. Currently she is a teacher with the Toronto Board of Education and chairs the senior division of a K–8 public school with a high proportion of ESL students. Her professional interests are in literacy, teachers as agents of change, and education as a principal means to achieve the ideals of personal and social development. email: genchang@oise.utoronto.ca

Anchalee Chayanuvat is an assistant professor at Chulalongkorn University Language Institute. She has twenty-four years' experience in teaching English both as a Second Language and as a Foreign Language. Her main interests are in teacher training and teacher research.

Marion Dadds worked in primary education in Nottingham for ten years and taught children of all ages from three to eleven years old. In-service Tutor in Educational Studies. She is currently at the University of Cambridge Institute of Education. For several years, she has been doing action research on the impact of her in-service work on teachers' classroom practices and the life of their schools. From this work, Marion has learnt that committed practitioners can develop their teaching by studying it carefully and working together with colleagues. She has written about this action research in numerous journal articles and edited works.

Susan (Sue) Davidoff is the Director of the Teacher Inservice Project based at the University of the Western Cape in Cape Town, South Africa. She works as an organization development consultant for educational institutions at local, provincial, and national levels. Her publications are primarily in the area of organization and school development in a South African context.

Christopher Day is a Professor of Education, Head of Research, School of Education, University of Nottingham. Prior to this he worked as a teacher, lecturer and local education authority adviser. His particular concerns centre upon the continuing professional development of teachers, teachers' thinking, leadership and school cultures. Recent publications include *Insights into Teachers' Thinking and Action* (co-edited with M. Pope and P. Denicolo) (1990) Falmer Press; and *Research on Teacher Thinking: Towards Understanding Professional Development* (co-edited with J. Calderhead and P. Denicolo) (1993) Falmer Press.

John Elliott is the Director of CARE. He has directed a number of action research projects involving local teachers and schools from the Centre. He has designed inservice courses for teachers which support reflective practices in schools and directed research projects on teachers' jobs and lives, pupil autonomy in learning with micros, the assessment of experiential learning, competency based professional education, and teachers as researchers in the context of award bearing higher education. He is a consultant for the OECD, helping to support international curriculum development in environmental education.

Andrew Gitlin is Professor of Educational Studies at the University of Utah. His research interests focus on alternative research methodologies, teacher education, school change and teachers' work. Recent writing projects include *Teacher Evaluation: Educative Alternatives* (with John Smyth), *Teachers' Voices for School*

Change: An Introduction to Educative Research, Power and Method; Political Activism and Educational Research and *Becoming a Student of Teaching: Methodologies for Exploring Self and School Context* (with Robert Bullough).

Ivor Goodson is Professor of Education at the Warner Graduate School, University of Rochester, USA and he holds a Chair of Education at the University of East Anglia in England. Professor Goodson is currently Scholar in Residence at Lovejoy Hall at the University of Rochester. He was recently awarded the W.D. Wilson Fellowship by the Anglo-American and De Beers Chairman's Fund to visit South Africa. The visit was hosted by the University of Wittwatersrand and the University of Capetown. He is the author of a range of books on curriculum and life histories.

Shirley Grundy is an Associate Professor in the School of Education at Murdoch University, Western Australia. Her research interests include curriculum theory, policy analysis, organisational leadership and management, school-based research and development, and school/university partnerships for teacher professional development. She is author of a substantial number of academic papers, including *Curriculum: Product of Praxis*? (1987, Falmer Press). She is a past president of the Australian Association for Research in Education and from 1994–96 was the joint national coordinator of the NPDP project: Innovative Links between Universities and Schools for Teacher Professional Development.

Johanna Hadden is a doctoral candidate in Educational Studies at the University of Utah. She has taught for fifteen years at both the elementary and secondary levels, and in rural, urban and Pacific Island schools. Her research interests include the economic, social and political antecedents of education reform and the impact reform measures have on teachers' work.

Sandra (Sam) Hollingsworth is the Division Head for Teacher Education at San Jose State University — the third of her academic homes. A former historian and classroom teacher, Dr. Hollingsworth took her first academic position at the University of California, Berkeley. There, she conducted longitudinal research on the impact of teacher education coursework on beginning teacher's professional needs in urban schools. In 1990, Professor Hollingsworth moved to Michigan State University where she was involved in Professional Development School arrangements. Her current research interests are urban partnerships in teacher education, the praxis of 'multiple literacies', and international social studies. Using the inquiry process of action research as a unifying theme across those areas, Professor Hollingsworth has published two books, coauthored many articles with teachers, spoken extensively, and organized national and international conferences. She continues to conduct research into the longtitudinal effects of her own teaching.

David Hursh is Associate Professor and Chair of the Teaching and Curriculum program at the Warner Graduate School of Education and Human Development at the University of Rochester. He has been involved in educational reform on several levels including organizing conferences on educational reform; founding, administrating and teaching in alternative educational programs at the elementary and postsecondary level; and consulting with schools. His publications focus on critical social studies, teacher education and action research.

Stephen Kemmis is Pro Vice Chancellor (Research) at University of Ballarat, Australia.

Kim Phaik-Lah (Ph.D., UNE, Australia, in curriculum studies) is a Lecturer in the School of Education, Universiti Sains Malaysia specialising in Literacy development, Curriculum studies and Research methodologies. Local consultant of IDP (Australia) on action research.

John Brown Lee qualified as a Social Worker in 1982 from Hull College of Higher Education (now Hull University). On qualifying he moved to Essex to work for the County's Social Services Department within a psychiatric hospital, working with adults with learning difficulties, older people and people with physical disabilities. He is currently Contracts Manager for the South West of Essex, monitoring quality of services provided by independent providers of domiciliary care to both adults and older people.

Robyn S. Lock began her twenty-six year teaching career in Iowa. She earned a Master's degree in Education from the SUNY-Albany, New York; and her PhD from the University of Iowa. Upon completion of the degree Robyn accepted a position at the University of Toledo in Toledo, Ohio, where she remained for eight years. While at Toledo, Robyn worked on developing an inclusive secondary physical education curriculum for the preservice teacher education students. She is currently teaching at both San Jose State University and San Francisco State University.

Bruno Losito currently works as a researcher in the European Centre for Education in Frascati, a research centre run by the Italian Ministry of Education. He has a PhD in Education. His research interests and activities are in the field of in-service teacher training and of school development evaluation.

Duangta Lukkunaprasit is an Assistant Professor at Chulalongkorn University Language Institute. Her twenty-five years' experience as a language teacher involves developing instructional materials for business and law students as well as conducting classroom research.

Rosaleen McGonagle is currently Senior Lecturer at South Bank University with responsibility for teaching English and Music to student-teachers. She taught for many years in primary schools before working in higher education. Gender issues in children's early reading development and young children's perceptions of school are among her key research interests. The use of action research in the inner city context is another important aspect of her work.

Christine McMillan has been a qualified social work practitioner since 1984. She went on to specialize in the field of Mental Health Further study led to a career change. She now promotes human growth and development through counselling, supervision, private consultancy and freelance training. She enjoys a wide variety of work from the private, public and voluntary sectors.

Mag Gottfried Mair is currently teaching at the University of Innsbruck, Austria, and is Science Teacher at the Bundesgymnasium Imst, Tirol. She is also member of the Austrian Team of the 'Environment and School Initiatives' (ENSI) Project; School Coordinator of the WHO-Project 'Healthy Schools'; Coordinator of the Network of Environmental Community Projects and of several local and regional 'energy projects'. She has written books and journal articles on action research studies and other issues. Her main professional interests are in environmental and health education, networking, school development and inservice education of teachers (especially in project management).

Maire Maisch is a Principal Lecturer in Social Work at Anglia Polytechnic University. She has worked as a field practitioner, team manager and training officer for statutory and voluntary organizations before entering Social Work Education she was former director of the ASSET Programme and is now BSc (Hons) Social Work Co-ordinator at Anglia Polytechnic University.

Michela Mayer is a former teacher of Physics and History of Science in a secondary school. She has worked at Rome University as a researcher and teacher educator, with her dissertation work on 'Scientific knowledge and common sense knowledge'. For the past ten years, her worked has focused on environmental education and the use of action research in supporting educational innovation. Her recent work includes being an associate editor of *Educational, Action Research* and a partner in the Managing Organizational and Human Development project sponsored by the European Community. In 1995, she was invited to deliver the Stenhouse Memorial Lecture during the European Educational Research Association conference.

Janet L. Miller is Professor in National-Louis University's National College of Education. She is the author of *Creating Spaces and Finding Voices: Teachers Collaborating for Empowerment* (State University of New York Press, 1990), and the Co-Editor, with William Ayers, of *A Light in Dark Times: Conversations in Relation to Maxine Greene* (Teachers College Press, forthcoming). Her publications focus on intersections of curriculum and feminist theories, teacher-research and issues of collaboration and school reform, and autobiography as a form of educational inquiry. She recently was elected Vice President of American Educational Research Association for Division B, Curriculum Studies, for the 1997–1999 term.

Leslie T. Minarik is currently teaching at Highland Elementary School in Richmond, California. Her undergraduate work was done at the University of California, Santa Barbara, and at the University of Bordeaux, France. In 1987 she received her elementary teaching credential from the University of California, Berkeley. Leslie credits her most important teaching skills to the nine years of support from the Learning To Teach Group, her husband, and an outstanding group of teachers at her school with whom she has had the good fortune to spend nine years, including breakfasts, lunches and dinners.

Susan Noffke was a teacher of elementary and middle school-aged children in Wisconsin (USA) for ten years. She is currently Assistant Professor of Curriculum and Instruction at the University of Illinois — Urbana/Champaign — where she teaches preservice elementary teachers as well as working with experienced teachers in graduate programs. She has worked over ten years with and about action research, and is co-editor (with Robert Stevenson) of *Educational Action Research: Becoming Practically Critical.*

Christine O'Hanlon is a Senior Lecturer at the School of Education, University of Birmingham, UK. She has used action research as a means of professional development with educational personnel for some years and is particularly interested in the way in which group discourse and journal writing can extend thinking to support life-long change. She is Reviews Editor of the *Educational Action Research Journal.*

Peter Posch teaches, studies and researches at the Universities of Innsbruck, Konstanz and Vienna; he is Professor of Education at the Institute of Education at the University of Klagenfurt in Austria since 1976 and Visiting Professor at the School of Education of Stanford University, USA (1992). Member of the Editing Boards of the *Journal for Teaching and Teacher Education* (TATE) and of the *Journal of the South African Association for Academic Development* (SAAD), *Cambridge Journal of Education, Environmental Education Research* (EER). Author of more than 130 articles and of several books. Main research interests are in action research, environmental education, school development, inservice education and professional development of teachers.

Graziella Pozzo: A former language teacher in Italian secondary schools (1966–1984), was seconded at IRRSAE Piemonte, a regional institute for teacher training and curriculum development, where she worked for ten years (1984–1994), organizing training courses and facilitating, among others, groups of teachers involved in action research projects. She now works as a free-lance consultant in education and has recently been involved in the MOHD project, partially funded by the European Community.

Lesvia Olivia Rosas C. is a researcher at the Center for Educational Research of Mexico. She graduated from the Universidad Nacional Autonoma de Mexico (National Autonomous University of Mexico), and holds a Masters degree in Education from Harvard University. She is currently working on her doctoral thesis about the improvement of the education of rural primary school teachers in Mexico. Her main research interest has been formal and non-formal rural education.

Judyth Sachs is Professor of Education within the Faculty of Education at the University of Sydney. Her research interests are in the areas of teacher professional development, women and leadership and school reform and restructuring. During 1997 she will be President of the Australian Association for Research in Education.

Susan Groundwater Smith is Adjunct Professor of Education within the Faculty of Education and the Arts at Griffith University — gold Coast Campus in Queensland. Her research interests lie in the areas of teacher professional development, primary assessment, and reporting.

Paula Sobieschowska has worked in the social work field for the past fourteen years; half of that time was in practice and the latter half in education. She is currently employed in Essex Social Services as a Trainer and has recently taken up lead responsibility for the ASSET Programme within the Bsc in Social Work at Anglia Polytechnic University.

Hugh Sockett is Professor of Education and Director of the Institute for Educational Transformation at George Mason University, and President of the Institute for Educational Transformation Inc. He came to GMU in 1987 as Director of the Center for Applied Research and Development and founded IET as a business-education partnership committed to transformative educational change in 1990. He has published four books and over thirty articles in refereed journals.

Bridget Somekh has extensive experience of action research in a range of roles (teacher-researcher, external facilitator, coordinator of a large project). From 1987 to 1995 she was Coordinator of the Collaborative (formerly Classroom) Action Research Network. The main focus of her research has been the process of innovation for individuals, groups and organisations. This has involved her in cross-professional work with health service personnel and employees in public and private companies, as well as teachers. In 1984, while working at the University of East Anglia, she worked in collaboration with local employers to establish new part time degree courses of which the core element was action research in the work place. In 1985 she became Deputy Director of the Scottish Council for Research in Education. Bridget was the international coordinator of the project, Management for Organisational and Human Development, funded by the European Community during 1994.

Michaela Thaler has a degree in Business Education and Personnel Management from the University of Innsbruck. From 1994–96 she was a Teacher Educator for pre-service Business Teachers in secondary schools and was involved in the evaluation of the implementation of the new policy for vocational education in higher education in Austria. In 1996 she worked at the Scottish Council for Research in Education as Research Fellow in the European MOHD project.

Angie Titchen: After ten years clinical experience as a physiotherapist, Titchen undertook an MSc in Rehabilitation Studies at the University of Southhampton in the UK. Shortly afterwards, she became the Continuing Education Consultant at the Chartered Society of Physiotherapy. As a Doctoral research student, supported by the National Institute for Nursing and registered at the Oxford University Department of Educational Studies, she is currently exploring the nature of the knowledge underpinning patient-centred nursing and its development.

Melanie Walker has extensive experience of teaching history in 'disadvantaged' schools in South Africa. She has also worked as a teacher educator with preservice and inservice teachers, and spent several years working with African primary school teachers on small scale curriculum development projects within a reflective practitioner approach. This work formed the action research study into her own practice as a facilitator of teachers professional learning. More recently, she has worked at a historically black South African university in the area of professional development, working alongside academic staff to develop their own teaching practice. Much of this work has incorporated a research-based approach to development. From January 1997 she will continue this work at the University of Glasgow as Director of the Teaching and Learning Service where she hopes to focus on gender and achievement in relation to 'good practice'. Her interests include the theory and practice of action research for fairer education and a more just society, professional learning and women in the academy.

Pauline Watts is currently a Senior Lecturer in Education at South Bank University. Her main interest is in looking at the way in which educators work with change in a variety of contexts. She has recently collaborated with colleagues to investigate issues concerning the integration of New Technologies into Education. Prior to her current position, she worked as a teacher and then advisory maths teacher in a number of primary schools in London. She became involved in Action Research as an effective means of examining processes of change within her own classroom and school, initially at Higher Degree level and then as a means of structuring inservice work with teachers.

Gaby Weiner is currently Professor of Educational Research and Director of the Educational Research Unit at South Bank University, London, UK. Involved with feminist issues since the late 1960s, she has tried to bridge the personal and public sides of her life by writing about feminist issues in education. She has published widely on social justice, equal opportunities and gender, writing and editing a number of books and research reports.

Gordon Wells is a Professor of Education at the Ontario Institute for Studies in Education in the University of Toronto, where, as a member of the Curriculum Department and of the Centre for Teacher Development, he researches and teaches in the fields of language, literacy and learning within a framework provided by sociocultural theory. In recent years, all these professional interests have come together in a number of collaborative action research projects which he has conducted with teachers in Ontario and further afield. He is currently engaged in a project entitled

'Developing Inquiring Communities in Education', funded by the Spencer Foundation, which aims to increase understanding and improve practice with respect to the use of spoken and written discourse in learning and teaching across the curriculum. email: gwells@oise.utoronto.ca

Richard Winter is Professor of Education at Anglia Polytechnic University. He taught English to adult students in the UK and in Malawi, and then worked for many years in teacher education before taking up a post in nursing and social work education in 1990. He began his career in action research with a project on the organization of teaching practice in the APU Education Department. Since then he has published various articles on action research methodology. He co-directed (with Maire Maisch) the ASSET Project, which is described in *Professional Competence and Higher Education* (Falmer Press, 1996).

Michal Zellermayer is the chair of the Literacy Education program at Levingsky Teachers College in Tel-Aviv, Israel, where she is currently responsible for designing a graduate program in teaching. Her research interests are related to enhancing thoughtful teaching and thoughtful teacher education within the context of literacy instruction. Her recent writings describe teacher-researcher collaborative construction of story; the use of video for critical reflection in collaborative action research; and the interview as a transformative space.

Index